The Definitive Guide to

MOMENTUM INDICATORS

MARTIN J. PRING

MARKETPLACE BOOKS®
GLENELG, MARYLAND

Publisher: Chris Myers

VP/General Manager: John Boyer

Executive Editor: Jody Costa

Production Editor: Courtney Jenkins

Art Director: Larry Strauss

Graphic Designer: Jennifer Marin

Graphic Design Intern: Ethan Gladding

This book, along with other books, is available at discounts that make it realistic to provide them as gifts to your customers, clients, and staff. For more information on these long lasting, cost effective premiums, please call us at 800-272-2855 or e-mail us at sales@traderslibrary.com.

Printed in the United States of America.

Library of Congress Cataloging-in-Publication Data
Pring, Martin J.
 The definitive guide to momentum indicators / by Martin Pring.
    p. cm.
 Originally Published in 2002 by The McGraw-Hill Companies as: Momentum explained.
 Includes index.
 ISBN-13: 978-1-59280-338-5 (casebound)
 ISBN-10: 1-59280-338-5 (casebound)
 1. Investment analysis. I. Pring, Martin J. Momentum explained. II. Title.
 HG4529.P7478 2009
 332.63'2042–dc22

                    2009016424

To my beloved wife, Lisa

Contents

Part II

Acknowledgments

The year 2009 will see the publication of this unique book CD-ROM tutorial combination by Marketplace Books. None of this would have been possible without the help of several key people.In particular I would like to thank Jimmie Sigsway, my wonderful mother-in-law, whose support of our busy family allowed both me and my wife, Lisa, to allocate sufficient time to work on this project.Without a doubt, a mighty thanks goes to Jeff Howard of Interactive Software Design, who has, as usual, pulled out all the stops and done a superb job creating the installation program and multimedia programming for the CD-ROM tutorials contained at the back of this book.I would also like to thank many of our subscribers, workshop attendees, and purchasers of our CD-ROMs, whose kind and constructive comments have greatly encouraged me to expand the "Pring library."Above all, a special thanks goes to my wife, Lisa, who, despite multiple pressures from major domestic construction work, minding the kids (including me), cooking the meals, and maintaining our Web site at pring.com, was still able to deliver the artwork for this book on time.

Preface

This two volume set covering the concept of momentum in financial markets is arguably the most comprehensive ever published in one work. Indeed the real value of this package lies in the combination of the text with the two CD-ROMs enclosed in the back cover. These little disks contain a complete multi-media presentation of the subject matter contained in the workbook. Years ago I published videos on technical analysis, but the CD-ROM format is far superior. Not only does each chapter play as a continuous presentation but also the need to fast forward or rewind is eliminated. Instead, the user can click on any subject matter in the contents and move instantly there. This format also allows for an interactive quiz, so the user can quickly move through multiple choice questions or chart examples, all of which are scored at the end. In this way, you can easily discover any area that needs brushing up. This two volume set is designed to expand on several of the subjects covered in the fourth edition of Technical Analysis Explained. Each of the book/CD-ROM combinations takes the reader into greater depth on the individual subjects. Diagrams and theoretical concepts are explained and then adapted to practical marketplace examples. It is normal in presentations of this nature to indicate the strong points of any indicator or concept, but these presentations also advise you of any known weaknesses of pitfalls they may have. Technical analysis is the art of identifying trend reversals at a relatively early stage and riding on that trend until the weight of the evidence shows or proves that the trend has reversed. The objective of this two volume set is to present a substantial amount of that evidence in the form of indicators and concepts, so that readers of the workbooks and viewers of the CD-ROMs will be in a stronger position to identify such trend reversals. Please take note of the fact that technical analysis deals in probabilities, never certainties. Armed with the information in this series, the probabilities should now move heavily in your favor.

With that in mind, good luck and good charting!

Martin J. Pring
Sarasota, Florida

The Definitive Guide to
MOMENTUM INDICATORS
PART I

1

Introduction

TECHNICAL ANALYSIS AND MOMENTUM

Before we begin our discussion on momentum, I would like to start off with a few words on technical analysis itself and how momentum fits in. My definition of technical analysis is—*the art of identifying a price trend reversal at a relatively early stage and riding on that trend until the* weight of the evidence *shows or proves that the trend has reversed.*

The key assumption in this definition is that once a trend gets underway, it will perpetuate. If it did not, then we would be unable to ride on it. There is a favorite saying of technically oriented managers: "the trend is your friend." And indeed, if we do not jump the gun by anticipating a reversal in trend when one has not been signaled, the trend will surely be our friend. Trends perpetuate because prices in any freely traded market are determined by crowd psychology, by the *attitude* of all market participants to the unfolding fundamentals. I have emphasized the word *attitude* because it is not the fundamen-

tals themselves that are important, it is *how* people feel about them. In the stock market, for example, traders are concerned with future profits of corporations. Normally, they buy because they think earnings will rise, and sell in anticipation of a decline or slower growth rate, and so forth. However, there are exceptions. Chart 1-1 shows the Standard and Poors (S&P) Composite in the 1973–1974 bear market. You would think that prices were declining because earnings were expected to drop. However, the chart clearly shows that earnings actually went up. Indeed, many stocks in the so-called nifty fifty peaked in 1973 and did not better those prices until the start of the 1980s; yet throughout the period, profits rose. Thus the importance of psychology; and, fortunately for technicians, crowd psychology moves in trends. Some trends, such as those found in the intraday charts, last for a few hours, and others, as reflected in the monthly charts, can extend for years. However, just as friends fall out from time to time, so we must admit that not all trends

1

"MOMENTUM" IS A GENERIC TERM

Over the years, technicians have developed many indicators that have attempted to measure the velocity of a price move, both upward and downward. These oscillators can be banded together under one heading: momentum. Momentum is one of the most frequently used techniques in technical analysis, but probably the least understood. In this section of the book, we will cover the basic principles of momentum interpretation, zeroing in on some specific indicators later on and describing how the principles apply to them. Part 2 will explore 25 other indicators in depth.

Momentum measures the velocity of a price move and is a generic term. Just as the word fruit encompasses apples, oranges, grapes, bananas, and so forth, so the expression momentum embraces a host of individual indicators, such as Rate of Change (ROC), relative strength indicators (RSI), moving average convergence divergence (MACD), stochastics, and so on (see Fig. 1-1). Each indicator has different attributes, but the principles of interpretation apply to them all. Think of it this way. A common characteristic of a fruit, for example, is that it is typically sweet and is almost always grown at the time of the year when the climate is warmest. Some fruits are sweeter than others, some require very hot temperatures, others a long growing season, and so on (see Fig. 1-2). Momentum indicators also have some common characteristics, but the indicators themselves, like the different types of fruit, differ in the way we interpret them. Some are more suited to specific rules

> Technical Analysis is the art of identifying a price trend reversal at a relatively early stage and riding on that trend until the *weight of the evidence* shows or proves that the trend has reversed.

perpetuate. If they did, technical analysis would be easy to apply and its application would be self-fulfilling.

If we go back to the definition, you can see that I have highlighted the words "weight of the evidence." This is the critical part, since technical analysis deals in probabilities and that is where the weight of the evidence comes in. To determine when a trend has reversed, we use a number of reliable indicators. When several of them are in agreement, the odds favor a trend reversal. Momentum analysis provides a substantial number of indicators that can be used in our weight-of-the-evidence approach.

Now we have established what technical analysis is, it is time to move on to the main part of the discussion.

Chart 1-1   S&P 1972–1974 Price versus Earnings

(Source: pring.com)

than others. We shall learn later, for example, that the rate of change indicator lends itself to trendline construction. So does the stochastic indicator, but that is not the way in which it is normally interpreted. The next few chapters are concerned with these common principles of interpretation. Once they have been examined, the individual indicators themselves can then be considered along with their underlying concepts, construction, and the specific peculiarities of interpretation.

The momentum indicator is normally plotted as an oscillator underneath the security that is being monitored. This enables a convenient comparison to be made. Occasionally, two or more indicators will be plotted along with the price. This enables a comparison of different momentum approaches or different time spans. The objective is always to ascertain the weight of the evidence in determining whether a trend has been reversed. The more evidence (indicators) that points in one direction, the greater the odds that a trend has changed.

Figure 1-1   Momentum versus Fruit

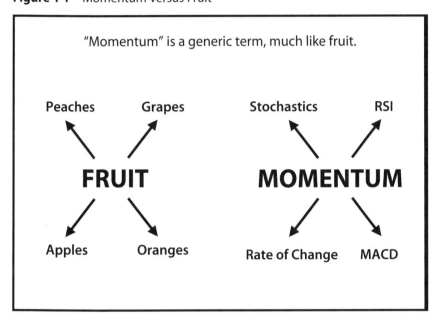

Figure 1-2   Momentum versus Fruit—characteristics

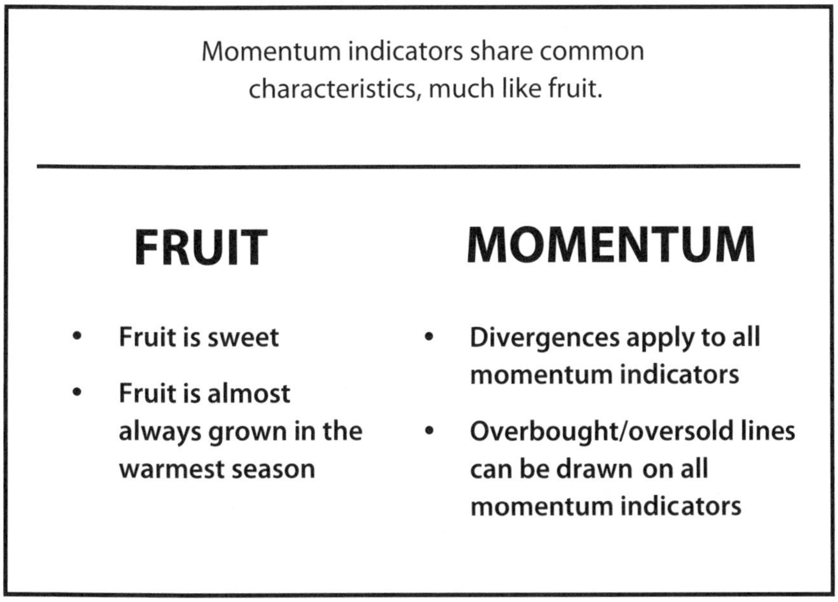

A FEW WORDS ON TIME FRAMES

In technical analysis, we are concerned with identifying trend reversals at a relatively early stage and, assuming that the new trend will perpetuate, riding on that trend until it reverses. It is always assumed that the prevailing trend is in force until *the weight of the evidence* proves otherwise. By this I mean that if one isolated indicator points to a trend reversal, this is insufficient. All indicators, however good, can and do fail from time to time. This means that we must take a consensus approach, using several indicators, each confirming the others. When the balance is in agreement, we can be more confident that the trend has indeed reversed. It is that part of the weight of the evidence provided by momentum indicators that primarily concerns us here.

There are many types of trends, but the most widely followed are short-, intermediate-, and long-term. They last approximately from 3-6 weeks, 6-39 weeks, and 1-2 years, respectively. When attempting to analyze a trend, it is of crucial importance to bear in mind the type of trend we are trying to measure. Turning an oil tanker around is a much more formidable accomplishment than reversing a sports car. So it is with markets: the reversal of a short-term trend takes less time and involves a substantially smaller change in collective psychology than the reversal of a long-term trend. This also means that a signal from a momentum indicator with a long-term time span has a far greater significance than a buy or sell alert from one with a 5- or 10-day span. Investment and trading decisions should be made with this same perspective.

> A weight-of-evidence approach is based on probabilities; we must critically evaluate the evidence presented by our mulitple indicators before making a decision regarding the trend.

Most of the material discussed later will focus on short and, to a lesser extent, intermediate trends. Nevertheless, it is still of paramount importance for any trader to gain some understanding of the current position in the long-term cycle. Just as the unwary swimmer finds it difficult to swim against the tide, so the short-term trader will certainly run into difficulties when positioned against the main trend. Time and time again we find that unprofitable signals from trend-following systems invariably come from contratrend moves. Short- and intermediate-term price trends that are swimming against the tide of a primary trend are likely to run into trouble. It is not always possible to ascertain the direction of the main trend, especially in its initial stages.

Nevertheless, it is very important, even for short-term traders, to try to get a fix on both its maturity and direction. If you know that the trend is down and you are also aware of the fact that contratrend moves are usually unprofitable, it will caution you from entering long positions when indicated by short-term momentum indicators. To do so only induces failure, however attractive the opportunity may seem at the time. This sub-

Chart 1-2   NASDAQ Composite 1999–2000, comparing oscillators

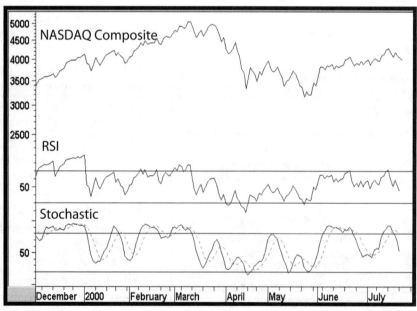

(Source: pring.com)

ject of short- and longer-term trends will be discussed at great length in Chapter 10.

THE CHARACTER AND MAGNITUDE OF AN OSCILLATOR SWING

The character and magnitude of an oscillator swing will depend on three factors. They are:

1. *The nature of the formula relating to the indicator's construction.* The formula is important because each calculation deliberately tries to reflect different characteristics. In Chart 1-2 we see a relatively volatile RSI index at the top and a smoother stochastic-based calculation in the lower panel. The RSI is designed for specifically identifying overbought/oversold read-

ings, whereas the stochastic is more concerned with moving-average crossovers. That is a fairly simplistic comparison, but the point is that each indicator was designed with a different objective in mind.

2. *The time span being used.* Time spans are also important in determining the magnitude of a swing in the momentum series. Figure 1-3 shows a 5-day oscillator (solid line) compared to a 65-day series (dashed line). You can see that the 5-day series contains a much narrower trading band and experiences a far greater number of swings compared to the 65-day indicator, where the cyclic movements are much more deliberate and pronounced. For instance, the price of a security could increase by 30 percent during the course of a year. Thus a 12-month rate of change may easily rally to the ± 30 percent area. However, it is highly unlikely, except in the case of a takeover or other

Figure 1-3 Momentum signals require price confirmation

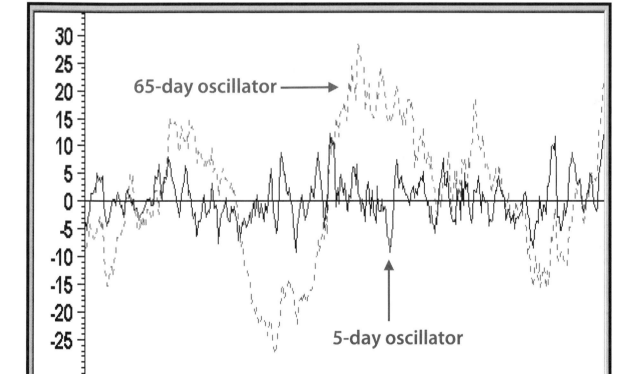

Chart 1-3   Newmont Mining versus Southern Company, comparing volatility of securities

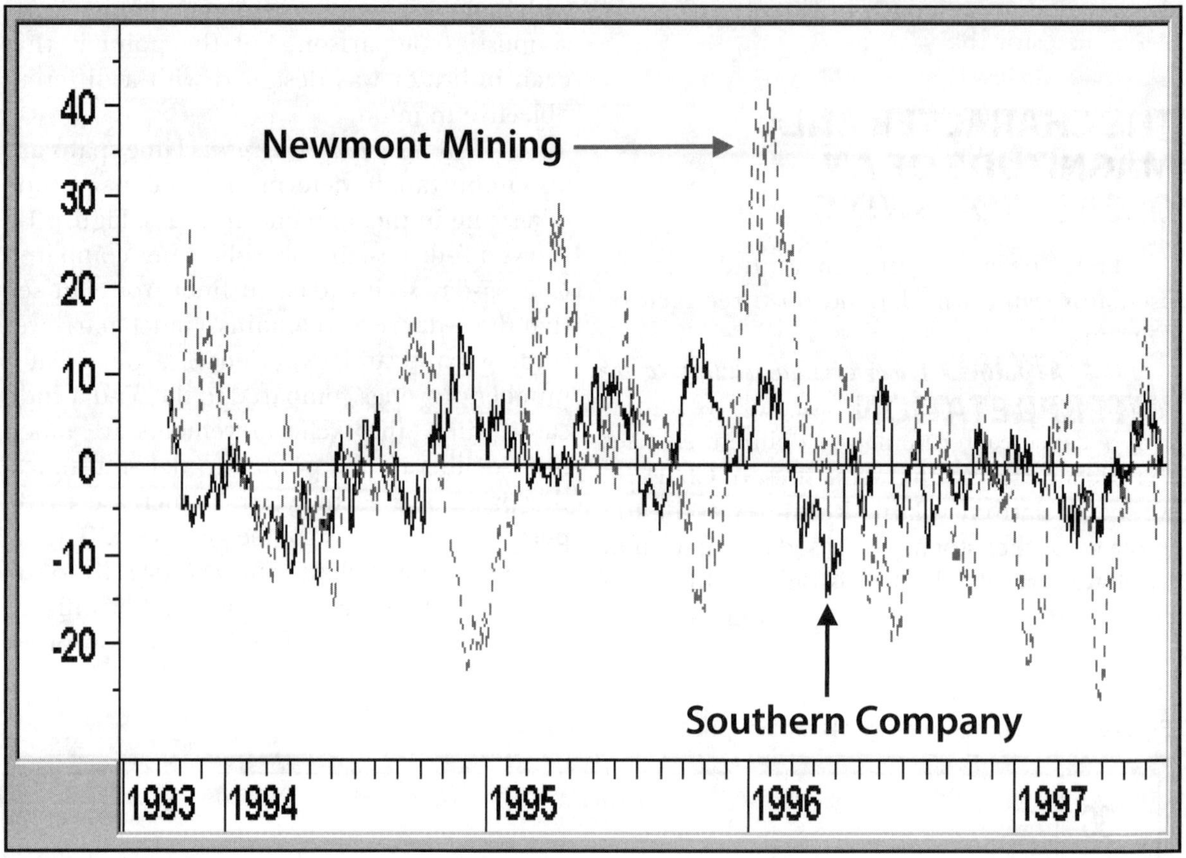

(Source: pring.com)

unusual event, for the price to rally 30 percent in the course of a 5-day period. While an oscillator based on a short-term time span will be subject to more oscillations than one constructed from a longer-term span, the magnitude of these fluctuations will be far less.

3. *The volatility of the security being monitored.* Finally, some securities are more volatile than others, and this also affects the character of an oscillator. Chart 1-3 features a momentum indicator for Southern Company, an electric utility (solid line) and Newmont Mining, a gold mining company (dashed line). It is fairly obvious that the dashed oscillator for the mining company is far more volatile than the narrower-swinging electric utility. Mining companies tend to be very volatile due to the fact that their earnings are more difficult to predict and fluctuate a lot more than those of the somewhat staid utilities. This results in greater

uncertainty, which, in turn, causes greater swings in opinions and attitudes toward such companies. Even when earnings can be predicted, mining company profits are much more volatile than those of utilities, so again this leads to greater price fluctuations. Finally, buyers of utility stocks are often looking for a consistent earnings stream and for safety. They, therefore, tend to be very conservative investors. In contrast, potential owners of mining stocks are more concerned with a quick capital gain and are, therefore, less stable holders, as a group.

Buy and sell signals only come from a reversal in trend of the actual price, not the momentum series.

Since the perception of what constitutes a sharp price move will be different for a conservative investor than for a trader or speculator, momentum levels between securities holding widely differing characteristics cannot be meaningfully contrasted. It follows, then, that the relevant momentum comparison is the current reading of a specific security to its historical range.

TWO BROAD CATEGORIES OF INTERPRETATION

There are a large number of interpretive rules. These principles can be roughly divided into two broad categories:

1. *Those that deal with overbought, oversold conditions, divergences and the like.* I will call these momentum characteristics. If you study momentum indicators or oscillators, you will find that they have certain characteristics that are associated with subsurface strengths or weaknesses in the underlying price trend. It is rather like looking under the hood of an engine. Quite a lot of the time, you can identify mechanical trouble before it becomes self-evident.

2. *Those that identify trend reversals in the momentum indicator itself.* In this case, we are making the assumption that when a trend in momentum is reversed, prices will sooner or later follow.

Trend-reversal techniques, such as trend-line breaks, moving-average crossovers, and so on, when applied to momentum, are just as valid as when they are applied to price. The difference, and it is an important one, is that a trend reversal in momentum is just that—*a reversal in momentum, not price.* Momentum typically reverses along with price, often with a small lead. But just because oscillators change direction does not always mean that prices will, too (see Fig. 1-4). Normally, a reversal in momentum acts as a confirmation of a price trend reversal signal. In effect, this momentum signal forms the act of supplementary witness in our weight-of-the-evidence approach. Momentum's valuable contribution is to tell us when the underlying technical structure is strengthening or weakening, thereby giving us an advance warning of when a reversal in price may be about to take place. For now, take special note of the fact that *actual buy and sell signals can come only from a reversal in trend of the actual price, not the momentum series.*

Technical analysis can be applied to any freely traded entity. Since there are numerous items traded in the world markets, such as stocks, market indexes, bonds, currencies, commodities, and so forth, I will use the generic term *security* to refer to *specific* price trends and concepts. This simplifies matters and avoids the need of repetition, and so on.

Figure 1-4 Time Frame Comparison

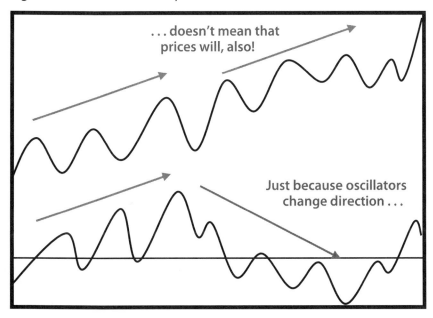

... doesn't mean that prices will, also!

Just because oscillators change direction ...

2

Overbought and Oversold Conditions

THE BASICS

All momentum series have the characteristics of an oscillator, as they move from one extreme to another. Figure 2-1 illustrates this point. These extremes are known as *overbought* and *oversold* levels. In my seminars, I often equate these zones with a person taking an unruly dog on a walk. The animal continually strains at the leash, moving from one side of the walk to the other. At one moment, the dog roams to the curb on his extreme left and the next he scampers back to the lawn on his right as far as the leash will allow him.

Market momentum works in a similar manner, so that when an oscillator is at an overextended reading on the upside, it is said to be *overbought*. When it reaches the opposite end of the spectrum on the downside, the condition is known as *oversold*. The horizontal line in between these extremes is known as the *equilibrium line*, since it is the point of balance between the two extremes.

Some indicators, such as RSI, are calculated in such a way that they have a finite extreme above or below which they cannot go. In such cases, there is an established default level for the overbought and oversold lines. For the most commonly used 14-day time span, these lines are drawn at 70 and 30, respectively. Conversely, other indicators, such as the rate of change, have no such theoretical boundary, at least on the upside. Instead, we must insert the overbought/oversold lines on a trial-and-error basis, using our best judgment. We will see how this is accomplished in a practical way later. For now, let us simply say that these lines should be drawn in such a manner that the space between them includes the vast majority of the trading activity, such as those in Chart 2-1. In this case, try to think of the oscillator as a rubber leash, which from time to time will inevitably be stretched beyond the normal limit. To draw lines that represent the extremes is not particularly helpful. What we must do is find the graphical equivalent of the end of the leash, that is, the points

(Source: pring.com)

which include most of the rallies and reactions for the price trend under study.

INTERPRETATION

The technical interpretation of overbought and oversold lines is that they represent an intelligent point for anticipating a trend reversal. An overbought condition is one in which you should consider taking profits or reducing your exposure (see Fig. 2-1). For example, if you are holding three gold contracts and the price rallies to where it is recording an overbought reading, you might wish to take some partial profits. Even though the trend may continue, the overbought reading indicates that the odds of a reversal have increased.

If the risks of a top have grown, then it makes sense to reduce your exposure. If press stories concerning the bullish nature of the

security are beginning to emerge and your emotions are telling you to buy more, use these signs as further confirming evidence that it is a good time to reduce rather than increase your exposure.

Alternately, if you believe that the main trend is down and you have been waiting for a short-term bounce as a time to sell, an overbought reading is as good a time as any. For the same reason, it would normally be a grave mistake even to consider making a purchase when an oscillator signals an overbought condition. The problem we all have is that this is precisely the time when most of us have the urge to buy,

Evaluate sentiment in the market as more evidence for overbought and oversold conditions.

because rising prices attract optimism, positive news stories, and bullish sentiment.

The opposite is true for an oversold condition. Few people want to buy after prices have been declining when the news is inevitably discouraging. Unfortunately, that is the time when we need to pick up our shaking hands and call our friendly broker. Such instances are shown by the upward-pointing arrows in Fig. 2-2. That

is the moment when we should avoid at all costs the temptation to put on a short position. In actual fact, the correct tactic is to cover part of any outstanding short position. At the time you may think that it is possible to make more money by holding on to your position, but believe me, taking some partial profits will put you in a far more objective frame of mind when that inevitable rally gets underway.

Figure 2-1 Overbought and oversold lines

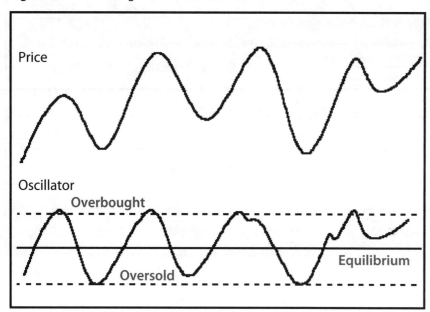

RE-CROSSOVERS OFFER BETTER SIGNALS

Quite often a price trend will continue so that the oscillator goes well beyond the overbought/oversold extremes. In that event, it is often a good idea to wait for the indicator to re-cross the overbought or oversold extreme on its way back toward the equilibrium area and then take action. Some possibilities are indicated in Fig. 2-2. See how selling at the time the indicator first touched its overbought zone at arrow 1 would have been premature. Waiting for it to re-cross the overbought level at arrow 2 would have been more profitable because this event took place at a higher price level.

The same was true of the oversold crossover at arrow 3. See how the momentum indicator re-crossed its oversold line pretty close to the low at

Figure 2-2 Used to take profits

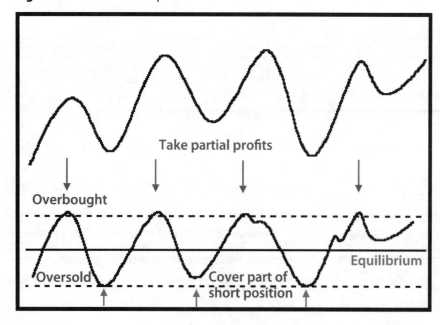

Chart 2-2 Comparing General Motors using two time frames

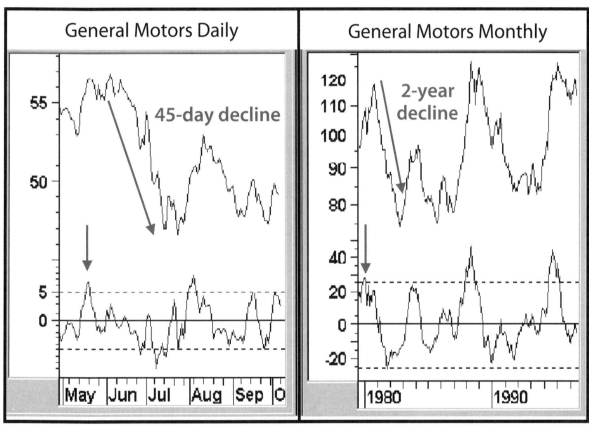

(Source: pring.com)

arrow 4. I am not going to say that it works this well every time, because it does not, but the momentum re-crossover technique is definitely a useful technique to employ.

THE IMPORTANCE OF TIME FRAMES

The importance of an overbought or oversold condition will depend on the time frame under consideration. For example, if the period used for the construction is 5 days, the implications from the extreme readings will be nowhere as significant as those from a momentum indicator spanning 12 months. Chart 2-2 shows an oscillator with a short time span on the left and a substantially longer one on the right. You can see how the overbought reading

Make sure you understand the big picture first—strong bull or bear market conditions will affect the use of overbought and oversold readings in your indicators.

in the first oscillator was followed by a decline of a few days, but the overbought reading in the one on the right was followed by a more substantial decline that took a lot longer to play out.

MOMENTUM CHARACTERISTICS IN BULL AND BEAR MARKETS

Momentum characteristics change with the direction of the primary trend oscillators, which move in the direction of the prevailing primary trend, and not only tend to reach more extreme readings but tend to maintain overbought conditions much longer than those that move against the trend. In Fig. 2-4 we see that the main trend is upward. Note how the overbought and oversold extremes are positioned equidistant from the equilibrium level indicated by the solid line. Rallies in the indicator have a tendency to move well into overbought territory and remain there for a longer time than do reactions. Reactions are almost always reversed at the oversold line, or even sometimes before the oscillator reaches that point. This trait is itself a strong characteristic of a primary bull

Figure 2-4   Characteristics of a bull market

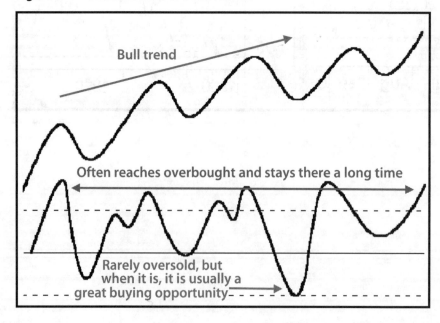

market.

The reverse is true in a bear market (Fig. 2-5). Rallies, when they are able to reach an overbought extreme, are usually terminated there. Reactions cause oversold readings to be much more extreme than normal. Whereas an overbought reading will normally generate a rally in a bull market, there is no such guarantee in a bear market.

Figure 2-5   Characteristics of a bear market

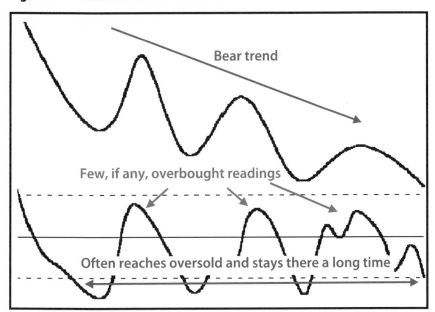

3

Divergences: The Basics

CLASSIC DIVERGENCES

In the description of overbought-oversold conditions, we assume that the oscillator peaks and troughs at roughly the same time as the price. That is not often the case, however. An equally likely possibility is that the momentum indicator will turn ahead of the price. Think of a pen thrown into the air. The pen reaches its point of maximum velocity the instant it leaves the hand. It continues to rise—but at a slower and slower rate—until it is overcome by the force of gravity. Only then does it fall back toward the ground.

All that a momentum indicator is trying to do, therefore, is to measure this acceleration and deceleration factor and present it in graphic format. Figure 3-1 shows how this works in practice for a rising price trend. In Figure 3-2, Point A marks the moment of maximum velocity, but the price itself continues to rally at a slower and slower pace until point C. This conflict between momentum and price is known as a *divergence*,

> Divergences occur when there is a discrepancy between price and momentum. Negative divergences accompany rising prices and positive divergences accompany falling prices; in both cases, prices are moving opposite to momentum.

since the oscillator is out of sync with the price. It is called a *negative* divergence because rising prices are supported by weaker and weaker underlying momentum. The deteriorating momentum represents an early warning of some underlying weakness in the price trend.

In one respect, markets are like houses: they take a lot longer to build than to tear down. Security prices spend most of their time advancing rather than declining. This means that *the lead characteristics of momentum indicators are usually more pronounced at market peaks than at troughs.*

Figure 3-1   Negative divergence

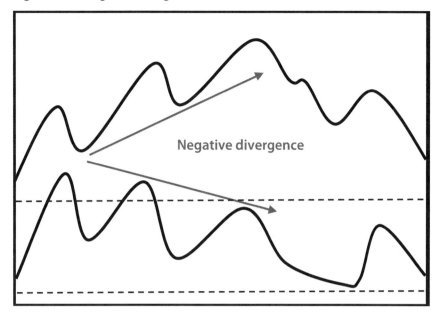

Figure 3-2   Positive divergence

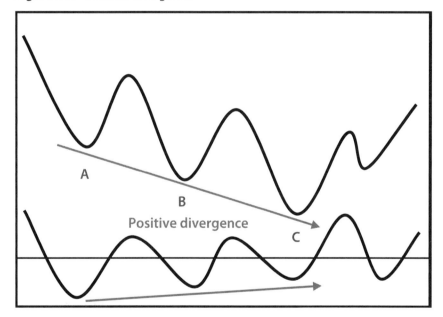

Even so, divergences also occur at market bottoms, where they are called *positive*, because momentum hits bottom before price. This phenomenon may be likened to a car in neutral gear being pushed over a hill. As the vehicle progresses down the slope, it gradually picks up speed or momentum. Then, as the gradient levels toward the bottom of the hill, the car slows down. Even though the speed is decreasing, the car itself continues to move before it finally slows to a halt. In this example, the speed of the car should be thought of as market momentum and its position as the price.

In Fig. 3-2 the price is declining between points A and C, but at a slower and slower rate. The technical position is said to be improving, or getting stronger. Indeed, if you think a market is in the process of reaching its bottom and you do not see a divergence, you may want to reconsider your analysis because most market bottoms for any time span are preceded by at least one positive divergence.

HOW TO TELL THE SIGNIFICANCE OF DIVERGENCES

There are three factors that help to establish the significance of a divergence. These are the number of divergences, the time span separating them, and the closeness of the momentum reading to the equilibrium level at the final turning point. Let us consider them each in turn.

Generally speaking, the more divergences that occur, the greater their significance. In the case of a market peak, the large number of negative divergences indicates a trend that is undergoing a very long and serious weakening process (see Fig. 3-3).

The same principle applies to positive divergences at market bottoms: the more plentiful they are, the stronger the technical position.

The length of time separating the divergences is important because it reflects the type of trend you are monitoring. For example, if traders are analyzing short-term price movements, they would expect the divergences to take place over the course of a week or so, at most. Alternately, investors are principally concerned with the primary trend, so they would look for divergences associ-

Figure 3-3   Multiple divergences

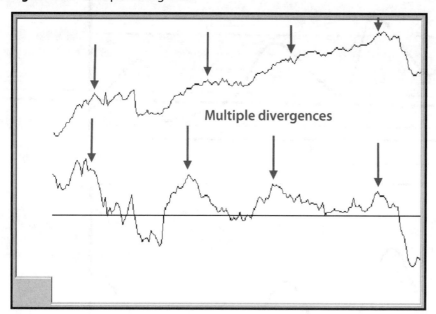

Figure 3-4   Short-term divergence

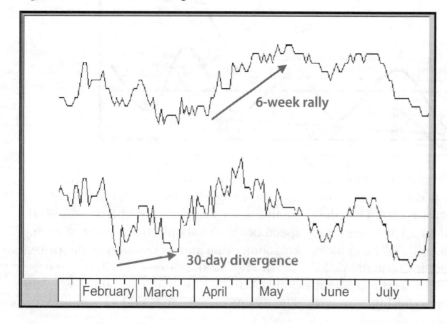

Figure 3-5 Intermediate divergences

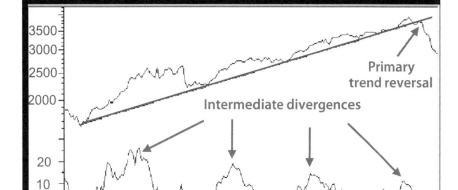

Figure 3-6 Lack of upside momentum divergence

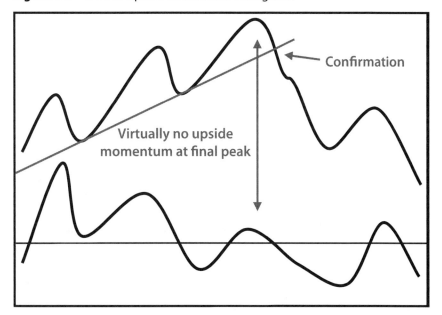

Figure 3-7   Lack of downside momentum divergence

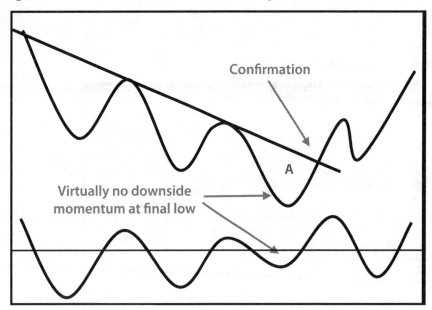

ated with a momentum graph constructed from an intermediate time frame. In this case, three divergences in an intermediate oscillator are obviously more significant than three divergences in a short-term momentum series. In this regard, compare Figs. 3-4 and 3-5.

A final important point relates to the level at which the last divergence takes place. Generally speaking, the closer the last divergence to the equilibrium line, the more significant the divergence. At market peaks, rallies in a momentum indicator, which are barely able to rally above the zero level, are often followed by very sharp declines. An example is shown in Fig. 3-6. This is one of the

few instances in technical analysis when a clue appears to be hinting at the *character* of the next price move. I must stress that such instances are not always followed by a sharp drop. Remember, technical analysis is far from perfect. However, in most cases, when weak momentum of this nature is confirmed by a trend break in the price, be on guard for a larger-than-normal sell-off.

The same principle in reverse holds for market bottoms. These occur when the price hits a new low following a number of positive divergences. In this case, though, the latest decline barely takes the oscillator below the equilibrium point. One such action has been confirmed by a positive trend break in the price itself, an explosive rally usually follows. Figure 3-7 shows the kind of situation I am driving at. See how the price makes a new low at point A. However, the momentum series barely falls below zero and a sharp rally follows.

> Remember the weight-of-the evidence approach: the more divergences (and other complementary technical signals) that precede a trend break in price, the more emphasis that can be placed on the significance and intensity of the price pattern completion.

DIVERGENCES *MUST* BE CONFIRMED BY PRICE

Perhaps the most important point to remember is that it is of paramount importance for a divergence to be confirmed by a trend break in the price itself, no matter how significant the divergence may appear on its own merit.

Think of it this way: the darker the clouds, the heavier the rain shower. However, you do not know it is going to actually rain until you

Figure 3-8 Momentum warning of trouble

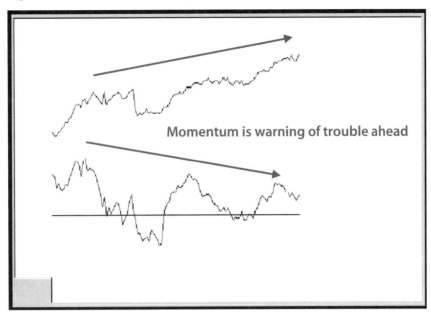

Momentum is warning of trouble ahead

Figure 3-9 Momentum confirmed by price

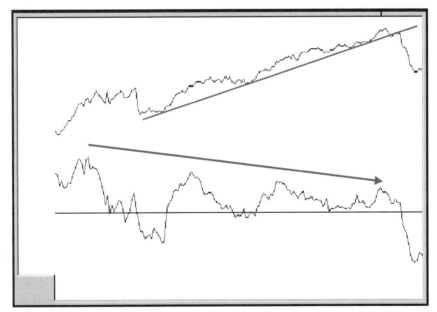

can hold out your hand and feel it, because there is always the chance that a new front will come in and blow the clouds away. The same is true for the relationship between price and momentum. One divergence can lead to another, and so forth.

Confirmation by a trend break in the price can come in many forms: trendline violations (see Figs. 3-8 and 3-9), moving-average pene-trations, price pattern completions, and more. For example, the completion of any reversal price pattern signals a change in the trend. However, the more divergences that precede this break, when combined with the other principles of momentum significance discussed above, the more emphasis is placed on the significance and intensity of the price pattern completion.

4

Divergence Variations: I

In this chapter and the next one, we will examine some more divergence possibilities, each of which warns of a potential change in trend.

PRICE DISCREPANCY DIVERGENCES

Another sign of a mature trend develops when the momentum indicator moves strongly in one direction and the price fails to follow through with any degree of gusto. This indicates that the price is tired of moving in the direction of the prevailing trend, for, despite the strong momentum thrust, prices are unable to respond. This is an unusual, but nevertheless powerful, phenomenon. Figure 4-1 shows such a situation for a market top. You can see how the price rally is anemic relative to that of the oscillator.

The same principle, but this time for a reversal from a downtrend to an uptrend, is shown in Fig. 4-2. In this instance, the oscillator is quite weak, but the price hardly slips. If lots of down-side momentum will not push prices lower, nothing will, so the result is a rally. In a true sense, this is not a divergence—because in many instances, neither series actually makes a new high or low. The point is that this is really a subtle sign that price and momentum are not in complete agreement and that when such discrepancies arise, the astute analyst or trader should be on the lookout for evidence that the price trend may be in the process of reversing.

REVERSE DIVERGENCES

NEGATIVE

We know that the oscillator either coincides with a top or bottom in the price, or, more typically, it will lead it, thereby setting up positive or negative divergences. *In technical analysis, we are always looking to see if two series are moving in sympathy with each other, that is, in gear, or whether there are discrepancies.* It is when discrepancies show up

20

that the technician is alerted to a probable change in trend. An unusual, but normally reliable, discrepancy occurs when the *price* leads the momentum indicator. This is the opposite of the norm, where it is the oscillator that leads the price. That is why I have termed this phenomenon a reverse divergence. Figure 4-3 features a *reverse divergence* at a market peak. See how the price makes its high at point A and then makes a lower high at point B, whereas the oscillator makes a higher high at B, thereby setting up a reverse divergence. I must strongly stress, however, that *reverse divergences do not operate for a momentum indicator that has experienced a great deal of smoothing.*

This is because the smoothing will have a natural effect of delaying the turn in an oscillator. Consequently, if you spot a reverse divergence with an indicator that has been smoothed by a moving average with a relatively long time span (relative in this case to the time span of the raw data) or one in which the indicator is a smoothing of a smoothing, take a little more care in coming to a conclusion. An example where a moving average is laid over the raw data is shown in Fig. 4-4. You can see that the average peaks at around the same time that the price is experiencing its secondary, lower peak. The peak in the smoothed oscillator is really associated with the whole upward price move contained in the left-hand part of the chart, so the reverse divergence is a statistical quirk, depending on the nature of the smoothing. Alternately, the raw oscillator definitely experiences similar wave fluctuations as the price, so its final peak is definitely diverging.

Figure 4-1   Bearish price discrepancy divergence

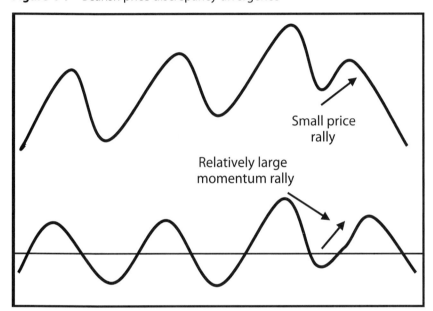

Small price rally

Relatively large momentum rally

Figure 4-2   Bullish price discrepancy divergence

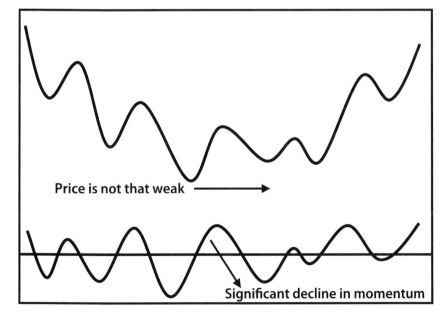

Price is not that weak →

Significant decline in momentum

Sometimes, the reverse divergence develops in a trading-range environment. In Fig. 4-5, for example, we see that the price is bump-

> Reverse divergences do not operate for a momentum indicator that has experienced a great deal of smoothing.

ing against a resistance trendline since each price peak is at the same level. However, the oscillator is not constrained by a horizontal trendline and reaches its peak toward the end of the trading range. This also qualifies a variation of the reverse-divergence principle and is typically followed by a price trend reversal.

POSITIVE

Finally, the same sort of thing can develop at a bottom, where the price keeps falling to the same level of support, but somewhere along the line, the oscillator drops to a new low. This, too, is a valid form of reverse divergence. It is important to bear in mind that the significance of the trend being reversed will depend on the time span of the oscillator. An oscillator constructed from monthly data will have a far larger trend reversal potential than one constructed from daily data, and so forth. An example is featured in Fig. 4-6. Note how the price once again makes its final low at point A and how the oscillator bottoms at point B. Figure 4-7 shows the same phenomenon but this time for a trading range where the price does not make a new low but touches it.

The reason why this concept seems to work so well is that price at

Figure 4-3   Bearish reverse divergence

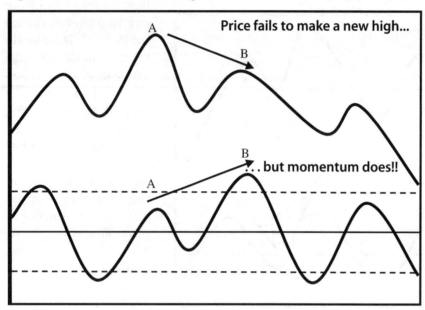

Figure 4-4   Bearish reverse divergence and MA

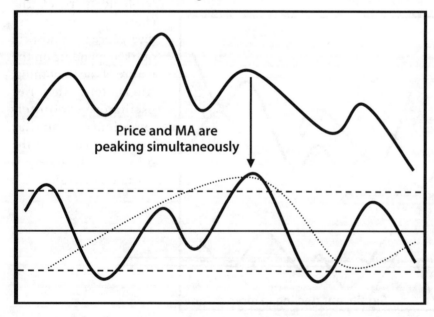

any one time is determined by a number of cyclic rhythms: a momentum oscillator with a specific time span can only reflect a very limited number of these cycles. This is similar in nature to the fact that a person is affected by everything going on around him, for 360°, in fact. However, he can see less than 180° in his field of vision at any one time and so needs to turn around to get the full picture.

The significance of the trend being reversed will depend on the time span of the oscillator.

The type of cycle being reflected by a specific oscillator, then, will depend on its time span. The longer the time span, the longer the

Figure 4-5 Bearish reverse divergence at similar price level

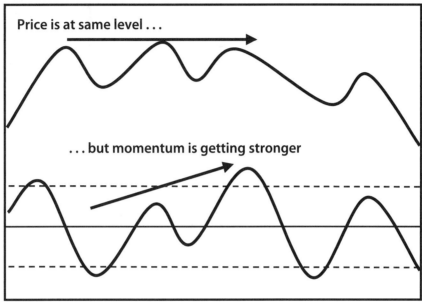

Figure 4-6 Bullish reverse divergence

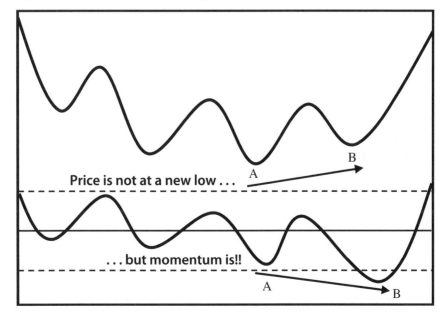

cycle being monitored. When a price peaks or troughs ahead of the ideal-cycle turning point, as reflected by the reverse divergence, this indicates underlying strength or weakness, depending on whether it is in a falling or rising trend. Perhaps some other cycle, not reflected by the specific momentum indicator being monitored, has now become dominant. At any rate, the bottom line is that when the price peaks or troughs ahead of the oscillator, expect a trend reversal to materialize.

COMPLEX DIVERGENCES

We learned earlier that price trends are determined by the interaction of many different time cycles. Most momentum indicators, however, only reflect one cycle since they are constructed from a specific time span. One way in which this problem can be approached is to overlay two momentum indicators constructed from different time spans, and then compare them.

Normally, both series will move in a broadly similar direction. It is when they diverge that we are given a signal of an impending trend reversal.

Figure 4-8 shows two oscillators. Most of the time they are moving in the same direction, which tells us very little. Alternately, when the shorter of the two (i.e., the dotted line in Fig. 4-9) reaches a peak and then falls toward the zero level, whenever the series with the longer time span continues to rally on to a new high, this indicates that the two cycles reflected by the oscillators are "out of gear" with each other. Remember our example of the car failing to operate on all

Figure 4-7   Bullish reverse divergence at similar price level

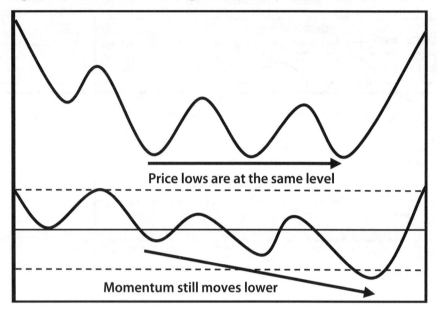

Figure 4-8   Two oscillators overlaid

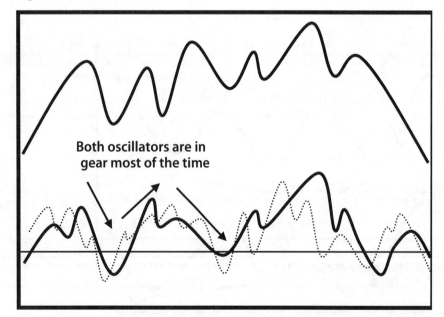

Figure 4-9 Bearish complex divergence

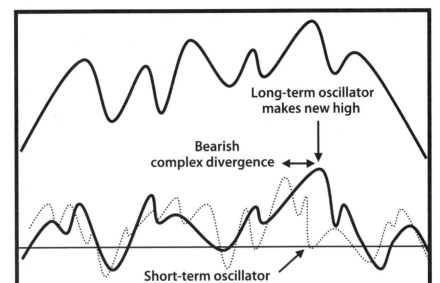

Figure 4-10 Bullish complex divergence

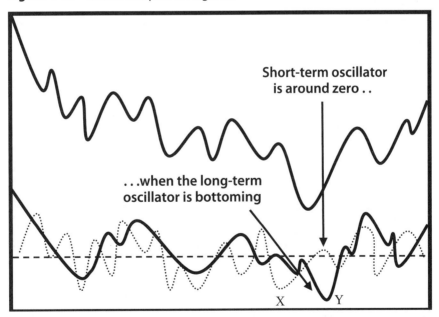

Figure 4-11   Bearish complex divergence confirmed

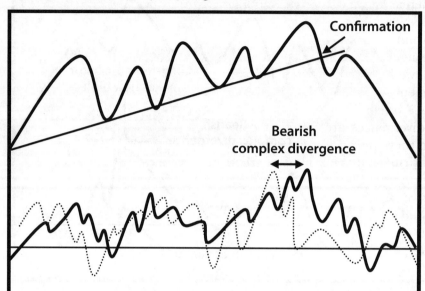

Figure 4-12   Positive complex divergence confirmed

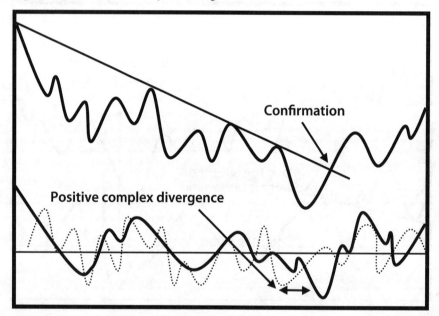

cylinders. The concept of complex divergences works in a similar way.

Complex divergences also appear at market bottoms. In Fig. 4-10 you can see the oscillator with the shorter time span reaches its low at point X, whereas the longer-term one bottoms at point Y. Note also that the short-term indicator is around zero at about the same time that its longer-term counterpart is bottoming. Again, we have the unusual situation of the two momentum series being grossly out of gear with each other.

Complex divergences are not that common, but when they appear, it is important to have them confirmed by some kind of trend reversal in the price. In Fig. 4-11 the negative divergence was confirmed by a violation of the uptrend line. And in Fig. 4-12 a positive divergence was confirmed by the violation of a downtrend line.

In Fig. 4-13 a complex divergence appears at point A, exactly as described above, but the price continues to rally. Here, the divergence is telling us that a large price movement is underway, but in this case it is in the *same direction as the existing one*. Note that in this situation no indication of a reversal in the price trend itself was given.

It is important to make sure that the two oscillators are separated by a sensible time span. If the periods are too close, such as a 10- and 12-day span (see Chart 4-1), they will reflect similar time cycles. Generally, I like to see one indicator with double the time span of the other, or pretty close to it. In that way, you can be sure that different cycles are being monitored.

SUMMARY OF COMPLEX DIVERGENCES

In sum, there are several factors to consider in complex divergence analysis.

1. *It is important to compare two time spans that are separated by a long interval.* In this sense, the term *long interval* is a relative one. What is lengthy for a short-term trend will, by definition, be brief for a long-term trend. For example, it makes sense to compare two oscillators based on a 10- and 20-day time span for a short-term trend because the indicators are separated by a substantial time span. As a result, they will reflect two totally different time cycles. If we compared a 10-day with a 12-day span, as in Chart 4-1, this would not be so, since the two are so close that they would reflect price trends caused by more or less the same cycle. A 10- and 12- day combination would also be counterproductive.

Even though the two indicators would be separated by 10 days, such indicators would, by definition, be trying to monitor intermediate-term price movements where a time difference of two weeks is immaterial.

Figure 4-13   Complex divergence unconfirmed

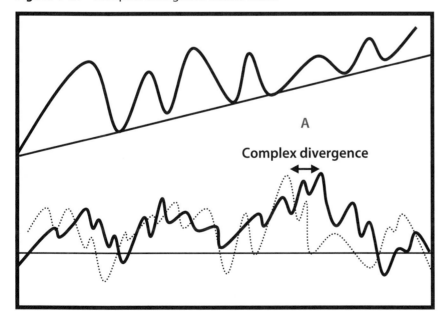

A

Complex divergence

In this case, a 10/20- day (as in Chart 4-2), or even 10/26-day, combination would make more sense.

2. *The peak in the longer-term indicator must represent a substantial one relative to the recent past.* For example, if a 13-week oscillator was being compared to one constructed from a 26-week time span, the latter should make a new high of at least a 6-month duration, usually much longer.

3. *The oscillator with the shorter time span must be at or close to an equilibrium reading at the time its longer-term counterpart is peaking.*

4. Perhaps most important of all, *complex divergences must be confirmed by a trend reversal in the price itself.*

Chart 4-1   Time spans are too close

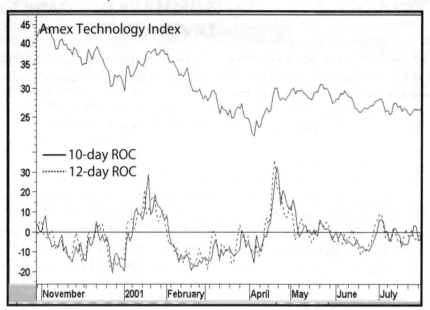

Chart 4-2   Time spans just right

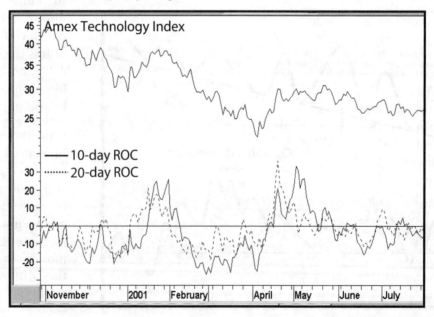

5

Divergence Variations: II

DIVERGENCE TRAPS

Most of the time, divergences proceed in a fairly orderly way, in that they get progressively lower or higher, depending on the direction of the trend. Figure 5-1 represents an exception. As you can see, the price experiences several negative divergences. Then, just as you expect the price to drop, as at point A, a final rally develops right out of the blue. This advance will normally push the momentum indicator back above at least one of the two previous peaks, typically causing the wary trader to give up his bearish sentiment. Quite often, this latest rally will prove to be a diver-

gence trap, after which the price will *then* fall in the manner previously expected. This final burst will probably be due to some unanticipated news event that results in short covering. When the

Figure 5-1   Negative divergence trap

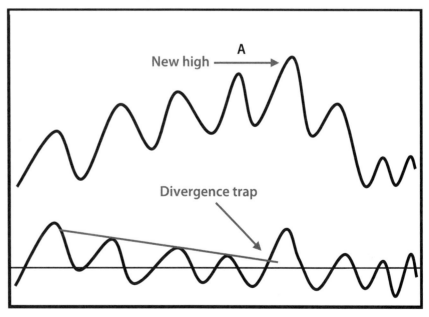

29

Figure 5-2   Positive divergence trap

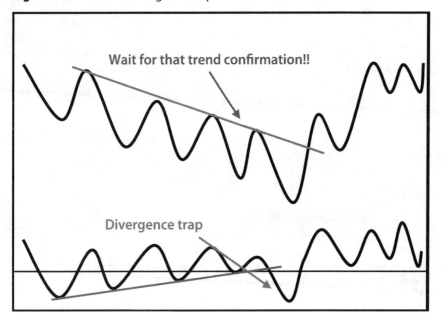

Wait for that trend confirmation!!

Divergence trap

short covering is over, there is very little to support the price and down it goes.

Figure 5-2 shows the same phenomenon, but this time at the end of a decline. See how the momentum diverges positively from the price. This looks to be a very constructive situation. Then, the price makes a new low, and the series of positive divergences gives way to an exhaustion-move on the downside. This is the move that turns out to be a divergence trap. These are clearly unfortunate characteristics, since they leave the technician totally confused until it is often too late to do anything about it. However, it does point out the importance of waiting for a positive or negative momentum structure to be confirmed by the price prior to taking any action in the market place itself.

ADVANCE BREAKDOWNS AND BREAKOUTS

Occasionally, an indication of an impending trend reversal in price occurs when the momentum indicator breaks a series of rising peaks and troughs but the price indicator does not. In Fig. 5-3a we can see that the price

experiences a series of rising bottoms, which terminate after the final peak has been seen. In Fig. 5-3b at point X, the oscillator breaks below its previous bottom. It is now *out of gear* with the price and is warning of possible trouble. This indicates that the next rally in the price is likely to be the last one for this particular trend. I term these momentum failures *advance breakdowns* because they represent very subtle warnings that the trend in momentum has reversed and that the price trend is likely to follow suit. The completed picture is shown in Fig. 5-3c together with a price confirmation.

A reversal from a downtrend to an uptrend, based on the same concept, is featured in Fig. 5-4a, where the price makes a series of lower peaks along with the oscillator. However, at point Y in Fig. 5-4b, the oscillator succeeds in rallying above its previous high. At this point,

> An advance breakdown occurs when the momentum indicator breaks below its previous bottom while price makes a higher low. An advance breakout occurs when the momentum indicator breaks above its previous high and price makes a lower high. These represent subtle warnings that the trend in momentum has reversed and that price will follow suit.

Figure 5-3a   Advance breakdown

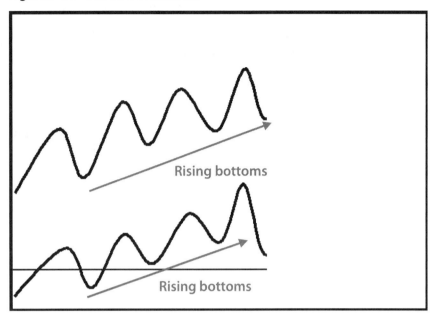

Figure 5-3b   Advance breakdown

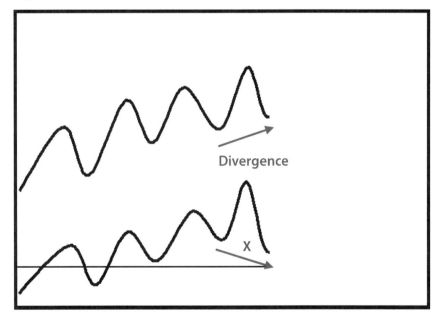

Figure 5-3c   Advance breakdown

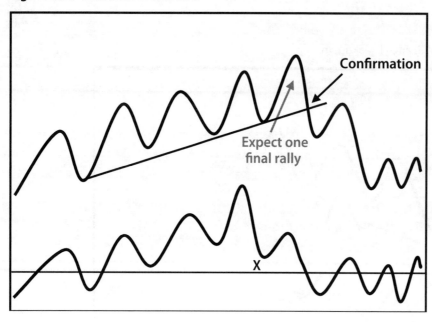

this one needs to be confirmed with a trend reversal in the price itself. Moreover, if the momentum series goes on to violate a trendline or complete a price pattern, and so on, this will add to the weight of the evidence, indicating that a new trend has begun.

DESTRUCTIVE BREAKDOWNS

Sometimes during a protracted decline, the technical position will start to evolve in what appears to be a very constructive way. For example, the momentum indicator might diverge positively with the price, as shown in Fig. 5-5a. Then the price successfully tests its low (point X) and eventually experiences an upside break from a trendline or price pattern and so on (Fig. 5-5b). On the face of it, this should be taken as a bullish sign, for indeed it is. The destructive breakdown comes when this very positive situation starts to unravel (Fig. 5-5c), after which the price typically experiences a very sharp decline. In effect, the upside breakout proves to be a whipsaw, and most whipsaws are followed by sharp moves in the *opposite* direction to that originally expected. In many, but certainly not all, cases, the destructive breakdown signals that the last decline in

Figure 5-4a   Advance breakout

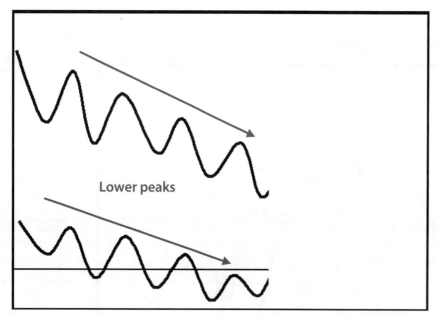

expect one more decline in the price and for that decline to be the last one. This type of reversal is termed an *advance breakout*, a completed form of which appears in Fig. 5-4c.

This advance breakdown-breakout concept is another method that helps to determine when the prevailing momentum trend has reversed. As with all the other techniques,

Figure 5-4b   Advance breakout

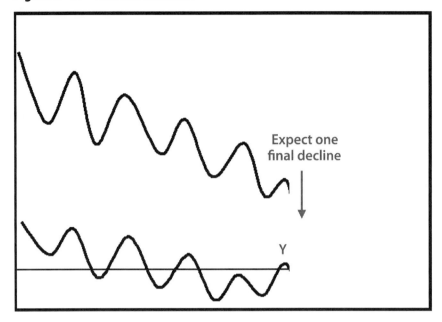

Figure 5-4c   Advance breakout

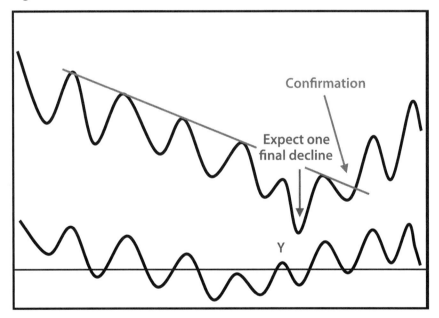

Figure 5-5a   Destructive breakdown

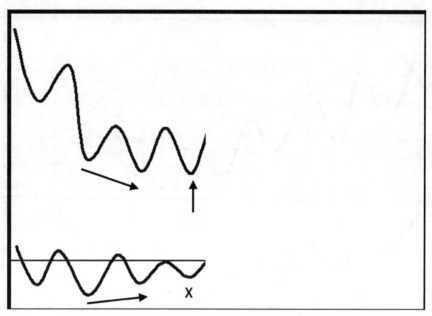

Figure 5-5b   Destructive breakdown

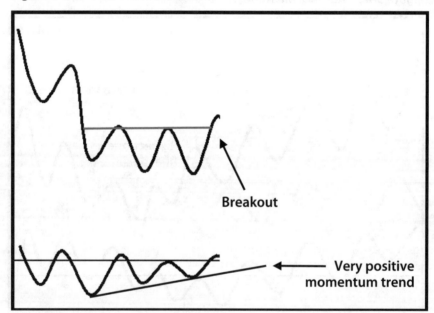

Figure 5-5c Destructive breakdown

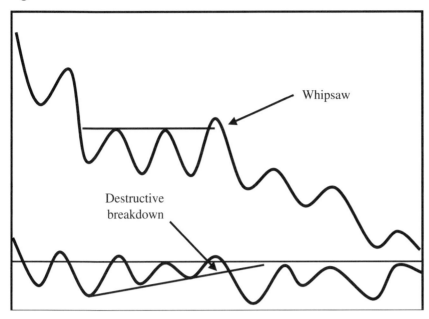

Whipsaw

Destructive
breakdown

Figure 5-6a Destructive breakdown

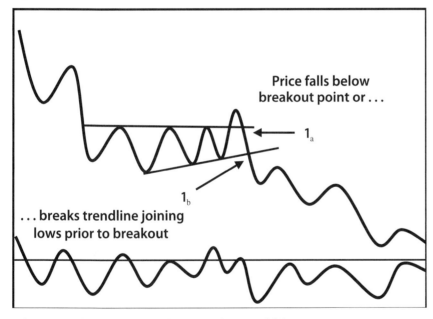

**Price falls below
breakout point or . . .**

1$_a$

1$_b$

**. . . breaks trendline joining
lows prior to breakout**

important corollary is that destructive breakdowns tend to occur as short-term corrections in primary bear markets. It is another sign of the principle that if a technical indicator is going to fail, it will usually do so when it develops as a countercyclical phenomenon.

There are several signs that indicate a destructive breakdown has taken place.

1. A break in the price below its breakout point and/or a break below a trendline joining the lows preceding the breakout (Fig. 5-6a).

2. A momentum indicator that either fails to confirm the breakout high in the price, or which experiences a violation of an up trendline joining the rising series of bottoms preceding the price breakout, or both (Fig. 5-6b).

3. In the absence of realistic trendlines, the momentum indicator and/or the price experiences a minor low below the previous bottom (Fig. 5-6c).

4. A subtle sign of weakness develops when the upside breakout is accompanied by an anemic level of volume and the downside-move attracts an expanding level of volume (Fig. 5-6d).

The destructive breakdown can also develop in a situation where there is no breakout but where the price looks as though it may

a bear market is now underway. This could be because the constructive-looking momentum characteristics that precede it reflect optimism by the bulls that the bear trend has run its course. Then, when prices break unexpectedly to the downside, this ushers in the "give up" phase, as sentiment swings pretty well universally to the bearish side. This final capitulation, then, lays the groundwork for a new bull market since all the serious selling is over. One

Figure 5-6b Destructive breakdown

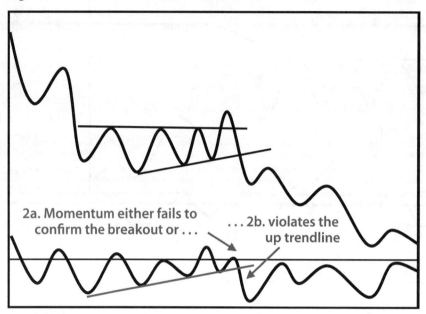

Figure 5-6c Destructive breakdown

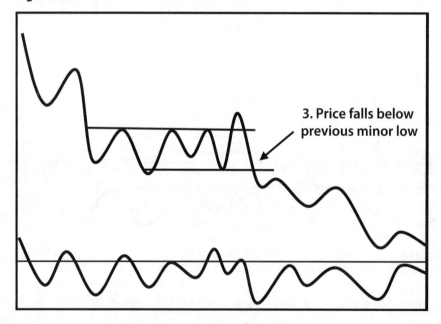

Figure 5-6d   Destructive breakdown

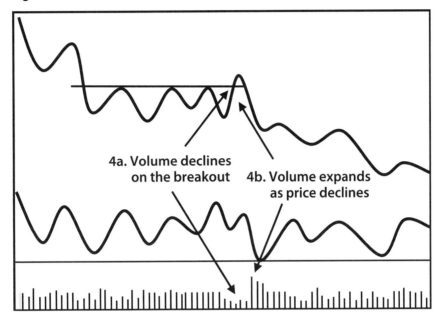

4a. Volume declines
on the breakout

4b. Volume expands
as price declines

Figure 5-6e   Destructive breakdown

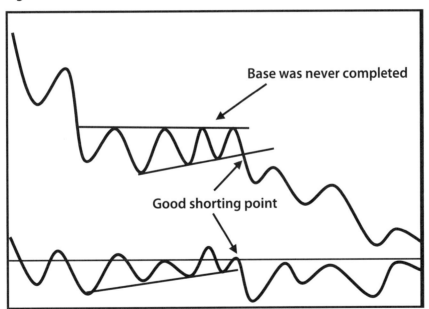

Base was never completed

Good shorting point

be forming a price pattern, as in Fig. 5-6e. If you follow the rule that a positive momentum characteristic should be confirmed by a price trend reversal, this type of situation will not cause any trouble. However, if you recognize that the trend is bearish and you are in a position to observe a breakdown taking place, then such situations can be used for the purposes of putting on a short position.

CONSTRUCTIVE BREAKOUTS

The constructive breakout is the bullish equivalent of the destructive breakdown. It typically develops in the course of a bull market where both the price and momentum configurations offer the impression of a market that is likely to decline. In Fig. 5-7a, for instance, you can see that the price makes a series of higher peaks accompanied by a declining set of momentum tops, a classic negative divergence, in fact. The price obliges by completing and breaking down from a head-and-shoulders top, Fig. 5-7b, and the scene is apparently set for a decline. However, it turns around and starts to rally, and momentum now breaks to the upside. The two trendline breaks in Fig.

5-7c are the signal that not only will the price fail to decline but is actually going to rally. This type of whipsaw is often followed by a very spirited rally. One clue that this may be the case could be provided by volume, which should ideally expand as the whipsaw is becomes apparent.

The reason why these characteristics are often followed by a strong rally is probably due to the fact that the breakdown develops as the shorts press the market. The breakdown also causes many of the technically oriented bulls to bail out. However, as it becomes apparent that the fundamentals for the bull market are still in place, more buying comes into the market. The shorts are then forced to cover, which just adds fuel to an already positive situation.

> Remember to use volume as a clue—ideally, volume should expand as the whipsaw becomes apparent.

Figure 5-7a   Constructive breakout

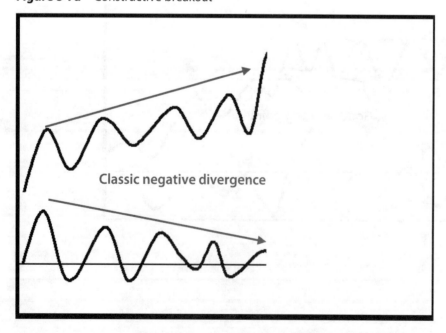

Figure 5-7b Constructive breakout

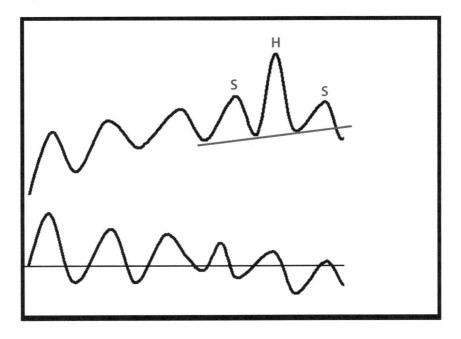

Figure 5-7c Constructive breakout

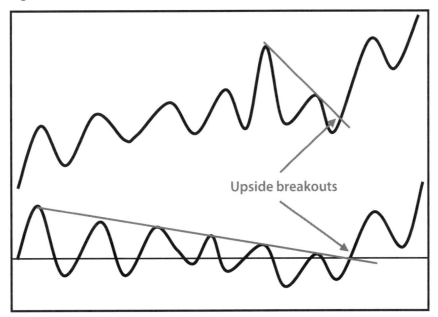

6

Trendline Analysis

MOMENTUM AND PRICE TRENDLINE VIOLATIONS

Momentum, like price, moves in trends. This means that the techniques used for analyzing price trends can be used for appraising trends in momentum. Despite this fact, we must keep in mind that a trend reversal in momentum is usually, though not always, associated with a similar reversal in the price itself. Occasionally, the analysis of an oscillator trend will actually tell us that momentum has reversed and that a reversal in price may, indeed, follow. However, the lag between the signal of a reversal in momentum and the actual turning point in price may be so great that trading decisions based on this signal will be unprofitable. That is why it is important to wait for confirmation of a trend reversal in the price itself.

Trendlines are perhaps the most easily invoked tool of technical analysis. After all, it is a relatively simple matter to pull out a ruler and draw a line connecting a series of peaks or troughs. Indeed, I never cease to be amazed at the effectiveness of this approach, despite its simplicity.

In Fig. 6-1 we see a momentum series for which it is possible to construct a trendline joining several momentum bottoms. The idea is that when the trendline is violated, the uptrend in momentum is reversed. This, of course, only tells us about momentum, nothing about the trend in price. For that, we must try to isolate some kind of trend reversal there, as well. I have found that *one of the most effective techniques in this regard is to try to match up a trendline violation in momentum with that of price.* When both are penetrated, the market usually reverses trend or, at the very least, consolidates for a while. In effect, the momentum signal represents additional confirmation in our weight-of-the-evidence theory of trend reversals discussed earlier.

The same principle holds true in downtrends. Figure 6-2, for instance, shows a couple

40

Figure 6-1 Momentum trendline break requires price confirmation (bearish)

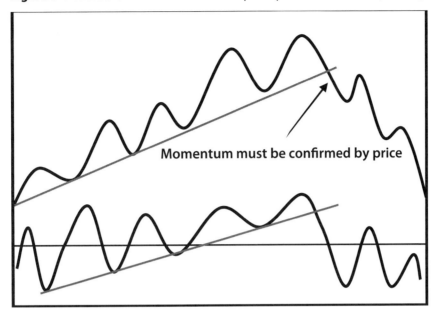

Figure 6-2 Momentum trendline break requires price confirmation (bullish)

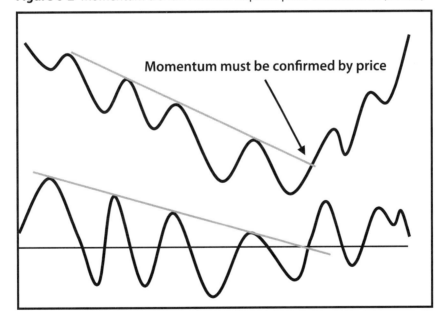

Figure 6-3 Reversal break

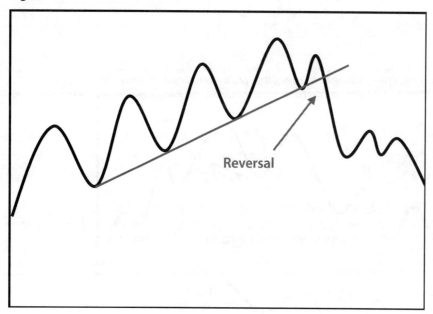

Reversal

In determining reversals of trend in momentum, one of the most effective techniques I've found is to try to match up a trendline violation in momentum with that of price.

---

of downtrend lines that join a series of peaks. When they are jointly violated, a buy signal is triggered.

In most situations, the trendline or another price confirmation signal will develop some time after the momentum trendbreak. However, when the breaks are more or less simultaneous, the signal tends to be a much stronger one.

TRENDLINE VIOLATIONS AS REVERSALS OR CONSOLIDATIONS

When trendlines are violated, one of two things normally happens. Either the price trend reverses, as in Fig. 6-3, or it is temporarily interrupted. The price is then free to resume its prevailing trend but at a slower pace, as in Fig. 6-4. Alternately, it then ends

up reversing once the consolidation is over. In momentum analysis, we find that the likelihood of a reversal (in the momentum trend) is much greater than the consolidation alternative. This is because the maintenance of a momentum trend requires a faster and faster velocity, whether on the upside or the downside. Therefore, it is a far greater task to maintain rising or falling velocity than a rising or falling price. (Remember our example of the pen being thrown into the air in chapter 3.) It is normally wiser, therefore, to *assume that a momentum trendline violation signals a reversal rather than a consolidation in the trend of momentum.*

THE SIGNIFICANCE OF A TRENDLINE

Any trendline obtains its significance from a combination of three factors:
- *Its length*
- *The number of times it has been touched or approached*
- *Its angle of ascent or descent*

Let us briefly touch upon each of these in turn. If we make the assumption that a trendline is a graphic way of portraying the underlying trend, then it naturally follows that the longer the period for which the line can be constructed, the more significant the trend. Since reversals of long trends have greater significance than the reversal of short trends, the same must hold true for the length of the lines reflected by these trends.

A trendline really represents a support or resistance point, depending on whether the

Figure 6-4 Consolidation break

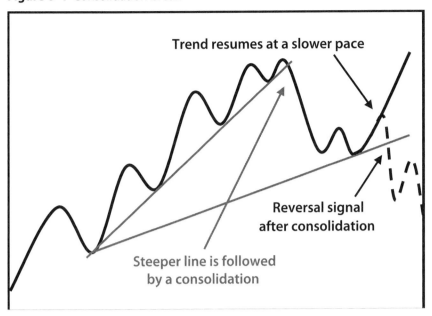

Trend resumes at a slower pace

Reversal signal after consolidation

Steeper line is followed by a consolidation

line is rising or falling. The more a line has been touched or approached, the greater the significance of that line as a support or resistance point and, therefore, the greater the implication of its violation. A line that has been touched or approached only twice, such as that in Fig. 6-5, has nowhere near the importance of one that has made contact with an oscillator (or the price) four or five times (Fig. 6-6). We tend to think of support and resistance as horizontal levels, but trendline analysis points out that support and resistance can alter their levels with the passage of time. A good trendline reflects this phenomenon.

Finally, the angle of ascent or descent is important in assessing the significance of a line. The sharp momentum downtrend line on the left of Fig. 6-7, for example, is not followed by any significant technical development. Alternately, when a line with a slower angle of

> Trendlines are actually support and resistance points—the more times they are touched and approached, the stronger the support or resistance and the greater the implication of any violation.

descent is drawn from the same level, a more meaningful trend-reversal signal is given. This is because a trend that rises or falls sharply is less sustainable than one that rises or falls in a more gentle fashion. Just think of a runner racing to victory in a 100- meter race. He can keep up this speed for a short period but could never maintain such a pace for a long-distance race. Markets are the same way. They can move quickly for short spaces of time, but then they have to rest.

A signal based on this quick dash will be less significant than if the price trend slowly advanced over a much longer period. We can now conclude that *if there is any time when it is wiser to assume that the violation of a line will be followed by a consolidation as opposed to a reversal in trend, it is the penetration of an unusually steep line.* This principle applies to both momentum and price violations.

EXTENDED TRENDLINES

Most people disregard a trendline once it has been violated. I believe this to be a mistake since an extended trendline has equally as much significance as it does prior to the violation. In Fig. 6-8 we can see that the momentum trendline was violated, but the price went on to make a new high. However, this advance was halted at the same time the momentum indicator rallied to resistance in the form of its extended trendline. This would have been an intelligent place to have taken partial profits. The actual sell signal would have come when the price itself violated its up trendline. Note that at the time of the final peak, the oscillator

Figure 6-5 Trendline as support area

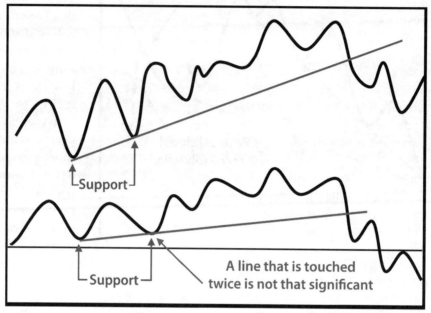

Figure 6-6 Trendline as support area

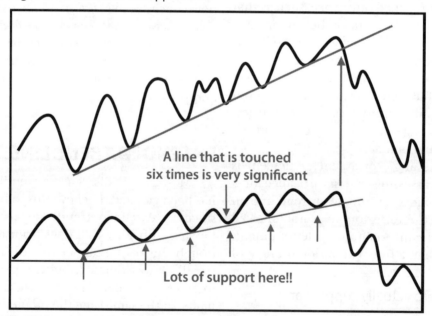

diverged negatively with the price, thus providing further evidence that the technical structure was deteriorating.

Just remember, *if a line was important prior to its violation, it will be equally as significant thereafter.* It merely reverses its role from support to resistance, or vice versa, in the case of a downtrend line.

It works the same way in the real world. For example, if you jump on a floor and the floor gives way, you will fall down to the level below. However, from your new position, the ceiling now becomes a barrier: it was support but has now become resistance.

When a momentum series experiences a rally, such as that indicated in Fig. 6-8, most traders naturally assume that the penetration was a whipsaw. However, if they took the trouble to *extend the line*, they would discover that this was an excellent place from which to anticipate a price decline.

Figure 6-9 shows the same type of situation for a reversal from a downtrend to an uptrend. Once again, it looked at first glance as if the momentum trendbreak was a whipsaw, but closer analysis in the form of extending the line shows that a good buy alert was signaled, as the momentum series found support at a trendline that was previously resistance.

If there is any time when it is wiser to assume that the violation of a line will be followed by a consolidation as opposed to a reversal in trend, it is the penetration of an unusually steep line.

Obviously, these rules are general in nature and need to be applied not blindly but with a dose of common sense. By and large, you will find that the penetration of lines that contain the elements of the three factors (length, number of touches and approaches, and angle of ascent or descent), will generally be followed by a commensurately significant move in momentum and price.

MEASURING OBJECTIVES

When dealing with trendline violations in price, in some instances it is possible to come up with measuring objectives. This concept can also be extended to momentum analysis, as shown in Fig. 6-10. For example, it is normal practice to measure the maximum distance between the trendline and the price, or in this case the trendline and the indicator, and extend it downward at the point of penetration. This objective then serves as an area to monitor from the point of view of a possible support point. If momentum reverses at such a juncture, that could also be a good place to expect the price to experience a similar phenomenon. Of course, the measuring objective may only have implications for the oscillator, but quite

Figure 6-7 Trendline — angle of descent

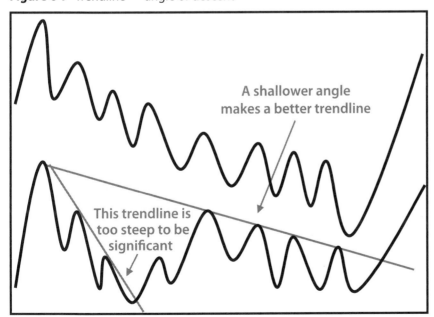

A shallower angle makes a better trendline

This trendline is too steep to be significant

Figure 6-8 Violated trendline reverses support/ resistance role

Figure 6-9 Violated trendline reverses support/ resistance role

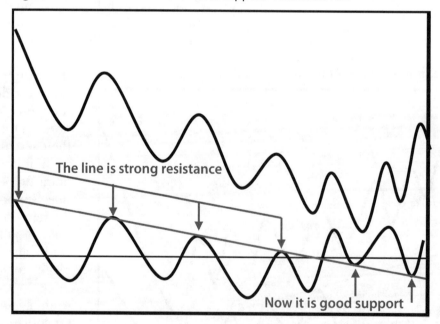

often momentum and price reverse simultaneously, as they did in this diagram.

It is also possible for the oscillator to reach multiple levels of the objective. In Fig. 6-11, for example, the objective is calculated from the maximum distance between the line and the oscillator. This is then projected downward, and we see the momentum reached support there. Then, if the objective is doubled, we see another support area for the oscillator. As it rallies, it subsequently finds resistance at the first objective. As you can see, the objective, or multiples of the objective, becomes *possible* pivotal points for the momentum indicator. I emphasize the word *possible* because these are really intelligent points for anticipating where a turn might come. Since the reliability of this technique is somewhat limited, it should *never* be used in isolation as a basis for making a forecast. So look around to see what the rest of the technical structure is saying.

Generally speaking, *the more significant the momentum trendline, the stronger the possibility that it will be followed by an important reversal in price.* If the trendline for price is just as impressive, then the odds of a major reversal relative to the time span under consideration will be that much greater.

> There are many ways to develop measuring objectives when dealing with trendline violations in price and momentum analysis. Use these in combination with other tools in order to get a big picture of the technical structure. Remember, this is our weight-of-the-evidence approach.

Figure 6-10 Trendline measuring objective

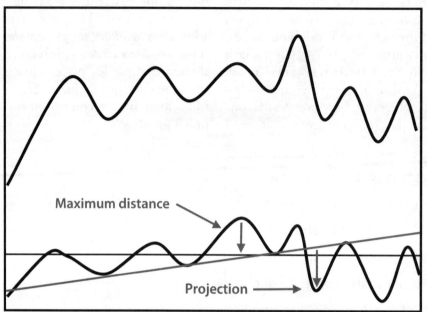

Figure 6-11 Trendline multiple measuring objectives

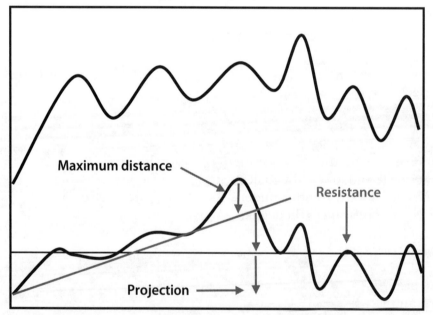

7

Peak-and-Trough Analysis and Price Patterns Applied to Momentum Indicators

PEAK-AND-TROUGH ANALYSIS: THE BASICS

The central building block of technical analysis is the concept that a bull trend consists of a series of rising peaks and troughs, and a bearish one of declining peaks and troughs. Peak-and-trough analysis can also be applied to momentum indicators, as represented in Fig. 7-1. When the prevailing trend of rising tops and bottoms is broken and the momentum experiences a lower peak and lower trough, it is assumed that a new downward trend is underway, and vice versa. Its significance will depend directly on the nature of the rallies and reactions. If they are of an intraday variety, the reversal will be of very short-term duration. Alternately, if the peaks and troughs are associated with rallies and reactions lasting for 6 weeks or more, then the reversal will be of a primary trend nature.

In Fig. 7-1 we see a series that is at first in an uptrend, as each succeeding peak is higher than its predecessor. Then a rally develops, which for the first time fails to exceed its predecessor. During the next reaction the indicator falls below the previous bottom, at point X, so the series of rising peaks and troughs has now reversed. This downtrend remains in force until the fluctuations signal rising peaks and troughs. This is shown in Fig. 7-2. In this instance, a rally off the final low is followed by a test. The test is successful, and the oscillator moves on to a new recovery high. It is when the price moves above the first recovery peak that a trend reversal at point Y, a rally, is signaled. This simple technique only signifies that the trend in momentum may have reversed: it *is not a signal that the price trend itself has changed direction*, though in most instances it eventually will. I should add that although this is a legitimate technique for both price and momentum analysis, it appears to work much more reliably for price trends. In most instances, trendline analysis is the most reliable method for identifying momentum trend reversals.

49

Figure 7-1 Upward peak-and-trough reversal

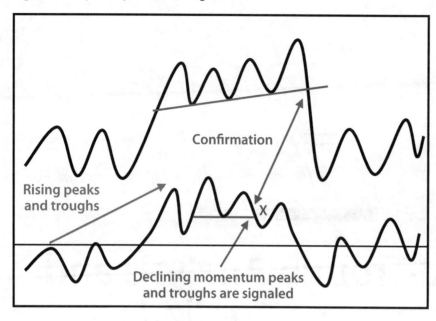

Figure 7-2 Downward peak-and-trough reversal

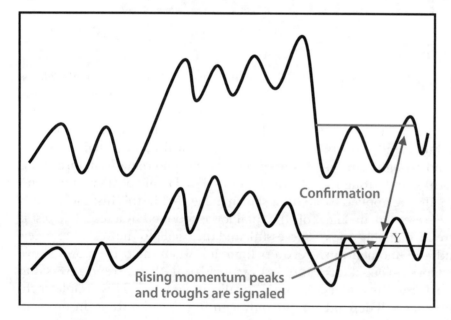

vided there is other evidence to back it up, it is perfectly legitimate. However, it is generally better to wait for the trend of both peaks *and* troughs to reverse since oscillators in their raw, that is, unsmoothed state tend to be far more random in nature than movements in the price itself. Because of this, it makes more sense to rely on trend-reversal signals that are more reliable.

The right-hand part of the diagram features another of these half-signal examples, but this time it reflects a reversal from a downtrend to an uptrend. The same principles should apply. Unless you are convinced from the action of other technical indicators, wait for the series of declining peaks and troughs at point YY to be reversed before concluding that the momentum trend has reversed.

CONFIRMATIONS

A reversal in a series of rising or falling peaks and troughs should, of course, be confirmed by the price. This is how it might work. In Fig. 7-1 we see a series of rising peaks and troughs. Then, at the horizontal line, the oscillator breaks to a new low, thereby confirming that the series of rising peaks and troughs has now been reversed. This only represents a sig-

Sometimes things are not so clear-cut, as we can see in Fig. 7-3. This is because it is possible for the first reaction in a new bear trend to take the oscillator below the previous bottom without interrupting the series of rising peaks. In this instance at point Y, the series of rising peaks is still intact but not that of the troughs. My view is that this represents half of a signal, but pro-

Figure 7-3 Half signal reversals

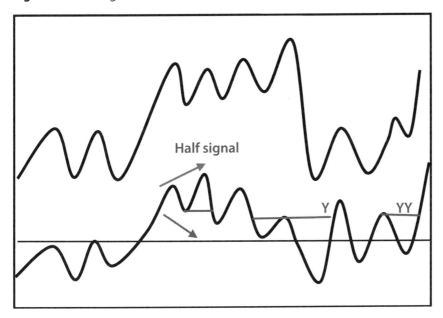

Figure 7-4 Head-and-shoulders top momentum reversal

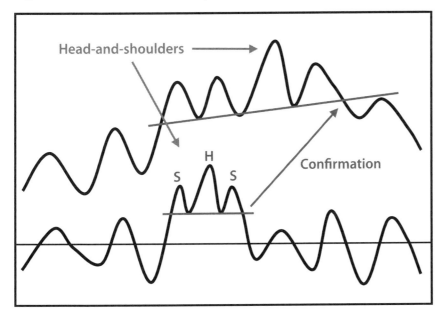

this instance, it comes when the price itself reverses a series of declining peaks and troughs. This signal is different from the others we have seen, where a trendline violation or price pattern was completed. Thus we can see that the peak-trough approach can be applied to momentum and price trends alike.

PRICE PATTERNS

Price patterns do not occur very often in oscillators, but when they do, it is time to sit up and pay attention. This is because these patterns usually result in worthwhile moves. I want to stress, once again, that the momentum reversal is just that—a reversal in momentum, not in price. However, when a momentum price pattern reversal is confirmed by a trendbreak in the price, it almost always has important consequences—relative to the time frame under consideration, of course.

Price patterns in momentum indicators take the standard forms: rectangles, head and shoulders, triple tops, triangles, and so forth. The same principles used in price analysis also apply. For example, any formation gains its significance from its size and depth. However,

nal that the trend of momentum has reversed. Consequently, we need to obtain a price trend confirmation. This comes a little later as the price breaks down below the up trendline.

In Fig. 7-2 we see a reversal from a downtrend to an uptrend. First, the oscillator makes a new high as it crosses the horizontal line. Then we must await a signal from the price. In

Figure 7-5 Inverse head-and-shoulders momentum reversal

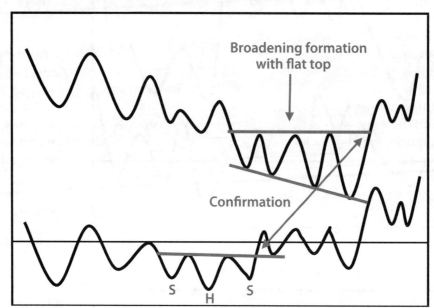

Figure 7-6 Overbought momentum breakout

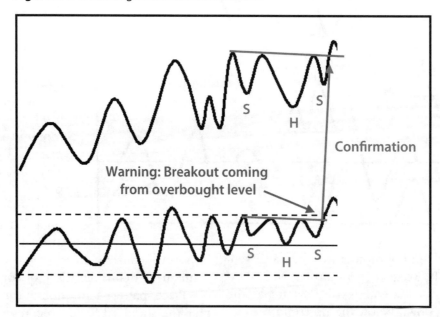

since trends in momentum are, generally speaking, less sustainable than trends in price, momentum configurations are not as large, and they are certainly far less plentiful. A possibility is featured in Fig. 7-4, where a head-and-shoulders top develops first in the oscillator and then is confirmed by one in the price series.

In Fig. 7-5 an example of a market bottom is shown. Here, the momentum base is completed and this is later confirmed by a trend-reversal signal in the price itself. It is very important to understand that there is usually a lag between the time the oscillator completes its formation and the actual trend confirmation signal by the price. The momentum series is nearly always giving *advance* warning that the underlying technical picture is improving or deteriorating.

FALSE BREAKOUTS

One very important principle that applies perhaps more to momentum formations than those that develop in a price series is that a pattern must have something to reverse. Consider for example, the situation in Fig. 7-6, where a breakout from a reverse head-and-shoulders pattern occurs close to an overbought line.

Based on the material discussed earlier, this is a point at which we should be thinking more about selling than buying; yet this particular configuration is indicating a "buy." In this way, the rule states that *the closer to an extreme a breakout in a momentum pattern takes place, the less reliable the signal will be.*

In effect, the rule is telling us to use a little common sense and not to blindly assume that every price pattern breakout will result in a reliable move. As a general guideline, I tend to ignore upside price breakouts in momentum that occur much above the equilibrium line and downside ones that develop much below it, because the further they break out from the equilibrium zone, the more likely they are to result in a whipsaw, even if the price confirms. In Fig. 7-7 the price action is extended, and you can see that both breakouts failed, anyway.

In conclusion, price patterns are a fairly rare occurrence in oscillator series. Provided they are not formed near an overbought or oversold zone, they generally represent a reliable indication that a trend reversal in the price is about to take place. As a result, when the price confirms with some kind of trend reversal signal in its own right, this is usually a reliable signal.

Figure 7-7 Overbought momentum breakout

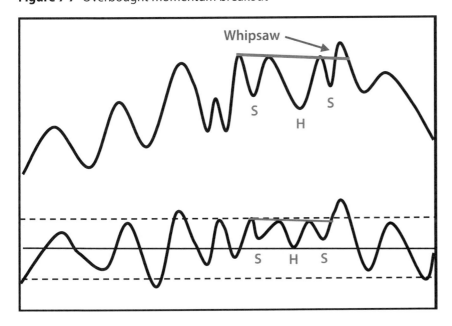

8

Moving Averages Applied to Momentum Indicators

INTRODUCTION

It is a good idea to combine momentum analysis and moving-average crossover techniques in a specific, non-general way. In other words, it is necessary to study the relationship between momentum and a moving average of momentum and see if the relationship works. In most cases, oscillator movements will be too jagged and trigger too many whipsaws to be of practical use, such as the example shown in Fig. 8-1. However, as long as movements in the raw momentum data are not too jagged, it is possible to use the moving-average crossover approach.

For example, a 12-month rate of change with a 6- or 9-month simple moving average seems to work reasonably well for most stock and bond markets. Alternately, it is unlikely that you will

Figure 8-1 MAs demonstrating whipsaws

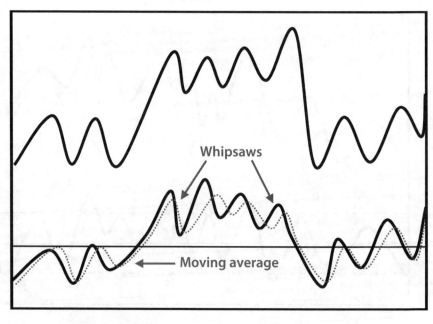

Whipsaws

Moving average

be able to find anything that works successfully in the day-to-day combat of the futures pits. Other concepts are, I believe, more practical for short-term trading.

There are three other ways in which moving averages can be used to greater advantage in momentum analysis. They are:

- *Double moving-average crossovers*
- *Moving-average directional changes*
- *Predetermined benchmark crossovers*

This may seem a bit of a mouthful to swallow, but if we take each concept in turn, you'll find that it is not that complex.

DOUBLE MOVING AVERAGE CROSSOVERS

We have already discussed the idea that the most obvious method of using moving averages in momentum analysis is to calculate some form of moving average of the oscillator, using the crossover points as indications of where the momentum trend has reversed, as in Fig. 8-1. As previously noted, this method is not generally successful because the momentum series is so jagged that more whipsaws than reliable signals are generated. This flaw typically

> It is important to keep in mind these major influences on moving average crossovers: the time span, the type of security, and the position of the momentum indicator at the time of the crossover.

recedes in importance as the time span of the raw momentum series increases. This is because the shorter the time span, the greater the influence of purely random factors. For example, an oscillator based on a 5-day time span is much more likely to be influenced by rumors and manipulation by floor traders than one calculated over a 30-day period. Such biases are nonexistent when considering periods of a year or more. This is not to imply that longer-term time spans are perfectly free from irregular fluctuations, merely that they are less likely to be subject to them.

A secondary influence will be the type of security being monitored. For example, pork bellies are notoriously volatile. Far more, for example, than 3-month Treasury bill contracts. As a result we may well find that it is possible to derive some kind of order from a moving-average crossover with a 30-day time span for the Treasury bill prices than it is for pork bellies. Once again, we can appreciate that the technical analysis requires the application of a little common sense and experimentation.

The position of the momentum indicator at the time of the crossover is also an important contributing factor to the reliability of the

Figure 8-2 MAs and whipsaw crossovers

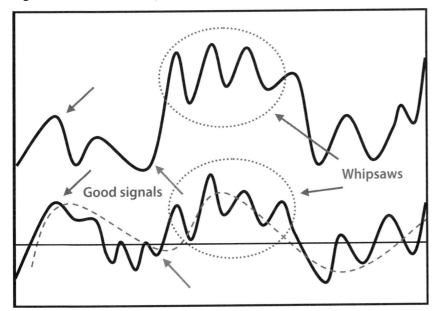

Figure 8-3   Using two MAs

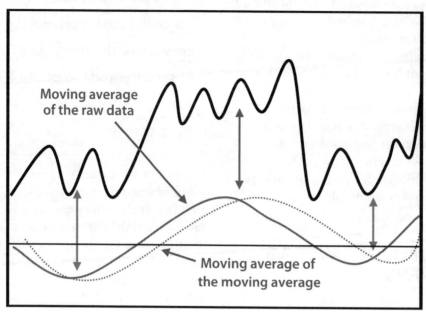

signal. The further away from the equilibrium line an indicator is, the more difficult it will be to maintain that trend. We should also note that reversals that develop closer to the equilibrium point after a divergence are often followed by very sharp moves, once confirmed by the price trend itself. Consequently, we can say that as a general rule, the more extreme the momentum reading at the time of the crossover, the more reliable that crossover is likely to be in signaling a trend reversal in momentum.

In Fig. 8-2 the first buy and sell crossovers offer reasonably timely signals for both the oscillator and the price. Then we run into some difficulties because there are no less than six whipsaws. This demonstrates that, when used with a volatile momentum series, this approach is often more trouble than it is worth. This example was put in deliberately to indicate that every rule in technical analysis is broken from time to time. It again emphasizes the need, indeed the requirement, to consider several indicators in a consensus, weight-of-the-evidence approach. Remember also that you should always relate the oscillator to your chosen moving average. Then check to see if it is a reliable method of identifying reversal trends in momentum. If it is not, either change the

time span for the moving-average time or the oscillator, substitute a different oscillator, or even try a new approach entirely. Once you are satisfied that momentum trend reversals can be fairly reliably identified, compare these signals to actual turning points in the price. After all, that is the ultimate test.

One solution to the whipsaw problem is to discard the raw momentum data, substituting the moving average instead. Then it is possible to bring in another moving average, either of the raw data or a moving average of the moving average. The idea, then, is to compare the two moving averages and use the crossovers as buy and sell momentum signals, as we see in Fig. 8-3. I call this the *double moving average method.* The whipsaws will definitely be reduced quite dramatically in some cases, but the timing of the signals will also be delayed a little. It should only be adopted if reliability is satisfactory, yet the loss in timeliness is not too great. Incidentally, this method forms the basis of the stochastics, trend deviation, and MACD indicators that are discussed later.

MOVING AVERAGE DIRECTIONAL CHANGE

An alternative moving-average approach is to use changes in direction as a mechanism for generating signals. In this case, it is important for the moving average either to be constructed from a long time span or, alternately, to be

Figure 8-4 Directional changes in smoothed momentum

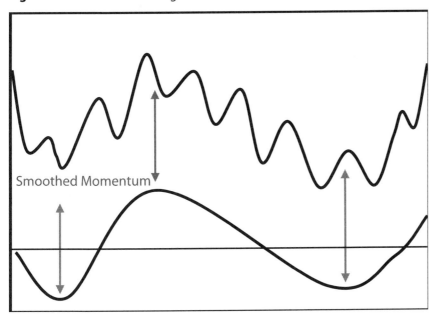

Figure 8-5 Directional change offering late signals

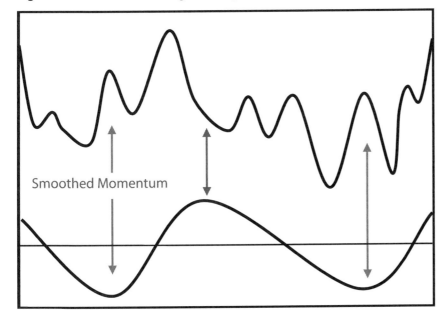

smoothed on at least one occasion; otherwise, a huge number of whipsaw signals will be triggered.

In Fig. 8-4 you can see that, by and large, the directional changes certainly offer good momentum reversal signals, and these correspond with changes in trend for the price as well. However, this is a concocted example.

Figure 8-5 shows a situation that is more reflective of probable market conditions. The first signal on the left, for example, is quite a bit late and develops well after the price has started to turn. The next sell and subsequent buy signal are also late. This is because the decline and fast upward reaction in the price are far too quick for this slow-moving, smoothed momentum indicator to pick up. Alternately, if you use changes in the direction of the oscillator purely as a filter, then this approach will be far more useful. For example, say the oscillator reverses direction at point A in Fig. 8-6. Then you would look at the price to see whether it was very far from its turning point or if it had, in fact, yet turned. If it was quite a way from the top or bottom, it would not make much sense to use the indicator as a timing device. However, if it was close to a turning point and you could spot some

Figure 8-6   Directional change requiring price confirmation

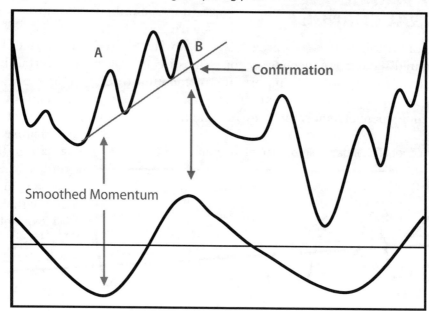

kind of trend reversal signal that had not yet transpired, then the combination of the oscillator and the trend reversal could be used to take some action. It would also be a good idea to consider the technical position of a couple of other oscillators to see if they were in agreement. If a turn in the price had not yet transpired, then the momentum reversal would alert you to look around again for a useful trend-reversal benchmark, a previous low, a trendline violation, and so forth. In Fig. 8-6 the first buy signal comes after the price has rallied quite a bit. It is usually better to ignore such signals from the point of view of entering a new position, even if they are confirmed by a trendbreak in the price. Alternately, the sell signal at point B was not only timely but was confirmed by a trendbreak in the price.

There are two other points worth noting. First, the *quality* of the signal will usually depend on the relative distance of the turning point from the equilibrium level. The further the distance, other things being equal, the more significant the signal. This does not mean that the signals that are generated from extreme levels are always reliable and those close to zero are always useless, merely that

there is a tendency for extreme reversals to be more reliable.

Second, it is occasionally possible to observe divergences between the smoothed momentum and the price series itself. In effect, the smoothing gives us a bird's eye view of specific rallies and reactions in momentum. In this way, it is easier to spot trends of improving or deteriorating momentum. Figure 8-7 shows a definite deterioration in momentum, as each successive peak is lower than its predecessor.

In some cases, it is even possible to construct trendlines joining a series of peaks or troughs in the smoothed oscillator (Fig. 8-8). When violated, these lines will generally have greater significance than those constructed from the raw data over a similar time frame.

> On occasion, it is possible to observe divergences between the smoothed momentum and the price series itself, and by doing so, you can give yourself a better view of a trend's improvement or deterioration.

Figure 8-7 Smoothed momentum and divergences

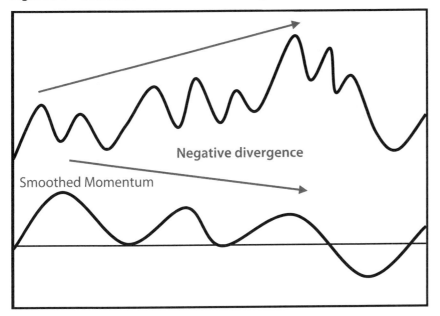

If the smoothed momentum series fails to give reliable signals from a change in direction and the object of the exercise is to make it do so, then the solution is to either expand the time frame or smooth the average with an additional exponent.

Figure 8-8 Smoothed momentum, divergences, and price confirmation

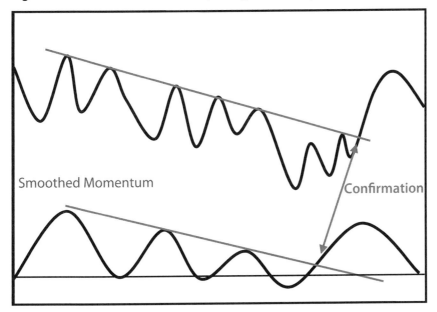

OVERBOUGHT/ OVERSOLD CROSSOVERS

There are other ways in which moving averages can signal reversals in the momentum trend. One approach is to establish overbought and oversold levels. As discussed earlier, this is typically done on a trial-and-error basis with regard to the specific security being monitored. The buy and sell indications are given when the average moves through one of the extremes and then recrosses back through it, on its return journey to the equilibrium level. Figure 8-9 features a

This is because the smoothing more accurately reflects the trend, so a penetration of the line has greater authority. Unfortunately, trendlines, or even price patterns, constructed from smoothed data are far less plentiful than those drawn from a raw series such as a 14-day RSI, and so on. However, when you can spot them, their violations are usually followed by a very worthwhile price move.

moving average with a relatively short time frame. Consequently, it experiences several whipsaws, as you can see from the signals on the left. That is why it is important to make sure that there is a trend confirmation signal from the price itself. The third signal in Fig. 8-9 was confirmed by a head-and-shoulders top completion.

Figure 8-9   Overbought/oversold crossovers

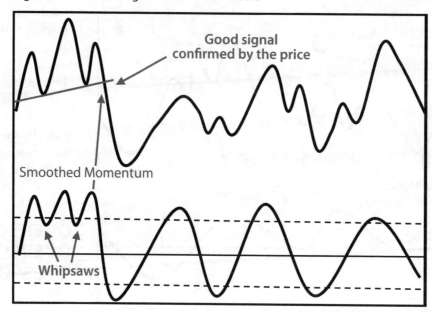

Alternately, when there is some indecisive action and the indicator does not experience an overbought/oversold crossover, the actual signal, when it finally does come, is that much more powerful because the overbought/oversold crossover realistically signals a reversal in the momentum trend.

This approach seems to work best on longer-term, smoothed momentum indexes constructed from monthly and weekly data. It is possible to get the same effect from daily and intraday charts, but the signals tend to be less reliable. In this instance, they may be a little late, but they are not normally associated with whipsaws.

There are two drawbacks to this method. The first is that price fluctuations in the security in question are often of insufficient magnitude to enable the momentum indicator to reach an extreme. In such instances, a buy signal is generated, but there is no countervailing sell signal and vice versa, as shown in Fig. 8-10. Sometimes, the indicator does not quite make it to the extreme, as with the potential sell signal at point A. It is important to remember that the overbought and oversold lines are not generally cast in stone, so a near miss such as this one certainly requires closer investigation. If other evidence, such as alternative momentum indicators, is throwing up warning flags and the price completes a price pattern, the near miss may turn out to be a great signal. In technical analysis, we are dealing in probabilities. Normally, the probability of a price reversal increases as the oscillator moves into an extreme zone. However, if it moves close to a zone and there are other reasons for suspecting a trend reversal, then this near miss should be treated with equal respect.

All of this means that this type of approach is not appropriate for a mechanical trading system, that is, unless subsidiary rules are developed to account for situations where a buy signal is generated from an oversold crossover, yet there is no countervailing sell signal, and vice versa. Nevertheless, it can be of invaluable help in picking out reliable buy and sell points in a more general way. In effect, pay attention to such signals when they occur and use the indicator in the weight-of-the-evidence approach. Do not necessarily wait for a countervailing signal to take you out of the market because it may very well fail to materialize.

Figure 8-10 Overbought/oversold crossovers

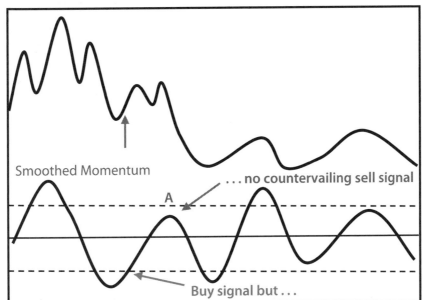

Smoothed Momentum

. . . no countervailing sell signal

A

Buy signal but . . .

Figure 8-11 Equilibrium crossovers and raw momentum

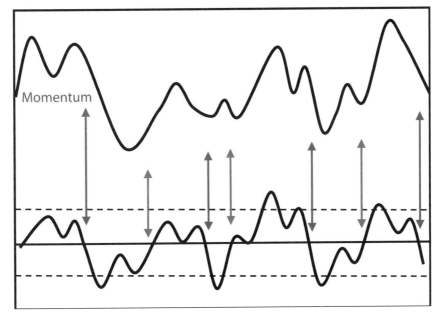

Momentum

Figure 8-12 Equilibrium crossovers and smoothed momentum

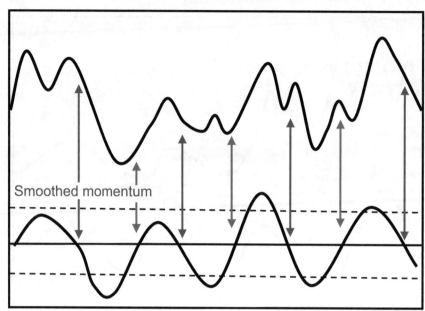

Smoothed momentum

EQUILIBRIUM CROSSOVERS

Another signal-generating possibility comes from an equilibrium crossover, as shown in Fig. 8-11. Buy alerts are given when the indicator moves above zero and sell signals when it moves below. This gets around the problem of countervailing signals from the overbought/oversold crossover method. Alternately, if the time span is too short or if you use raw data, it is likely that lots of whipsaws will be generated. I have found that on some commodity indexes, positive zero crossovers of a raw 12-month ROC have been quite helpful. The reason probably lies in the fact that commodities are very cyclical in nature and often experience a test of their bear market lows. Just as they are coming off this secondary low, the momentum series is also moving above zero.

Figure 8-12 shows a smoother version. Usually, the zero crossovers represent reliable signals that the trend in momentum itself has reversed. However, it may not be that timely for the price unless the reversal in momentum leads that of the price by a wide margin. Some securities lend themselves very well to this approach, others to the overbought/oversold crossovers. It is really a question of examining the characteristics of each one over a pretty long period of time to see if it works.

Momentum and the Primary Trend

WHY SHORT-TERM TRADERS NEED TO KNOW THE DIRECTION OF THE PRIMARY TREND

There is an old expression that tells us a rising tide lifts all boats. The same principle also applies to markets, in that short-term buy signals in a primary bull market usually result in a worthwhile move. By the same token, a sell signal in a bull market is often followed by a consolidation or no decline at all. The same concept applies to bear markets, but in reverse. For example, a sell signal will usually be followed by a worthwhile shorting opportunity, whereas buy signals more often than not will result in consolidations or whipsaws rather than a good tradable opportunity. In effect, and this is extremely important to understand, *if a whipsaw is going to arise, it will invariably develop in the manner of a contrary trend*. For the record, a primary trend is defined as lasting from as little as 9 months to 2 years, or sometimes longer.

The horizontal bars at the top of Chart 9-1 indicate primary bull and bear market environments. A positive environment is signaled by a dashed line and a bearish one by a solid line. You may have noticed that the price has been highlighted in alternating thick and thin lines. These changes in thickness are triggered by a short-term momentum signal. That signal takes place as the 14-day RSI crosses above and below its equilibrium line, that is, the 50-level. If you do not know what an RSI is, do not fret; I will cover this indicator in a later chapter. Also, I am not touting this RSI crossover as the greatest thing since sliced bread. Instead, what I am trying to do is make a point about short-term signals that develop in the direction of the main trend and those that develop in a contrary direction. If you look at all signals contained in the ellipses, you will see, first, that they are all whipsaws and, second, that they are all triggered in a direction that moves against the primary trend. Look at the buy signal at point A, for instance; it occurs during a bear market and turns out to

63

be a whipsaw. The sell signal at point B is also a contratrend signal and turns out to be a whipsaw.

Chart 9-2 features German Government Bonds, known as *Bunds*. The principle is the same, in that the arrows mark the primary trends, but this time the triggering mechanism is a 10-week moving-average crossover. The average itself is also represented on the chart next to the price. However, to maintain a balanced explanation, it is important to understand that not all pro-trend short-term signals result in worthwhile moves. Those in the two dashed ellipses indicate trading ranges where neither pro- nor contratrend signals work. Finally, the signals in the solid ellipses point out that the majority of whipsaw situations do develop in a contratrend fashion.

Since the odds generally favor most pro-primary trend short-term signals as being profitable, and contratrend ones as being suspect, it is very important that short-term traders at

> If a whipsaw is going to arise, it will invariably develop in the manner of a contrary trend.

least make an attempt to identify the direction of the main trend.

If we could quickly identify every primary trend reversal, we would have it made. Unfortunately, it is not as simple as that. Often, the indicators we are using do not signal reversals until well after the fact. One useful method is to take a 12-month moving average crossover as a signal of a primary trend reversal. In Chart 9-3, featuring the S&P Domestic Oil Index, you can see that there were some good signals, but there were also numerous whipsaws. Also, the buy signal in Spring 1999 was unduly late. This is only one of a number of techniques for identifying long-term trend reversals. We may, for example, observe the completion of major

Chart 9-1 Hartford Steam B, 1991–1995, Contratrend signals

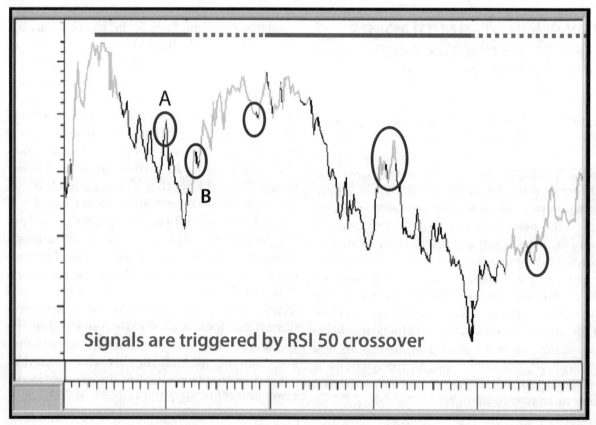

Signals are triggered by RSI 50 crossover

(Source: pring.com)

Chart 9-2 German Bunds, 1990–1997, contratrend signals

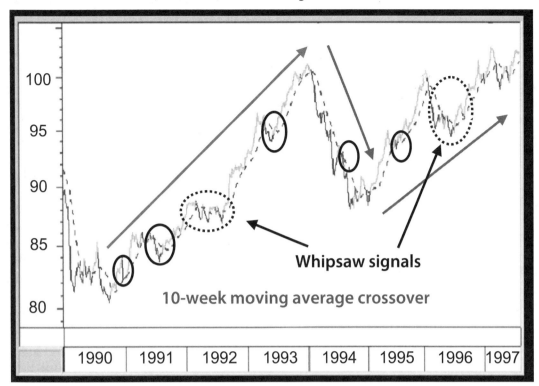

(Source: pring.com)

Chart 9-3 S&P Domestic Oil Index, 1992–2000, and 12-month MA crossovers

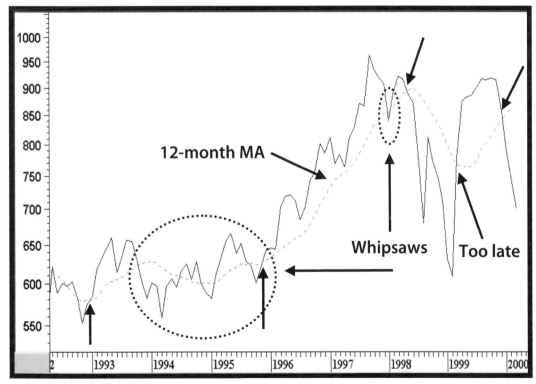

(Source: pring.com)

> Market sentiment is the tone or feeling of the market, evidenced by the movement of prices. Remember the major assumption to technical analysis studies: prices are determined by the psychological attitude of market participants towards the underlying fundamentals.

THE LINK BETWEEN MARKET SENTIMENT AND MARKET MOMENTUM

At this juncture, I would like to reiterate a point made in the introduction that relates to an important assumption made by technical analysis: *prices are determined by the psychological attitude of market participants to the underlying fundamentals.*

Let me show you what I mean. Chart 9-4 features KeyCorp, a money center bank. The solid line represents the growth in the company's earnings. As you can see, it is a more-or-less steady increase from the left- to the right-hand part of the chart. Alternately, the price of the stock fell between 1998 and 2000. This decline indicated that although profits were expected to grow, people's attitude toward those profits changed for some reason. Perhaps it was rational, in the sense that this was a period of rising interest rates and bonds or

price patterns, trendline violations, and so forth. In the next chapter, we will examine some ways in which short-term oscillators can be used for identifying changes in primary trends at an early stage, but first it is important to understand the link between changes in sentiment and movements in oscillators.

Chart 9-4   KeyCorp, 1991–2000, price versus earnings — Telescan

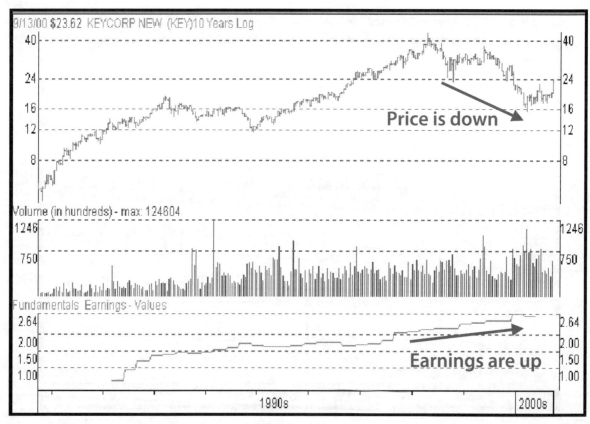

(Source: pring.com)

that money market instruments became a more attractive alternative. Alternately, it may have been irrational due to unwarranted fears. Whatever the reason, these trends in psychology, once begun, have a tendency to perpetuate. I am sure that you are saying to yourself, this is all well and good, but what does it have to do with momentum? For an adequate answer, we need to refer to a couple of charts.

SENTIMENT AND MOMENTUM IN THE STOCK MARKET

Every week, Investors Intelligence out of New York (chartcraft.com) tallies the percentage of newsletters that are bearish, bullish, or undecided on the market. The series in the upper panel of Chart 9-5 features the percentage that are bearish. Since this series is the opposite direction to the market, I have plotted it inversely to correspond with the direction of stock prices. Consequently, when the

inverted series is at a high level, it indicates few newsletters are bearish, and from a contrary aspect, we should expect to see the market decline. This, then, is a good measure of market sentiment. Underneath is a Friday close of the S&P Composite divided by its 13-week moving average. This is a trend deviation oscillator about which I will have more to say in Chapter 15.

The significant thing to note is that the peaks and troughs in the sentiment indicator correspond pretty well with those in the oscillator. Nothing is perfect and there are a few exceptions, such as the mid-1995 high reading in the S&P, which was not confirmed by the inverted bears. By and large, though, momentum and sentiment are obviously correlated. You might say that this relationship holds true just for the stock market, but take a look at Chart 9-6 featuring the Market Vane bond bulls.

Chart 9-5 Investors Intelligence bears (inverted) versus S&P momentum

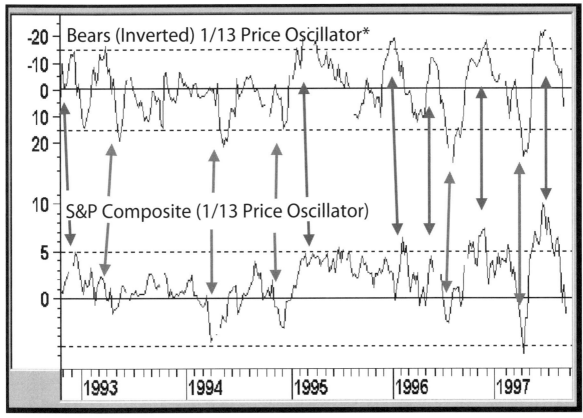

(Source: Investors Intelligence)

Chart 9-6   Government 20-year bond yield (inverted) versus Market Vane bond bulls

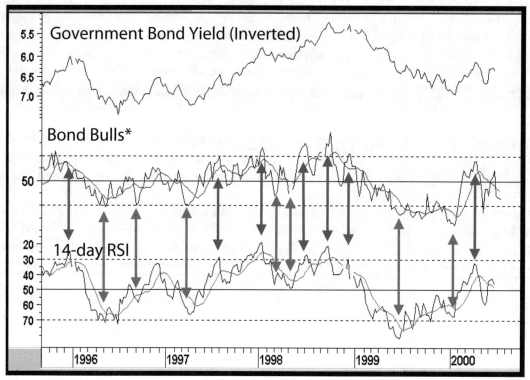

(Source: Market Vane)

Chart 9-7   Government 20-year bond yield (inverted) versus Market Vane bond bulls

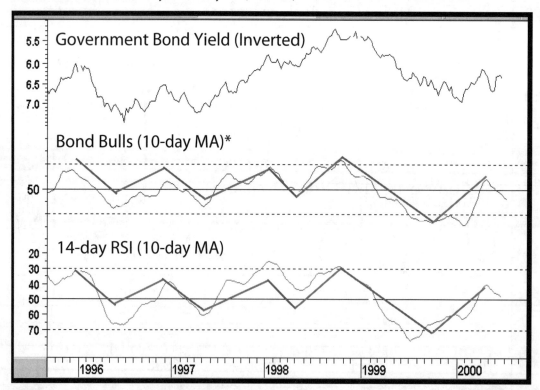

(Source: Market Vane)

SENTIMENT AND MOMENTUM IN THE BOND MARKET

The series in the top panel of Chart 9-6 is the Lehman Government Bond Index, and the series in the middle one is a percentage of traders that are bullish on the bond market, as measured by Market Vane. Finally, a 14-day RSI of the Lehman Index is featured in the bottom panel. See how the arrows connecting the peaks and troughs of the two series are pretty closely aligned and are even more closely correlated than the bears in Chart 9-5. Now look at the smoother lines traversing the RSI and Market Vane Bulls. These are 10-day moving averages. In Chart 9-7 the raw data have been removed to reveal the moving averages on their own. I approximated the actual wave forms of the averages for the Bulls and made an exact copy for the RSI. As you can see, there is an almost identical fit right up until the end of the chart in the summer of the year 2000.

The important point to grasp is that sentiment and momentum are really two different ways of reflecting the swings in the emotions of market participants.

> Sentiment and momentum are really two different ways of reflecting the swings in the emotions of market participants.

CHANGES IN PRIMARY TRENDS REFLECT CHANGES IN MASS PSYCHOLOGY

Now to return to our original assumption that primary trend reversals are really a reflection of important changes in market psychology. If that is so, then we should be able to observe character changes in the oscillators as the primary trend is reversing. It is these character changes in momentum that we will be examining in Chapter 10. However, before we do so, I would also like to add that not every primary trend reversal experiences these phenomena, just as we do not observe the formation of price patterns at every turn. However, whenever you see some of the character changes described in Chapter 10, they can legitimately be used as one relatively reliable indication that a primary trend has reversed direction.

10

How to Identify
Primary Trend Reversals with
Short-Term Oscillators

In the previous chapter, we established the close relationship between momentum and sentiment and held out the idea that changes in primary trends are brought about by major changes in psychology. Since sentiment and momentum are reflections of the same thing, it is possible to observe major changes in the character of an oscillator as the primary trend itself reverses. These character changes really fall into two categories. First, what we might term *subtle character changes*, and, second, *violent character changes*.

Before we examine the first category, it should be pointed out that the time frames for the oscillators being described fall within the 8-day to 10-13-week range. Generally, we would be looking at something in the middle, say, 20-30 days.

SUBTLE MOMENTUM CHARACTERISTICS

1. *Momentum has different characteristics in bull and bear markets.* I mentioned at the very beginning of the book that the character of an oscillator alters according to the price environment. In a bull market, oscillators tend to move into an overbought condition very quickly and stay there a long time. In a bear market, they can, and do, remain in an oversold condition for a long time. In effect, an oscillator is not unlike a migrating bird in the Northern Hemisphere. I have divided the price action in Fig. 10-1 into a bear market, followed by a bull, and finally another bear market. Note where the dashed overbought and oversold lines have been plotted in relation to the equilibrium line. As the price enters the bear phase, the true range of the oscillator is shifted south toward the bottom of the chart, in a way similar to a bird in the Northern Hemisphere migrating south to escape the cold northern winter. Then, when the bull

Figure 10-1 Oscillator characteristics in a primary bull market

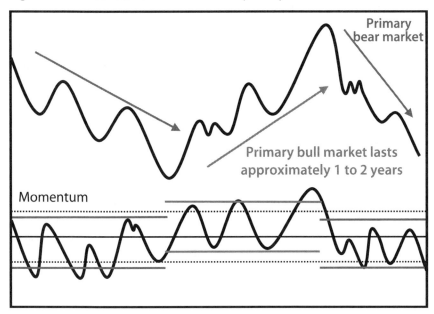

Primary bear market

Primary bull market lasts approximately 1 to 2 years

Momentum

Figure 10-2 Oscillator characteristics in a primary bull market

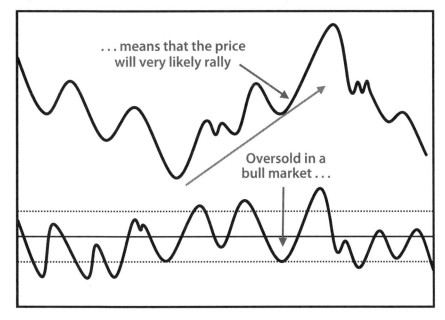

. . . means that the price will very likely rally

Oversold in a bull market . . .

nature of the migration if you will.

2. *Contratrend signals often result in whipsaws.* The second point is that if you have an idea of the direction of the primary trend, you can anticipate what might come from a specific overbought or oversold reading. In a bull market, the price is extremely sensitive to an oversold condition (see Fig. 10-2). That means that when you are lucky enough to see one, look around for some confirming signals that the price is about to rally. An example might be the violation of a downtrend line, and so on. The reason for this sensitivity lies in the fact that the oversold reading very likely reflects an extreme in short-term sentiment. Market participants are focusing on the latest bad news and using that as an excuse to sell. Since this is a bull market, they would be better served by remembering the positive long-term fundamentals that will soon emerge and using this weakness as an opportunity to buy.

market starts, the true range of the oscillator shifts north, just like the bird, finally shifting south again as a new bear market begins.

This is useful information in itself, for if it is possible to draw parallel horizontal lines like these against a momentum indicator, it can provide a valuable clue as to whether we are in a primary bull or bear market. In effect, a simple observation can often point up the

The same thing happens in reverse during a bear market. Traders are focused on bad news, which sends the price down. Then, some unexpectedly good news hits the wires and the price rallies. However, when it is fully digested, most people realize that things really have not

> Oscillator characteristics in a bull market—higher probability signals show in oversold conditions versus overbought. Oscillator characteristics in a bear market—higher probability signals show in overbought conditions versus oversold.

changed at all, and the price declines again. Thus, the overbought reading more often than not will correspond with the top of a bear market rally. An example is shown in Fig. 10-3.

Looking at it from another perspective, during a bull market the price will be far less sensitive to an overbought condition. Often, it will be followed by a small decline or even a trading range, as in Fig. 10-4. The rule, then, is: do not count on a short-term overbought condition to trigger a big decline because the odds do not favor it.

Finally, people often point to an oversold condition and use that as their rationale for a rally. Your favorite financial column might say, "analysts point out that the market is deeply oversold and a snap back rally is expected." Well, once again, it very much depends on the

environment. In a bull market, yes, that is true. But the column is more likely to say that "despite a short-term oversold condition, analysts are expecting lower prices because.. ." and then go on to list a load of bearish factors justifying their position. In a bear market, though, a market or stock is far less sensitive to an oversold reading, often failing to signal a rally, or possibly being followed by a trading range, as in Fig. 10-5, or virtually no rally at all, as in Fig. 10-6.

Now it is time to look at some of the more violent momentum characteristics that can help identify primary trend reversals at a relatively early stage. Let us start off with the overbought/oversold character changes, or OCCs, as I call them.

OVERBOUGHT/OVERSOLD CHARACTER CHANGES (OCCS)

Sometimes, after a price has been in a primary bull or bear trend lasting about a year, the oscillator changes character. This takes the form of the oscillator moving to an extreme reading in the opposite direction to the previous trend. In Fig. 10-7, for instance, the price starts off in a bull trend, which then goes bearish. During the declining phase, the oscillator is contained within its overbought zone and experiences several deeply oversold readings. This is a typical bear market characteristic for a momentum indicator. Then, the indicator rallies to an overbought reading and goes through it, thereby registering its most extreme reading since the bear market began. Please note that is not merely a regular overbought reading. Indeed,

Figure 10-3 Oscillator characteristics in a primary bear market

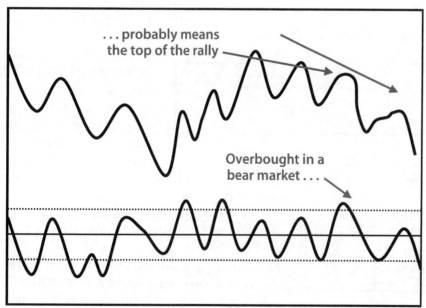

... probably means the top of the rally

Overbought in a bear market ...

Figure 10-4 Oscillator characteristics in a primary bull market

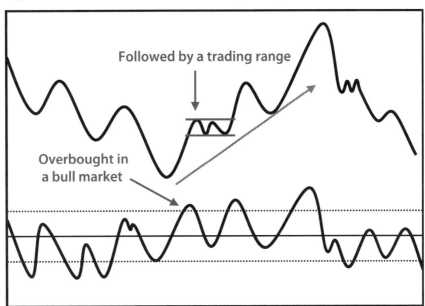

Figure 10-5 Oscillator characteristics in a primary bear market

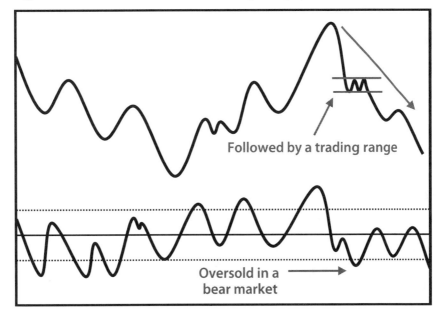

Figure 10-6   Oscillator characteristics in a primary bear market

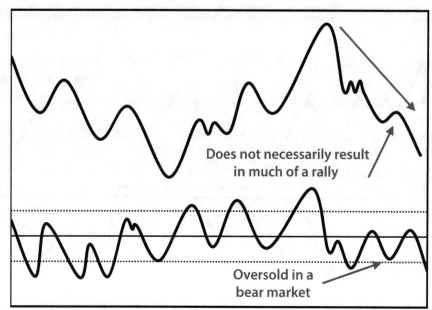

Does not necessarily result
in much of a rally

Oversold in a
bear market

Figure 10-7   Overbought character change

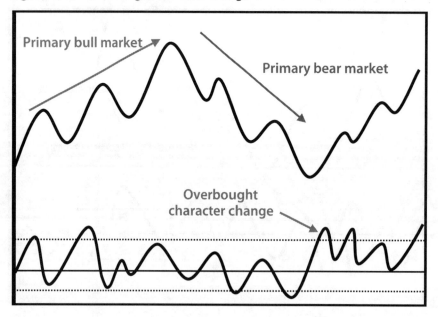

Primary bull market

Primary bear market

Overbought
character change

the oscillator should move some distance above this level to qualify. I have termed this phenomenon an *overbought character change*, or OCC, since action of this nature indicates that the underlying character of the security in question has changed. When you can identify an OCC, it usually means that the primary trend has reversed from a bearish to a bullish one. The strong underlying momentum indicates that short positions are being covered and that strong new buying is coming into the marketplace. Just as a young person on the verge of adulthood can run and swim faster than a middle-aged person, so an oscillator at

> Overbought/Oversold Character Changes (OCCs) happen when an oscillator moves to an extreme reading in the opposite direction of the primary trend. This type of extreme movement warns that a fundamental change in the psychology of the buyers and sellers has occurred.

the start of a bull market can put on an incredible turn of speed that surprises everyone.

Figure 10-8 shows the same concept, but this time for a reversal in a bull-to-bear trend. This time the *O* in OCC stands for *oversold* character change. The oversold reading is the strongest since the bull trend started and, once again, warns of a fundamental change in psychology between buyers and sellers.

MEGA OVERBOUGHTS AND OVERSOLDS

Sometimes, as a security experiences the first rally in a bull market, the initial thrust off the final low is associated with what we might term a *mega-overbought condition* (Fig. 10-9). This is a reading in the momentum indicator that takes it well beyond the normal overbought condition witnessed in either a bull or bear market. It should, for example, represent a multi-year high for the oscillator concerned, perhaps a record overbought reading. The principle is exactly the same as with the OCC: the difference is one of degree. The mega-overbought is far stronger and a much more reliable and powerful signal of a major shift in psychology. Such conditions are usually a sign of a very young and vibrant bull market. The very fact that an oscillator is able to generate such a reading can be used, along with other trend reversal evidence, to signal that a new bull market has begun. Such action represents a sign that the balance between buyers and sellers has unequivocally shifted in favor of buyers. It is something like a person using all his strength to crash through a locked door. It takes a tremendous

Figure 10-8   Oversold character change

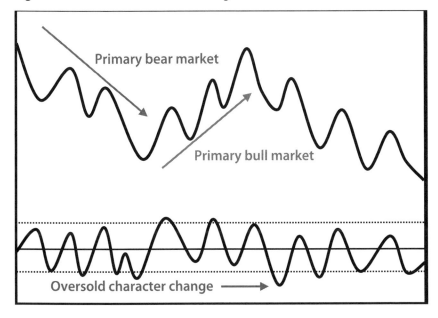

amount of energy to achieve, but once the door is finally shoved open, there is nothing to hold that person back any longer. In the same way, a mega-overbought removes the price from its bear market constraints, leaving it free to experience a new bull market.

This is about the only instance when opening a long position from an overbought condition can be justified. Even so, it can only be rationalized by someone with a longer-term time horizon. This is due to the fact that whenever an oscillator experiences a mega-overbought, higher prices almost always follow after a short-term setback or consolidation has taken place. A highly leveraged trader may not be able to withstand the financial pressure of the contratrend move, whereas the long-term investor can. In most instances, you will probably find that the correction following the mega-overbought is a sideways, rather than a downward, one, but there are just enough exceptions to cause the over-leveraged trader a lot of sleepless nights. Since a mega-overbought is associated with the first rally in a bull market, it is a good idea to check and see if volume is also expanding rapidly (see Fig. 10-10). If it takes the form of record volume for that particular security, the signal is far louder, because record volume coming after a major decline is typically a reliable signal of a new bull market. Expanding volume is a more-or-less necessary condition since it is consistent with the idea that buyers now have the upper hand and that the psychology has totally reversed.

Having said that, there are occasions when a mega-overbought is followed not by a reversal but by a change in trend. In

Figure 10-9 Mega overbought

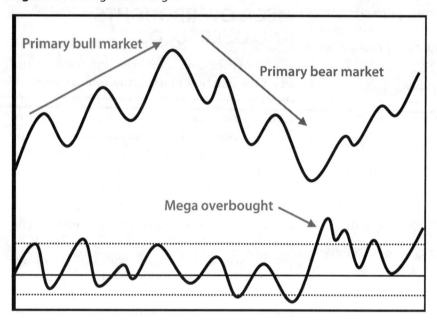

Figure 10-10 Mega overbought

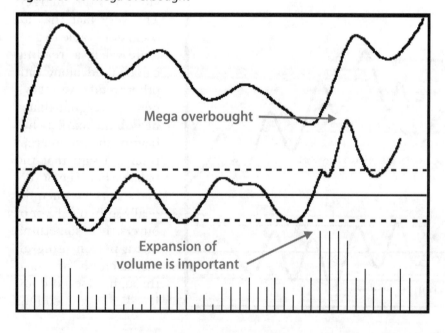

Figure 10-11 Mega oversold

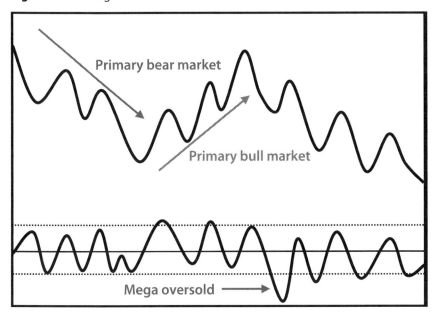

other words, the previous bear market emerges into a multi-year trading range rather than a full-fledged bull market. The point here is that normally, the low preceding the mega overbought is not decisively violated for many years.

The same concept also appears in reverse for oversold extremes (Fig. 10-11). In other words, a characteristic of a bear market is an oscillator that tends to move beyond the accepted norm and remain in an oversold state for an extended period. If the oscillator moves toward, or briefly touches, an oversold zone and then rallies, this is more a sign of a bull market or trading range.

Consequently, when a price decline, following a new bull market high, pushes a momentum indicator to a new extreme low, well beyond anything witnessed either during the previous bull market or for many years prior to that, the implication is that sellers now have the upper hand. The fact that it is possible for the momentum indicator to fall so sharply and

> Don't neglect volume readings—for instance, an expansion of volume is a necessary ingredient in a new bull market.

so deeply is in itself a sign that the character of the market has changed. When you see this type of action, you should at the very least question the bull market scenario. Look for tell-tale signs that a new bear market may be underway. What are the volume configurations on the subsequent rally? Does volume now trend lower as the price rises, compared to previous rallies that were associated with trends of rising volume? And so forth. The same possibilities of a change, as opposed to a reversal in trend, also apply, in the sense that a mega-oversold is typically the first decline in a bear market, but occasionally it can also signal a change in trend from a primary bull market to a multiyear trading range.

The difference between an OCC and a mega condition is a moot point. It is really a question of degree. While OCCs are pretty reliable, the mega conditions, being so much more powerful and unusual, offer a much better warning of a primary trend reversal.

THE CANCELLATION EFFECT

Occasionally, it is possible to spot a mega, or OCC, situation that does not work. This typically develops when the extreme psychology reflected by the momentum indicator is quickly canceled by a swing in sentiment in the opposite direction. In Fig. 10-12 we see a bull market where the momentum indicator never reaches an oversold reading. Then the price experiences a sharp decline and the oscillator falls to an extreme oversold reading. Normally, we would expect this to signal a bear market since the oversold reading indicates a change

Figure 10-12   Mega oversold cancellation

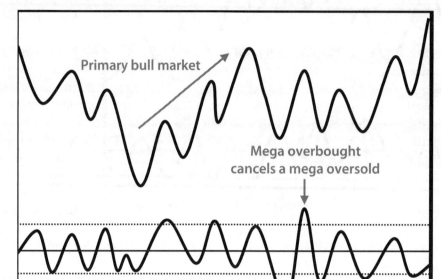

Figure 10-13   Mega overbought cancellation

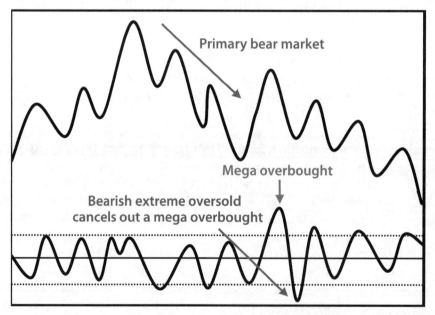

in psychology. However, in this case, the price experiences a trading range, and this is followed by a strong rally, which results in an extreme overbought reading. In effect, the second extreme reading cancels out the first and the all-clear is given for prices to work their way higher. Normally, we would expect to see the oscillator recover from the extreme oversold condition with a small bounce that takes it back to the equilibrium level, or perhaps beyond. This would be consistent with bear market activity, of course. However, the very fact that the oscillator moves immediately to an overbought extreme tells us that this is not typical bear market activity and warns us that the bearish implication of the deeply oversold condition has been neutralized. An example of this nature developed after the 1987 U.S. stock market crash, which was responsible for a mega-oversold condition. Since this developed after a long and protracted advance under the rules, the oversold reading should have signaled the start of a bear market, but it did not. This was because the oversold condition was then followed by an extreme overbought one.

The opposite set of circumstances are also valid (see Fig. 10-13). In this case, an OCC, or mega-overbought, after a bear market would be followed by an extreme oversold reading.

The oversold condition signaled that the bullish overbought reading had been canceled and that the bear market was alive and well.

CHECKLIST FOR MEGA OVERBOUGHTS/OVERSOLDS

1. A mega condition must be preceded by a primary trend lasting at least 1 year.

2. The short-term oscillator must move to a multi-year extreme.

3. Mega-overboughts should be accompanied by heavy volume.

THE EXTREME SWING

The extreme swing is a variation of an OCC, or mega-overbought/oversold. The difference is that some primary trend reversals are signaled by a swing from unbelievable exuberance, as the bull market reaches its peak, to one of complete despondency and depression, as the first bear market set-back gets underway. The opposite is true of a transition from a primary bear to a primary bull market.

To observe an extreme swing, it is necessary to experience a prolonged up or downtrend. The extreme swing then appears in a momentum indicator by an extra strong move in the direction of the then-prevailing trend. This is then followed by an extreme reading in the opposite direction. In Fig. 10-14 we see a blow-off to the bull move, as the oscillator reaches a very overbought reading. This is subsequently followed by a price decline that pushes the oscillator to

Figure 10-14　Bearish extreme swing

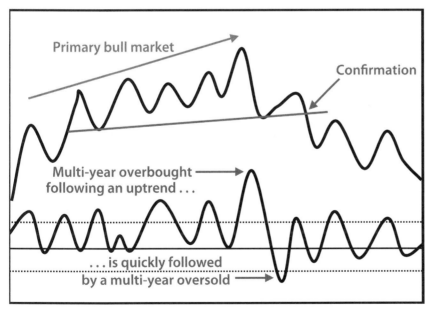

Figure 10-15　　Bullish extreme swing

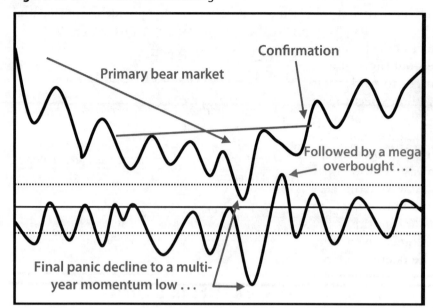

the other extreme. Such action indicates a dramatic shift in sentiment, as market participants change from a mood of euphoria to one of despondency, as the market eventually reacts in the opposite direction to that originally expected.

To qualify as an extreme swing, the first swing must represent the strongest move in several years, certainly the strongest since the initial thrust from the previous bear market bottom. It is really a climax move for the bull market. The second swing to the downside should really be a mega-oversold, though, in some cases, an OCC will suffice.

This phenomenon undoubtedly develops because the first swing encourages the participants who have been right about the prevailing trend and discourages those who have been wrong. In the case of a bull market, the final rally also squeezes out all of the remaining shorts, so when the trend reverses, there is virtually no buying activity from speculators covering short positions. The preceding sharp advance also encouraged buyers, who could see that there was only one way prices could go, and that was up. As a result, decisions on the buy-side are made carelessly and without thought for the fact that prices may move the other way. When they do, such individuals are flushed out of the market with no quarter given. Since there are few short sellers able to pick up the pieces, the price drops ferociously.

Extreme swings also develop between a bear and bull primary trend (see Fig. 10-15). In this case, though, the mood swing is from total despondency and depression, as the bear market squeezes out the last of the bulls, to one of disbelief, as the market reverses to the upside. At market bottoms, the shorts gain confidence from the sharp and persistent downtrend. Even the strongest bulls are forced to capitulate, and eventually there is no one left to sell. Then, during the rally phase, the shorts are forced to cover, and new buying comes in because of the perceived improvement in the fundamentals. Since there is virtually no one left to sell, prices shoot up, and an OCC, or more likely a mega-overbought, is registered.

Needless to say, extreme swings are quite unusual, but when you can spot them, it really pays to follow their lead since a new trend invariably results.

CHECKLIST FOR EXTREME SWINGS

1. The extreme swing starts with an extreme oscillator reading in sympathy with the then-prevailing primary trend.

2. This is then followed by an extreme reading in the oscillator in the opposite direction.

11

Interpreting the Rate of Change: I

THE CALCULATION

The rate of change (ROC) is probably the easiest momentum indicator to construct. Do not let this fool you, however, as it is one of the most effective. Many people believe that a mathematically complex indicator will be superior to one derived from a simple formula. This is not the case. Some may be, but most are not. We all have the tendency to substitute the crutch of complexity for the effort of thinking. The golden rule of technical analysis is: *do not cast away an indicator because it is simple; reject it because it does not work.*

The rate-of-change calculation compares the price today with the price "n" periods ago. For example, a 10-day ROC is calculated by comparing the price today with that 10 days ago. Tomorrow's price would be compared to that 9 days ago, and so forth. The result is then plotted as a continuous series that oscillates above and

> **Rate of Change = Today's Closing Price / Closing Price "n" Days Ago**
>
> If the prices are equal, the equation equals 1. If today's price is higher, the equation is greater than 1. If the price "n" days ago is higher, the equation is less than 1. When plotted as a series, the ROC will oscillate above and below the equilibrium level.

below the equilibrium level, as shown in Chart 11-1. The longer the time span used, the greater the fluctuation of the indicator in terms of both magnitude and duration.

Chart 11-1 Phelps Dodge, 1992–1996, a 13-week ROC, and overly narrow
overbought/oversold lines

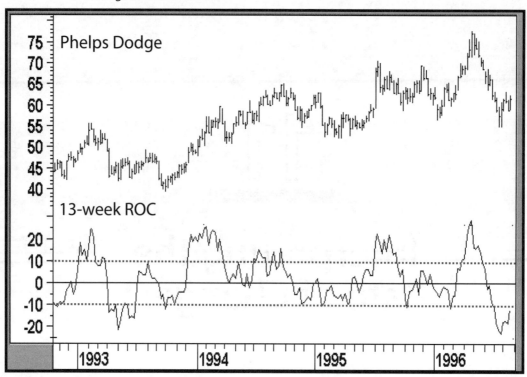

Chart 11-2 Phelps Dodge, 1992–1996, and a 13-week ROC with overly wide
overbought/oversold lines

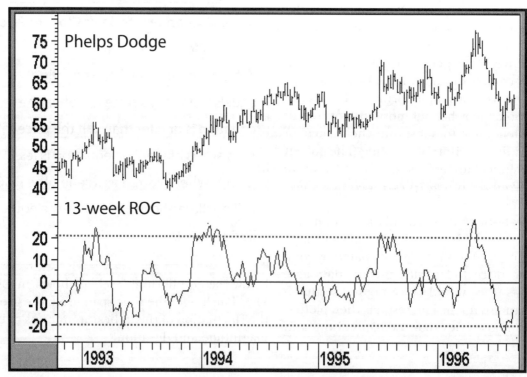

OVERBOUGHT AND OVERSOLD LEVELS

The ROC indicator lends itself handsomely to overbought and oversold interpretation. The problem is that there are no hard-and-fast rules about where the lines should be drawn, since the magnitude of the oscillations will vary according to the volatility of the underlying security and the time span being considered.

For this reason, overbought and oversold lines are constructed on a custom or judgment basis. Wherever possible, it is important to place them equidistant from the equilibrium level. This is because fear and greed tend to move in proportion and should be represented graphically in this way.

In general, we want the overbought/oversold extremes to correspond with the end of the dog leash described in chapter 2.

Unfortunately, the ROC oscillator represents a "rubber" leash, so it is necessary to be a little creative. Ideally, the lines should be drawn at such a level that they encompass as many large rallies and reactions as possible yet do not include so many fluctuations as to dilute the terms *overbought* and *oversold*. The lines in Chart 11-1, for instance, are too close to the equilibrium level since they include virtually every rally and reaction. Overbought and oversold readings, therefore, have no real practical use.

Alternately, those in Chart 11-2 are too far apart. They certainly include the very short rally at the beginning, but nothing else is included. They are also of little practical use.

Those in Chart 11-3 are not perfect, but, in a common-sense way, they are a reasonable compromise since they are close to most of the extreme points.

Chart 11-3 Phelps Dodge, 1992–1996, and a 13-week ROC with better placed overbought/oversold lines

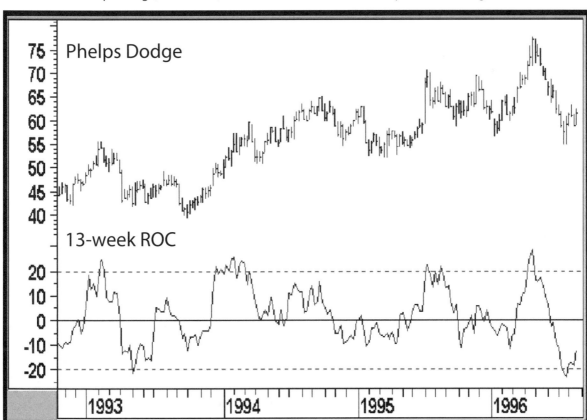

(Source: pring.com)

OVERBOUGHT AND OVERSOLD CROSSOVERS

Once overbought or oversold zones have been established they can be used for signaling reversals in the momentum trend and, presumably, price. It is very important to have some indication of the direction of the primary trend, since oversold readings are few and far between in a bull market, and overboughts a rare phenomenon in a bear market. Chart 11-4 features

> Use common sense when drawing overbought and oversold lines; you want them to be wide enough to include as many large rallies and reactions as possible while not diluting the meaning of the terms overbought and oversold.

the S&P Composite and a 39-week ROC. Note that the oscillator never reaches the oversold-minus-40-percent zone. Alternately, downside crossovers of the overbought-plus-40-percent zone provide relatively timely signals. Since this is a linear bull market and corrections are few and far between, some of the signals result in sideways trading ranges. They are nevertheless useful filtering devices that indicate when things are overdone, and they alert the technician to look out for other signs of an impending top.

Chart 11-5 for the British pound does offer some buy signals. In this case, you can see that the overbought/oversold zones have been adjusted to reflect the price action. Instead of being at plus and minus 40 percent, they have been reduced to a more practical plus and minus 20 percent in keeping with the volatility characteristics of the currency. Notice that in many instances, it is possible to construct trendlines for both the price and the oscillator, so the overbought/oversold crossovers

Chart 11-4   S&P Composite, 1989–1997, and a 39-week ROC

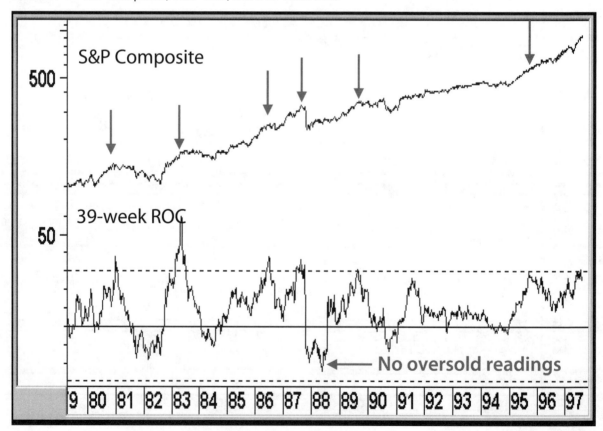

(Source: pring.com)

Chart 11-5 British pound, 1982–1997, and a 39-week ROC

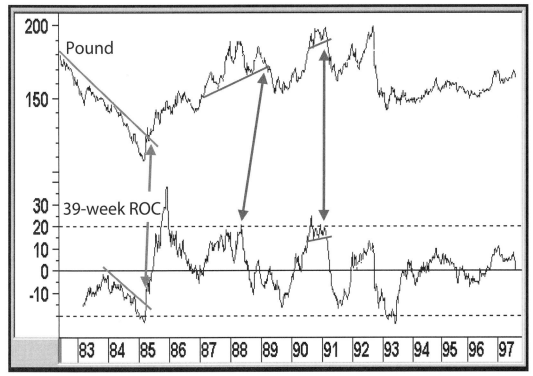

(Source: pring.com)

Chart 11-6 German DAX Index, 1950–2000, and an 18-month ROC

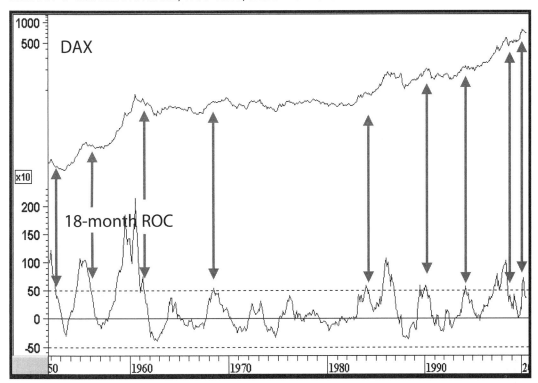

(Source: pring.com)

have some additional confirming evidence of trend reversals.

Chart 11-6 demonstrates that this type of analysis is also applicable to monthly charts. The German DAX Index has had a habit of undergoing a correction or bear market once its 18-month ROC crosses below the over-bought-plus-50-percent zone. With the exception of the premature signal in the early 1990s, this indicator has worked remarkably well during the almost 50 years covered by the chart.

Finally, Chart 11-7 features an example of a short-term ROC. It is a 30- day period plotted for the Nikkei. The arrows point out the buy and sell indications as the indicator crosses above and below the overbought/oversold zones. Most of the signals work pretty well, but there are some that do not. The cluster of buy signals in early 1995 offers several failures. Also, the two sell signals in mid-1995 were only followed by a consolidation, not a decline. Let us take a closer look at these signals in detail.

I will deal with the arrows contained in the two ellipses and rectangle later. One thing to note from all of the remaining momentum buy and sell signals is that each was confirmed by a trend signal in the price. These are shown in Chart 11-8. The mid-1995 low was a small double bottom formation. The late-1995 signal was followed by a trendline break, as was the April 1996 overbought reading. A double top was also signaled in July 1996, as the Index broke below the horizontal trendline. Finally, the early 1997 bottom was a small, reverse head-and-shoulders pattern. What then, of the signals contained in the ellipses Chart 11-7? Well, the first two arrows in the early-1995 ellipse in Chart 11-9 were not confirmed by any kind of trend-break, so they should not have been acted on in any event. The third at point A in Chart 11-9 was followed by a breakout from a small double bottom formation that would have classified it as a legitimate signal. However, it turned out to be one of those unfortunate

Chart 11-7   The Nikkei, 1994–1997, and a 30-day ROC

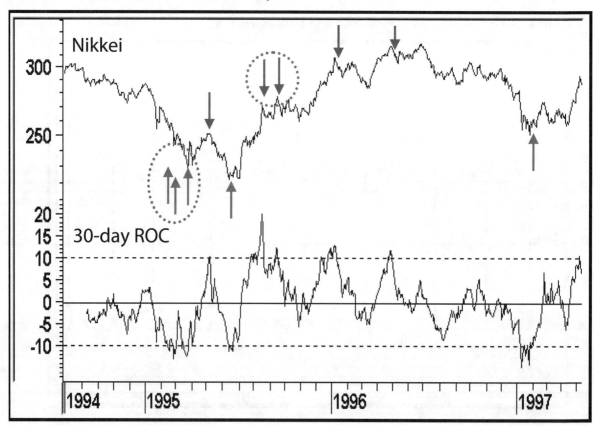

Chart 11-8 The Nikkei, 1994–1997, and a 30-day ROC

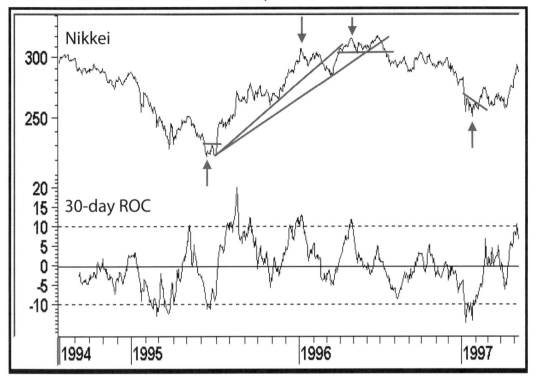

(Source: pring.com)

Chart 11-9 The Nikkei, 1994–1997, and a 30-day ROC

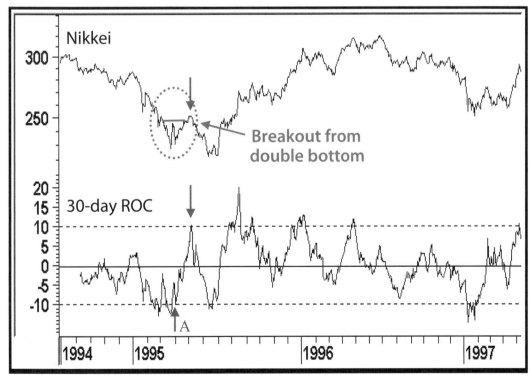

(Source: pring.com)

Chart 11-10 The Nikkei, 1995–1996, and a 30-day ROC

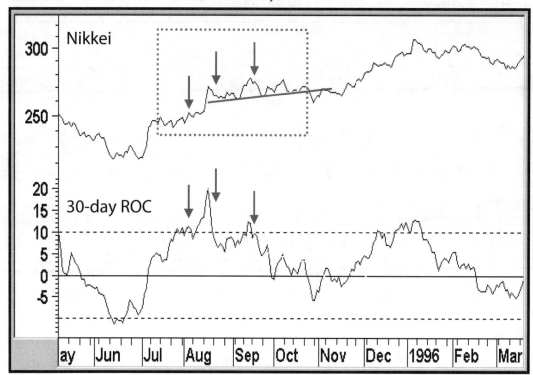

(Source: pring.com)

Chart 11-11 The Nikkei, 1995–1996, and a 30-day ROC

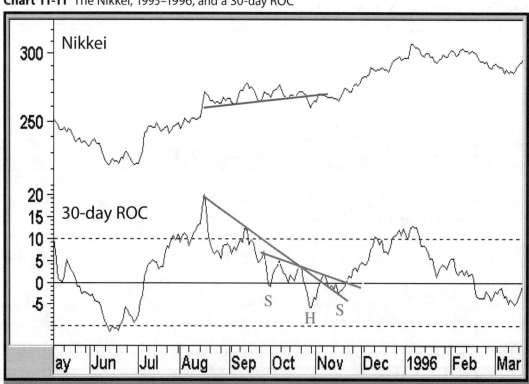

(Source: pring.com)

Chart 11-12 Lowes, 1994–1995, and a complex divergence

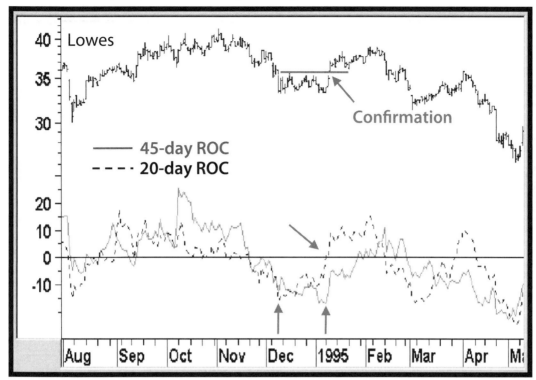

(Source: pring.com)

examples where even those signals that follow the rules fail from time to time. The May sell signal of the downward-pointing arrow preceded the final low and would have provided a warning that the double bottom formation was unlikely to work. Even so, there were no serious trend reversals that could have been used as a basis for action. The signals contained in the second ellipse in Chart 11-7 are reproduced in greater detail in Chart 11-10.

In actual fact, there were three, not two, signals. The third sell signal was later confirmed by the completion of the small top. As it turned out, this was a whipsaw since the price declined for a couple of days and then reversed direction. Fortunately, it would have been reasonably easy to spot the trend reversal to the upside. This is because the oscillator first violated a downtrend line in early November and then completed a reverse head-and-shoulders pattern later on in the month (Chart 11-11). These two events were later confirmed by the price, which was able to rally above a horizontal resistance trendline later at the end of November.

> Remember to use time spans that are spaced by a relatively wide margin so that different characteristics can be examined. If you choose two time spans that are close in value, the results will be too similar and you won't learn anything from the relationship.

COMPLEX DIVERGENCES

Now it is time to take a look at the relationship between two ROC indicators that are overlaid on each other. Using this method of display allows us to more easily compare the indicators for possible complex divergences and other phenomena that more readily lend themselves to the overlaying process.

Chart 11-12 features a 20- and 45-day ROC. The time spans have been deliberately spaced by a fairly wide margin to bring out different

Chart 11-13 Lowes, 1994–1995, and a complex divergence

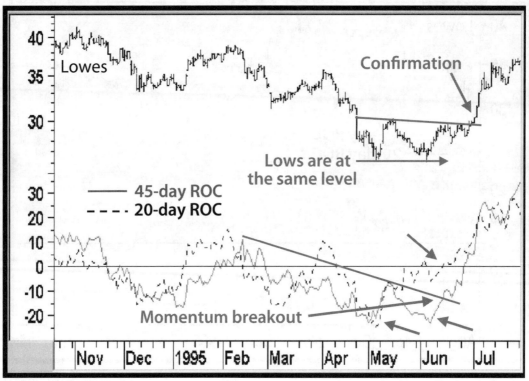

(Source: pring.com)

Chart 11-14 Lowes, 1996–1997, and ROC crossovers

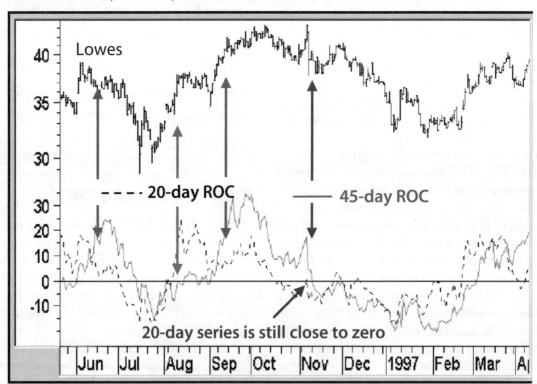

(Source: pring.com)

characteristics from the various time cycles that the ROCs are reflecting. Had I used a 20- and, say, a 25-day ROC, there would not have been much difference between the two series and nothing could have been learned from their relationship.

Chart 11-12 shows that there is a positive complex divergence that develops at the end of 1995. The 20-day series bottoms at the beginning of December, and by the time its 45-day counterpart reaches its low water mark in early January 1995, the 20-day ROC is close to the zero level. Complex divergences need to be confirmed by a price trend signal, and this was forthcoming when it broke out from a double bottom formation later in the month. Remember, the rule for a complex divergence calls for the longer-term momentum to be at an important low. Earlier, we used a 26-week ROC and suggested that the low be a record one over a 12- to 18-month period. In this chart, we are considering a much shorter period. A 45-day span is approximately one-third of a 26-week period, so the record low should be at least one-third of the minimum suggested for the 26-week series, that is, one-third of a year or, in this case, 4 months, or more. This time frame falls well within our range, so the divergence in the chart would have met the tests for a complex divergence.

> Remember, a momentum indicator that cannot experience much of a rally at a time when the price is at or close to a major high indicates a serious lack of upside momentum.

Chart 11-13 shows that Lowes forms another complex divergence later in 1995. Notice how the 20-day series bottoms in May and how the 45-day ROC makes a low at exactly the same level as its very early May bottom. Since this counts as a multi-month low and the 20-day ROC is around zero, all that was required was

confirmation from a price trend reversal. That came at the end of June in the form of a breakout from an accumulation pattern. In a sense, it could be argued that this was not a complex divergence because the second bottom for the 45-day series did not exceed the first and, therefore, is not a multi-month low. However, the key ingredient was certainly present, and that was the divergence between the short and long ROCs, which reflected the different characteristics of the two cycles.

Actually, if you take a close look, you can see that the early June low developed at approximately the same level as the one in May. However, the position of the 20-day ROC is remarkably different and represented a very strong signal in its own right. As far as this indicator was concerned, there was virtually no downside momentum at the time of the second bottom. Typically, when a price makes or closely tests a new low, and the momentum indicator is barely able to move below the equilibrium level, this is a very powerful sign that downside momentum has dissipated as far as the cycle being monitored by the oscillator is concerned. This is typically followed by a sharp rally, which was certainly true in this case. Finally, it would have been possible to construct a creditable downtrend line for the 45-day series, which was penetrated in the middle of June. This was not, in and of itself, a signal to buy, but it certainly added to the bullish scenario when the price broke out from its accumulation pattern in late June.

Sometimes, an overlaid ROC chart will yield other useful technical phenomena that are not readily apparent when the two series are plotted separately. In virtually every situation, the short-term ROC will reverse ahead of its longer-term counterpart. In fact, you can generate buy and sell signals when the short-term oscillator crosses above and below the longer-term one. These are shown by the arrows in Chart 11-14. See how this happens in June 1996, as the 20-day series crosses below the 45-day series. Then it jumps above it in late July. On the surface, this looks to be a pretty good idea. There are two problems, though.

Chart 11-15 Spot copper, 1984–1987, and a complex divergence

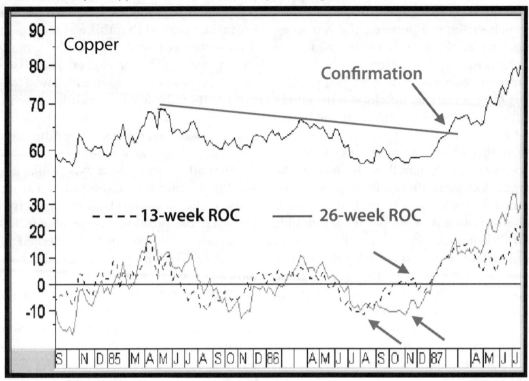

(Source: pring.com)

Chart 11-16 Cash corn, 1979–1982, and a complex divergence

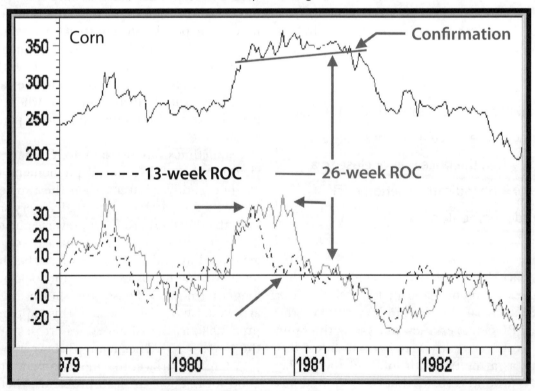

(Source: pring.com)

First, both series are volatile, which means that a lot of whipsaws are generated. Second, in trending markets the short-term series will cross prematurely, as it did in late August, thereby missing the September rally. I have tried differing time spans, even smoothing them with different averages, but the results are usually pretty disappointing. However, this chart shows something that is unusual and powerful in its effect.

For instance, the sharp rally in November 1996 takes the price of Lowes to a marginal new high. At that time, the rally was reflected by a sharp move up in the 45-day ROC. Certainly not to a new high, but given time, there was no reason to suppose that it would not have moved up to an overbought reading, had the rally extended. However, look at the 20-day series. It could not even muster an advance above the zero level. Remember, *a momentum indicator that cannot experience much of a rally at a time when the price is at or close to a*

major high indicates a serious lack of upside momentum. Typically, this is followed by a sharp decline when confirmed by a trendbreak in the price. In this case, the decline did materialize, but there was no sensible pace to construct a trendline following this false upward break. The other point to bear in mind is that the short-term series almost always leads the longer-term one at important turning points. In this instance, there was absolutely no upward leadership by the 20-day ROC. This again signified an important discrepancy and indicated that the upside break was suspect.

Now we turn our attention to some examples with a longer time frame. Chart 11-15 features the spot copper price with a 13- and 26-week ROC. This example shows a complex divergence at a bottom. The 13-week series bottomed in August 1986 and the 26-week ROC bottomed in November. Since this was a 12-month low in the 26-week series and its 13-week counterpart was close to the zero level,

Chart 11-17 Three-month Commercial Paper Yield, 1944–1964, and a complex divergence

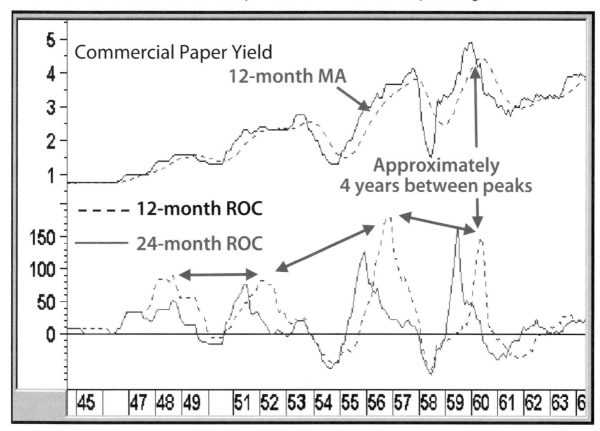

(Source: pring.com)

Chart 11-18 Cash cocoa, 1977–1988, and a complex divergence

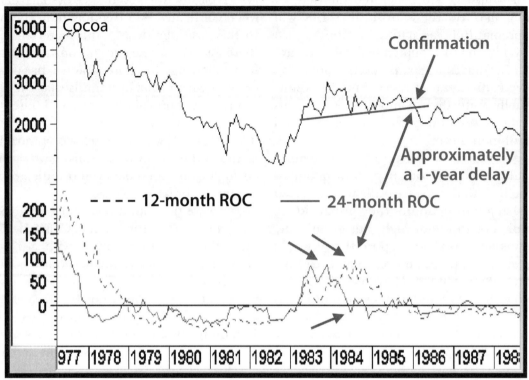

Chart 11-19 Philadelphia Gold and Silver Share Index, 1996–1997, and a reverse divergence

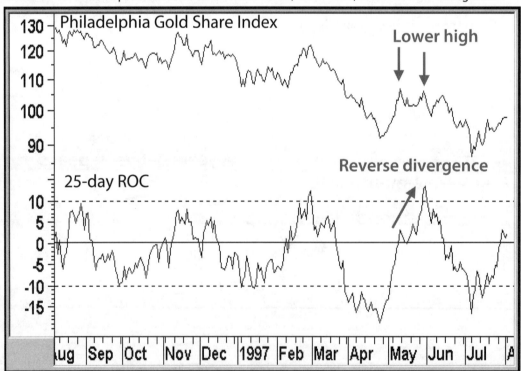

this met the test of a complex divergence. It was later confirmed as the price rallied above its 1985–1987 downtrend line right at the beginning of 1987. This was just the start, as the price tripled from its low point by the time the advance terminated.

Chart 11-16 shows a similar ROC combination but this time for corn, and the divergence appears at a top. In this instance, the 13-week series peaks in mid-1980, its longer-term counterpart tops in the fall, as the 13-week ROC is struggling around zero. There is no problem with the high in the 26-week indicator because it is certainly a record, one over at least a 2-year period. This complex divergence was then confirmed by the price, which completed a top in early 1981. The other point worth noting arises from the fact that the price was extremely close to its high in early spring 1981, yet the two ROCs were very close to the zero level. This in itself indicated a complete lack of upside momentum, which, when confirmed by the

price break, was followed by a very nasty decline.

Complex divergences also show up on the monthly charts. The 3-month Commercial Paper Yield and a 12- and 24-month ROC are featured in Chart 11-17. It is fascinating to see that the three peaks in the 1950s were all associated with complex divergences. In this particular instance, we are dealing with a 24-month ROC, so it is important that the time frame separating these peaks should be at least four years (that is, four times the minimum set for the 6-month, or 26-week, series). In all three cases, the separation between the peaks is approximately four years. Note that there are no meaningful trendlines that can be drawn against the price for a trend confirmation. Instead, I have used a 12-month moving-average crossover as the signal. Historically, this time span has worked remarkably well for this yield in the post-war period. In the case of the last peak in 1960, the crossover comes before

Chart 11-20 Lubrizol, 1996–1997, and a reverse divergence

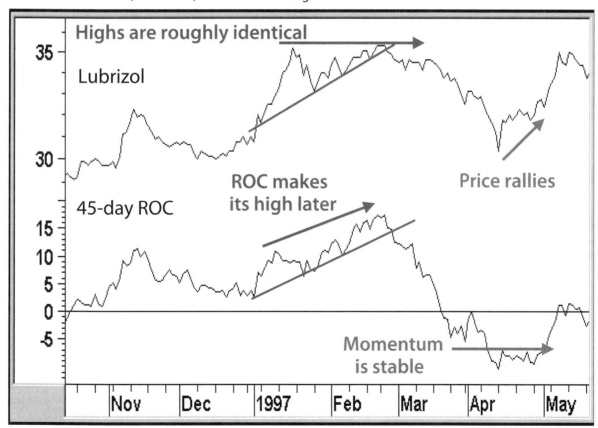

(Source: pring.com)

the peak in the 24-month ROC, and the ROC peaks after the yield. This is a most unusual situation because momentum usually tops out either simultaneously or after price. This is a reverse divergence, similar to the concept discussed earlier. The cocoa price in Chart 11-18 uses a similar 12-24-month ROC combination. Once again, we see the 12-month series peak and then retreat to the zero level at a time when its 24-month counterpart is also topping out. In this instance, the 24-month ROC is at a 6-year high, so it qualifies as a complex divergence. This is then confirmed by the price, which breaks an up trendline in late 1985. Note that the trendbreak in the price does not coincide with the complex divergence but takes place about a year later.

REVERSE DIVERGENCES

When the price makes a new high or low, this is normally preceded by one or several peaks or troughs in the momentum indicator. These are the standard positive and negative divergences where the new price high or low is not confirmed by the oscillator. Occasionally, it works the other way, in that a new high in the momentum indicator is not confirmed by the price. In a sense, this is a reverse divergence where the price is unable to reach a new high, even though the underlying momentum is strong. Chart 11-19 shows a fine example. See how the Philadelphia Gold and Silver Share Index makes a high in early May 1997. This is then followed by a small reaction and later by a rally that is not quite as strong as the previous one. However, the 25-day ROC goes on to

> Contrary to what you might first think, reverse divergences are not limited to momentum indicators with longer time frames; these patterns apply to all time spans.

make a significant new high. This is the reverse divergence. This situation can be explained by saying that the time cycle being reflected in the 25-day ROC peaked along with the oscillator. However, the price peaked ahead of the cycle, not as it normally would in a coincidental or lagged mode. A price trend that peaks ahead of a cycle peak is indicating a very tired market. Perhaps another, more bearish cycle is dominant.

Chart 11-20 features Lubrizol together with a 45-day ROC. In this instance, the secondary price peak is about the same level as that achieved in January 1997, but the ROC moves on to a significant new high. The sell signal came on a very timely basis, as both the price and ROC violated their respective up trendlines pretty close to the high. This, of course, was not a reverse divergence in the strict sense because the price reached the approximate level of the first peak. However, the same principle applies, that is, that the price is unable to respond to the strong momentum by reaching a new high. Somehow, other cycles are more dominant and are holding it back. It is a small, unusual sign, but usually a significant one. Later on, we see the same kind of phenomenon, but this time at a bottom. The price reverses on a dime, yet the ROC is unable to respond because it remains in an oversold level around the mid-April low. This seems to be the way that reverse divergences operate around market bottoms. Rather than the momentum indicator making a new low as the price rallies, it appears to move sideways. It doesn't really matter; the effect is the same. I am not saying that the momentum indicator never makes a new low, merely that it seems to prefer the sideways action as the price moves higher.

In Chart 11-21 Luby's Cafeterias experienced a sideways trading range in summer and early fall, 1994. The price was unable to rally above the resistance trendline, but the 45-day ROC was able to make a new high in August and October. This was followed by a small decline and another trading range. During this sideways price action, the same sort of thing happened, as the price was unable to

Chart 11-21 Luby's, 1994–1995, and a reverse divergence

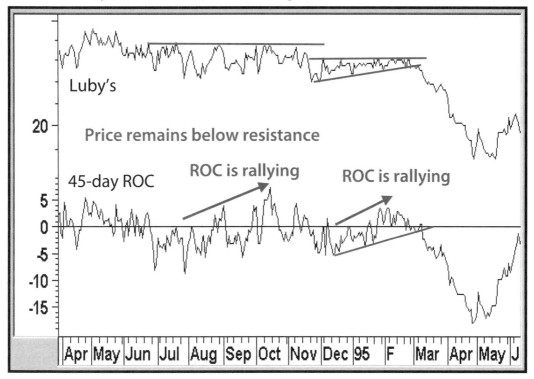

(Source: pring.com)

Chart 11-22 British pound, 1986–1995, and a reverse divergence

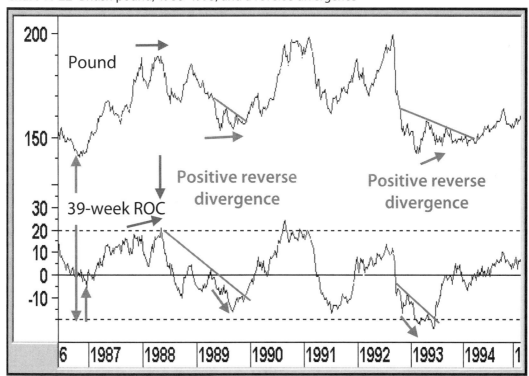

(Source: pring.com)

Chart 11-23 Emerson Electric and a reverse divergence

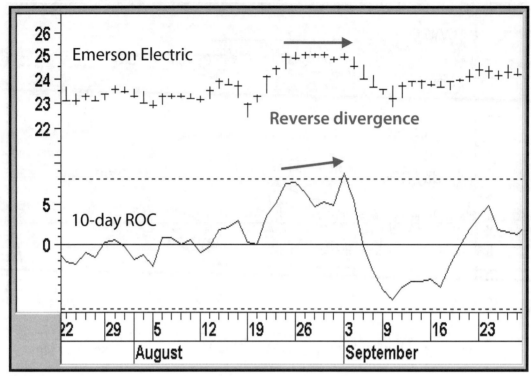

(Source: pring.com)

Chart 11-24 Emerson Electric and a reverse divergence

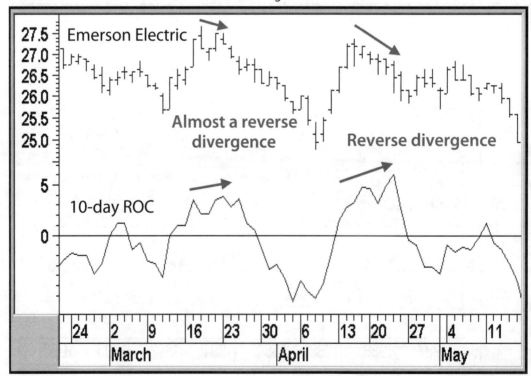

(Source: pring.com)

break to the upside but the ROC did. A pretty severe decline then followed. This again was a variation on the reverse divergence principle since the divergences did not come after an advance or decline but were formed during a trading range.

Chart 11-22 shows the British pound, featuring some truly great examples of reverse divergences. Right at the end of 1986, hardly noticeable on this scale, you can see that the arrow marking the momentum low is ever so slightly to the right of that marking the price low. Later on, at the 1988 peak, the reverse divergence is more obvious, since the ROC clearly makes a high by the arrow, yet the pound was only able to rally back to its late 1987 high. In 1989 the currency was forming the second bottom in a double bottom formation at a time when the oscillator was touching a multi-year low. The same sort of thing happened in mid-1993. The pound did experience a move to the $1.70 area later, but the event

following this reverse divergence was that the currency held above the 1993 low for many years.

You might think that reverse divergences are limited to momentum indicators with a longer time frame, long enough, for example, to peak or trough after the price series. However, this principle applies to all time spans. For example, Chart 11-23 features a 10-day ROC. You can see how the price for Emerson Electric is at approximately the same level for seven sessions, but the ROC makes a new high. This is then followed by a decline. Note, however, that the decline is relatively short, this being a function of the short time span in the 10-day ROC.

Chart 11-24 shows another example of a different period, again featuring Emerson. The example on the left has been labeled an "almost" reverse divergence because the momentum does not quite make a new high as the price starts to slip. A decline nevertheless

Chart 11-25 Cash cocoa, 1981–1992, and a reverse divergence and price patterns

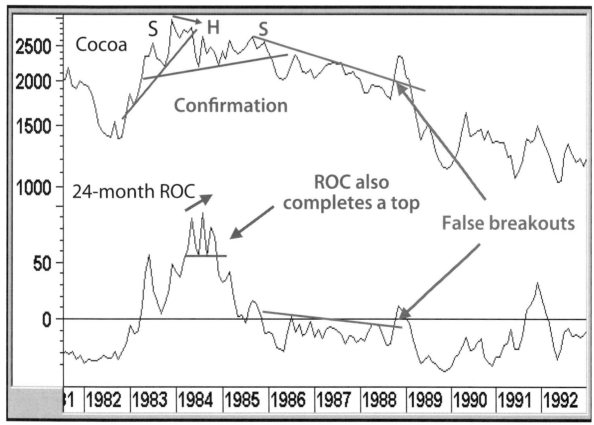

(Source: pring.com)

Chart 11-26 Three-month Commercial Paper Yield, 1944–1964, and a reverse divergence

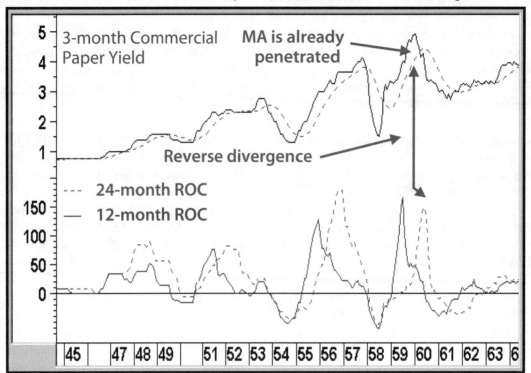

(Source: pring.com)

Chart 11-27 Philadelphia Gold and Silver Share Index, 1994–1996, and an advance breakdown

(Source: pring.com)

followed. This was not true of the momentum peak that was achieved in April, because there definitely was a reverse divergence at play during this period. You can see that in both situations it was not possible to construct a trendline or identify a price pattern. These breakouts gave us our required price trend reversal confirmations. If you are a trader, it is often a good idea to lighten up a little, even if there is no price trend confirmation, because these negative characteristics are usually strong enough to trigger some kind of negative reaction.

We now move from the relatively short 10-day time span to a very long 24-month period (Chart 11-25). The same reverse divergence momentum principles apply, but this time the trend reversal signals are far more significant. See how the cocoa price peaks right at the beginning of 1984, yet the ROC does not peak until the middle of that year. The confirmation had actually come earlier on the violation of the 1983–1984 secondary up trendline. Another confirmation arose a year later, as the price broke down from a head-and-shoulders top. Notice that the momentum series experienced a similar top formation back in 1984.

The final point to consider in this chart is that price and momentum both violated downtrend lines in 1988, but the breakout failed. The reason? If an otherwise perfect breakout results in a whipsaw, it is usually because the breakout is of a contratrend nature. This one certainly was because the bullish breakout developed in an ongoing bear market.

Chart 11-26 features the 3-month Commercial Paper Yield. The failure of the yield to make a new high along with the 24-month ROC represented a major sell signal since the 12-month MA had already been violated. Note how much longer and larger this decline was compared to the reverse divergences that were associated with the 10-day ROC that we saw earlier.

ADVANCE BREAKDOWNS AND BREAKOUTS

Advance breakdowns and breakouts are another form of divergence. An advance breakdown develops when a price is in an established uptrend with a recognizable series of rising bottoms. It is also necessary for the ROC to experience a series of in-gear rising bottoms. Chart 11-27 features the Philadelphia Gold and Silver Share Index. Both the price and 65-day ROC experience a low at the end of 1995. Each series then registers two more lows, each one higher than its predecessor. The price subsequently declines sharply into May 1995. The low at point Y breaks the previous low (point X). But look at the ROC: it holds at exactly the same level, so a positive reverse divergence is experienced. A new rally is, therefore, being signaled by the oscillator. The rally materializes and the next low in the ROC again holds at the same level, but this time the price low (point C) is higher than the previous one. The failure of the ROC to experience a higher low at this time becomes a cause for concern. Then, after a small rally the momentum falls to a new low, as the price experiences a higher bottom. This takes place in June. Now we have an advance breakdown because the price is experiencing rising bottoms, but the series of rising bottoms for the oscillator has now been reversed. The rule states that when a market experiences an advance breakdown, you should normally expect one more price rally, and when it peaks, the trend is then reversed. That is exactly what happened in this case.

> The rule states that when a market experiences an advance breakdown, you should normally expect one more price rally, and when it peaks, the trend is then reversed.

Chart 11-28 features Tootsie Roll. The price makes a low at point A, then rallies and

Chart 11-28 Tootsie Roll, 1990–1992, and an advance breakdown

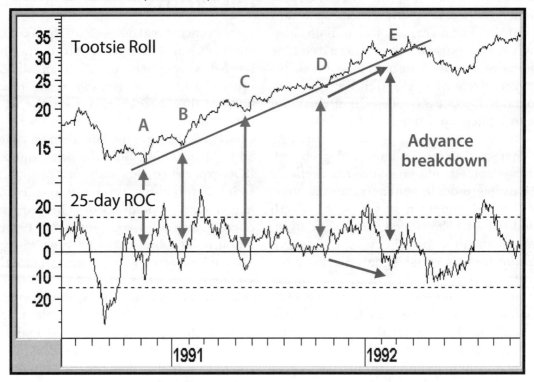

(Source: pring.com)

Chart 11-29 CRB Spot Raw Industrials, 1991–1997, and an advance breakdown

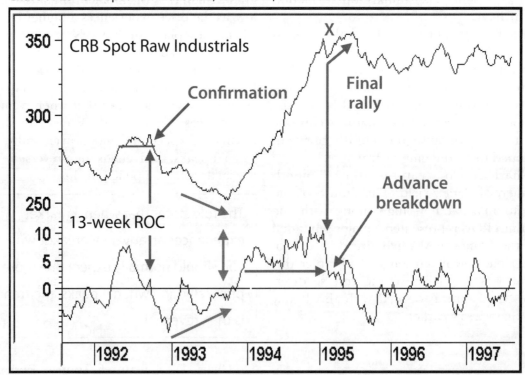

(Source: pring.com)

makes another, but higher, bottom at point B, as does the oscillator. The next decline bottoms out at point C and the oscillator is basically unchanged from its low at B. Then, both series make a higher low at point D. So far, all the lows for both the price and oscillator are in gear. Then, at point E, the oscillator breaks below the low set at D but the price does not. The break in momentum indicates that a final rally to a new high is called for. Once this has taken place, we should expect a major correction, and that is exactly what happens. Normally, the ensuing reaction is quite prolonged, but in this case it is limited, and the price then goes on to make a new high. This idea of an advance breakdown is quite rare, but when you can spot one, they often give a timely signal that an extended uptrend is over. The idea of the "final" rally is also useful, since you can mentally prepare yourself to take a closer look at the technical position when the price appears

to reach an extreme. For example, it might rally up to an extended trendline. This would then be an intelligent place to take at least some partial profits.

The CRB Spot Raw Industrial Material Index and a 13-week ROC are shown in Chart 11-29. The Index itself makes its low at the end of 1993, whereas the oscillator experiences a positive divergence. Both series then go on to register a series of higher lows until point X, where the oscillator breaks below its previous bottom. This is the signal to expect the next rally to be the final one for the move, which it is. This time, though, the price experiences a sideways trading range rather than a full-fledged decline. There is one other feature that I would like to draw to your attention, and that is the little rally that led up to the 1992 peak. See how the ROC was barely able to rally above zero, thereby indicating a potentially very weak technical position. It is of little won-

Chart 11-30 DuPont, 1994–1995, and an advance breakout

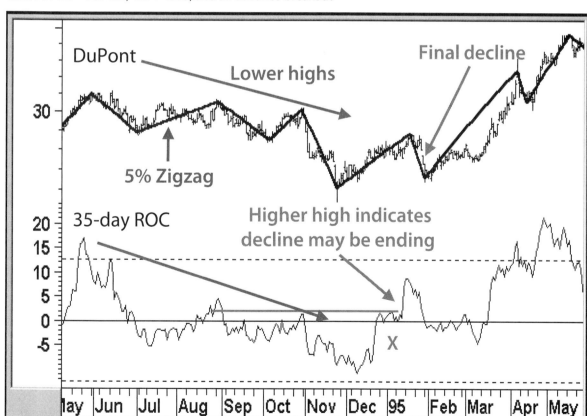

Chart 11-31 30-year yield, 1996–1997, and MA momentum crossovers

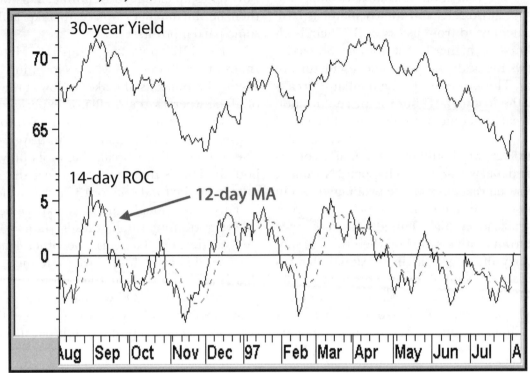

(Source: pring.com)

Chart 11-32 Swiss franc, 1981–1997, and momentum MA crossovers

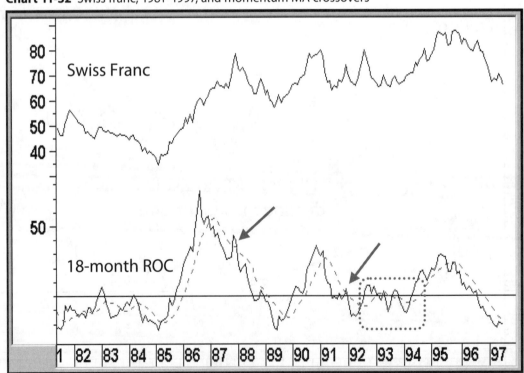

(Source: pring.com)

der, therefore, that when the price slipped below the minor low that preceded the final run-up, a sharp decline followed. In the absence of a trendline violation, this downward penetration of the minor low would have qualified as the confirming price trend reversal signal. The same type of situation developed at the late 1993 bottom, but in reverse. This time, the price barely fell below zero at a time when the Index was recording its bear market low. Unfortunately, it was not possible to construct any meaningful trendline or identify a price pattern. The best approach would have been to wait for the penetration of a moving average, say, a 40-week simple or a 65-week exponential moving average (EMA).

Now we turn to an advance breakout. Chart 11-30 compares a series of declining peaks in the price and the momentum indicator. To keep the analysis as objective as possible, I have

plotted a 5-percent zigzag. A zigzag is merely a wave that, in this case, monitors price movements of 5 percent or greater. Now it is fairly easy to spot the series of declining price peaks and then to make sure that the oscillator is in gear. Incidentally, a zigzag can be plotted for any size of price move: I just happened to choose 5 percent in this particular instance.

In this case, everything is in gear on the downside until point X. See how each momentum peak is lower than its predecessor. Then at X the oscillator rallies above its October peak, but the price does not. This is the signal to expect the final decline once the next reaction gets underway. In this case, though, the final decline is a test of the previous November low rather than a new one.

Chart 11-33 30-year yield, 1996–1997. Regular versus advanced MA

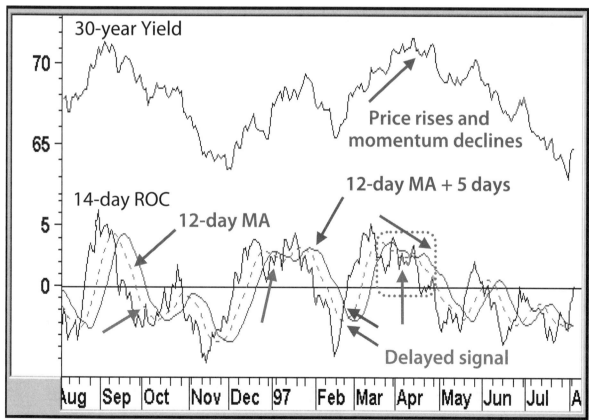

(Source: pring.com)

Chart 11-34 30-year yield, 1996–1997, and double MA crossovers

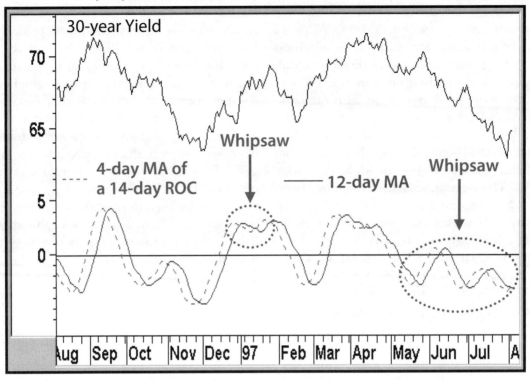

(Source: pring.com)

Chart 11-35 U.S. Dollar Index, 1996–1997, and double MA crossovers

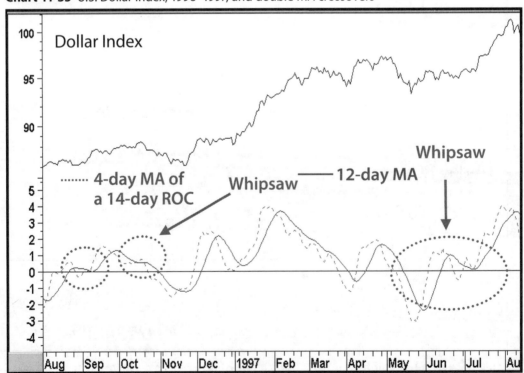

(Source: pring.com)

RATE OF CHANGE USING MOVING AVERAGES

Moving averages are used to identify reversals in the momentum trend. The most obvious method is to run a moving average through a ROC and wait for the crossovers to generate buy and sell signals, as indicated in Chart 11-31. The problem, especially with ROCs that have a relatively short time span, is that a substantial amount of whipsaw signals are generated.

Chart 11-32 of the Swiss franc, an 18-month ROC and its 9-month moving average contains fewer whipsaws, but even here we see a couple of nasty ones in the 1986–1989 decline and also in 1990–1991. When the raw ROC series does not experience much swing movement, such as the 1992–1994 period, there is even more confusion. Generally speaking, therefore, moving-average crossovers by the raw data are generally too volatile and unpredictable to be of any use.

One partial solution is to advance the average by a few periods. Chart 11-33 takes the 12-day moving average from Chart 11-31 and advances it by 5 days. This has the effect of delaying the signals a little, but often eliminates a lot of the whipsaws.

The solid, smoothed line is the delayed or advancing moving average, and the dashed one, the actual moving average. I have highlighted three whipsaws that were eliminated in the case of the advanced moving average. But if you look carefully, you will see that there were still quite a few left. The March–April period in the dashed square, for example, contained several. The price paid for this better reliability is a loss in timeliness. Sometimes, this works in a beneficial way, as the momentum indicator leads the price. An example of this developed in March 1997, when the price continued to rally after the momentum peaked. Alternately, the February 1997 low developed more or less simultaneously with the oscillator,

Chart 11-36   U.S. Dollar Index, 1990–1993, and overbought/oversold crossovers

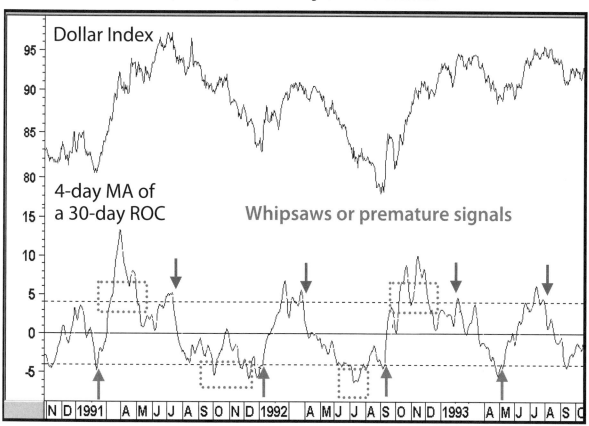

(Source: pring.com)

Chart 11-37 U.S. Dollar Index, 1990–1993, and overbought/oversold crossovers

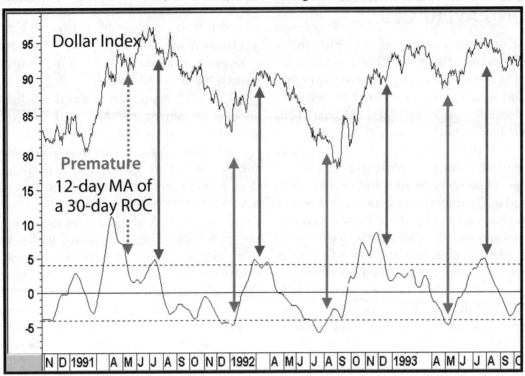

(Source: pring.com)

Chart 11-38 NASDAQ Composite, 1989–1997, and overbought/oversold crossovers

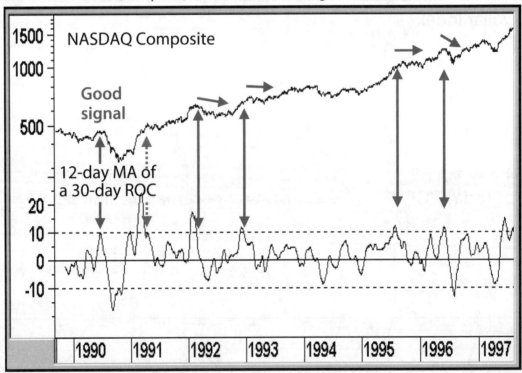

(Source: pring.com)

so the delayed signal by the advanced MA was a negative.

One approach that appears to offer a better solution is combining two moving averages of a rate-of-change indicator and using their crossovers as buy and sell momentum triggering points.

Chart 11-34 features a 4-day MA of a 14-day ROC (that is the dashed line) and a 12-day MA of the same 14-day ROC. They certainly give good signals, in the sense that they reflect reversals in the momentum indicator itself. In several cases, this also works out fine for the price, but there are far too many late and misleading signals for this approach to work consistently well.

The strong trending U.S. Dollar Index in Chart 11-35 does not fare at all well with this same combination.

One way of improving the results is to expand the time frame for the ROC. This is done in Chart 11-36 with a 30-day period. The indicator displayed is a 4-day simple smoothing of the ROC. I have also introduced an overbought and oversold zone. As you can see, the overbought crossovers work reasonably well in principle, but there are still a number of whipsaws.

If the time span for the moving average is expanded to 12 days, the results are pretty good. The arrows next to the price in Chart 11-37 show when the 12-day MA of the 30-day ROC crosses below its overbought zone and above its oversold level. What I have done here, of course, is a little bit of curve-fitting, with the benefit of hindsight.

This approach is not going to work as well in clear trending markets, such as the example of the NASDAQ composite shown in Chart 11-38. See how the indicator gives a sell signal at the start of 1991. It correctly forecasted a small decline but would have totally missed the

Chart 11-39   NASDAQ Composite, 1989–1997, and overbought/oversold crossovers

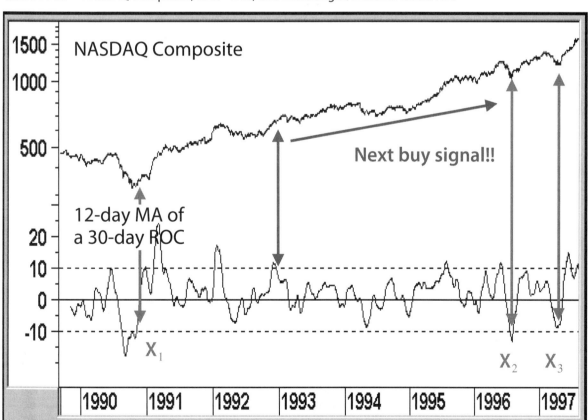

(Source: pring.com)

strong rally, because the advance was well underway by the time it reversed direction. Because this period encompassed a linear bull market, most of the sell signals were followed by consolidations rather than declines. The mid-1990 signal was an exception. However, even the sideways movement in early 1996 was severely truncated and in summer 1997, nonexistent. The three bottoms at points X1, X2, and X3 (Chart 11-39) were all very timely signals. By and large, though, this 12-day MA, 30-day ROC combination performed pretty well. Always remember that these are momentum buy and sell signals and would need to have been confirmed by some kind of reversal signal in the price. Also, even if you could rely on momentum to signal price reversals, this type of approach cannot generate automatic buy and sell signals. This is because a sell signal, such as that at the end of 1992, can develop, but the market does not correct sufficiently to

trigger a countervailing buy signal. In this instance, the next buy signal developed 4 years later in 1996.

For monthly data, I find that smoothed ROCs of 9-, 12-, and 18-month time spans offer a good long-term perspective of what is going on. In Chart 11-40 we see a 9-month MA of a 12-month ROC for the Toronto Stock Exchange Gold and Silver Share Index adjusted for U.S. dollars. This is a fairly smoothed series, so when it reaches an extreme and reverses, there are rarely any whipsaws. Other markets may not be so obliging. The arrows above and below the Index indicate those periods when the ROC reverses direction. The two ellipses indicate whipsaw signals in a major bull market. No momentum indicator is going to be able to continue its trend without some kind of whipsaw when the price trend is as powerful as this. Any series that would have kept going up would have most probably paid the price by being

Chart 11-40   TSE Gold and Silver Share Index and smoothed-momentum directional change

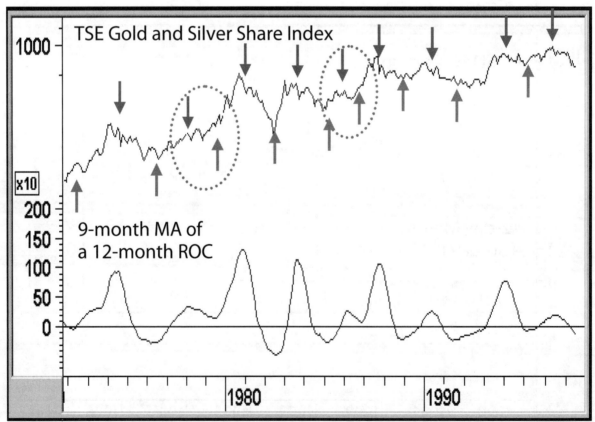

(Source: pring.com)

unduly late in turning at many of the spiky turning points. By and large, then, this particular smoothing worked very well in the almost 30 years covered by the chart.

Chart 11-41 features the same arrangement, but this time I have displayed a 12-month MA for the U.K. short-rate series and a 4-month simple MA for the oscillator. The idea is that the oscillator is not always so well behaved as it was with the TSE Gold Share Index. Occasionally, it changes direction and then quickly changes back. That is where the moving average comes in. See how the ROC moved to the upside at the beginning of 1980. However, it did not decisively cross above its 4-month MA, so the downtrend was preserved. Also, the ROC crossed below its moving average in June 1979, many months ahead of the Index. However, the Index remained above its 12-month MA for quite a while.

Remembering our rule about waiting for a price trend reversal signal after a momentum sell signal, well, that is where the 12-month MA crossover of the Index comes in. In this case, it would also have been possible to construct a secondary trendline and use that for the sell confirmation. One must always be flexible in these interpretations.

Chart 11-41 U.K. short rates and smoothed-momentum MA crossovers

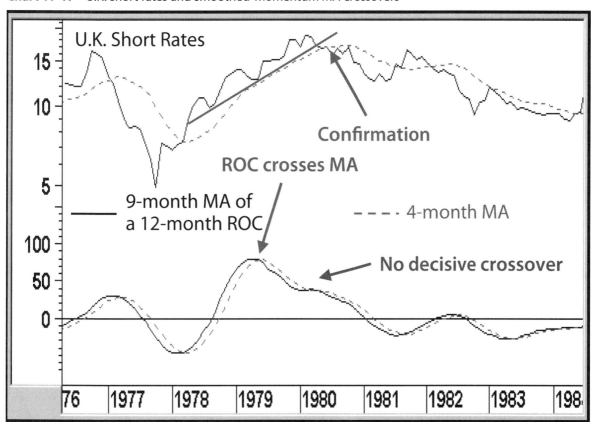

(Source: pring.com)

12

Interpreting the
Rate of Change: II

MOMENTUM ARRANGEMENTS

One of the most useful arrangements I know of is to place two or three momentum series of differing time spans on the same chart. There are several advantages to this. First, one indicator may not reflect certain signaling characteristics, such as price patterns, whereas another might. This then alerts you to the possibility of a trend reversal that would not have been brought to your attention were you just studying one indicator in isolation. Another aspect is that several momentum indicators may be offering trend reversal signals simultaneously. Again, if you do not have the benefit of having them displayed, this kind of evidence may be missed, as well. This is important because each time frame represents a different cycle. The more oscillators that are indicating a turnaround, generally speaking, the more significant the reversal. This is because the oscillator reversals are signaling that several time cycles are also turning. Even so, it is still possible to get a major reversal where

Technical analysis deals in probabilities. The greater the probabilities, in this case the number of signals, the greater the chances that the signal will not only be reliable but also that it will be followed by a stronger price move than normal.

only one momentum series is signaling a change of trend. By the same token, four or five indicators may offer signals, yet the reversal does not turn out to be that extensive. The point I am trying to make is that *technical analysis deals in probabilities. The greater the probabilities, in this case the number of signals, the greater the chances that the signal will not only be reliable but also that it will be followed by a stronger price move than normal.*

Chart 12-1 features a 10-, 20-, and 45-day ROC. When plotting three series, it is always a good idea to make sure that they are of significantly differing time frames. In that way, the chart is more likely to throw out some interesting signals since the time frames will be reflecting different time cycles. If the ROCs in this chart were separated by a day, say, or 10, 11, and 12 days, I doubt if we would be able to notice much that is different about them. The first thing to observe in Chart 12-1 is the top completion in the 10-day series for Long's Drugs in late September. Nothing was happening in the 20-day ROC, but its 45-day counterpart experienced an up-trendbreak. The price also confirmed these two events and the result was what we might call a *consolidation with a downward bias.*

Later on, we see a four-line event. First, the 10-day ROC completes a base. Notice how the top of the base develops around the zero line. Sometimes, zero, or equilibrium resistance,

lines can be quite effective, when penetrated. Normally, the 10-day series whips back and forth across it, but when the equilibrium level turns back several declines or acts as resistance for rallies, as in this case, then it is an area to be reckoned with. Remember, zero is the point of balance between advancing and declining trends. Consequently, when an equilibrium crossover develops after it has become a support or resistance point, the breakout has a fairly powerful effect of signaling a reversal in trend. The second aspect to notice is the fact that the 20-day ROC breaks above a downtrend line more or less simultaneously with its 10-day counterpart. At this time, the price is still confined below its trend-line, so the two momentum signals are only warning of an impending advance. The actual signal comes in mid-November, when the price rallies above the trendline. During this whole process, the 45-day series is barely reversing its downward trend. However, as the price is breaking out

Chart 12-1   Long's Drugs, 1995, and three ROCs

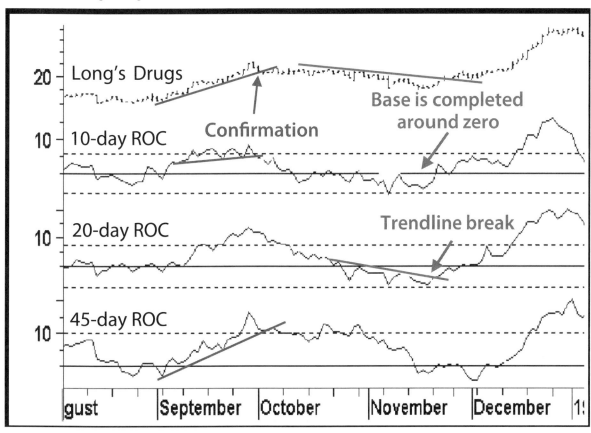

(Source: pring.com)

from the sideways trading range following the trendline violation, the 45-day ROC completes a double bottom formation. Interestingly, the top of this accumulation pattern is in the zero zone. In actual fact, this breakout point, so far as the price is concerned, is one that takes it above a horizontal level of resistance, as we can see from Chart 12-2. Thus we have four pieces of evidence confirming that a new uptrend has begun; three momentum signals, and the one price signal. The right-hand part of the chart indicates that the momentum series may be in the process of peaking again. Let us take a look at that situation in more detail.

What happens is that the 10-day series makes an 8-month high (Chart 12-3). Actually, if we were to take the chart back further, it would be much longer than that. However, the point is that this is a record high over a very substantial period for a daily chart. Then it immediately turns on a dime and moves to a multi-month extreme but this time on the

downside. The positive psychology following the triple momentum breakout earlier has now been completely reversed. According to our rules, this suggests a major change in trend. In the immediate future, you would expect to see a rally from this oversold condition–but wait a minute. If the trend has now reversed from a bullish to a sideways or bearish one, surely this will be a weak rally. Also, take a look at the 45-day ROC; it is still around the overbought zone whereas the 10-day series is experiencing a multi-month low. Let us see what happened.

Chart 12-4 shows that an important decline followed. It lasted for about eight months, so it was too short to be classified as a strong bear market. This was nevertheless a period to avoid, at least from the long side. Also, take a look at the quality of the rallies during this downward trend. It is true that the 10-day series is able to reach to the overbought zone, but it does not stay there very long and spends far more time hugging its oversold level. The 20-day series

Chart 12-2   Long's Drugs, 1995, and three ROCs

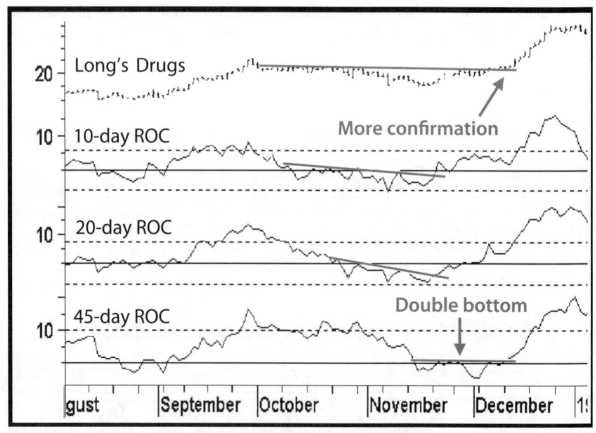

Chart 12-3 Long's Drugs, 1995–1996, and three ROCs

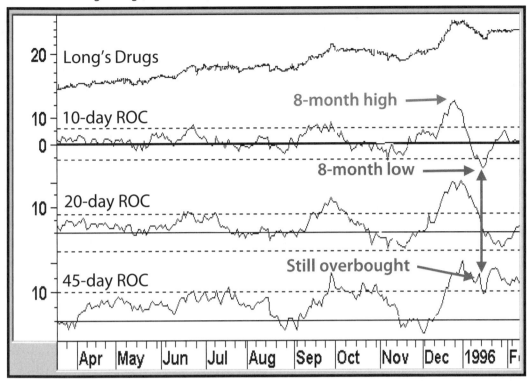

Chart 12-4 Long's Drugs, 1995–1996, and three ROCs

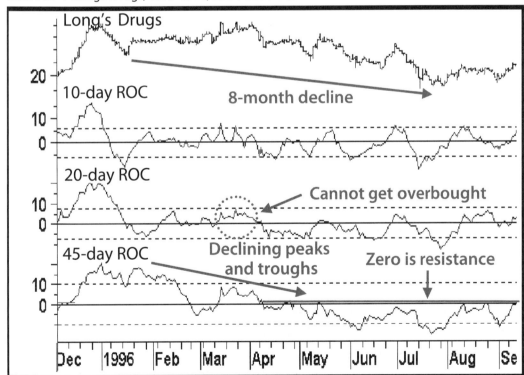

can barely touch overbought in March 1996 and is unable to generate any real form of rally. These are, of course, strong bear market characteristics. Finally, watch how the 45-day ROC experiences a series of declining peaks and troughs throughout the December 1995 to July 1996 period.

Later on, in August, the 45-day rate of change rallies to the zero level. But notice one more thing. Zero is now a major zone of resistance for this indicator. You can see what happens when the 45-day series moves into positive territory in Chart 12-5.

A major rally is signaled and confirmed by a double trendbreak in the price. Also, look at the late August test of the low. It is not exactly a new low, so we cannot say that the 20-day ROC experienced a positive divergence. But look at how closely it is hugging the zero line. At this point, the indicator is signaling that there is virtually no downside momentum whatsoever. Once again, we have this very pos-

itive 45-day ROC and price trend-breaking action confirmed by another momentum indicator, in this case the 20-day series. At the end of Chart 12-6, the price trend is still positive, but two of the momentum indicators are not in agreement. So what happened next?

First, it was possible to construct three trendlines, one for each momentum series. Later on, Chart 12-7 shows that the uptrend in the price was also violated. What followed was a change in trend, but this time to a sideways, not a declining, one. A good idea, once a trendline has been violated, is to extend it, to see whether it will reverse its role. In this case, we have four trendlines, each of which was acting as a support level. Now, if we move forward in time once again to Chart 12-8, you can see that some of the extended lines did, in fact, reverse their roles. The price itself peaked just below its extended line, but the 20-day ROC topped out right at the line. This would not have represented an actual signal to sell. Instead, it

Chart 12-5   Long's Drugs, 1996, and three ROCs

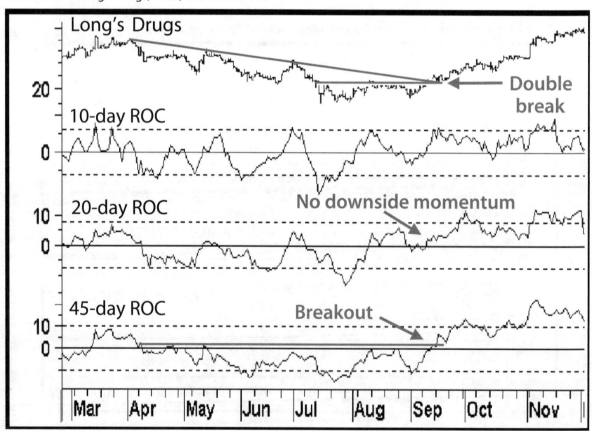

(Source: pring.com)

Chart 12-6 Long's Drugs, 1996, and three ROCs

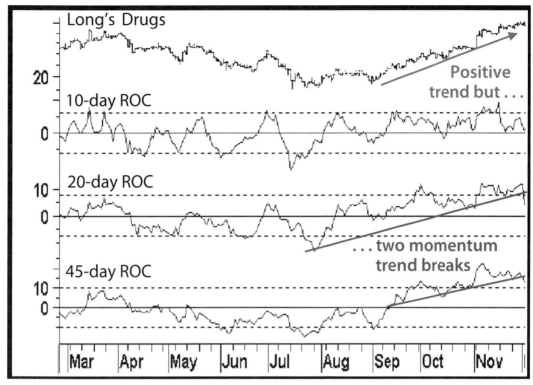

Chart 12-7 Long's Drugs, 1996–1997, and three ROCs

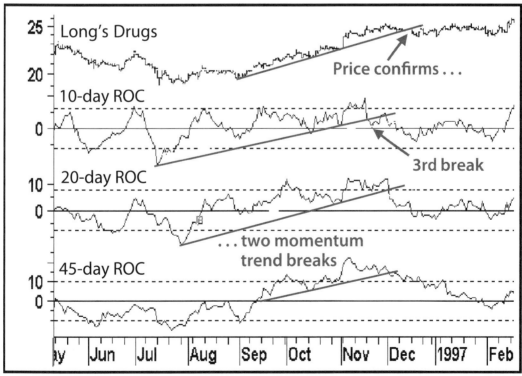

would have acted as an intelligent place to look around to see what confirming evidence, if any, could signal a probable trend reversal. Interestingly, the next peak in the price, achieved in early May, was touched by the extended line for the 10-day series and almost touched by its 20-day counterpart.

MEGA OVERBOUGHTS AND OVERSOLDS

To qualify as a mega overbought condition, an oscillator must rally to a multi-year high following a bear market. The idea is that the mega overbought indicates a complete change in the negative psychology associated with the bear market. This means that the first rally after a prolonged decline of a year or more is associated with an extreme overbought condition.

The example of Beckton Dickinson in Chart 12-9 meets all the requirements. First, we

have a bear trend between 1983 and 1984. Then, the 14-day ROC rallies to a multi-year high. Note also that this overbought reading dwarfs anything seen either in the bear market or the 2-year trading range preceding it.

In many instances, the rally associated with the mega overbought is extremely strong and there is no second chance to buy at bargain basement levels. That certainly proved to be the case in this instance, as the price just experienced a small consolidation. A mega overbought is one of the few examples when long-term investors are advised to purchase when an oscillator is in an overbought condition because there may not be a test of the low. In this instance, it may have been wiser to have bought once the price rallied above the mega overbought high. This move would also have signaled a series of rising peaks and troughs.

The next example, in Chart 12-10, features the Philadelphia Gold and Silver Share Index, the XAU. As the chart opens, the index is in a

Chart 12-8   Long's Drugs, 1996–1997, and three ROCs

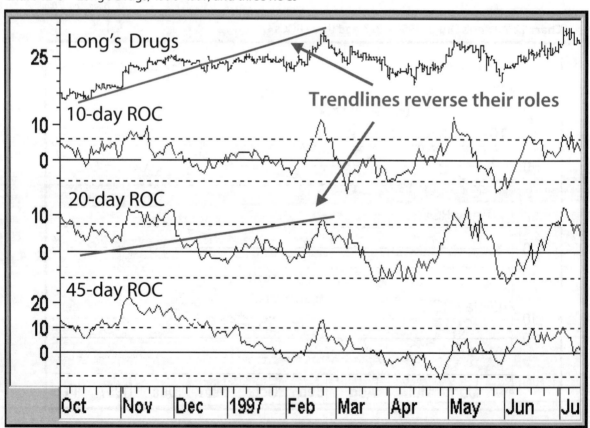

(Source: pring.com)

Chart 12-9 Beckton Dickinson, 1981–1986, and a mega overbought

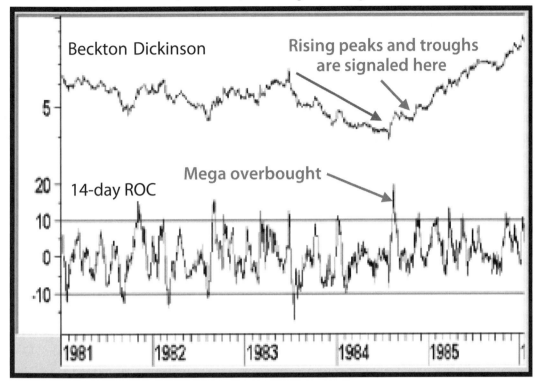

(Source: pring.com)

Chart 12-10 The Philadelphia Gold and Silver Share Index, 1983–2000, and mega overboughts

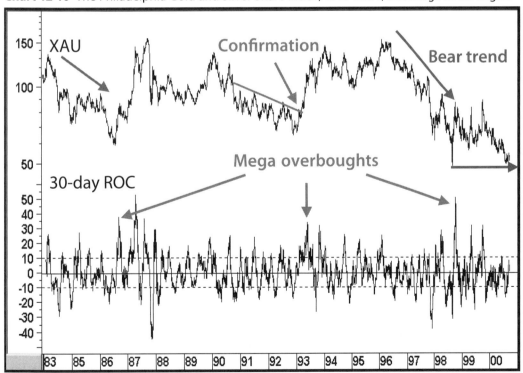

(Source: pring.com)

bear market, and this is then followed by a mega overbought and a small bull market. Later on, in 1993 we see another mega overbought condition. This time the evidence of a forthcoming rally is greater because the price confirms with a break above this trendline. Finally, in 1999, the oscillator again rallies to an overbought condition; however, the change in psychology is not an actual reversal but a change in trend from down to sideways. This example is a good one because it reminds us that whereas a mega overbought is usually followed by a *reversal* in trend, it is occasionally followed by a *change* in trend.

Even then, we also have to say that there is no such word as "always" in technical analysis, and mega overboughts can, and do, fail. Our final mega overbought example in Chart 12-11 features the S&P Composite at the 1982 market low. See how the oscillator reaches a multi-year high following the 1981–1982 bear market.

Even more impressive is the fact that the volume reached record levels as the price lifts off its lows. This record volume combined with the very high ROC reading offers two very strong pieces of evidence that the trend had reversed from bearish to bullish.

Now it is time to look at an example of a mega oversold condition. Chart 12-12 shows a bull trend lasting at least a year between 1994 and 1997. This is followed by an extreme oversold reading in the 10-day ROC and, therefore, qualifies as a mega oversold condition, and, indeed, it was followed by a bear market.

Now take a look at the extreme reading in fall 1998. Even though this was a multi-year high, it did not qualify as a mega overbought, because it was only preceded by a decline lasting several months, not the 1-2 years normally associated with a bear market. Chart 12-13 shows the 1987 crash. You can see how the oscillator recorded a multi-year low following

Chart 12-11 S&P Composite, 1982–1986, and a mega overbought

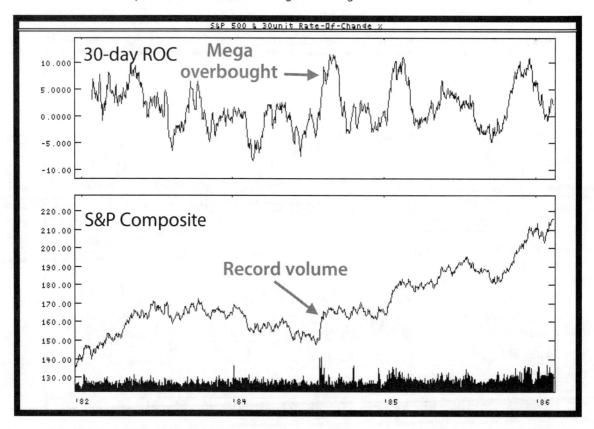

(Source: pring.com)

Chart 12-12 Bemis Co., 1994–2000, and a mega overbought and oversold

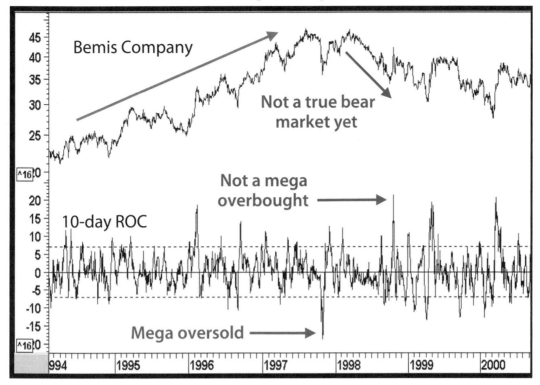

Chart 12-13 S&P Composite, 1984–1988, and a mega oversold

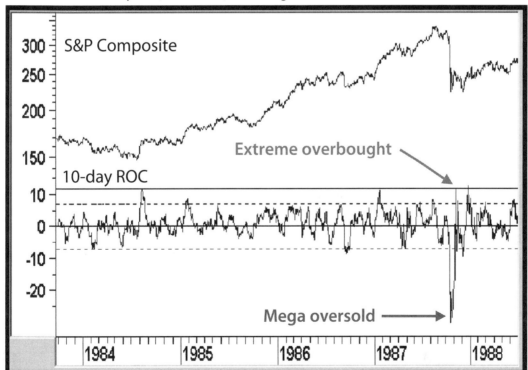

a long bull market. There is no question that the psychology changed here. However, we all know that October was the low for the bear market, so what went wrong?

We could always say that the mega oversold just failed. But there is a better answer, and that lies with the quality of the next rally because the oscillator reached a multi-year high. In effect, the bearish mega oversold was being cancelled by the extreme overbought reading. From that point on, prices gradually worked their way higher. *This is a stark reminder that people can, and do, change their minds, as do market participants.* However strongly you may feel that an indicator or series of indicators is signaling in a certain direction, always be on the lookout for a change. Although trends have a tendency to perpetuate and allow you to ride on them, sometimes they do not. You may think you have just met a compatible person who is likely to be your friend for life. But something may happen

It is extremely important that you are vigilant for changes when analyzing a trend. Market participants do change their minds, which is why it is imperative, no matter how strongly you may feel about a trend, to be on the lookout for change.

to expose a flaw in that person; the same is true in markets. The trend is definitely your friend, but it is still necessary to constantly make sure that your friendly trend is still intact and has not signaled to the contrary.

EXTREME SWINGS

Chart 12-14 shows an example of a bullish extreme swing for VF Corp. This phenomenon

Chart 12-14   VF Corp., 1989–1993, and a bullish extreme swing

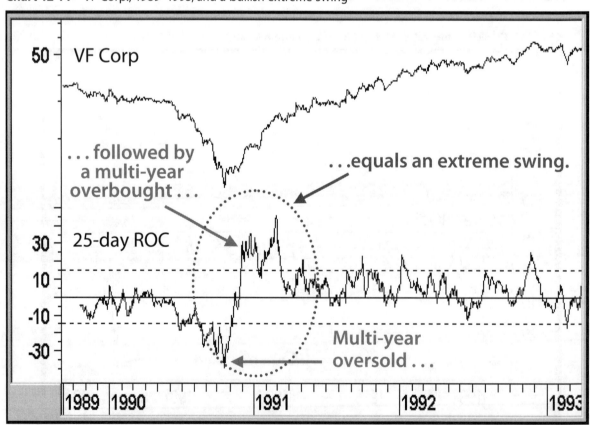

(Source: pring.com)

develops when a momentum indicator swings from one multi-year extreme to the other. In this case, it indicates a change from a bear to a bull market. The reason is that this extremely unusual oscillator action reflects a complete reversal of psychology. All the weak holders sell out during the selling climax, and short sellers and new buyers rush in together as the price rebounds. The new uptrend is not always as strong and deliberate as this. Sometimes, there is some kind of test of the lows or volatile action at higher levels before the price takes off. The main points are that most of these extreme swings trigger a change in the prevailing primary trend and that change typically takes the form of a reversal.

To qualify, the two extremes must be something quite extraordinary. The example of General Motors in Chart 12-15 meets the criteria because the overbought and oversold conditions were multi-year extremes and this was the bottom for a number of years. However, they are what I would call *marginal* extremes. They did not scream out at the casual chart watcher as something really extraordinary.

Chart 12-16 of the Mexico Equity Fund, alternately, is closer to what I mean. In this instance, an advance was not immediately forthcoming because it was necessary to experience some base-building. The extreme readings nevertheless indicated a basic change in psychology.

Extreme swings are not as common at market tops as they appear to be at bottoms. The Korea Investment Fund in Chart 12-17 is an exception. The extreme swing marked a multi-year top. This characteristic occurred at the first top and subsequent rally. Even though the price went on to make a marginal new high, the extreme swing in emotions was sufficient to result in a major change in psychology concerning this fund.

Chart 12-15 General Motors, 1990–1994, and a bullish extreme swing

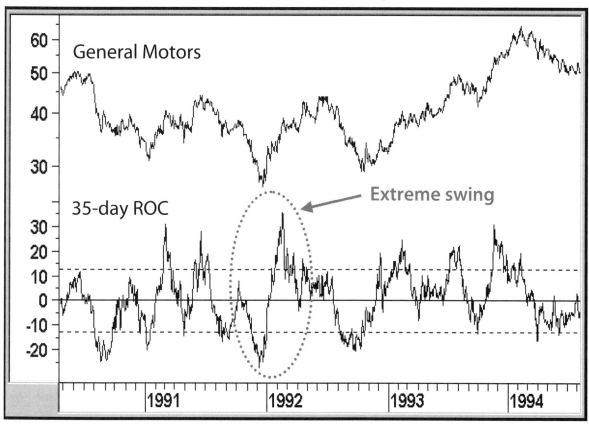

(Source: pring.com)

Chart 12-16 Mexico Equity Fund, 1992–1997, and a bullish extreme swing

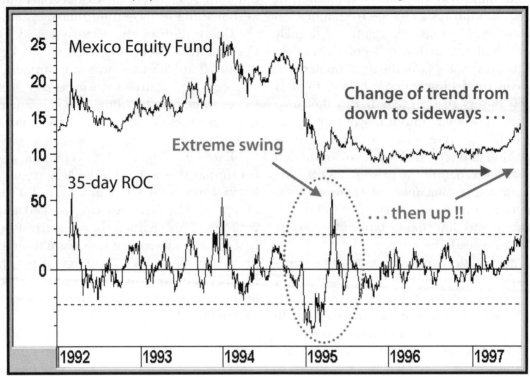

(Source: pring.com)

Chart 12-17 Korea Investment Fund, 1992–1997, and a bearish extreme swing

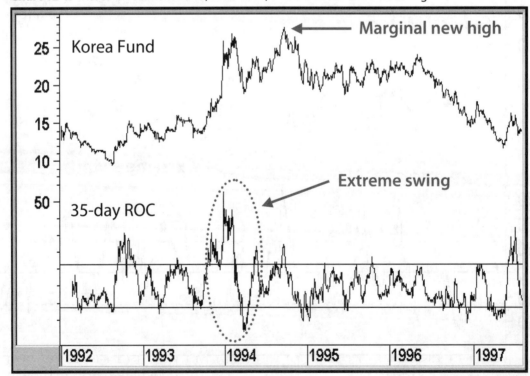

(Source: pring.com)

13

RSI: Theoretical Considerations

INTRODUCTION

The RSI indicator, commonly known as the *relative strength indicator*, was first introduced by Wells Wilder in his 1978 book *New Concepts in Technical Trading*. It is a momentum indicator as plotted in Chart 13-1 and should in no way be confused with the principle of comparative relative strength, where *one series is divided by another*. Relative strength is most commonly used to compare the performance of a stock to a market average. It is plotted as a continuous line underneath the series it is monitoring. In Chart 13-2 we see the Amex Biotech Index in the top panel and its relative strength against the S&P Composite in the lower one. A rising line means that biotech stocks are outperforming the market, and vice versa. The RSI, alternately, is a front-weighted price velocity ratio for a specific security (Chart 13-1). In effect, it is a momentum indicator that *compares the price of a security relative to itself.*

THE CALCULATION

The formula for the RSI is:

$$RSI = 100 - (100/1 + RS)$$

In this case, RS equals the average of the closes of the up days divided by the average of the closes of the down days. In the standard calculation originally presented by Wilder, the time span for the total was set at 14. Thus, RS would be the average of the closes of the up days over a 14-day time span divided by the average of down days over a 14-day span. This 14-day period represents half a lunar cycle of 28 days. The time parameter can, in fact, be set for any measure. The 14-day span was chosen because Wilder considered the 28-day cycle to be the dominant one for short-term market movements. Since the original introduction of the RSI, traders have experimented with a number of alternative time spans. In this respect, 9- and 22-day spans have become very popular.

Chart 13-1 Japanese Yen, 1989–1992, and a 14-day RSI

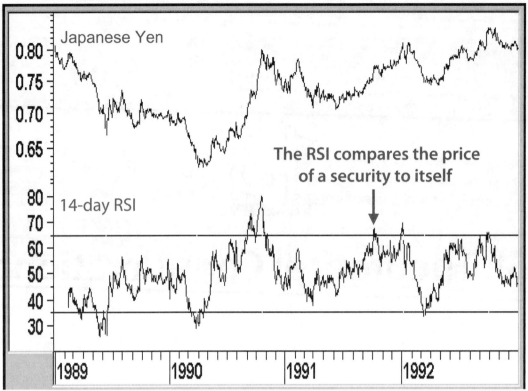

(Source: pring.com)

Chart 13-2 Amex Biotech Index and comparative relative strength, 1993–1997

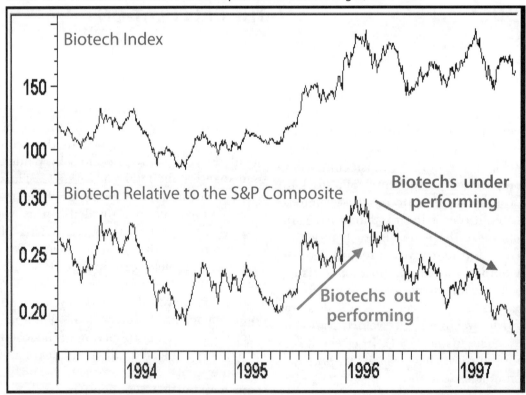

(Source: pring.com)

RSI BENEFITS

The RSI has several advantages over a simple ROC calculation. That is not the same thing as saying it is a better indicator because the ROC has some benefits that the RSI lacks. The RSI benefits are as follows.

1. *It is less volatile.* Consider the example of a 10-day rate of change, as shown in Table 13-1. In this example, the price falls sharply between Day 11 and Day 12, that is, from 102 to 80. The ROC calculation calls for Day 12 to be divided by Day 3. Since the closing price was identical on both days, this would have resulted in a reading of 100, up from the previous day's reading of 79, yet the price was in a declining trend. Of course, a lot will depend on the specific day of comparison, and the ROC will not usually give such a distorted picture.

Since the RSI averages the up and down days, it is less affected by a specific day and, therefore, has a tendency to be less volatile.

2. T*he RSI falls within the finite boundaries of 0 and 100.* In chapter 2, we discussed the analogy of a dog on a leash and its relationship to overbought and oversold levels. We also saw in the previous chapter that one of the problems with the ROC is that it is possible for this indicator to move to unusual extremes, in effect reflecting a "rubber" leash. Additionally, some securities are more volatile than others, that is, the leashes vary in elasticity. This means that it is often not possible to compare the volatility of two different securities because their oscillators are plotted on different scales. To quote Wilder, "There must be some common denominator to apply to all commodities so the amplitude of the oscillator is relative and meaningful."

The RSI does not suffer from this drawback since its absolute levels are set at 100 and 0, as shown in Chart 13-1, although in practice these extremes are rarely attained. With the RSI, it is possible to gauge whether one security is more volatile than another by comparing their vertical movements, both up and down. A more important benefit that flows from this phenomenon is the fact that it is much easier to establish universal standards for the overbought and oversold benchmarks. Using the 14-day default, these levels are traditionally set at 30 for oversold and 70 for overbought. Chart 13-3 compares a 45-day ROC to a 45-day RSI for the Dow Jones Utility Average and the Philadelphia Gold and Silver Share Index. The dashed line represents the Philadelphia series, which is clearly much more volatile than the utilities in the upper ROC panel. However, the comparison is far less pronounced for the RSI in the lower panel. Generally speaking, the longer the time span, the greater the difference between the two momentum indicators.

> Two key benefits distinguish the RSI Indicator from the ROC; 1) it is less volatile and 2) it has finite boundaries of 0 and 100, making it easier to establish universal overbought and oversold conditions. All this being said, my preference is for the ROC, although both are highly recommended technical tools.

Having made these points, I would like to add that my own preference is for the ROC because it lends itself better to price pattern and trendline construction and experiences more reverse divergences. Since the RSI falls in the 0-100 boundary, it cannot signal mega overbought and oversold signals, which is a further disadvantage versus the ROC. Having said that, both are excellent indicators and are highly recommended as technical tools.

OVERBOUGHT AND OVERSOLD LINES

It is important to note that the volatility of the RSI moves inversely to that of most other momentum series. This means that for very

Chart 13-3 DJ Utilities vs. the Philadelphia Gold and Silver Share Index, 1992–1995,
           comparing the RSI to the ROC

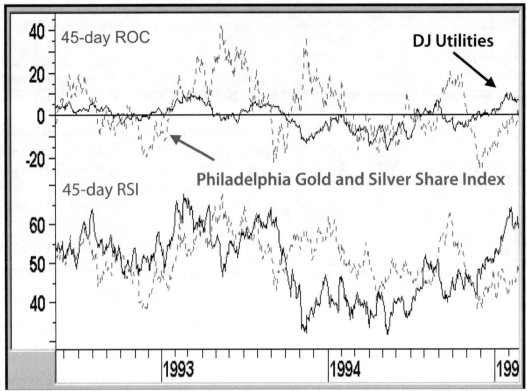

(Source: pring.com)

Chart 13-4 Eurodollar, 1994–1997, comparing RSI time spans and overbought/oversold levels

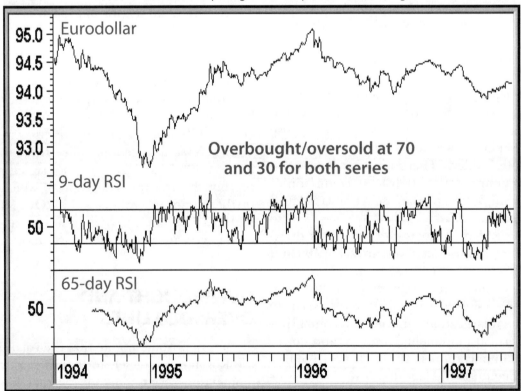

(Source: pring.com)

Chart 13-5 Eurodollar, 1994–1997, comparing RSI time spans and overbought/oversold levels

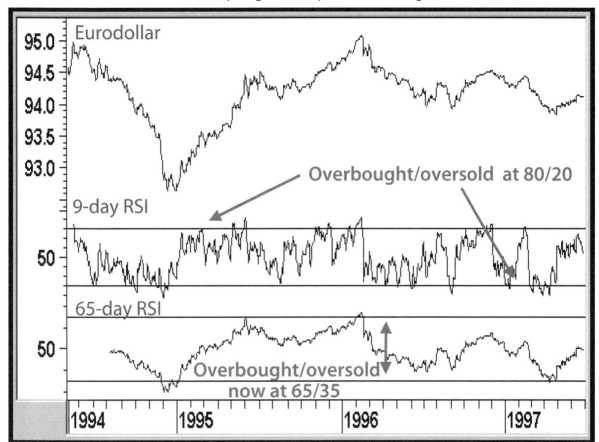

short time periods, the fluctuations are much greater. For example, Chart 13-4, featuring a 9-day RSI, indicates that the 30/70 oversold and overbought readings are often attained and usually well exceeded. Now look at the 65-day RSI. The indicator never reaches the overbought and oversold zones. This means that you should narrow these bands for longer-term time spans. Something in the order of 65/35 would be more appropriate for the 65-day series and 80/20 would work for the 9-day period. Chart 13-5 shows some more appropriate overbought/oversold boundaries for both series.

TIME FRAME CONSIDERATIONS

The terms *long* and *short* time spans refer to the type of data under consideration in a relative sense. For example, a 60-day RSI would represent an extremely long span for daily data, but for monthly numbers, a 60-day (i.e., two-month) span would be very short. That is why in Fig. 13-1 the 2-month RSI in the top panel sports the 80/20 combination, whereas the 60-day series underneath has its overbought and oversold lines drawn with a 60/40 combination. Some consideration should, therefore, be given to this factor when the choice of a specific RSI time span is being made. Ideally, you want to choose a span where the peaks and troughs of the RSI occur more or less simultaneously with tops and bottoms in the actual price. Alternately, a shorter time span, which

Figure 13-1   Comparing two RSI time frames

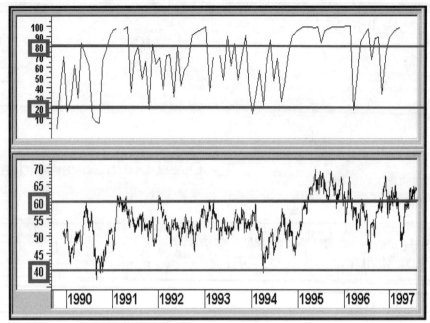

Chart 13-6   Japanese yen, 1989–1992, and negative divergences

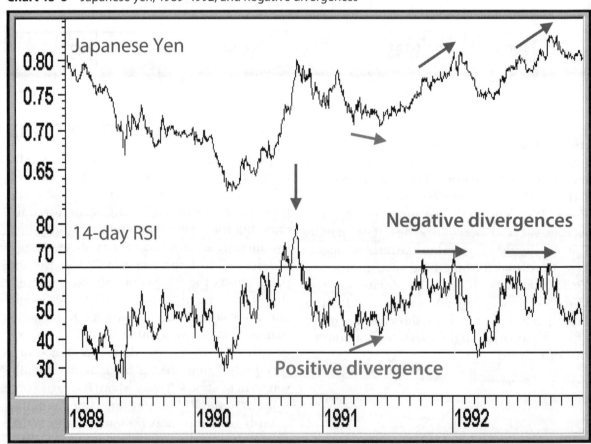

(Source: pring.com)

Chart 13-7 Japanese yen, 1990–1992, and a 60-day RSI

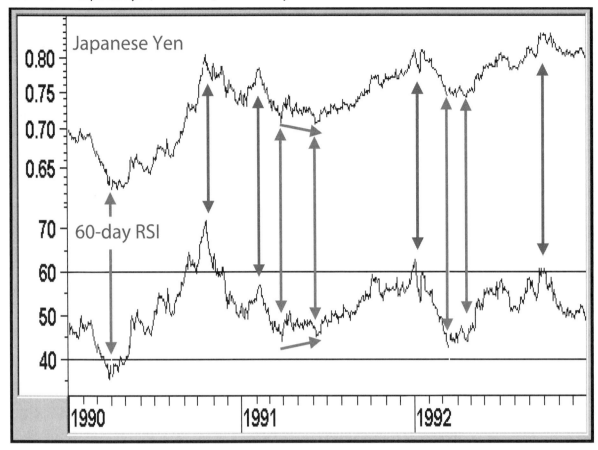

allows for the buildup of divergences, might also be selected. In the real world, where the duration of any given price trend classification (i.e., short-, intermediate-, or long-term) fluctuates, it is not possible to come up with the perfect span for either instance. A good way of allowing for this fact is to display two or three RSIs on one chart, each calculated with substantially different time spans.

For example, Chart 13-6 shows that the RSI is continually moving from one extreme to another, but the tops and bottoms do not consistently signal important reversal points. The late 1990 peak is one example, but generally speaking, the 14-day RSI used here is more suitable for the analysis of divergence or near-divergences.

Chart 13-7, alternately, takes the same data but expands the time span to a 60-day period.

Now we can see that the peaks and troughs in the RSI more or less correspond to those in the yen. There is a definite and deliberate way in which it moves in conjunction with these major rally highs. Occasionally, the 14-day series also peaks more or less simultaneously with the currency, but the path to that high was extremely jagged. Even here, the record is not perfect, since the early 1991 bottom is associated with a positive divergence. Nevertheless, a comparison of these two time spans does not indicate that one is relatively more suited to divergence analysis than the other.

SIX PRINCIPLES OF INTERPRETATION

Many of the basic principles of momentum interpretation described in the previous chapter apply to the RSI. Six of them are discussed below.

Figure 13-2 RSI tops and bottoms

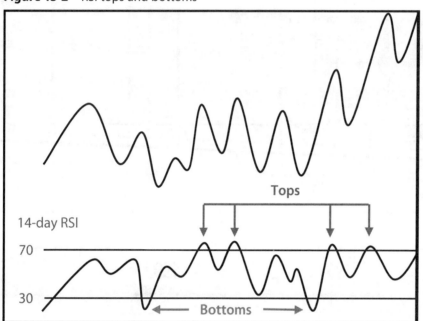

1. *Tops and bottoms.* Wilder points out that tops are indicated when the indicator goes above 70 and bottoms when it falls below 30 (Fig. 13-2). This, of course, is another way of expressing the overbought and oversold characteristics described earlier. Since momentum typically turns ahead of price, these "tops" and "bottoms" often give advance warning of a strengthening or deterioration in the underlying technical structure. The 70/30 combination assumes a 14-period time span, so longer-term time spans, say, above 25 periods, would use a narrower overbought oversold zone.

2. *Chart formations.* The RSI is one of the few indicators that lends itself to chart pattern construction (Fig. 13-3). Formations do not appear to develop as plentifully as they do with the ROC, but they nevertheless represent a useful addition to the RSI analysis. Chart 13-8 shows a classic example using a 14-day RSI for the pound. Note how the September 1992 peak was associated with a giant head-and-shoulders top in the RSI. Once the neckline at 50 was penetrated and the trendline in the currency itself was violated, there was only one way in which the currency could go.

3. *Negative failure swings.* The failure swing in a rising trend

Figure 13-3 Price patterns and the RSI

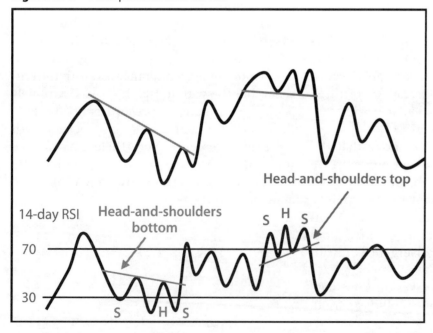

Figure 13-4   The RSI and a bearish failure swing

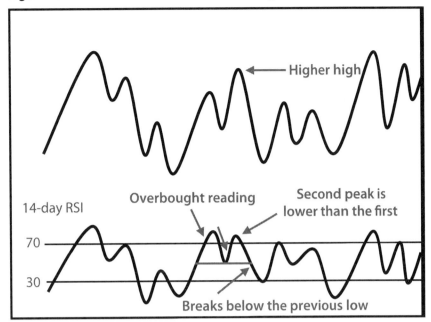

Chart 13-8   British pound and an RSI price pattern

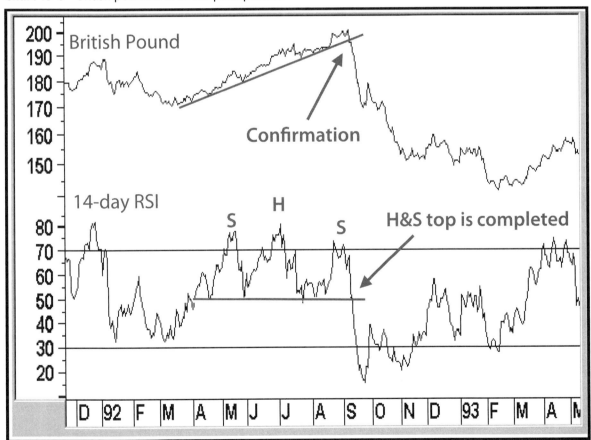

(Source: pring.com)

occurs when the RSI moves toward the equilibrium level, having already registered an overbought reading. It then moves back to overbought territory, but this swing fails to reach the peak of the first, even though the price makes a new high (Fig. 13-4). The actual RSI signal comes when the indicator falls below the low point of the initial overbought swing.

Figure 13-5 represents a failure swing at a market bottom. First, the RSI moves below 30 then back above it. Then, a subsequent reaction takes the RSI back below 30 again but not as far as the first swing. Finally, it rallies back above 30, and when it betters the previous peak, a positive failure swing signal is triggered. Generally speaking, the more extreme the reading that the failure swing is experiencing, the greater the significance. Always remember that this is a momentum signal that should also be confirmed with a reversal signal in the price trend itself.

4. *Positive failure swings.* Positive failure swings develop at bottoms. The principles are identical but reversed. An example of a positive failure swing is shown in Fig. 13-5.

5. *Divergence.* One of the most useful functions of the RSI is to point out divergences between the price and momentum. Examples of divergences are pretty widespread, but in particular we might consider the August–September bottom in the British market, shown in Chart 13-9. The actual low in late August was preceded by an RSI that had begun to walk uphill. Even more impressive was the fact that each time the index itself touched the 2375 area, the RSI continued to record higher numbers. While this characteristic does not represent an actual divergence, it does reflect the concept that the longer the trend of improving momentum following a sharp setback, the more bullish the technical position.

6. *Trendlines.* Experience in the marketplace demonstrates that the concept of RSI trendline construction is an unquestionably valid approach, as demonstrated by Chart 13-10. However, because of the constraints of the formula, which limit the up- and downside extremes to 100 and 0, respectively, trendline construction is less applicable in a relative sense to the RSI than to the ROC. The RSI seems to come into its own more as an overbought/oversold and divergence indicator.

Figure 13-5 The RSI and a bullish failure swing

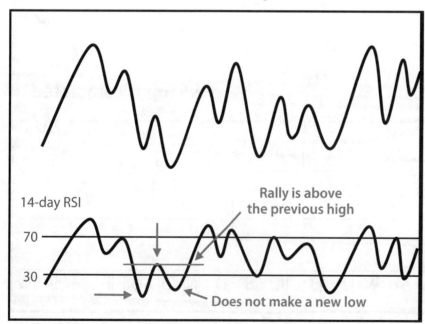

Chart 13-9 The FTSE Index, 1992–1993, and a positive RSI divergence

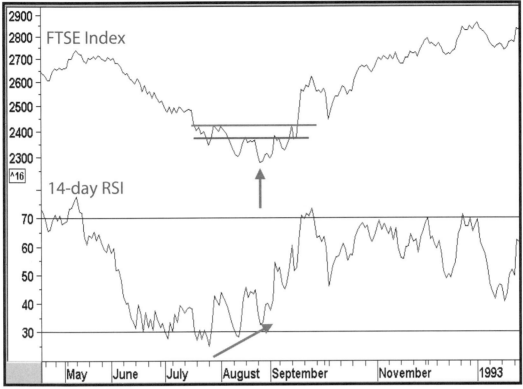

(Source: pring.com)

Chart 13-10 German Bunds, 1995–1996, and RSI trendline breaks

(Source: pring.com)

14

RSI Marketplace Examples

PEAK-AND-TROUGH ANALYSIS

Peak-and-trough analysis can sometimes be applied to the RSI. Chart 14-1 features a series of waves. The dashed lines indicate a trend of declining peaks and troughs, whereas the solid ones reflect rising peaks and troughs. The thick horizontal lines show where the RSI itself experiences a reversal of trend as defined by the peak-and-trough method. It is not always possible to identify such zigzags, but it is surprising how well they work when they can be identified. Even so, I would certainly not rate this form of interpretation as useful as trendline or price pattern analysis in momentum interpretation.

SUPPORT AND RESISTANCE

Support and resistance zones are more apparent in the RSI than the ROC indicator. This arises because the 0–100 confinement of the RSI means that the same points are crossed

and recrossed a greater number of times. Wilder makes the point that the support and resistance lines constructed from the indicator often correspond to trendlines drawn on the price series itself. In *New Concepts* he does not differentiate between support and resistance levels as actual numbers, such as 50, 35, and so on, and support and resistance as reflected in trendlines or moving averages. *Support* and *resistance* as described here refer to actual horizontal levels.

An example is shown in Chart 14-2, where the lines have been drawn to correspond to the approximate 35/45-, 55-, and 65-levels. The traditional overbought and oversold zones for the 14-day time period of 30 and 70 also serve as support and resistance areas. Smaller lines have also been placed at various other points where the index finds support or resistance. It is apparent that the 30- and 70-levels can act as pivotal points on occasion. The August/September 1994 period shows how the 65-level acts as resistance on numerous occasions. Then, the next level down at 55 acts as support and resistance

Chart 14-1 SunTrust banks, 1997, and peak-and-trough analysis

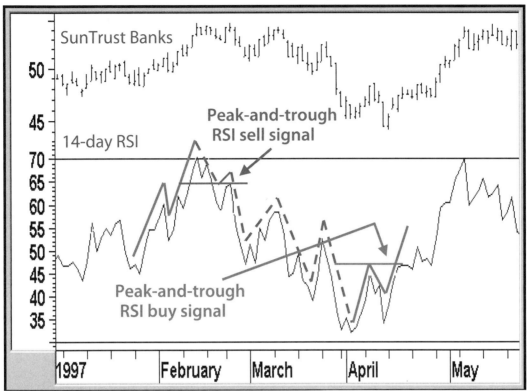

(Source: pring.com)

Chart 14-2 Orient Industries and RSI support and resistance

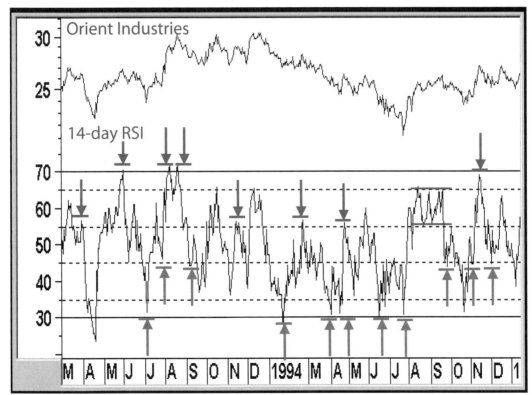

(Source: pring.com)

to a subsequent rally. The 35-area also acts as support three times between September and December. The earlier periods on the chart show that these dashed lines acted as support and resistance on numerous occasions. This is not to suggest that you should buy or sell solely because the indicator reaches one of these levels. What you could do, though, is look around at the other indicators or the technical position of the price when the RSI reaches a proven support or resistance area. This exercise then becomes a kind of filtering device. Since their repetition is often quite random in nature, I do not consider support and resistance characteristics to be a particularly helpful concept, except in this filtering context.

RSI AND MOVING AVERAGES

It is possible to extend the idea of moving-average crossovers to the RSI. However, even though this indicator is "tamer" than the ROC, in the sense that it is less erratic, it is still not smooth enough to avoid a significant number of whipsaws. A more reliable alternative appears to be a smoothing of the RSI by a moving average. The raw data are then discarded, and the moving average itself is used to trigger buy and sell alerts. There are, of course, a whole host of possible combinations. My personal preference for short-term charts is an 8-day moving average of a 9-day RSI. Normally, I would use a 20/80 overbought/oversold combination with a 9-period RSI. However, since the smoothing has the effect of dampening the fluctuations, I use the 70/30 combination. In Chart 14-3 we have a more-or-less linear uptrend for General

Chart 14-3   General Motors and a smoothed RSI

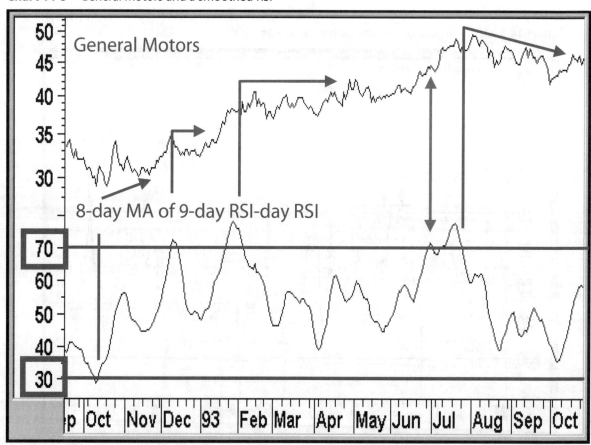

(Source: pring.com)

Chart 14-4 Alberto Culver, 1992–1997, and a 21-week RSI

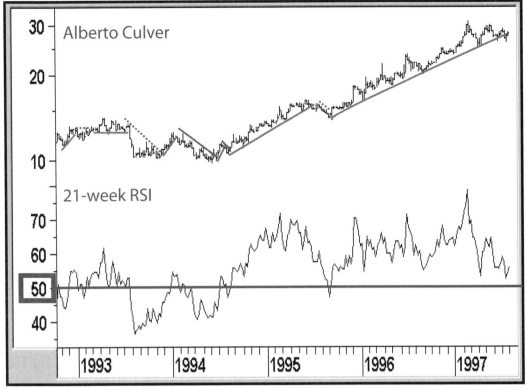

(Source: pring.com)

Chart 14-5 Alberto Culver, 1990–1995, and a 21-week RSI

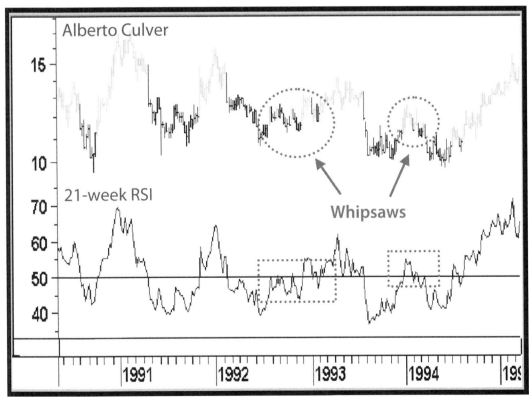

(Source: pring.com)

Motors in the early 1990s. Even so, the indicator does manage to signal a small consolidation in December 1992, a larger one in February 1993, and an intermediate decline later on that year. There can be no mistaking the fact that the June whipsaw was a loss-making proposition. The October 1992 low was also signaled, but in the interest of fairness it should be pointed out that this was a long decline, and this signal was preceded by a false bullish one several weeks earlier.

EQUILIBRIUM CROSSOVERS

In their book *Encyclopedia of Technical Indicators*, Robert Colby and Thomas A. Meyers tested for various combinations of overbought/oversold crossovers by the RSI. Their research was based on weekly periods over a couple of decades of stock market data, but they were unable to find any combination of time span and overbought/oversold levels that resulted in significant profits. This is not surprising, given the comments in the previous section concerning bull and bear market momentum characteristics. Technical analysis is an art rather than a science, which, in this case, means that it is very important to consider the way in which an indicator moves into an overbought or oversold zone rather than treat the signal in a totally mechanistic way.

Indeed, they found that the best results came from a simple equilibrium (50) crossover: buy when the RSI moves above 50 and sell when it crosses below. The best time spans clustered either side of 20-weeks, with the

> It is important to remember that indicators are not used in a vacuum—you need to consider the way an indicator moves into overbought and oversold conditions rather than mechanically act off a specific number.

21-week span providing the highest profit of all. Of the 75 trades, 21 (28 percent) produce a profit. Chart 14-4 of Alberto Culver shows that this approach would have worked pretty well for this stock in the more-or-less linear uptrend of the mid-1990s. The solid bars indicate bullish periods and the dashed ones bearish periods. Chart 14-5 shows the same stock but in a period of greater volatility. Even here, the approach appears to work quite well, except for the periods contained in the ellipses, where the price seems to move back and forth on an almost weekly basis. Not surprising, when you look at the whipsaw equilibrium action of the RSI.

The reason why this method is effective is because it keeps you in during trending markets and keeps losses fairly well under control in most trading-range environments.

RSI CHARACTERISTICS IN BULL AND BEAR MARKETS

Occasionally, the use of a smoothed RSI, such as the 8-day MA of a 9-day series, can help to identify what kind of primary trend is currently underway. This is because the indicator has a habit of performing differently in a primary bull market than a primary bear market. Chart 14-6 shows a 9-day RSI smoothed by an 8-day moving average for the Australian dollar. The buy and sell alerts based on the overbought/oversold crossover principle also appear to work reasonably well. However, a study of the chart also brings out some other very useful ideas with respect to the bull and bear market characteristics. First, note how the early 1990 reaction (A) was only associated with a moderately oversold condition, yet this was sufficient to stem the decline. Contrast this *bull* market action with the late 1991 decline (B). In this instance, a deep oversold condition, far greater than anything seen in the recent past, failed to trigger a meaningful rally. This was even truer of the two mid-1992 oversold readings (C and D) and is a characteristic of *bear* market activity.

Chart 14-6 Australian dollar, 1989–1992, and primary trend oscillator characteristics

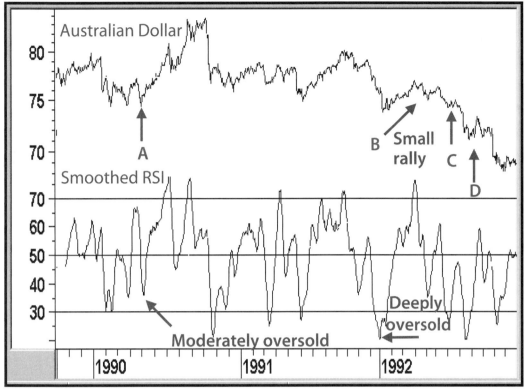

Chart 14-7 Australian dollar, 1989–1992, and an advance breakout

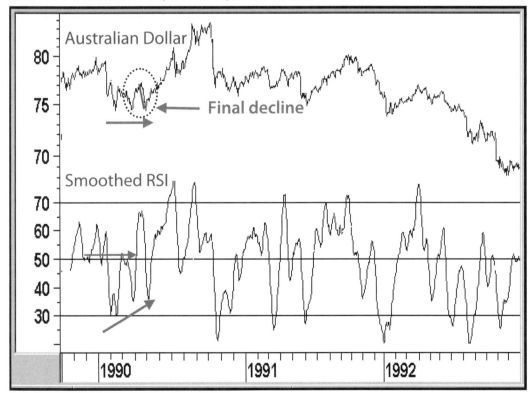

Figure 14-8   Australian dollar, 1989–1992, and smoothed RSI overbought/oversold crossovers

(Source: pring.com)

Now let us take a closer look at the early 1990 trading range in Chart 14-7. See how the currency touches the lower part of the trading range on three occasions, yet the RSI experiences a series of successively higher lows. It even traces out an advanced breakout as it makes a new high at the second peak in the trading range. The rule states: expect one more decline after this point. And that's exactly what transpired, as the Aussie dollar then embarked on a very strong rally. Another point arises from the fact that the first overbought rally in summer 1990 (E in Chart 14-8) did not result in a sell-off of any magnitude. Such action is indicative of *bull* market activity and is in stark contrast to the RSI decline that followed the three rallies in Chart 14-8 (F, G, and H) that did not penetrate the 70-area in 1991 and 1992. This extreme sensitivity to an over-

bought condition is again characteristic of a bear market.

The turning point between bull and bear was signaled loud and clear in fall 1990 (Chart 14-8). The rally peak as flagged by the two vertical arrows was barely able to push the RSI above the 50-level (equilibrium). When this was followed by a trendbreak in both the indicator and price, it suggested that the currency would experience a very sharp setback, which it did. It is important to reiterate these points.

Finally, look at the way in which the bear market rally terminated. The 1991/1992 advance was signaled by an overbought crossover and was confirmed by a trendline break. The currency finally completed a small top, as indicated by the violation of the horizontal trendline right at the middle of 1992.

Chart 14-9 Motorola, 1990, and three RSIs

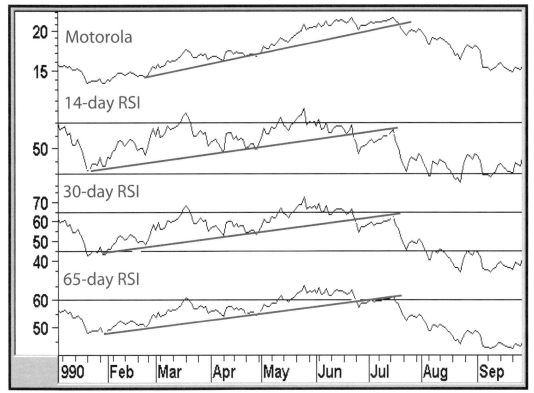

(Source: pring.com)

Chart 14-10 Motorola, 1990, and three RSIs

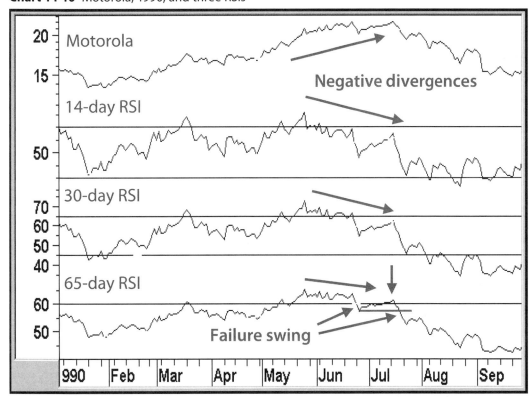

(Source: pring.com)

RSI ARRANGEMENTS

Quite often, it can be instructive to plot two or three RSI series on the same chart. In that way, it is possible to identify characteristics that are not necessarily available by studying one indicator on its own. Also, if two or three RSIs are in agreement, this gives us higher odds that the signals they are generating are indeed valid.

Chart 14-9 features a 14-, 30-, and 65-day RSI for Motorola. Note how the July top was beautifully signaled by a triple RSI trendbreak, later to be confirmed by a similar penetration by the price. It is unusual to get such a good combination. Normally, trendlines can only be constructed for one, or at the most two, oscillators. The fact that all three acted in the same way reinforced the validity and the strength of the signal. You can even see a small failure swing in the 65-day series (Chart 14-10). See how the

> Remember, we want to improve the probabilities on each trade; this is why it can be instructive to plot two or three RSI series on the same chart. If two or more are in agreement, we have greater odds that the signal is valid.

RSI falls below the overbought zone, then rallies above it, finally sinking to a new low.

Also apparent is the fact that all three series experienced negative divergences with the price. Finally, note how at the final July peak in the price, all three RSIs rallied back to resistance at the extended trendlines that they had previously violated (Chart 14-9).

Chart 14-11 shows another period for Motorola. This time it is a reversal from a

Figure 14-11   Motorola, 1991–1992, and three RSIs

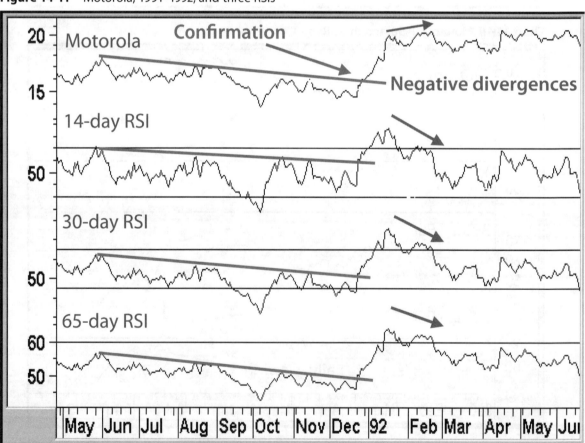

(Source: pring.com)

Chart 14-12 Motorola, 1991–1992, and three RSIs

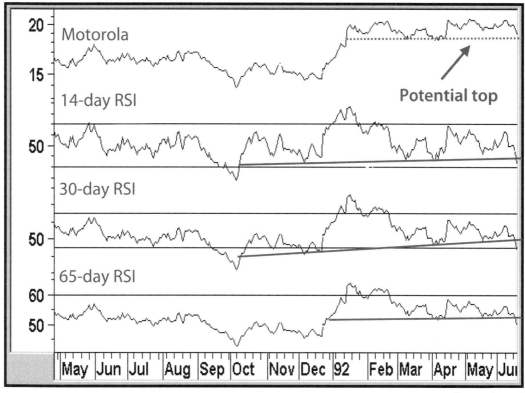

(Source: pring.com)

Chart 14-13 Motorola, 1991–1992, and three RSIs

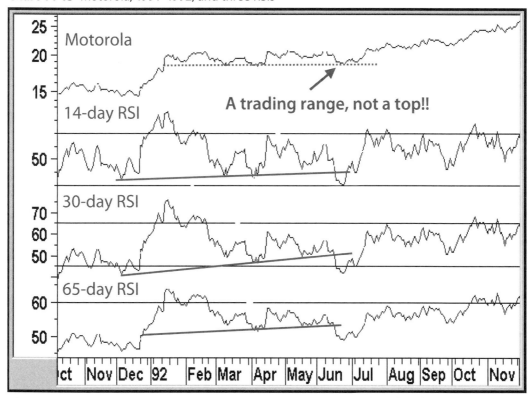

(Source: pring.com)

declining to an advancing trend. The trend-line breaks are more or less simultaneously confirmed by the price. This was still a powerful signal since the trendlines were over 7 months in length, an unusually long time, especially for an RSI with a 30-day time span. The subsequent rally is very steep and is followed by a trading range. As this consolidation gets underway, we find that each of the RSIs experiences a negative divergence with the price. Then, in June each of them slips below trendlines (Chart 14-12), and the price begins what looks to be the beginning of a sharp downtrend. At first glance, this is clearly a point to be taking some action, because the weak momentum will surely result in the price trend breaking, as well.

However, price remains above the dashed trendline and has not confirmed the divergences at this point.

Chart 14-13 demonstrates the wisdom of waiting for a price trendbreak, because Motorola never violated the dashed line. Indeed, as Chart 14-14 testifies, it completed the trading range by breaking out on the upside. There were some upside trendbreaks in the RSI indicators that confirmed the price action. However, the breakouts came from readings that were uncomfortably close to an overbought zone. For anyone entering a new long position, this signal would have been pretty high risk. However, if the original position had been maintained because the price never broke below the dashed trendline in Chart 14-12, the moderately overbought breakouts would not have been a problem. Our challenge would be to protect a higher level of profits, not the profit earned after a relatively high-risk upside momentum trendbreak.

Figure 14-14 Motorola, 1991–1992, and three RSIs

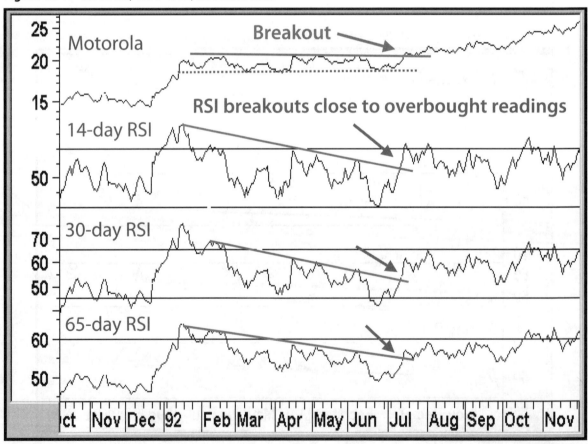

(Source: pring.com)

Chart 14-15 D-mark, 1987–1991, and three RSIs

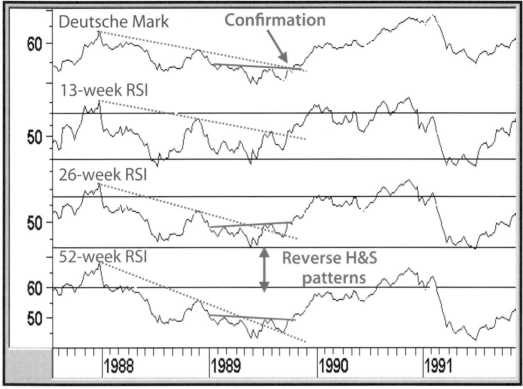

(Source: pring.com)

Chart 14-16 D–mark, 1987–1991, and three RSIs

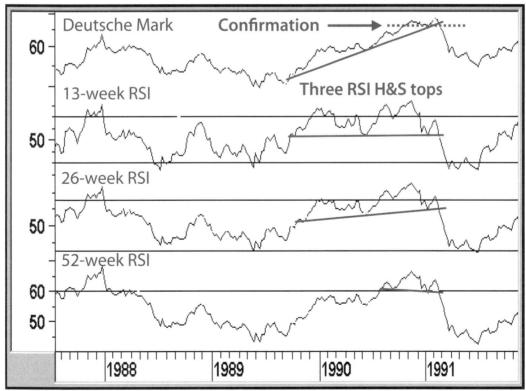

(Source: pring.com)

Chart 14-15 shows another RSI arrangement but this time using weekly data. The time frames are all based on quarterly periods: 13, 26, and 52 weeks. The overbought-oversold zones have been narrowed, as in the previous chart, because of the longer time span. You can see that the 26- and 52-week RSIs both completed reverse head-and-shoulder patterns and broke above 2-year trendlines. The price confirmed by completing a similar formation, and a very powerful rally followed. This was a classic signal since just about everything was working in tandem. The trendline break by the three RSIs indicated that all the cycles reflected by these indicators were in a positive mode.

The top of Chart 14-16 was just as interesting since all three RSIs completed and broke down from head-and-shoulders formations. The price did not trace out a head and shoulders, but it did violate a 11/12 up trendline and completed a kind of double top formation. The principal difference between this arrangement and the previous one is that here we are monitoring pretty long-term trends lasting a year or more, whereas the daily chart featuring the 14-, 30-, and 65-day RSIs reflected short and smaller types of intermediate trends. The trend reversals from the weekly data were, therefore, much more significant.

Signals from monthly charts are even more noteworthy. In this respect, Chart 14-17 features a 9-, 18-, and 24-month RSI. These indicators offer us even greater perspective than the weekly charts. See the three tops completed between 1985 and 1988. They were confirmed by a 12-month MA crossover in the currency and followed by a small 2-year decline. Also, the arrows indicate when one or more of these series reach an overbought or oversold area and then cross through it on their way back to

Figure 14-17 D-mark, 1984–1997, and three RSIs

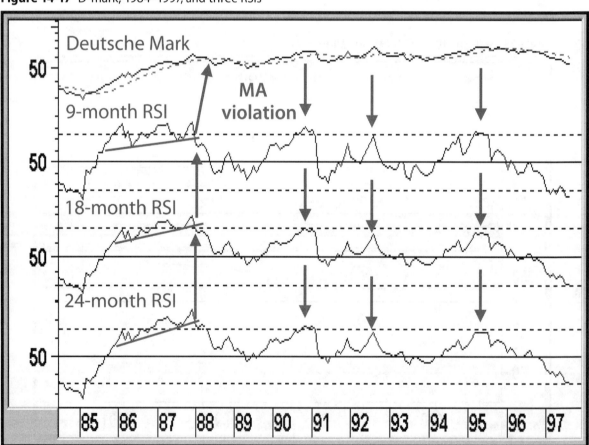

(Source: pring.com)

zero. They were all reasonably effective. One important point concerning the three tops is that when they were being formed, the RSIs crossed below their overbought zones. I did not draw any arrows to indicate these false moves, because it would have made the chart too busy. Even so, you can see that the 12-month moving average was not penetrated following the first two whipsaw signals. Only after the completion of the tops was the MA violated, that is, did the price confirm.

15

Trend Deviation and the MACD Indicator

INTRODUCTION

So far, we have limited our discussion to indicators that are constructed from a comparison of the current price to a previous one. Another possibility is to relate the current price to some form of trend measurement. This concept works on the assumption that although prices move in trends, they do not move in a straight line but rather fluctuate around that trend. These are the fluctuations that form the rationale for trend deviation momentum oscillators. Trend deviation oscillators can be calculated from price, volume, or even another oscillator. When calculated from price, trend deviation indicators are sometimes called *price oscillators. The types of trend and the way in which the price is related to them give rise to the variety of methods by which these oscillators are calculated.*

When a rate-of-change momentum indicator is compared to a trend deviation series, the results are more or less the same, provided that the timeframes are identical. However, there are some subtle differences. Chart 15-1 features a 25-day ROC and an oscillator calculated by dividing the daily close by a 25-day simple moving average. The ellipses flag some of the periods when one or the other crossed below the equilibrium level but not both.

If your zero crossovers are used to generate signals, this would be of critical importance. That is why it is often a useful idea to compare indicators based on these different construction methods.

> When trend deviation oscillators are calculated using price, they are sometimes called price oscillators. The types of trend and the way in which the price is related to them give rise to the variety of methods by which these oscillators are calculated.

Chart 15-1 S&P Composite, 1996–1997, comparing an ROC to a trend deviation indicator

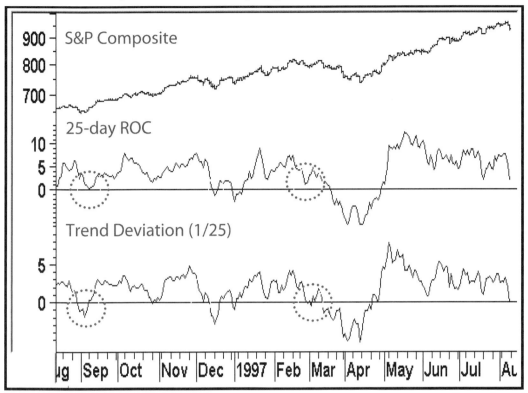

Chart 15-2 S&P Composite, 1996— How trend deviation is calculated

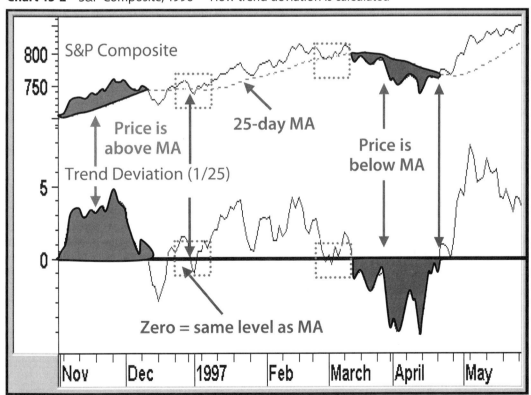

TREND DEVIATION AND A MOVING AVERAGE

The simplest form of trend deviation calculation involves the relationship between the current price and a simple moving average. The oscillator is constructed by comparing the latest price by the average. An example for a 25-day simple moving average is shown in Chart 15-2. When the price is at the same level as the average, the oscillator experiences a reading of zero. When it is above the average, the oscillator is above zero, and vice versa. The vertical lines indicate some of the points where the price and moving average are at identical levels. The two rectangles show when the price moves in an inconsistent way around the average. You can see that the same thing happens around the zero line for the oscillator. A trend deviation oscillator can be calculated either by subtracting the price from its MA or dividing it. For very short-term trends, there is little difference, but for longer-term price movements, the division calculation is much preferred since it reflects proportionate price movements.

This approach has an advantage over the ROC method, in that *zero crossovers also offer a price trend reversal signal in their own right.* In effect, simple trend deviation oscillators represent *both* momentum and trend reversal signals in one indicator.

Trend deviation methods are not limited to simple moving averages. Indeed, they can be applied to any form of trend measurement. This could, for example, be a variation on a moving average, such as a weighted or exponential average or a linear regression line, and so on. We will concentrate here on the moving-average approach. Trend deviations based on linear regression are featured in the second volume of our momentum series.

The principles of momentum interpretation outlined earlier apply to oscillators constructed from the trend deviation method. We shall cover this later, but first it is important to consider the implications of the length and type of moving averages used in the construction of these indicators. I would like to start with a few words on moving averages themselves.

DIFFERENT MOVING-AVERAGE VARIATIONS

The sensitivity of the various methods of moving-average calculation differs, which means that this will also affect the character of the trend deviation indicator. Chart 15-3 features three possibilities, each based on a 25-day time span. The first two, simple and weighted, are very similar. Since the weighted moving average is weighted toward the more recent data, it is more sensitive than the simple average. This means that it also reverses direction and crosses the equilibrium point more quickly. Most signals derived from this method are more timely, but that also comes with a price: more whipsaws. The arrows connecting the two series in Chart 15-3 point up those times when the weighted trend deviation oscillator crossed below zero, but the simple average did not. Generally speaking, I prefer the simple average relative to either the weighted or exponential, since whipsaws are reduced and timeliness is not unduly delayed. This principle does not just apply to zero crossovers but for overbought/oversold crossovers and for systems where the oscillator consists of two moving averages crossing each other, and so forth.

The characteristic of the oscillator constructed from a 25-day variable MA is very different. The movements, using zero crossovers as a benchmark, are far less volatile. In this chart, we see just two crossovers, compared to four for the simple moving average and seven for the weighted variety. This is not just an isolated example but is typical of the variable average. This means that the variable MA offers good signals for declines of an intermediate nature. However, it does suffer from the fact that with this particular time span, a negative zero crossover sometimes comes right at the bottom of a smaller decline, thereby resulting in a whipsaw.

Chart 15-3 S&P Composite, 1996–1997 — Three trend deviation indicators

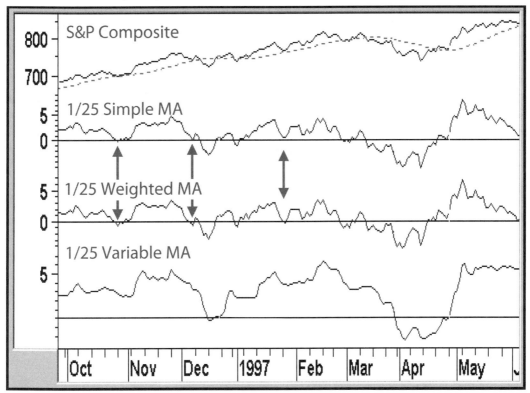

(Source: pring.com)

Chart 15-4   Amex Biotech Index and two trend deviation indicators

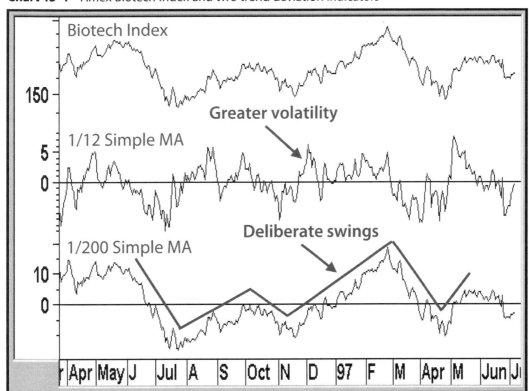

(Source: pring.com)

MOVING AVERAGES AND TREND DEVIATION

We discovered earlier that the magnitude of an ROC oscillation was, other things being equal, a function of the time span under consideration. The longer the span, the greater the swing, and vice versa. A similar principle applies to trend deviation oscillators, but in this case, the time span is determined by the length of the moving average. The longer the average, the greater the fluctuation. Chart 15-4 demonstrates two extremes: a 12- and a 200-day trend deviation. You can see how the 200-day series experiences more deliberate swings or waves than its relatively volatile 12-day counterpart.

The characteristics of a trend deviation indicator will also depend on the nature of the moving average calculation. There will never

be tremendous differences between simple and exponential methods. In Chart 15-5, which compares a close divided by a 200-day average, the swings are fairly similar. There are some differences in the actual levels. For example, the rectangle to the left shows that the exponential moving average (EMA) experienced a whipsaw, unlike the simple MA. Alternately, the rectangle on the right shows that the simple MA oscillator uncharacteristically experienced a whipsaw, when the EMA-based one did not. My own belief is that the EMA is more popular because it offers "faster" signals in the highly leveraged short-term-oriented futures arena. The more complicated math used in its construction also has some appeal. Working on the theory that there is no holy grail and that "simple" is superior to "complex," I have tended to use simple moving averages in my work much more than exponentially based

Chart 15-5   Amex Biotech Index and two trend deviation indicators

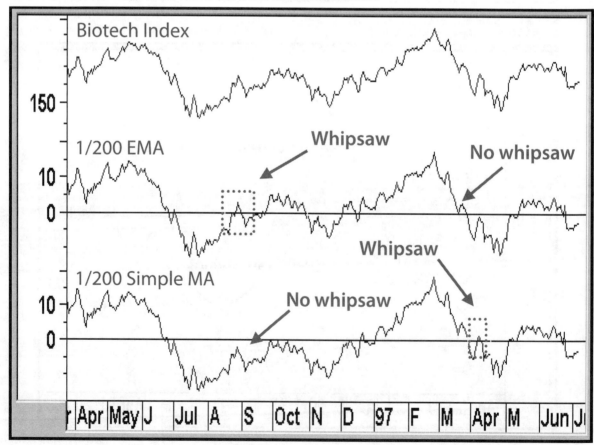

(Source: pring.com)

indicators. Indeed, in their book *The Encyclopedia of Technical Market Indicators*, Robert Colby and Thomas A. Meyers show that there was no meaningful difference using simple or EMA crossovers for the S&P Composite between 1960 and 1980. The range of time spans was 1–75 weeks, using weekly data.

We must also bear in mind that even though it makes sense to search for a time span or method of construction that avoids inferior results, it is doubtful whether the time spent on ultrafine-tuning, or debating the advantages of simple versus exponential calculations, will result in significantly greater profits. Always use indicators that you yourself feel comfortable with. If you do not have confidence in your indicators, you will lack the conviction to maintain a perfectly good position when things go against you.

One of the best ways to gain faith in an indicator is to test it out to your own satisfaction. Do not take my word for it, prove it to yourself first. After all, it is you who will be losing money if things do not go according to plan. If the indicators *you* use tested reasonably well in the past and are not overly complex, they are likely to be of assistance in the future.

> Remember, you need to trust the indicators you use. You need to test them yourself in order to make sure that they are the right tools for you.

Chart 15-6 S&P Composite, 1996–1997, comparing an ROC to a trend deviation indicator

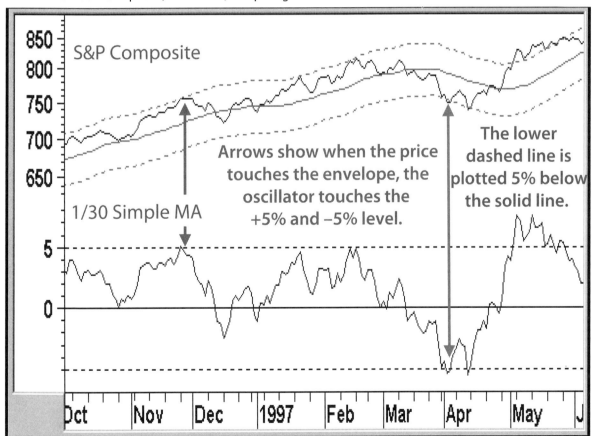

(Source: pring.com)

TREND DEVIATION AND ENVELOPES

As we have already seen, the simplest form of the trend deviation method is to compare the closing price to a moving average. The graphical representation of this calculation is really another way of representing a price series and moving average surrounded by an envelope, as featured in Chart 15-6. The envelopes occur at a vertical distance that is 5 percent above and below the 30-day MA for the S&P Composite. The two envelopes can be seen to be acting as support and resistance areas. The lower panel shows the oscillator constructed by dividing the close by the average. The overbought and oversold lines have been drawn at the same level as the envelope, that is, at ±5 percent of the 30-day MA. When the closing price falls below the upper envelope on its way back to the moving average, the oscillator also drops below its +5 percent overbought line on its way back to zero. Bearing in mind the dog and leash example from chapter 2, the placement of the envelopes will vary just as it does for overbought/oversold lines because the principle behind the envelope and trend deviation calculations is identical.

Obviously, if we just consider zero crossovers as buy and sell signals, we are merely substituting an oscillator for a moving-average crossover system, since the moving average and the equilibrium level basically amount to the same thing. In some respects, looking at the oscillator can prove to be quite frustrating, since it shows more vividly the significant number of zero-whipsaw crossovers that can, and do, happen. Normally, when we look at information on a price chart, such as the relationship between the price and a moving average,

Chart 15-7   S&P Composite, 1996–1997, comparing an envelope to a trend deviation indicator

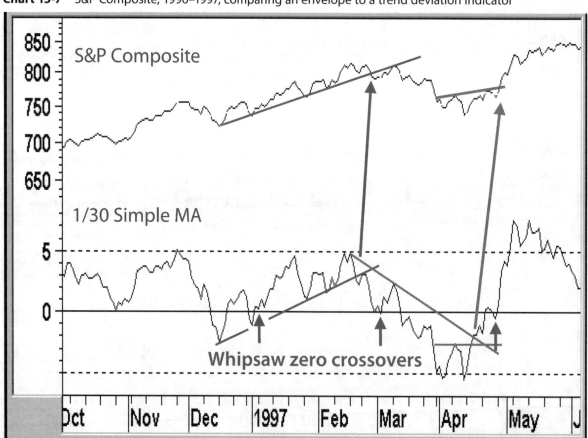

(Source: pring.com)

Chart 15-8 Verizon, 1986–1991 — A trend deviation indicator and trendline violations

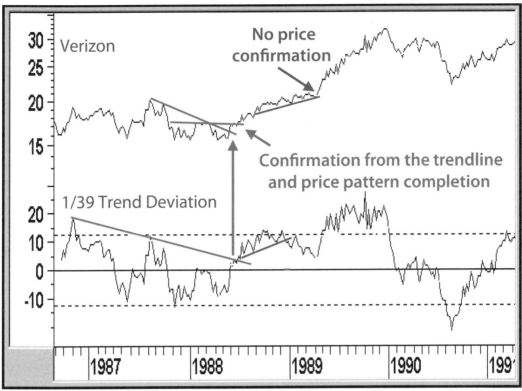

(Source: pring.com)

Chart 15-9 Verizon, 1986–1995 — A mega oversold

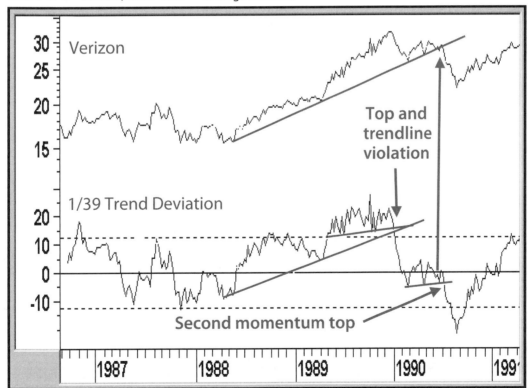

(Source: pring.com)

our eyes and minds conveniently gloss over the inconvenience of whipsaw signals. It is not so easy to do this with the price oscillator.

Apart from keeping us honest, the oscillator also offers an additional advantage over a simple-price-versus-moving-average presentation. This arises because the oscillator gives us an inside look at the dynamics in the relationship between the price and the average. Remember, it is a very simple matter to analyze trends in momentum through trendline construction, divergences, price patterns, overbought/oversold analysis, and so on. The utilization of these techniques, therefore, gives us some *advance* warning of when a moving average (that is, the zero level) might be penetrated.

Chart 15-7 represents the same data as that in 15-6 but without the envelope. It is fairly obvious that the oscillator lends itself nicely to trendline construction. First, there is a joint

downward penetration of price and momentum in February 1997. This is later followed by an upside trendline violation and the completion of two price patterns, one by the price and the other by the oscillator.

Trend deviation indicators can be used for any type of data: daily, weekly, monthly, or even quarterly and annually. In Chart 15-8, featuring a 1-week/39-week simple moving-average oscillator of Verizon, the first sign of a reversal arises from a violation of a downtrend line in the oscillator. The price subsequently confirms, first, as it breaks a trendline, and later, as it completes a double bottom formation. Later on, the oscillator completes a perfectly legitimate top, but the price refuses to confirm. This shows the wisdom of waiting for a price confirmation, since Verizon experienced a very sharp rally after this point. At the end of 1988, the indicator completes a top for-

Chart 15-10   Verizon, 1986–1995 — A mega oversold

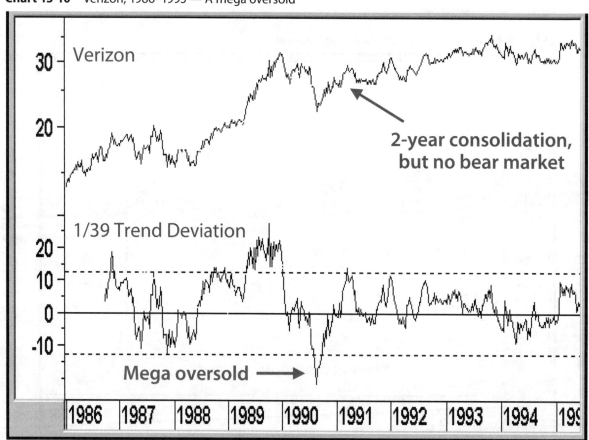

(Source: pring.com)

Chart 15-11 Amex Broker's Index and two MAs

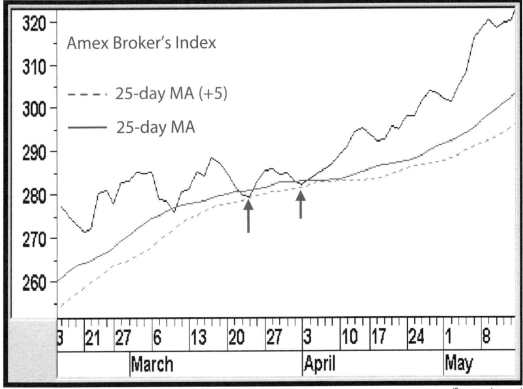

Chart 15-12 Amex Broker's Index and a regular and advanced MA

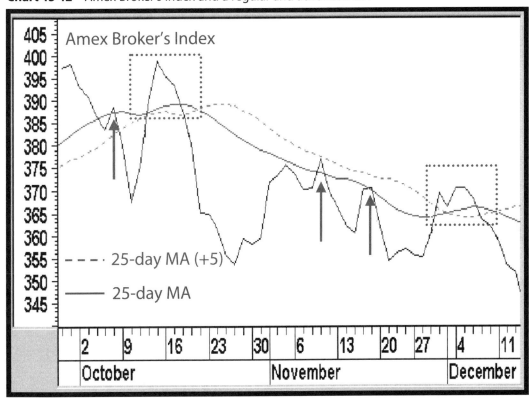

mation, and both series violate their 1988–1990 up trendlines (see Chart 15-9). This trendbreak proves to be quite tricky for a while, because the trendline violation in the price is delayed until early 1990. As the price breaks below its early 1990 low, the oscillator completes another top just below the zero level. This was the signal for the final decline. The low in the oscillator would qualify as a mega oversold (Chart 15-10). As a trend reversal signal, it does not work out, but as a change of trend signal, it does. This is because the mega oversold was not followed by a decline, but as you can see in this chart, by a sideways movement lasting a couple of years.

ADVANCING MOVING AVERAGES

If we are planning to use the trend deviation for zero crossover or overbought/oversold crossover signals, there is a useful technique that can often make the process more effective. This is to lead or advance the moving average for the purpose of the deviation calculation. Chart 15-11 features two simple MAs with a 25-day time span. The solid line is a straight average plotted in the normal way. The dashed one is an average that is plotted 5 days ahead or advanced by 5 days. Using this approach does mean that crossover signals of the advanced series are delayed a little bit, but at the same time, the number of whipsaws is usually reduced significantly. In Chart 15-12 there are two arrows that point up when the

Chart 15-13 Amex Broker's Index and advanced momentum MA

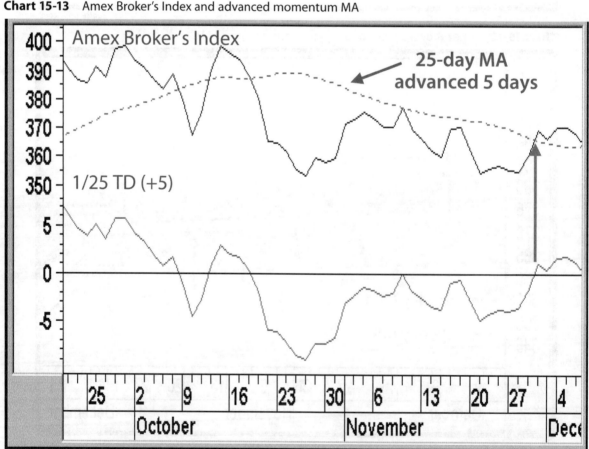

(Source: pring.com)

regular series experiences a whipsaw signal, but the advanced one does not. It is also possible to see how the regular MA (solid) reverses direction ahead of the regular one (dashed).

This method really comes into its own after a rally takes place following a sharp decline. See how the regular average experiences a double whipsaw in November. Of course, nothing is perfect, and the advanced series is not immune to whipsaws, either. In this respect, the rectangles contain periods when both series whipsawed. I have used 5 days in this example, but there is nothing sacrosanct about this particular period. Normally, though, I would use a span that is somewhere between 10 and 20 percent of the moving-averages span. For example, a 40-week MA would be advanced by somewhere between 4 and 8 weeks, and so forth. Another possibility is to take an approximate square root of the time span and to use

that for advancing purposes. Thus, for a 40-period MA, 6 (the square root of 36) or 7 (the square root of 49) for a 45-period MA would be appropriate.

When calculating a trend deviation indicator using the advancing technique, today's close is divided by the average *five days ago*, instead of today's average. Chart 15-13 features a 25-day average advanced by five days in the upper panel. The lower one contains the closing price divided by this average. The oscillator crosses above and below zero whenever the price crosses the average. An additional advantage of this approach is that the moving-average value for the next few days is known *ahead of time*. This means that for trading purposes, stops can be placed several days in advance.

Moving-average crossover signals from jagged oscillators are notoriously plagued with whipsaws. Using the advancing technique with

Chart 15-14 Amex Broker's Index, 1995–1996, and a regular and advanced momentum MA

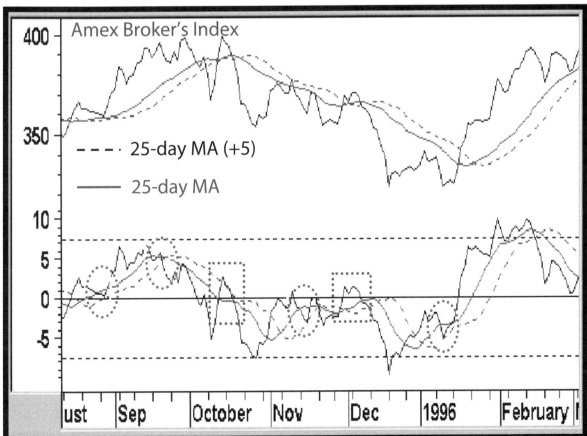

trend deviation indicators helps to eliminate many of these false signals. In this respect, Chart 15-14 shows a trend deviation indicator, together with two moving averages of the indicator, a straight 25-day simple MA (the solid line) and one that has been advanced by five days (the dashed line). The ellipses indicate periods when the 25-day trend deviation oscillator would have whipsawed across its 25-day average. Notice that in all these situations, the advanced moving average did not experience a crossover. This advanced series does not come out of the situation lily white. In this respect, the rectangles flag those periods when both series experienced whipsaws. The instances of the advanced average whipsawing are, in general, much less than a straight MA crossover.

A trend deviation indicator with an advanced average will usually cross back below an overbought zone or above an oversold zone after the straight moving average. The significance of this will depend on how much lead time the oscillator has over the price. Generally speaking, though, I prefer the straight moving average when using overbought/oversold crossovers, since the crossovers often occur just after, or coincidentally with, price peaks and troughs.

VARYING THE TIME SPANS

An alternative method of calculating price oscillators is to vary the time spans of the two moving averages being compared. As we know, a one-period moving average, that is, the close divided by a 25-period average, results in a fairly jagged series. Alternately, if the spreads are too narrow, the oscillator will not have much cyclic rhythm to its character. An example of a 20-divided by a 25-day average is shown in the

Chart 15-15   Amex Broker's Index, 1995–1997, and two smoothed trend deviation indicators

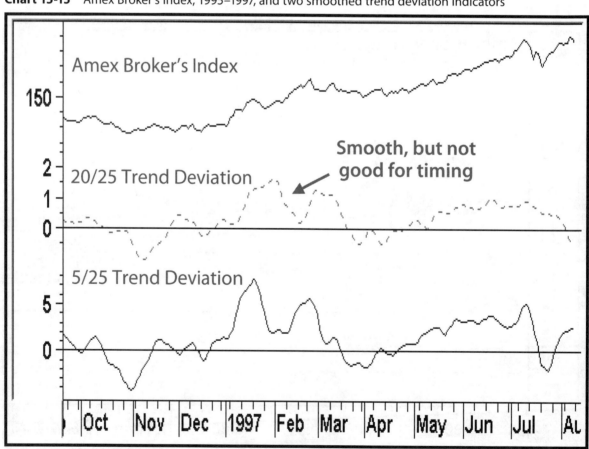

(Source: pring.com)

Chart 15-16 CBOE Latin Index, 1996–1997, and a 5/25 trend deviation indicator

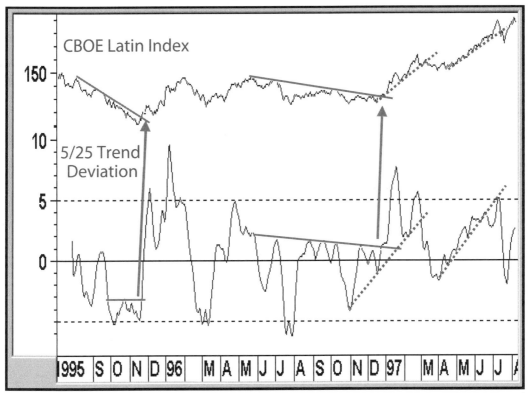

(Source: pring.com)

Chart 15-17 CBOE Latin Index, 1996–1997, and a 5/25 trend deviation indicator

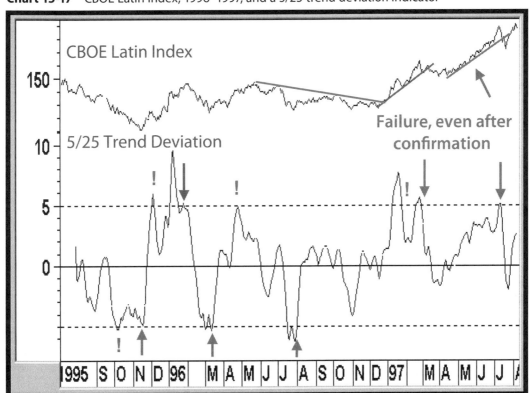

(Source: pring.com)

middle panel of Chart 15-15. Lengthening the time spans certainly smoothes out the oscillator, but it becomes useless as a timing device.

The optimum combination of averages can only be determined by trial and error with regard to the type of trend being monitored. Substituting a 2-day moving average for the closing price in a 25-day deviation will not be of much help, since the resulting oscillator will still be quite jagged. This is fine from the point of view of constructing trendlines and price patterns, and to some extent overbought/oversold crossovers, but that is about it. An alternative approach seems to be to arrange the calculation so that the spread between the averages is somewhere between two and five times.

A commonly used combination is a 5-period divided by a 25-period average, for instance. The resulting oscillator generates its best signals from reversals in trend, divergences, and

so on. It is also possible to run a moving average through such an oscillator, using crossovers as buy and sell signals.

Because of their characteristic smoothness, these indicators do not normally lend themselves to trendline construction or price pattern completion. However, on those rare occasions when it is possible to construct a trendline and observe its violation, such signals are usually followed by a significant trend reversal. Chart 15-16, for example, shows how a 5/25-day oscillator for the CBOE Latin Index lends itself to trendline construction. All of the examples featured work pretty well, with the exception of the two (dashed) trendline breaks on the extreme right-hand side of the chart. Fortunately, this type of failure is the exception rather than the rule. It was more than compensated by the very good signals that preceded it, especially the December 1996 mas-

Chart 15-18 DJ Consumer Noncyclical Index, 1983–1988, and two trend deviation indicators

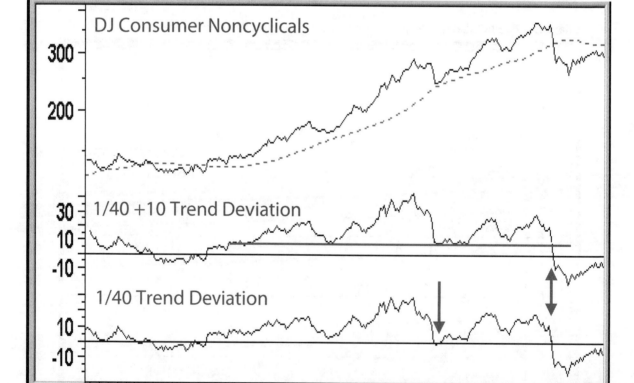

Chart 15-19 DJ Consumer Noncyclical Index, 1983–1988, and two trend deviation indicators

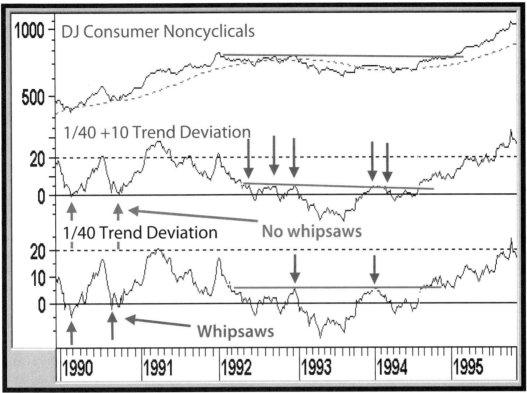

(Source: pring.com)

Chart 15-20 DJ Home Furnishing Index, 1982–1997, and a 26/40 trend deviation indicator

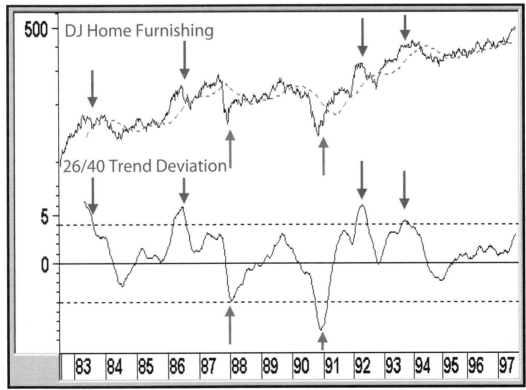

(Source: pring.com)

sive, reverse, head-and-shoulders breakout in the TD indicator itself.

Chart 15-17 shows the exact same data, but this time those periods when the oscillator crossed below its overbought zone and above its oversold level have been highlighted. The arrows flag periods where such action could have been confirmed by a trendline violation in the price. Again, we get some pretty good signals. The exclamation marks, alternately, indicate those overbought and oversold crossovers that were not associated with a price trend confirmation. Once more, the principle that the best momentum buy and sell signals are confirmed by price is reinforced. After all, you cannot buy and sell momentum, only price.

TREND DEVIATION FOR WEEKLY AND MONTHLY CHARTS

So far, we have just considered trend deviation measurements for short-term movements, but the technique can just as easily be applied to weekly and monthly data. Technicians have long used 40-week moving-average crossovers as a sign when the primary trend of the market has reversed. Chart 15-18 compares a weekly close to a 40-week MA trend deviation in the lower panel. The middle panel features the same thing, but this time the 40-week MA has been advanced by 10 weeks. You can see the whipsaw zero crossover at the end of 1986 for the straight series, yet the advanced indicator is nowhere near a crossover. When the price broke, the advanced series violated a support trendline and the straight series crossed below its zero level. The advanced series was clearly superior in this instance.

Chart 15-19 shows another example using the same combination of indicators. Notice how the advanced series is not immune from whipsaw zero crossovers, but it is certainly better than the regularly plotted average, because it does not suffer the two 1990 whipsaws.

Once again, both series break above their respective trendlines more or less simultaneously. In fact, if you look carefully, in this particular instance the trendline for the advanced series has been touched on more numerous occasions, thereby making it that much more significant.

It is also possible to smooth the trend deviation series by dividing a relatively long-term moving average by another long-term one. A 26-week or 6-month MA is divided by a 40-week or 9-month MA in Chart 15-20. This series seems to lend itself to extreme reversals. When the indicator reverses direction from an overbought/oversold level, this is an alert to buy or sell. Examples are flagged by the arrows. Note that we are using reversals of direction rather than an overbought/oversold crossover for this example. These signals need to be confirmed by some kind of trendbreak in the price. The basic principle is that the reversal from an extreme reading alerts you to the strong probability that a major trend change may be at hand. Such signals then act as a filter for further investigation to see if there is any confirming evidence.

Chart 15-21 features the Dow Jones Biotech group. The overbought/ oversold lines have been drawn at the same levels as in Chart 15-20, though I feel in retrospect that they could have been widened a notch. This underscores the point that each series needs to be assessed on its own volatility merits to come to a decision as to where the lines should be placed.

The Biotech group seems to lend itself well to this approach, except for the premature sell signal in mid-1990. If you will notice, the Index

> Reversals from an extreme reading alert you to the strong probability that a major trend change may be at hand. Such signals then act as a filter for further investigation.

Chart 15-21 DJ Biotech Index, 1983–1997, and a 26/40 trend deviation indicator

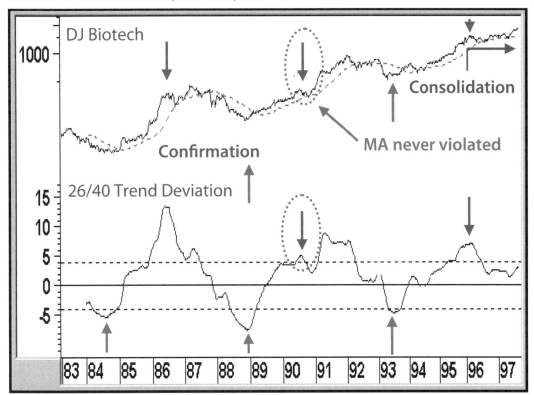

(Source: pring.com)

Chart 15-22 DJ Medical Supplies, 1982–1997, and two trend deviation indicators

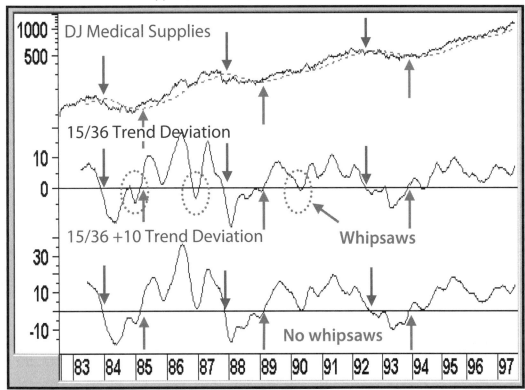

(Source: pring.com)

did not break below its 40-week MA during this period. Even though the 1986 sell was followed by a rally, the bulk of the bull market had already been seen.

Indeed, had we waited for the confirmation by the price, it would not have come until the 40-week MA had been violated some time later. Finally, note how the early 1996 signal was only followed by a consolidation prior to the Index going on to register a new high. This demonstrates the weakness of all momentum series, in that they will almost always give premature signals in a long-term linear uptrend. This was true of many stocks and industry groups in the 1990s bull market.

When Colby and Meyers tested for the best combination of moving-average crossovers using weekly data for the NYSE Composite, they found that between 1968 and 1986, the combination of a 15/36-week simple moving average worked best. They used the division, as opposed to the subtraction calculation, basing buy and sell signals on a zero crossover. An example of this combination is shown in the center panel of Chart 15-22. By and large, the signals work quite well, but there is the occasional whipsaw, such as those in 1984, 1986, and 1990. This technique tends to maintain positions during long, trendy moves. An even better approach seems to evolve when the 36-week average is advanced by 10 weeks in the calculation of the trend deviation oscillator. This is shown in the lower panel, where no whipsaw zero crossovers whatsoever are generated. This technique lends itself particularly well to the long-term linear uptrend, since it requires quite a decline before the 15-week MA crosses below the advanced 36-week series.

Chart 15-23 DJ Mining Index, 1982–1997, and a 15/36 trend deviation indicator

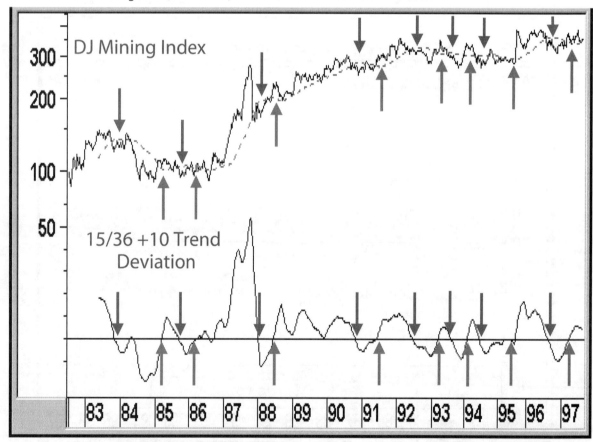

(Source: pring.com)

Chart 15-24 Spot gold, 1993–1994 — Calculating the MACD

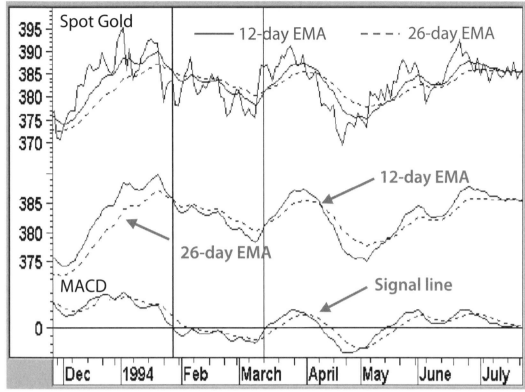

(Source: pring.com)

Chart 15-25 Spot gold, 1993–1994, and an MACD histogram

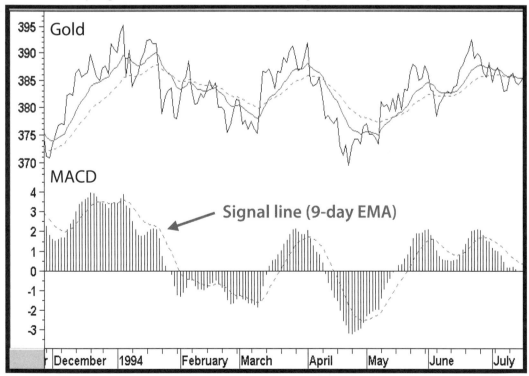

(Source: pring.com)

I am not going to say that this combination works well all of the time because nothing does. Just to prove the point, Chart 15-23, featuring the Dow Jones Mining Group, is indicative of what happens with a volatile security. It clearly does not lend itself to the 15/36 zero combination.

THE MACD INDICATOR

The acronym MACD stands for *moving average convergent divergent* method. This technique is really another way of expressing a trend deviation oscillator. This means that all the comments in this chapter relating to trend deviation indicators incorporating two moving averages apply equally as well to the MACD. The system obtains its name from the fact that the two moving averages used in the calculation are continually converging and diverging from each other. Normally, they are calculated on an exponential basis. Chart 15-24 serves as both a figure and marketplace example. It features the gold price together with a 12- and 26-day EMA. The middle panel shows the relationship between the two averages, but this time the closing price has been eliminated. The lower panel shows the oscillator derived from the division of the 12- by the 26-day average. This oscillator is, in fact, the MACD.

The zero line represents those periods when the two EMAs are identical. When the MACD is above the equilibrium line, the shorter average is above the longer, and vice versa. The dotted line represents a 9-day EMA of the MACD and is known as the *signal line*. It gets this name because MACD crossovers generate buy and sell signals. In my own experience, I have not found these crossovers to be particularly reliable, and I regard them as overrated.[1] I prefer to use the MACD from the

point of view of trendline violations or even price pattern construction. Another possibility is to use the MACD signal line crossovers as an alert that smoother oscillators, based on a longer time span, may be poised to give a signal. In this respect, I am thinking specifically about the short term. Obviously, MACDs can be constructed from many different combinations. Gerald Appel of Signalert, arguably its chief exponent, has done a substantial amount of work on the indicator. He recommends a combination of 8-, 17-, and 9-day EMAs but feels that sell-signals are more reliable using a 12–25–9 combination. This is interesting because the "selling" MACD contains a longer time span. It reflects the point made in an earlier chapter that markets spend more time in a rising than in a falling mode. The longer time span, therefore, has the effect of delaying the sell indications, so they will be more timely.

The MACD can also be plotted in a histogram format (see Chart 15-25). It has the advantage of emphasizing the peaks and troughs, but suffers from the disadvantage that it is more difficult to identify price pattern formations and trendline violations.

---

1 This comment relates to the default parameters of 12 and 26 periods. However, if a smoother series is calculated—say, a 65–125 combination—the signal line (20) approach works a little better for daily charts. Also, the default 12/26 periods work well when applied to monthly data.

16

Stochastics

INTRODUCTION

This indicator gained a lot of popularity in the 1980s, probably because its simple, deliberate style, on the face of it, appears to offer profitable and easy-to-follow signals. The concept rests on the assumption that prices tend to close near the upper part of the trading range during an uptrend and near the lower part during a downtrend. The range in this instance refers to the trading period under consideration. For example, daily data would embrace a trading range for a day, weekly for the week, and so forth. As the trend approaches a turning point, the price closes further away from the extreme. Figure 16-1 shows an uptrend. The horizontal bars, representing the closing price, develop close to the high at the start of the rally. However, as it matures, the closing price develops closer to the low of the day. The objective of the stochastics formula, therefore, is to try to identify those points in an advancing market when the closes

> The stochastic indicator is displayed as two lines, the %D and %K. The %K is the more sensitive, faster-moving line while the %D carries more weight and gives the major signals.

are clustered nearer to the lows than the highs, since this indicates that a trend reversal is at hand. For down markets, the process is reversed. Figure 16-2 shows that the stochastic indicator is displayed in the chart in the form of two lines, known as "PercentD" and "PercentK." The %K is the more sensitive of the two, but it is the %D line that carries the greater weight and gives the major signals. I always get confused between the two, but a simple reminder is to think of "K" standing for Kwick and "D" for Dawdling.

The *slow stochastic* is a smoothed variation of the regular series. In this calculation, the original %K line is eliminated and the old %D substituted for it. This renamed, or "slowed," %K is then averaged to form the "%D slow." Since the regular formula is more subject to whipsaws, the slowed version will be used from here on.

The %K is usually plotted as a solid line and its slower %D counterpart is expressed as a dashed or dotted line. The stochastic indicator always falls in the range from 0 to 100. A reading near 80 is generally regarded as overbought and 20 as oversold. These are the default lines that most charting packages and chart services use.

Figure 16-1   Price characteristics at a market peak

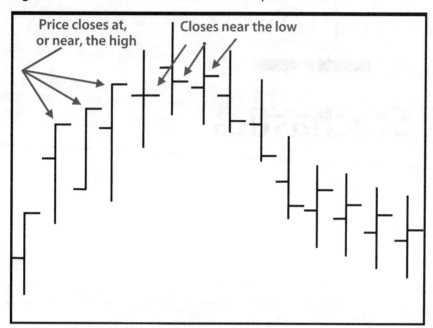

THE FORMULA

The formula for the %K is as follows.

$$\%K = \text{Raw Value} = \frac{100 \times [(C - Ln\text{close})}{(Hn - Ln)]}$$

In this expression, C is the most recent close, Ln the lowest low for the last *n* days, and Hn the highest high over the same *n*-day trading period. For short-term trading purposes, Gregory Lane recommends that *n* should be 3. A 5-period %K line has also become quite popular. Since the time span is longer, the indicator is less volatile than the formula using the 3-period calculation. There is, of course, no reason why other time periods cannot be used. In the March 1991 edition of *Technical Analysis of Stocks and Commodities*, former editor Thom Hartle uses a 14-day span and makes the point that

Figure 16-2   Stochastic %K and %D

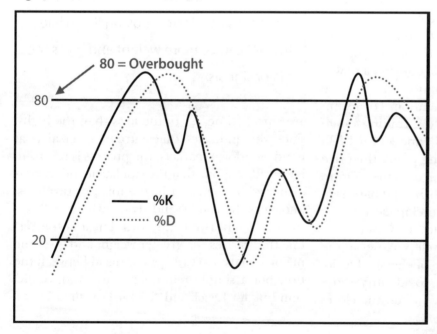

some traders go as far out as 28 days.

It is important to note that stochastics differs from the other indicators that we have so far considered in that it requires the high and low for the trading period in question, as well as the closing price. The %D line is a smoothed version of %K. Its calculation uses the following formula.

$$\%D = 100 \ x \ (H3/L3) \ I$$

In this expression, H3 is the 3-period sum of (C - L5) in the %K calculation and L3 is the 3-period sum of (H5 - L5). In a sense, you could equate the %D line with a 3-period smoothing of %K.

MORE ON THE SLOWED STOCHASTIC

It was mentioned earlier that the slowed stochastic is a smoothed version of the regular indicator and is used more often. In this calculation, the original %K is eliminated and the original %D substituted in its place. A new %D is then added to the indicator. The indicator in the center panel of Chart 16-1 is a regular version of the %K with a 5-period smoothing. The smoothing, represented by the dashed line, is %D. The lower panel contains the former %D, which now becomes the new or slowed %K.

Chart 16-2 shows the same series, that is, the slowed %K, but this time I have included the %D, featured as the dashed line. The numbers in parentheses next to the two legends refer to the time factors used in the calcula-

Chart 16-1 WM Wrigley, showing slowed stochastics

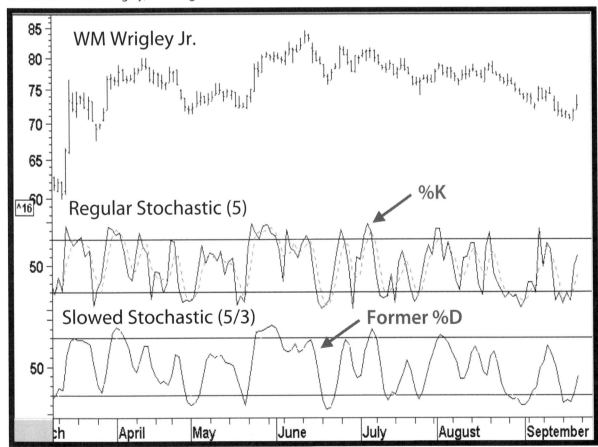

(Source: pring.com)

Chart 16-2 WM Wrigley, showing slowed stochastics

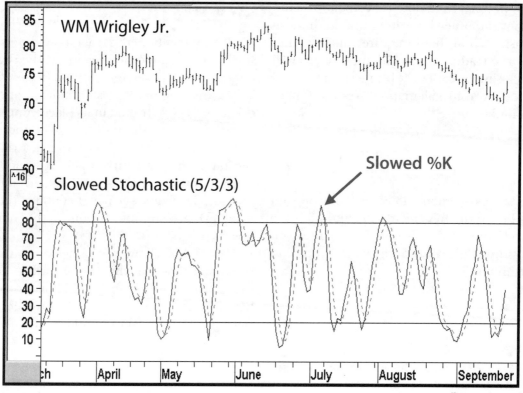

(Source: pring.com)

Chart 16-3 Placer Dome and two stochastic indicators

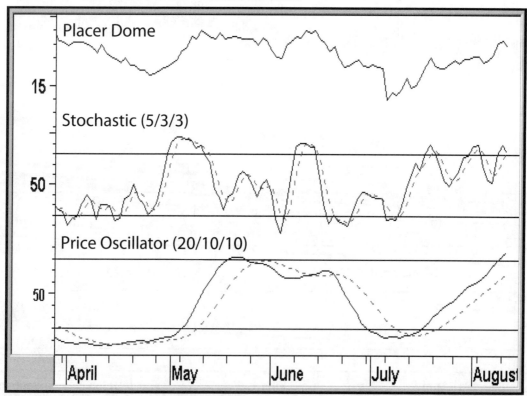

(Source: pring.com)

tion. Thus, the "5/3/3" in the center panel means that the %K is a 5-period smoothed by a factor of 3. The final 3 refers to the %D. The process need not stop there, of course, since there is nothing to prevent the innovative trader from experimenting with other smoothings and time period comparisons.

In Chart 16-3, for instance, the 5/3/3 combination we saw earlier has been plotted against a 20/10/10 price oscillator. Since the smoothing factors are that much larger, the resulting indicator experiences slower, more deliberate swings that are more useful in monitoring longer-term price trends.

INTERPRETATION

1. *Divergence.* Divergences between the %D and the price are similar to those discussed in the previous chapter. The principal difference between, say, a stochastic and an RSI divergence is that there are usually less of them. In fact, it is probably true to say that in the vast majority of cases, the %D only experiences one, or at the most two, divergences. Divergences are indicated in Fig. 16-3.

Figure 16-3 Stochastic divergences

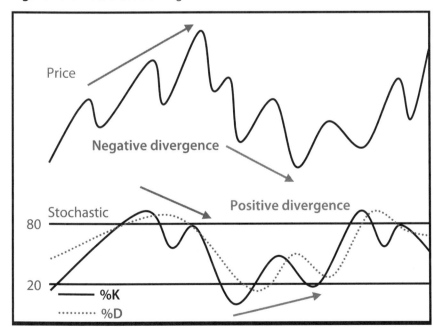

2. *Crossovers.* Normally, the more sensitive, or "Kwick," %K will turn and cross the "Dawdling," or slower, %D before the D changes direction. See how K crosses below D before D peaks in the left-hand part of Fig. 16-4. This is normal because K is more sensitive. According to George Lane, the inventor of the indicator, the strongest stochastics signal comes when the %K crosses from the *right*-hand side of the peak in the %D line; that is, K crosses D *after* D changes direction. Examples are also shown in Fig. 16-4. Lane also emphasizes that these right-hand crossovers are more reliable.

3. *The hinge.* The hinge is a slowing down in the velocity of either line. This implies a reversal in the next trading period, that is, the next day for daily data, the next week for weekly data, and so forth. See how the line, and here we are talking about %K, falls sharply on the left of Fig. 16-5; then downside momentum dissipates as the descent of %K becomes noticeably less pronounced. In this case, the hinge is represented by the dotted part of %K. The example on the right shows the same characteristics for a short-term top.

4. *Warning.* In the case of an advancing market, a warning occurs when the %K line has been rising for a while, and then one day (or week or month, depending on the time frame being used) reverses sharply (Fig. 16-6). This offers a signal that only one or two more days of rising movement are likely prior to a reversal in trend. The opposite condition would offer a buy signal in a declining market.

5. *%K reaching an extreme.* Normally, when an indicator reaches an overbought or oversold extreme it indicates a possible trend reversal. However, when the %K

line moves to the extreme of 0 percent or 100 percent this indicates *pronounced strength or weakness*. In the case of an overbought situation, a move to 100 percent or very close to it indicates that once the overbought condition has been worked off, the next rally is likely to take the price higher, as in Fig. 16-7. Typically, the %K will retreat 20 percent to 25 percent from the 100 percent level, later rallying back toward it again. It is when this testing process is underway that the actual price should work its way to new high ground.

The opposite is true of falling markets in relation to the 0 percent extreme. First, expect a rally, and then a reaction to new lows. Although these extreme readings are, on the one hand, telling us that things are overdone for the time being, the very fact that the stochastic has been able to reach it indicates an underlying strength. Once the correction has run its course, expect a new high following a 100 percent reading or a new low, for a 0 percent.

6. *Bullish and bearish failures.* At market bottoms, the failure occurs when the %K line crosses above the %D and then falls back for a couple of days but manages to remain above the %D line. It represents a kind of test that, if successful, indicates that the new uptrend is likely to continue. The example on the left of Fig. 16-8 shows this concept for a market top and that on the right for a bottom. See how the K-line crosses above the D, then falls back, successfully holds above %D, and then goes on to recover to a new high.

Figure 16-4 Stochastic crossovers

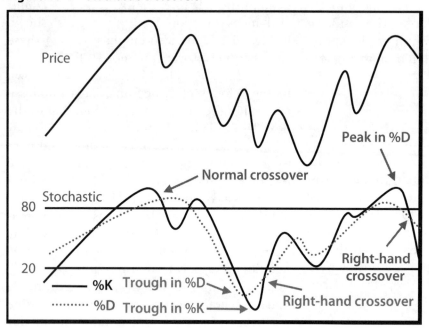

Figure 16-5 Stochastic hinges

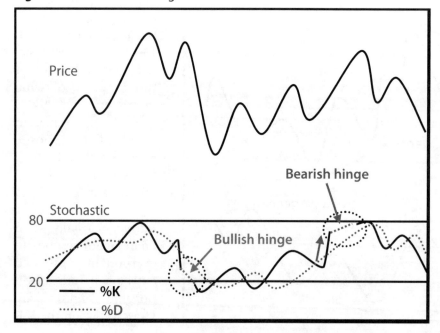

Figure 16-6 Stochastic warning

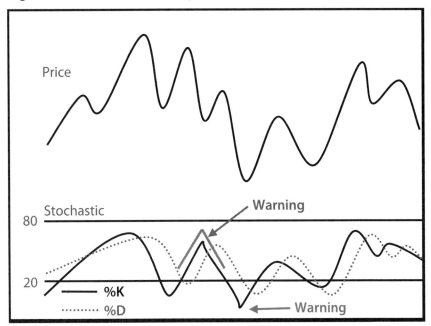

Figure 16-7 Stochastic extremes

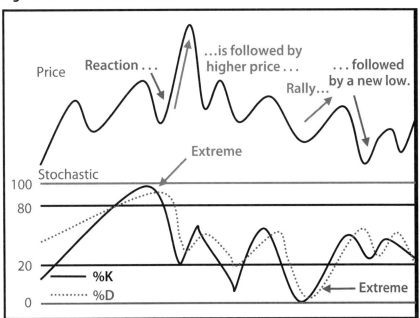

Figure 16-8   Stochastic failures

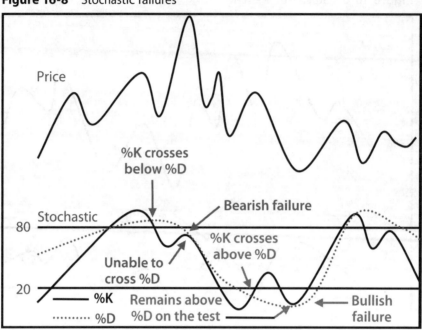

Figure 16-9   Stochastic bearish setup

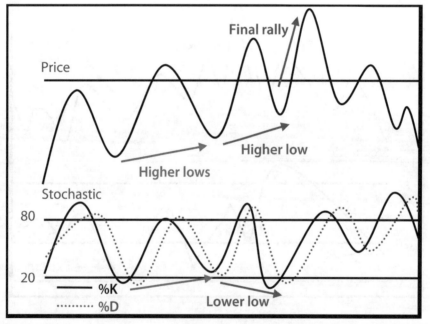

Figure 16-10 Stochastic bullish setup

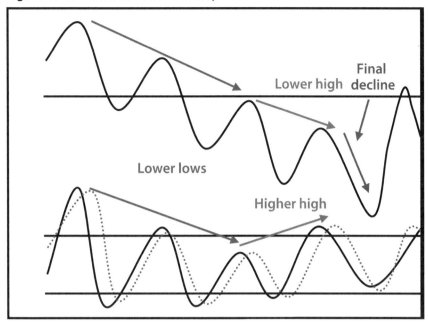

Chart 16-4 Norfolk Southern and some stochastic characteristics

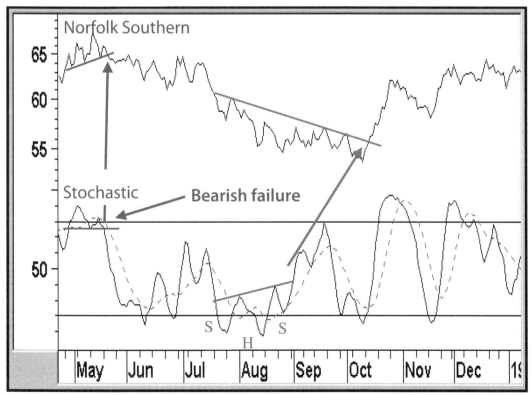

Chart 16-5 Northwest Corp. and some stochastic characteristics

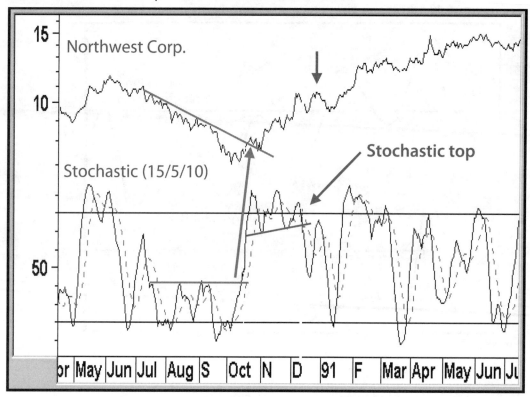

(Source: pring.com)

Chart 16-6 Northwest Corp. and some stochastic characteristics

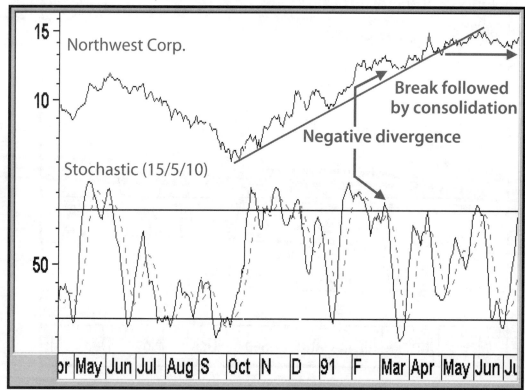

(Source: pring.com)

7. *The setup.* A setup is really the same thing as the advance breakdown or breakout discussed in the principles of momentum earlier. A bullish setup corresponds to the advanced breakout and a bearish setup to an advanced breakdown. In a rising market, the setup occurs as the *price* makes a low simultaneously with the %D. Both series then go on to make a new high, but on the subsequent reaction, the %D breaks below its previous low, but the security does not. The implication is that the next rally in price will *probably* turn out to be an important top. This is known as a *bear setup*. It is shown in Fig. 16-9.

Figure 16-10, on the other hand, shows a bull setup. In this case, both the price and %D trace out a series of declining peaks. Then the %D makes a higher high, but the price does not. This represents an advance signal that one more price drop is likely before the trend is going to reverse.

PRICE PATTERNS

Price patterns occasionally show up in a stochastic. In Chart 16-4 we see a reverse head and shoulders that was later confirmed by a nice trendline break in the price. The May top shows up as a bearish failure in the stochastic that is also confirmed by a small top in the price.

Chart 16-5 shows another example featuring some price patterns. The July/September base, when used in conjunction with the downtrend line violation in October, provides a very good buy signal. However, the top that formed between late October and early December in the stochastic was not followed by a price decline at all. There was a small decline that took place in January 1991, but that was about it. Even the negative divergence that materialized in the February/March period was not followed by a decline (Chart 16-6). It took a trendline break by the price in April to halt the uptrend. Even

Chart 16-7 Northwest Corp. and some stochastic characteristics

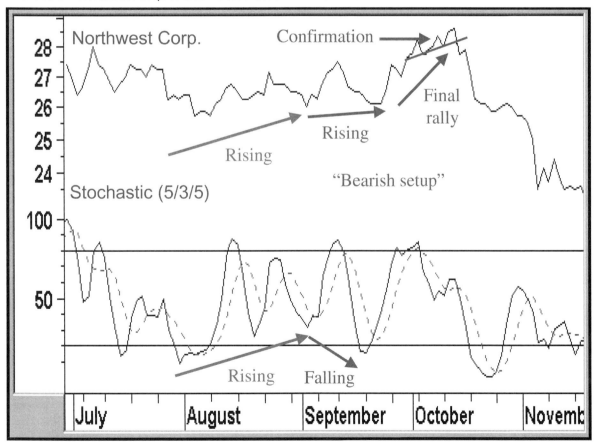

(Source: pring.com)

Chart 16-8 Northwest Corp. and some stochastic characteristics

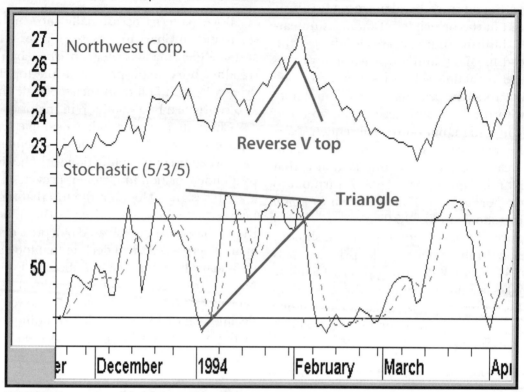

Chart 16-9 Northwest Corp. and some stochastic characteristics

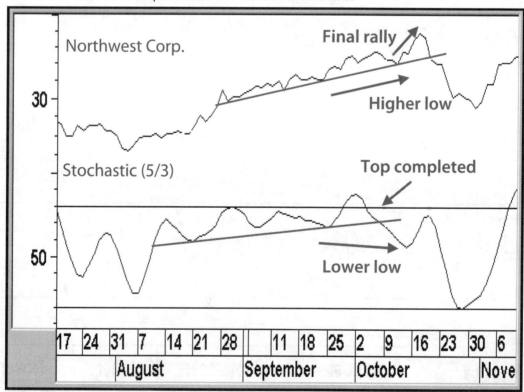

then, the price just experienced a temporary consolidation. I show this example to demonstrate that following the principles outlined here does not always guarantee that the security price will respond in the expected way.

Chart 16-7 shows a stochastic calculated from a shorter time frame, a 5/3/5 combination to be exact. It contains an example of a bearish setup. See how the oscillator makes a series of rising bottoms between August and early September. Then, the mid-September low takes it below the early September bottom, but the price experiences a higher low. This was the signal for a probable final rally. In this case, the top was signaled by the violation of a small trendline, a negative divergence, and a reversal in the direction of the %K and %D.

There was no trend confirmation by the price in the example shown in Chart 16-8, since it was not possible to construct a mean-

ingful line with the inverted V-type top. However, I really featured it to demonstrate how a stochastic sometimes experiences a kind of triangle formation. Often, when the downside breakdown develops, a sharp correction sets in. Remember, this was only a 5/3/5 stochastic, so the trends being monitored are relatively small.

Chart 16-9 features another example of a short-term top using the 5/3 combination for %K. There are two things worth noting. First, the stochastic completes and breaks down from a top formation. The price also confirms with a trendline violation. Second, the stochastic experiences a bear setup. You can see how the %K makes a lower low in mid-October: lower, that is, than its mid-September bottom. The price does not exactly make a low in mid-September, but the principle of rising prices relative to the break in the stochastic certainly

Chart 16-10 Hartford Steam, 1991–1997, and a 39/26/13 stochastic

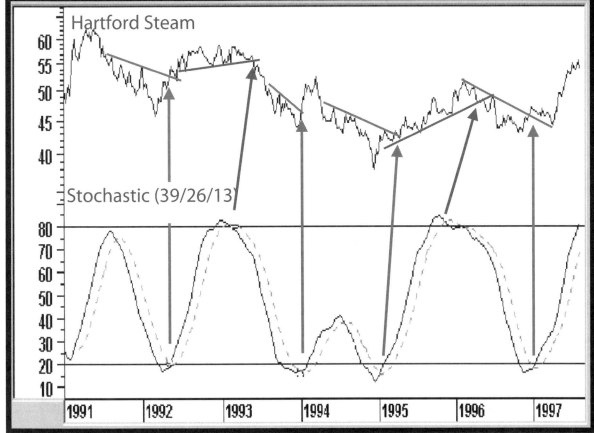

(Source: pring.com)

Chart 16-11 Hewlett-Packard, 1990–1997, and a 39/26/13 stochastic

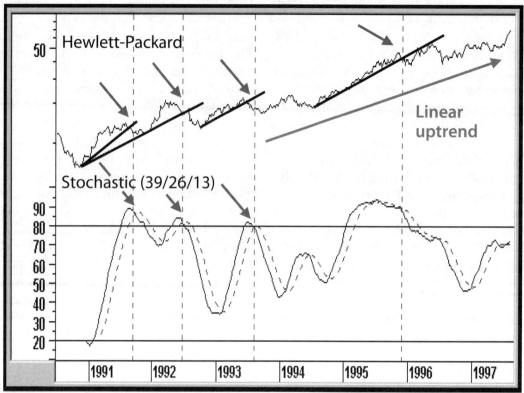

(Source: pring.com)

Chart 16-12 Placer Dome and three stochastics

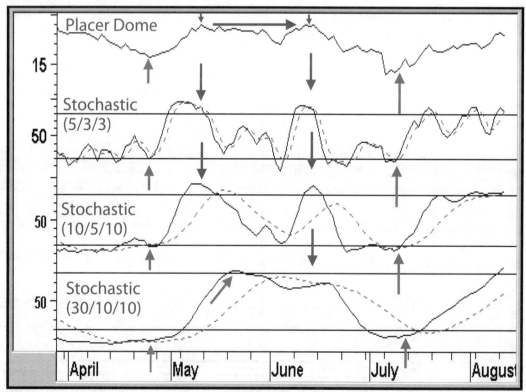

(Source: pring.com)

holds true. Once the mid-October decline has run its course, the price embarks on its final rally.

Chart 16-10 features a much longer time span. It is a 39/26/13- combination and is calculated from weekly data. The indicator has a deliberate swing to it, as it is able to reflect all of the major price changes that took place between 1991 and 1997. The vertical arrows point up when the %K crosses above or below the %D and when this has been confirmed by a trendline break in the price. This can be a highly effective method in a good range-bound market like this but will obviously fall down during a trending one.

Chart 16-11 represents Hewlett-Packard in a trending market. Three confirmed sell signals develop between 1991 and 1993, but the strong linear uptrend that follows experiences a false stochastic sell at the very end of 1995. Notice that after 1991, the oscillator never falls back to its oversold condition.

STOCHASTIC ARRANGEMENTS

These oscillators can sometimes be used fairly effectively by arranging several of them with different parameters on the same chart. The principle is identical to that explained earlier for the ROC and RSI indicators. The idea is to plot three stochastic indicators with differing time spans. Each will then reflect different cyclic rhythms. The advantage is that, occasionally, one of the indicators will point out a specific technical characteristic that the others may not. If only one indicator was being monitored, this may not have been picked out. The other advantage is that the longer-term stochastic gives the analysis some perspective.

The arrows in the bottom panel of Chart 16-12 identify three major turning points. Note that at the April price-low, all three stochastic oscillators have either bottomed or are in a bottoming phase. This means that each of the cycles they are individually reflecting is in an up-phase. Now look at the June peak. Two series peak out, but the 30/10/10 combination

in the lower panel has only just emerged into a bull phase. Consequently, there is a standoff as the shorter-term cycles battle against the longer-term one. It is not until the June high that all three are in declining modes, along with the price. The two shorter-term oscillators try to bottom in late June, but the longer-term one is still falling. Again, the price-low does not develop until July, when the 30/10/10 series reverses its downtrend and begins to rally.

The 10/5/10 series in the third panel of Chart 16-13 experiences a reverse head-and-shoulders formation at a time when the other two are in the process of bottoming. Note that the price also violates a downtrend line. This turned out to be a bear market rally but was nonetheless a worthwhile advance from a trading point of view.

An important characteristic of this chart is represented by the two up trendlines for the two shorter oscillators that were violated in late February in Chart 16-14. This is an example of a destructive breakdown. Destructive breakdowns arise in a bear market, when the price consolidates and rises for a while. It is an interlude from the persistently declining prices associated with a primary bear trend. During this pleasant interlude, the momentum takes on some very constructive characteristics, but when the bear market resumes, this otherwise bullish price and volume scenario is destroyed. Hence, it is a destructive breakdown. All breakdowns are destructive, but usually they develop from a situation that looks as if it is deteriorating rather than improving. In this example,

> Plotting three stochastic indicators with differing time spans gives you two advantages: 1) you may pick up on a technical characteristic that would have otherwise been missed, and 2) the longer-term stochastic will give the rest of the analysis some perspective.

Chart 16-13 Placer Dome, 1996–1997, and three stochastics

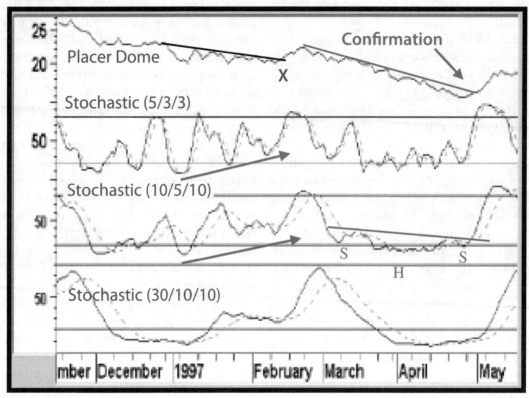

(Source: Market Vane)

Chart 16-14 Placer Dome, 1996–1997, and three stochastics

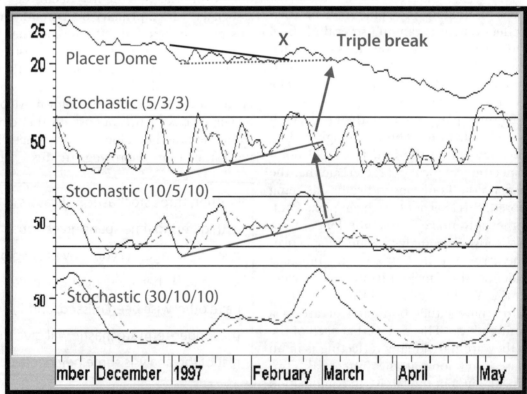

(Source: Market Vane)

> Destructive breakdowns happen when price consolidates and rises for a short while in a bear market. Momentum may seem to be improving during this period; however, when the bear resumes, all of it will be taken out.

the price was finding support during the January/February period at the dashed horizontal line. As this development was unfolding, the two shorter-term oscillators were experiencing a series of rising bottoms. This was the constructive part, especially as the price broke out on the upside at point X. At this juncture, things looked pretty good. Then the support trendline for the price and the two up trend-

lines for the oscillators were more or less simultaneously violated, and the bear market resumed.

Finally, one of the best ways of looking at the stochastic, and for that matter any of the other oscillators discussed here, is to plot three series, one reflecting the short term, another the intermediate term, and finally one monitoring the primary trend. That is what I have done in Chart 16-15, which is constructed from weekly data. The thick lines in the bottom panel roughly correspond with the primary trend swings as reflected by the 39/26/15 stochastic. From an investment point of view, it is desirable to be accumulating as the trend reverses from down to up, and to be selling when the trend reverses from up to down. Traders should also be aware of the direction of the main trend. In this respect, reactions in bull markets are weak

Chart 16-15 Bay St. Gas, 1992–1997, and three stochastics

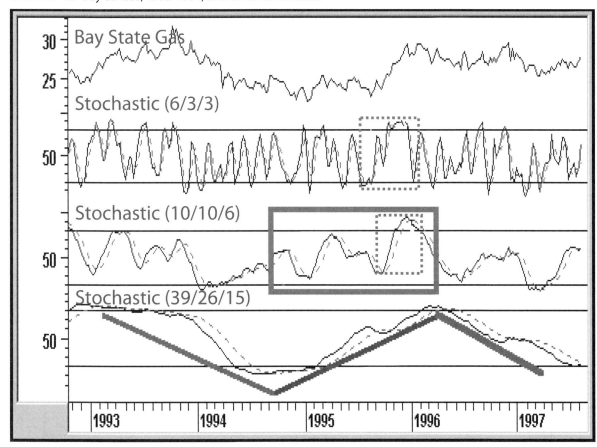

(Source: pring.com)

Chart 16-16 Hartford Steam, 1990–1993, and three stochastics

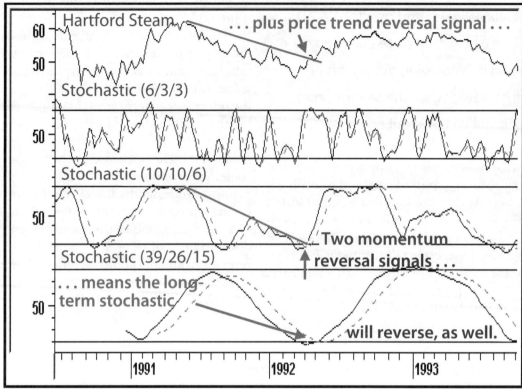

(Source: Market Vane)

Chart 16-17 Hartford Steam, 1990–1993, and three stochastics

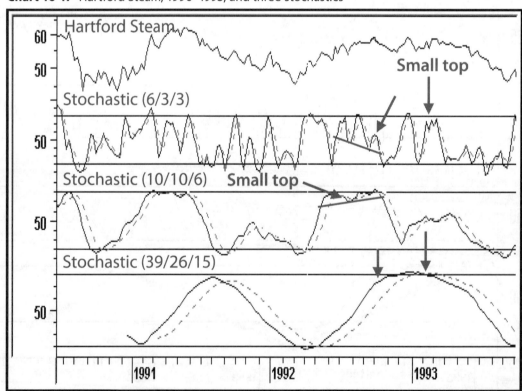

(Source: Market Vane)

and short-term rallies are strong. Rallies in bear markets either turn out to be weak or develop as consolidations. A trader is, therefore, foolish to go long in the anticipation of a bear market rally or to go short in anticipation of a bull market correction.

The solid rectangle approximates the 1994–1995 bull market. This trend contains two intermediate rallies, as reflected by the price action of the center series. The lower dashed rectangle contains the final intermediate advance and the upper dashed rectangle a couple of short-term rallies. When analyzing any market situation, therefore, it is a very good idea to try to gain some perspective. Your analysis may not be correct, or more likely the market may not respond in such a clear-cut way as that shown on this chart, but at least you could make the effort.

This approach can also be used to assess what I call the *domino effect*. For statistical reasons, the longer-term, smoothed momentum signals often come *after* the final turning point, sometimes with far too much of a delay. However, if you can see that the oscillator measuring the primary trend is at an extreme and starting to slow down, the short-term momentum indicators can be sometimes used to anticipate a reversal. If it is pretty obvious that the short-term oscillator has changed trend, then this may well be enough to reverse the direction of the long-term indicator—hence the domino effect. Look at the 1992 bottom in Chart 16-16. See how the intermediate series in the center panel not only reverses from an oversold condition but also violates a 1-year downtrend line. It is not normally possible to draw a trendline of this length or one that has been touched so many times on a stochastic indicator, so this was a big event in its own right. The point here is that the reversal of a shorter-term oscillator, combined with the trendbreak in the price, would have been sufficient to conclude that the long-term series and, therefore, the primary trend in the price itself had reversed to the upside.

We see a similar type of domino effect at the top. This is marked in Chart 16-17. In early fall 1992, the long-term oscillator is approaching an overbought condition. However, the short-term series completes a head-and-shoulders top, the intermediate oscillator also breaks down from a top and the price violates an up trendline. This turned out to be the actual peak, but the price moved in a sideways band for a while. However, the momentum and price breaks were sufficient to halt the short bull market in its tracks. Even then, the final peak in the long-term series was heralded by an overbought short-term reversal, as signaled by the two downward-pointing arrows.

THE STOCHASTIC MOMENTUM INDICATOR

The stochastic momentum indicator is a variation on the stochastic oscillator. It was developed by William Blau and introduced in a January 1993 *Stocks and Commodities Magazine* article. Normally, the stochastic is calculated by relating the close to the session trading range over an *n*-period time span. The stochastic momentum indicator, alternately, relates the close to the midpoint of the range. The result is a series that moves in a similar manner to the regular stochastic for any given time span. However, the movements are less erratic.

Chart 16-18 features two stochastic indicators, the regular oscillator and the stochastic momentum series. Their time spans are identical. The vertical lines show that in most cases, they each reverse direction at around the same time. The arrows above and below the price indicate that when they do not, it is the momentum series that leads. The dashed arrows correspond with the momentum series and the solid ones with the regular stochastic. In general, the extra timelines of the oscillator do not usually cost it in terms of whipsaws. The one possible exception for this particular example developed at the start of 1996, when a buy

Chart 16-18 Hewlett-Packard, 1991–1997, a stochastic versus a stochastic momentum indicator

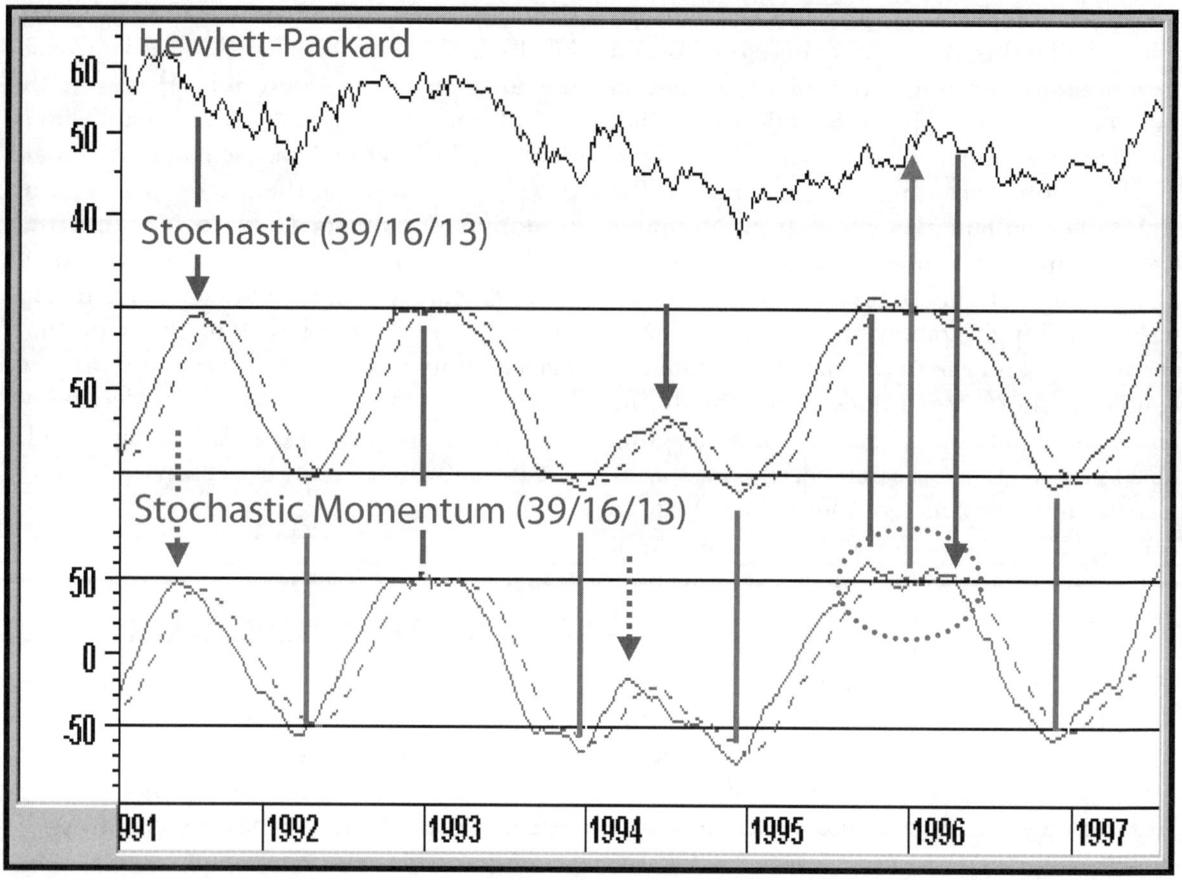

crossover by the momentum oscillator was quickly reversed. In this instance, the trade would have basically been a breakeven one. However, the fact that the crossover came from such an extreme level should have warned that it was probably suspect anyway.

HOW DOES IT TEST?

In The *Encyclopedia of Technical Market Indicators*, Colby and Meyers tested the stochastics for a variety of rules and parameters and found the vast majority to be unprofitable. This research was not only based on 1977–1986 weekly data for the NYSE but also drew on the experience of Schwager and Strahm (July 1986, *Technical Analysis of Stocks and Commodities*). Colby and Meyers finally came up with a prof-

itable combination, although this did not compare favorably with most of the other indicators that they tested. The rules they established called for a buy signal when the 39-week unsmoothed %K line (*n* = 39, with no moving averages) crosses above 50 percent and the %K and closing price are *both* above their previous closing levels. Sell and sell short when these conditions are reversed; that is, %K moves below 50 percent and the %K and closing prices are below the previous week's levels. They note that fairly consistent profits were achieved for periods (that is, the *n*-value) ranging from 38 to 66 weeks, but the 39-span proved to be the best. Note that the %D was not used in this particular rule. Chart 16-19 features the 39-week stochastic as tested. The arrows above and below the price indicate the buy and sell signals, as determined by a simple 50-stochastic crossover. These periods clearly generate good returns. However, we would also have to contend with the whipsaw periods. Some of the worst are contained within the rectangles. If you are in a strongly trending market, this approach is going to work well for you. However, in a volatile environment, this is not going to be a very successful system, as is apparent from the chart.

Chart 16-19 Bay St. Gas, 1986–1997, and stochastic %K (39) and 50 crossovers

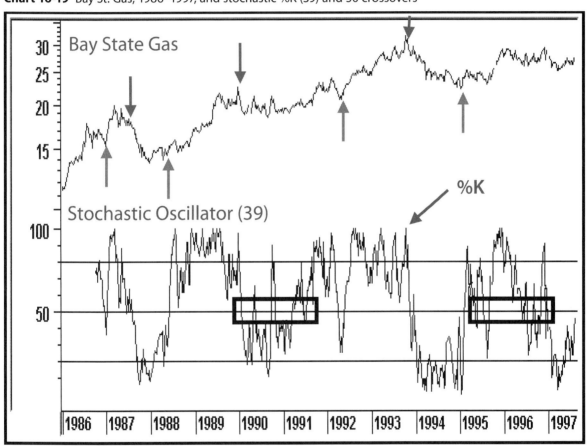

(Source: pring.com)

17

Real-Time Examples

TIME FRAME CONSIDERATIONS

In this section, we will be looking at some real-time momentum examples. I think it is important to note that for all intents and purposes, the principles of technical analysis apply to all time frames. This means that a confirmed divergence or an overbought/oversold condition have the same effect on an intraday chart as they do on the weekly, or even monthly, charts. The only difference is that an overbought condition on an intraday chart will only have an effect on the price trend for a few hours or a day or two at the most. Alternately, an overbought condition on a monthly chart can have an effect as long as a year or more. The principles are the same, but the lasting strength of their effect is not. Also, because intraday action is so fast, the time lags in which to take action are much more compressed, this means that, occasionally, different entry-and-exit tactics are required.

You will find that we can apply many of the principles set out in earlier chapters to real-time data, though I believe less reliably, due to the prevalence of more random noise and the greater significance of opening gaps.

One other time frame consideration lies in the fact that daily charts are just that—charts containing bars or closes of daily trading sessions. Similarly, a weekly chart contains data normally based on five trading sessions of data. Once we move to intraday charts, the choice of time span becomes greater, since it is possible to construct bars from, say, 1 minute of data, 5 minutes, 30 minutes, and so forth. Momentum time frames must be adjusted accordingly. For instance, the ROC contained in Chart 17-1 is based on a 1-minute bar for the NASDAQ 100. The time span is 200, and the overboughts and oversolds are constructed at ±2. This would appear to be a pretty good setup, based on these particular data for September 2000.

Chart 17-2, alternately, shows virtually the same period, but this time it is a 5-minute bar with a 200-period time span. The effect is totally different. And that is not surprising, for if we were to plot a daily chart with a 30-day ROC, we would get a very different picture than a weekly chart with a 30-week ROC. Obviously, we need to tailor-make the time frame of the indicator to the periodicity of the data.

The normal overbought/oversold crossovers are, of course, used in intraday charts. In Chart 17-3 (a 5-minute bar of IBM) we can see some overbought crossovers from the 14-period RSI. Because of the volatility of these short-term charts, traders are often advised to move as soon as the RSI moves to an overbought condition. We can see that is true for the first two sell signals. The third, on the 22nd, barely reaches overbought before a massive decline sets in. The same principles of waiting for a price trend confirmation should apply to intraday charts as those featuring longer-term timeframes. However, the greater volatility of intraday trends means that it is often a good idea to protect at least part of the profits when an indicator reaches or reverses from an over-

bought condition. This point is well demonstrated from all three sell signals in Chart 17-3. By the same token, none of them was associated with a trendline break or price pattern completion that would have served as a reliable confirmation of the action from the RSI.

The same observations could also be made for the buy signal on the 15th. It developed during a long-term downtrend and did not generate any form of a rally. This was only evident after the fact, of course. However, the astute trader would have noted that what normally would be a bullish factor, that is, the oversold condition, was not working. *When an indicator or a characteristic fails to work, more often than not this turns out to be a countercyclical phenomenon.* In effect, the very observation of the failed oversold would have warned us that the technical position was in a pretty precarious shape.

In the middle of the 18th, we get another buy signal, this time following a failure swing.

Chart 17-1 NASDAQ 100 1-minute bar and a 200-period ROC

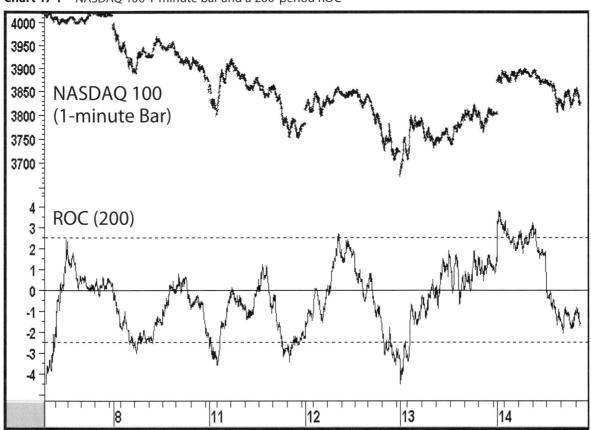

(Source: pring.com)

Chart 17-2 NASDAQ 100 5-minute bar and a 200-period ROC

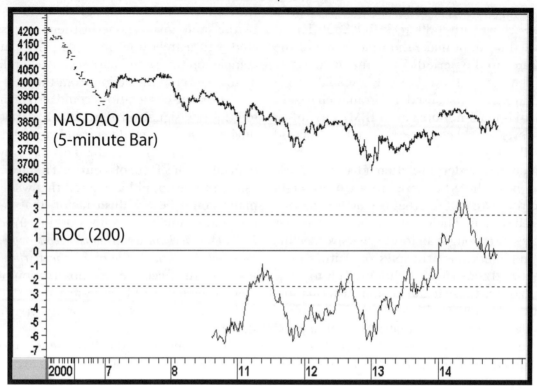

(Source: pring.com)

Chart 17-3 IBM 5-minute bar and a 14-period RSI

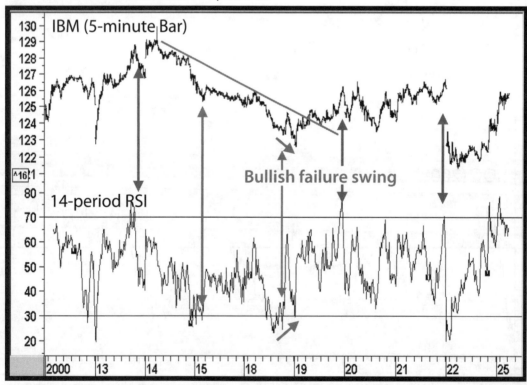

(Source: pring.com)

> When an indicator or a characteristic fails to work, more often than not this turns out to be a countercyclical phenomenon. In effect, the very observation of the failed oversold would have warned us that the technical position was in a pretty precarious shape.

It is later confirmed by a price trendbreak, but the situation is so weak that this positive action is only followed by a sideways trading range.

You may notice some gaps on the chart. These arise because of violent overnight action, whereby the price trades well beyond the previous night's closing price in Asia and Europe.

These gaps represent a tremendous risk for highly leveraged traders who wish to hold overnight positions. At first glance, you may think that these are random events and, therefore, untradeable. However, look at the RSI and price action following these events. On each occasion, the extreme reading is followed by a trend reversal. The first one develops at the opening of the 13th (Chart 17-4). It is even confirmed later on by a trendline break. The problem, of course, is that the breakout comes when the RSI is in an overbought condition. No wonder it was not followed by much of a rally. The second gap-opening develops just afterward, on the opening of the 14th. While this may have looked to be an explosive situation at the time of the opening, a few minutes later it was obvious that the RSI was going to diverge negatively with the price. There was no trend-break confirming their reversal. However,

Chart 17-4   IBM 5-minute bar and a 14-period RSI

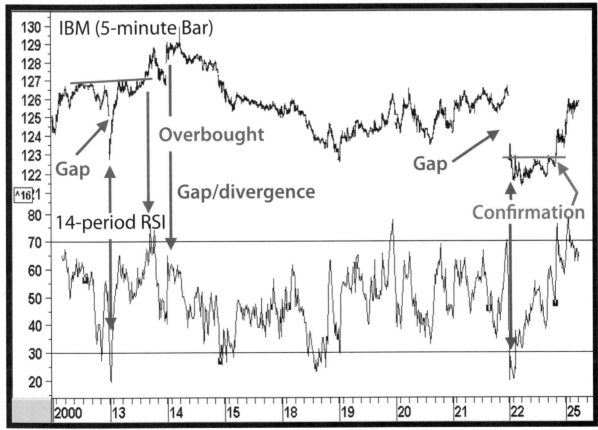

(Source: pring.com)

anyone who was long should have realized from the lack of upside momentum that the gap-opening was not as good as it may have looked on the surface.

Finally, the downside gap on September 22 registered an oversold condition. This would have signaled to anyone who was lucky enough to own a short position that it was time to take profits. Later on, a long position could have been justified, since the price broke above a small horizontal line marking a consolidation.

This gap was caused by a report of reduced profit expectations by Intel that resulted in a ripple effect throughout the technology sector. The news was bleak, indeed, but to observers of the RSI, it was apparent that the emotions of the crowd had probably reached an extreme. At the time when you least want to buy, deeply oversold momentum readings can often indicate that then is the time when you probably should buy.

TRENDLINE ANALYSIS

Chart 17-5 features a 1-minute bar of the S&P Composite. Also included are 32- and 65-period ROCs. The 32-period series completes a triple top around 11 A.M. and the 65-period indicator violates an up trendline. This looks like a top, but it does not fall into a classifiable category because each peak is substantially higher than its predecessor. This action is later confirmed by the price but is not followed by a reversal. Instead, the price moves sideways for a while. Chart 17-6 shows that the 65-period ROC completes a head-and-shoulders top. This looks pretty ominous, but the price does not confirm since it is not possible to construct a trendline. Also, the series of rising peaks and troughs remains intact. However, it was possible to construct the neckline of a head-and-shoulders top in the price. This combination looked pretty ominous, but the head

Chart 17-5 S&P Composite 1-minute bar and two ROCs

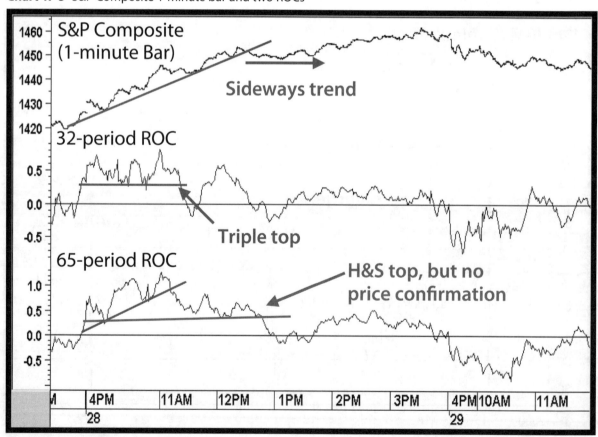

Chart 17-6 S&P Composite 1-minute bar and two ROCs

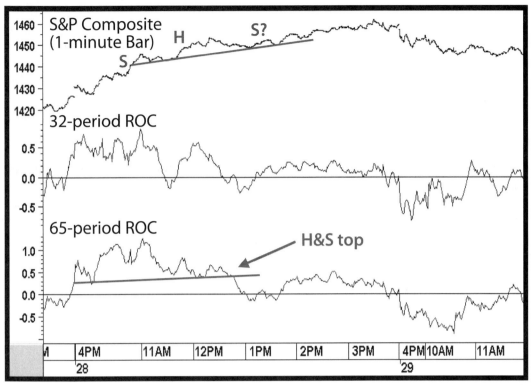

Chart 17-7 S&P Composite 1-minute bar and two ROCs

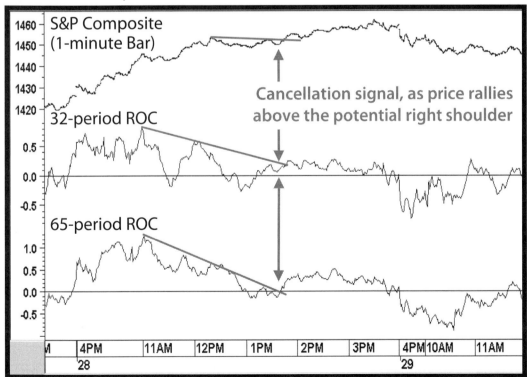

and shoulders for the S&P is never completed. This is a classic reminder of why, even in the face of the worst-looking momentum, it is important to await some kind of price confirmation. After this, Chart 17-7 shows that the head and shoulders are replaced by a triple trendline violation, but this time it happens on the upside, as the price rallies above the line joining the potential head and the potential right shoulder.

Later on, both momentum series complete small tops. It is also important to note that there was virtually no upside momentum from the 32-period ROC at the time of the final peak (Chart 17-8). Later, this is all confirmed by the price, as it violates a pretty good up trendline. I say it is a good line because it lasts for quite a long time, 5 hours, in fact—remember, this is a 1-minute bar and in this case 5 hours is a lifetime. Second, the line is touched or approached on many occasions. Finally, its

angle of ascent is relatively mild. Note also that the line is preceded by multiple negative divergences emanating from both ROCs. Now we move to Chart 17-9, which features a 10-minute bar for American Express. This time, the two ROCs are based on a 65- and 130-period. As the chart opens on the left the 65-period series diverges positively with the price. Then it breaks above a small base and this is confirmed by the price. You may notice that I drew the trendline through the rally peak at the end of the 20th of September. This is, strictly speaking, incorrect. However, I prefer to use a common sense approach, and for me, this line best reflects the underlying trend, as a correctly drawn trendline should.

Later on, the shorter ROC experiences a negative divergence and completes a small top. The 130-period ROC then goes on to complete a more ominous head-and-shoulders pattern, and this is confirmed by the price.

Chart 17-8 S&P Composite 1-minute bar and two ROCs

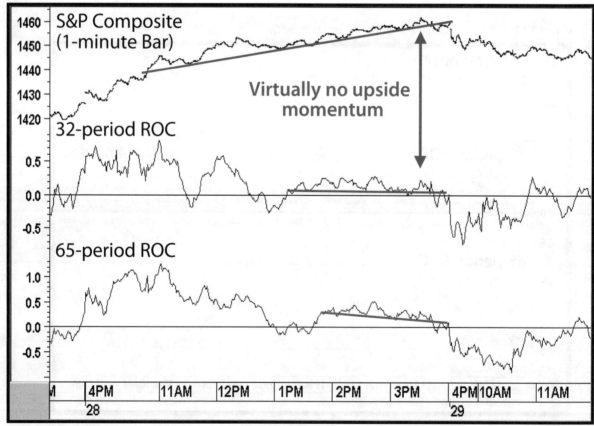

(Source: pring.com)

Chart 17-9 American Express 10-minute bar and two ROCs

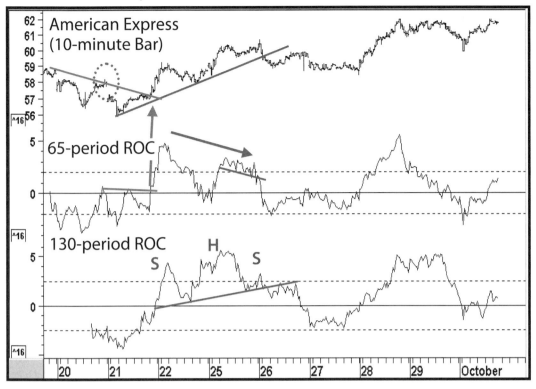

(Source: pring.com)

Chart 17-10 American Express 10-minute bar and two ROCs

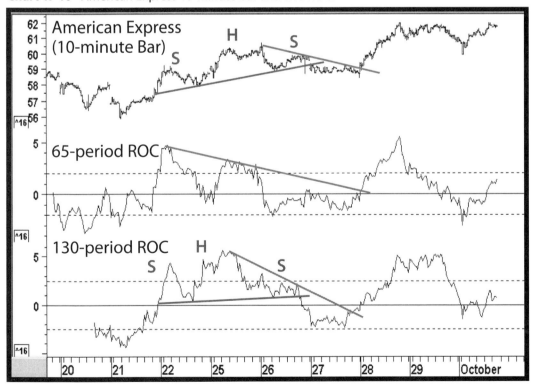

(Source: pring.com)

In actual fact, it is really part of an even larger one (Chart 17-10). The price experiences a head-and-shoulders top, but there is no really strong follow-through on the downside. Indeed, after a small pause, it reverses trend. This again emphasizes the need to be extremely flexible in any trading situation, especially intraday ones. As soon as a new trend is signaled, we must be looking over our shoulders continually for a possible reversal, for one will probably develop when we least expect it.

Both ROCs violate downtrend lines, and this is confirmed by the price around the opening of the 28th. Also, the two ROCs and the price each complete a base, as shown in Chart 17-11. At this point, all of the negative evidence indicated by the two head-and-shoulder tops is canceled by this new influx of positive action. Maybe this quick change in evidence is too overwhelming for a reversal of positions, but it

would certainly have been a strong warning for any who were short to cover their positions.

ARRANGEMENTS

In our daily, weekly, and monthly analysis, we found that the chart arrangements, spreading three indicators over widely differing time cycles, were very useful. The same applies to intraday data.

Chart 17-12 shows three ROCs for Eastman Kodak in September 2000. This is a 5-minute bar with 32, 65, and 130 time spans. I am not suggesting that this is the absolute best arrangement, but it does appear to work quite well. The important thing to note is that the three oscillators are widely separated in time, basically doubling as we move down the chart. There are two interesting bottoms, one at the

Chart 17-11 American Express 10-minute bar and two ROCs

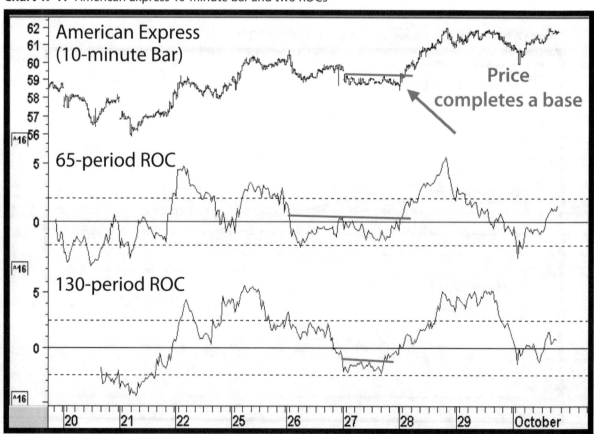

(Source: pring.com)

Chart 17-12 Eastman Kodak 5-minute bar and three ROCs

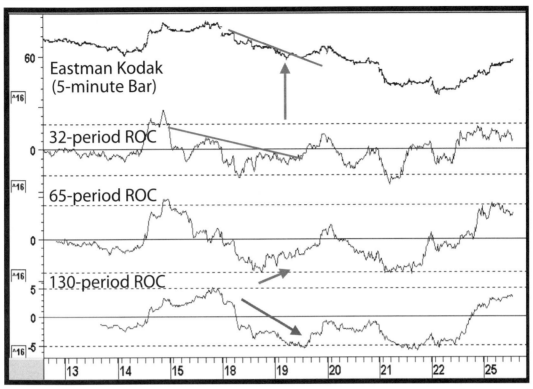

Chart 17-13 Eastman Kodak 5-minute bar and three ROCs

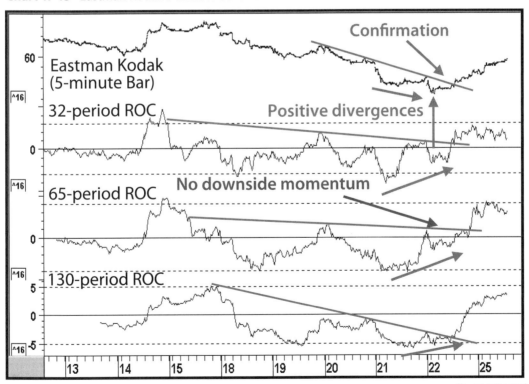

opening of the 19th and the other at the opening on the 22nd. The first is followed by a trading range and later lower prices, the second by a good rally. The questions to ask are: could our arrangements have warned us of these reversals, and secondly, could they have indicated that the second low was going to be a more important one than the first? Let us take a look at the first situation on the 19th. At this time, the 32-period ROC violates an up trendline, then the 65-period ROC experiences a positive divergence. These are confirmed by the break in a downtrend line for the price. In effect, we have several pieces of evidence that the price had stopped going down. It did but not for long. Why was this so? Well, first of all, the 130-period ROC was still in a downtrend by the time of the two trendline breaks. This is not overwhelming evidence that the price would act weakly but a thin reed indication.

There is a more compelling reason, but I will explain that later.

At the time of the second signal (Chart 17-13), all three ROCs broke pretty significant downtrend lines. Also, the 65-period ROC was barely below zero at the time of the low. This is normally a very strong signal when confirmed by the price. The confirmation was indeed given, and the price exploded upward. Thus, the second signal was supported by three strong trendline breaks, indicating that all three cycles were in gear on the upside. The first signal, you may recall, was only associated with one trendbreak.

However, there is another reason why the first signal did not work very well. That can be seen from Chart 17-14, which contains daily data for Eastman Kodak. The period to the right of the vertical line is that shown in our intraday chart. The first low, featured in Chart

Chart 17-14 Eastman Kodak daily and two indicators

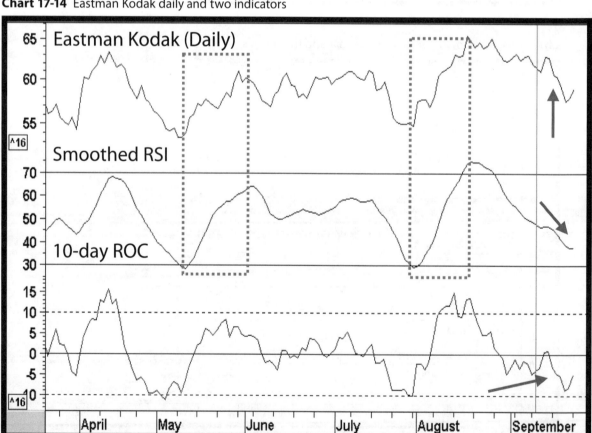

(Source: pring.com)

Chart 17-15 Eastman Kodak 10-minute bar and three ROCs

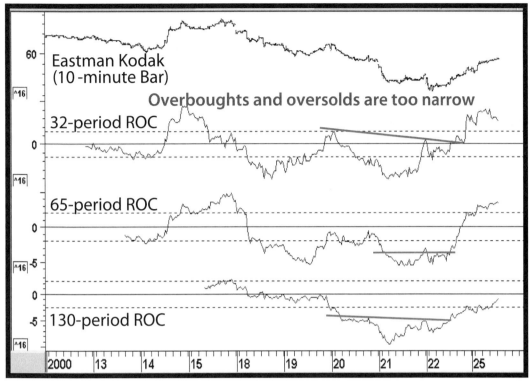

(Source: pring.com)

Chart 17-16 Eastman Kodak 10-minute bar and three ROCs

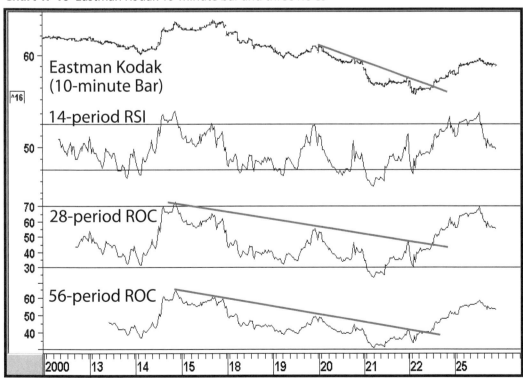

(Source: pring.com)

17-12, barely shows up as a blip on the chart. But notice how the whole period covered by the intraday data develops as the smoothed RSI is in a downtrend. Also, the 10-day ROC is not much below zero at the time of the first bottom. In other words, the first low develops as a countertrend move. Just as short-term buy signals in a primary bear market have a habit of failing, so do intraday buy signals that develop in a short-term downtrend. We know that at the time of the second signal, the smoothed RSI was still falling, but at least it was closer to an oversold condition than at the first signal. A better method, I believe, is to wait for a short-term buy signal, such as a reversal in the smoothed RSI, and then go to the intraday charts and look for buy signals. The two rectangles, for instance, both embrace short-term rallies. It is much better to act on positive intraday signals during this environment than when the smoothed RSI is in a declining phase.

Chart 17-15 shows a 10-minute bar using the same arrangement and time period.

We can see three trendbreaks in the ROCs at the second bottom. Again, this shows first of all that overbought/oversold lines need to be drawn differently for each time span. Secondly, these new momentum indicators add additional evidence in our weight of the evidence trend reversal case.

The same concept of varying overbought/oversold zones also applies to the RSI. Chart 17-16 features a 14-, 28-, and 56-period RSI, based on a 10-minute bar. The 14-period appears to be appropriately plotted with the standard solid 70/30 combination. The 28-period RSI is stretching it a bit. However, the 56-period RSI only contains an oversold band because the indicator never reaches the overbought zone.

Finally, to make another point, it is also possible to construct two very good downtrend lines

Chart 17-17 Merrill Lynch and two indicators

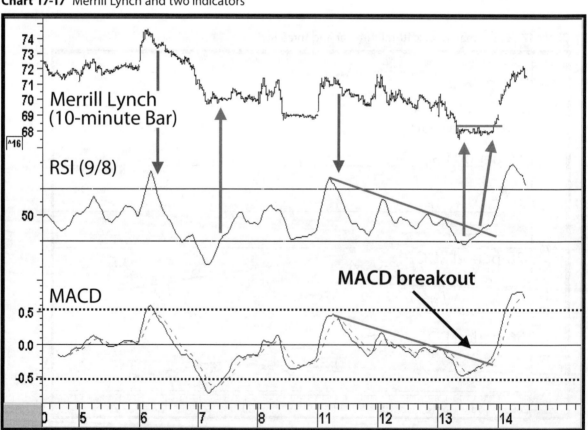

Chart 17-18 Merrill Lynch 10-minute bar and two indicators

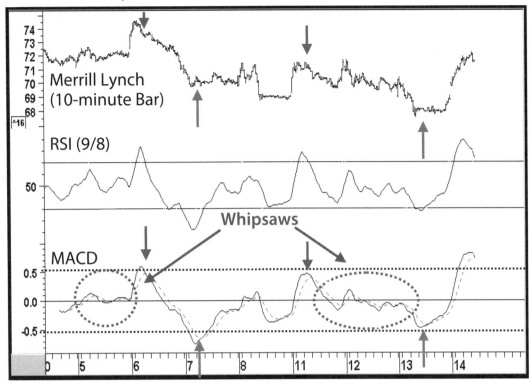

(Source: pring.com)

Chart 17-19 Merrill Lynch 10-minute bar and two indicators

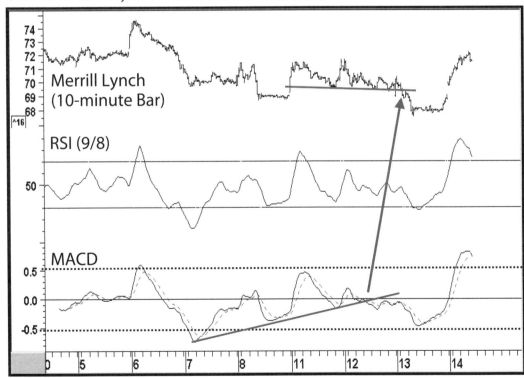

(Source: pring.com)

for the 28- and 56-period RSIs, which reinforce similar action by the ROC in Chart 17-16.

SMOOTHED OSCILLATORS

Chart 17-17 features a 10-minute bar of Merrill Lynch, together with a smoothed RSI and MACD. The RSI is an 8-period MA of a 9-period RSI. The first thing to notice is that it is possible to use overbought/oversold crossovers of the 70- and 30-levels as buy and sell alerts. For instance, there is a momentum sell signal on the 6th of September, and another one on the 11th, then a buy signal on the 7th, and another on the 13th. This latter one is quite special since it was later possible to construct a trendline for the MACD and another for the smoothed RSI. They were both quickly confirmed by the price completing a small base.

The MACD gave several timely buy and sell signs based on the signal line crossover, as we can see in Chart 17-18. However, the problem I have with this indicator is that you never know when you are going to run into a series of whipsaws. That statement can be said of any technical indicator, but with the MACD, it seems to stick a lot more strongly. In this case, the whipsaws are contained in the two ellipses.

I prefer to use the MACD with trendlines, and an up trendline was violated on the 12th, and confirmed by the price (Chart 17-19). The line in this case was penetrated when the MACD was around zero, and a reasonable decline followed.

Chart 17-20 shows that the RSI also violates an up trendline. This, too, is confirmed by the price, but the downside potential is nonexistent. This was a pretty good trendline for the RSI, so why the failure? Look where the penetration took place: very close to the oversold zone. It is not surprising, then, that it failed.

Chart 17-21 features a smoothed oscillator arrangement using three price oscillators, that

Chart 17-20 Merrill Lynch 10-minute bar and two indicators

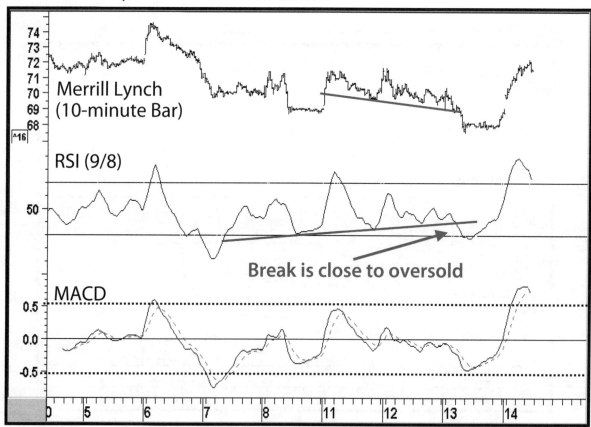

(Source: pring.com)

Chart 17-21 Disney 5-minute bar and three indicators

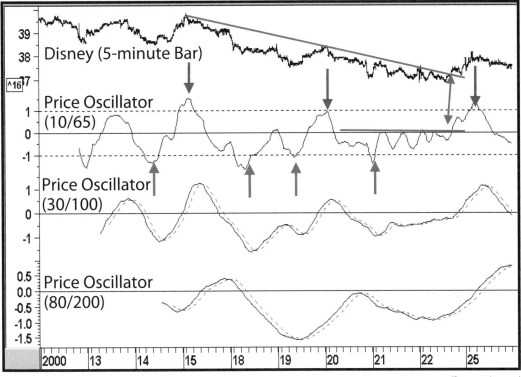

(Source: pring.com)

Chart 17-22 Disney daily and a smoothed RSI

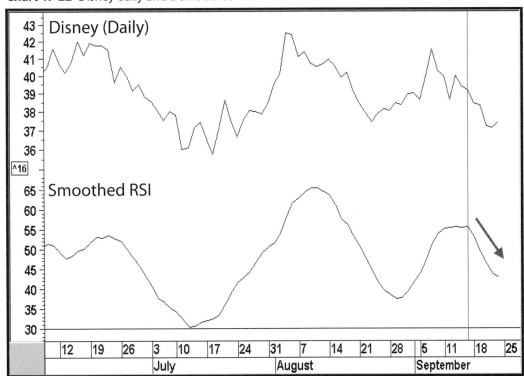

(Source: pring.com)

is, trend deviation indicators. Each one monitors a progressively longer time span as we move down the chart. The top one divides a 65-period simple moving average by a 10-period one. In this case, the periods are measured in 5-minute bars. This is a short-term measure and can be used for overbought/oversold crossover signals and trendlines. Here is a good joint trendline break on the 22nd. Some overbought crossovers are also flagged by the arrows. They work quite well. However, success with the oversolds is not so good. The first one was followed by a worthwhile rally, but the other three were not.

The reason can be seen in Chart 17-22. As you can see, the smoothed RSI at the vertical line had started to roll over, and all the buy signals on the intraday chart developed during this down-draft. In effect, they were contra-trend signals.

The two longer-term price oscillators in the lower panels did not work very well in terms of positive moving-average crossover signals because this whole period was basically a linear downtrend.

In a trading-range environment, things are different. Chart 17-23 features Merrill Lynch. See how the negative moving-average crossovers of the 30/100 series in the middle panel generate some good signals. Even though this period has a downward bias, the buy signals are also successful, in that they point up the transition from down to sideways.

The other point worth noting is that this is exactly the same arrangement we saw earlier for Disney. However, since Merrill Lynch tends to be far more volatile, the overbought and oversold lines constructed against the 10/65 series, which were fine for Disney, are too narrow on this chart and need to be widened.

Chart 17-23 Merrill Lynch and three indicators

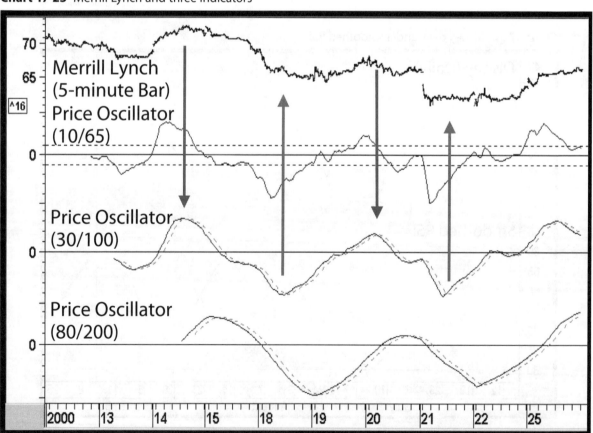

(Source: pring.com)

Our final example in Chart 17-24 features an 80-by-400-period price oscillator. This is a much longer-term series and is useful for identifying reversals in trends that form over, say, a 5-day period. When it reaches an extreme and crosses below its 100-period simple MA (that is the dashed line), some timely momentum sell signals are generated. Momentum buy signals are triggered in a similar way. The biggest decline on the chart was signaled differently. However, the oscillator reversal was quickly followed by a trendline break in both the momentum and price series. If the oscillator fails to reach an overextended reading, I think it is important to monitor for trendline breaks in the price, otherwise there is a great danger of whipsaw buy and sell signals developing, as shown in the two ellipses.

Chart 17-24 S&P Composite 5-minute bar and 80/400 price oscillator

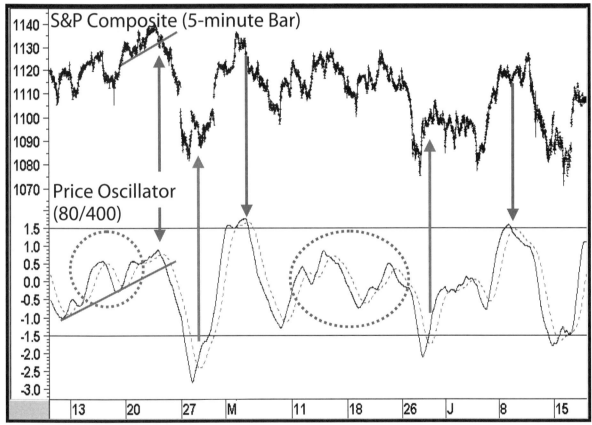

(Source: pring.com)

Part I Quiz

For answers, go to
www.traderslibrary.com/TLEcorner

PRINCIPLES OF MOMENTUM (CHAPTERS 1–10)

1. Which of the following statements is correct?

   (A) "Momentum" is a generic term that includes all oscillators.

   (B) Momentum measures the velocity of a price move.

   (C) Momentum can be equated to an orange.

   (D) A and B are correct.

2. Which of the following statements is incorrect?

   (A) You cannot buy and sell momentum, only price.

   (B) Momentum signals are generally given ahead of price.

   (C) If you have a dog on a leash, you are bound to interpret momentum correctly.

   (D) There are more than five momentum principles.

3. Which chart in the following figure has the best overbought/oversold zone?

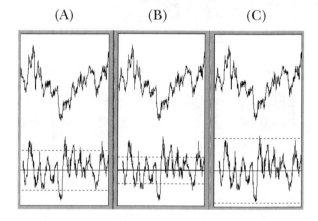

4. Which arrow indicates the most intelligent place to take profits from a long position?

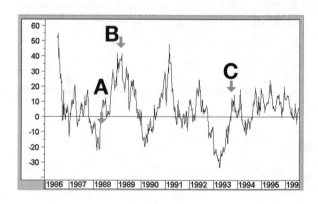

5. Which arrow indicates where newspaper and TV stories are likely to be the most bullish?

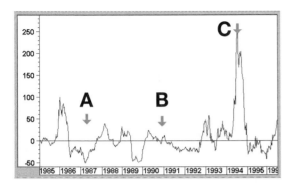

6. When an oscillator moves well above the overbought zone, the odds favor a reversal in the price trend. Under which condition are the odds the greatest?

   (A) Immediately as it crosses the overbought zone.

   (B) When it exceeds the overbought zone by 10 percent.

   (C) When it crosses back below the overbought zone on its way toward the equilibrium level.

   (D) Any time it is above the overbought zone.

7. Momentum characteristics are:

   (A) Different in a primary bull and bear market.

   (B) Oscillators stay more in an overbought condition during a bull market and in an oversold state in a bear market.

   (C) Oversold conditions are much more likely to generate rallies in a bull market and overbought conditions to trigger sell-offs in a bear market.

   (D) All of the above.

8. Divergences are:

   (A) Buy and sell signals.

   (B) Only relevant for bull markets.

   (C) Only relevant for bear markets.

   (D) Signs of latent strength or weakness that need to be confirmed by a trend reversal in the price.

   (E) Always in pairs.

9. A momentum indicator calculated with a long time span is:

   (A) Likely to reflect short-, intermediate-, and long-term trends.

   (B) Only monitoring long-term price movements.

   (C) Not very useful for measuring short-term trends.

   (D) Both B and C.

10. Based on the principles described in the text, which chart has the most significant divergence or set of divergences?

   (A)   (B)   (C)

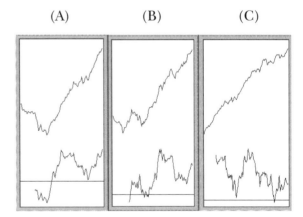

11. Based on the principles in the text, which chart offers the potential of a powerful rally once a reversal in the price trend offers confirmation?

(A)   (B)   (C)

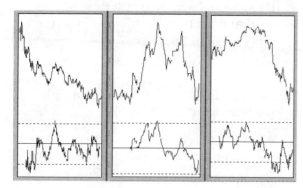

12. Which chart offers the most valid buy signal?

(A)   (B)   (C)

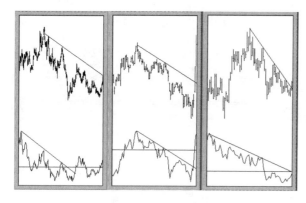

13. Which chart has the most valid sell signal, based on the action of both the price and momentum?

(A)   (B)   (C)

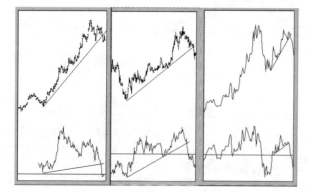

14. Chart formations in oscillators are rare events. When you see one, you should:

(A) Immediately take action.

(B) Take action only when this is confirmed by a reversal in the price trend.

(C) Take no action until you see a divergence.

(D) Wait for a trendline break in momentum to confirm.

15. Bearing in mind the principles discussed, which chart offers the most reliable signal?

(A)   (B)   (C)

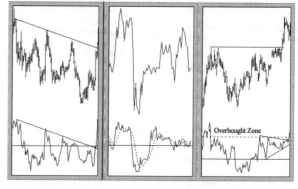

16. Which oscillator is likely to be more volatile?

(A) One constructed from an electric utility.

(B) One constructed from a commodity.

(C) One constructed from a mining stock.

(D) Both B and C.

17. Which of these statements is correct?

(A) When momentum reverses trend, so will price.

(B) A negative divergence guarantees lower prices.

(C) A positive divergence, when combined with a momentum trend break, will usually signal a price trend reversal.

(D) None of the above.

18. The nature of an oscillator's calculation is the sole factor in determining its volatility.

    (A) True

    (B) False

19. What phenomenon is being represented in the following diagram?

    (A) A positive complex divergence.

    (B) A negative complex divergence.

    (C) A regular positive divergence.

    (D) A positive reverse divergence.

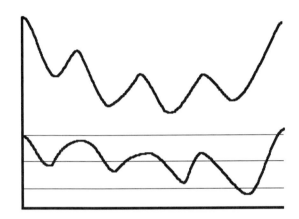

20. What technical concept is being represented in the following diagram?

    (A) A complex divergence.

    (B) A constructive breakout.

    (C) A destructive breakdown.

    (D) A negative divergence.

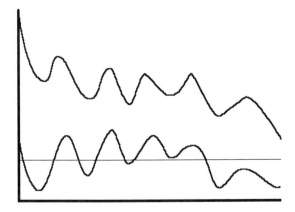

21. The character and magnitude of an oscillator swing depends on:

    (A) The nature of the formula.

    (B) The time span.

    (C) The volatility of the security.

    (D) All three.

22. Divergences signal that a trend has reversed.

    (A) True

    (B) False

23. Other things being equal, which figure is likely to be followed by the strongest rally?

    (A)   (B)

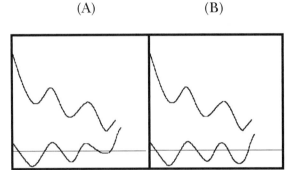

24. Which figure features a reverse divergence?

    (A)   (B)

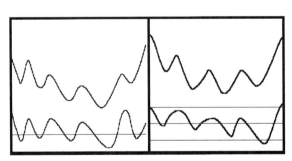

25. A mega-overbought condition is:

    (A) A deeply overbought reading that develops after an advance of at least one year.

    (B) An overbought condition that follows an oversold reading.

    (C) A multiyear overbought condition that develops after a decline lasting about a year or, usually, longer.

26. Which rectangle in the following figure contains an oversold reading most closely resembling a mega-oversold condition?

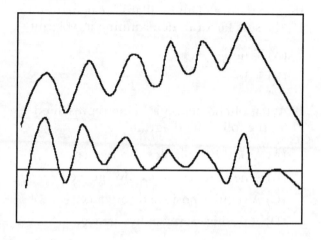

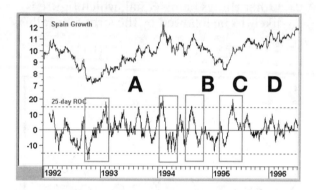

27. Which phrase best describes a bullish divergence trap?

    (A) A series of negative divergences followed by a final rally that disrupts the series of declining momentum peaks.

    (B) A sharp decline that experiences a mega-oversold condition.

    (C) A momentum indicator that barely falls below zero as the price is making a final low.

    (D) A series of positive divergences followed by a final decline that disrupts the series of rising momentum bottoms.

28. The following figure features:

    (A) A bearish divergence trap.

    (B) A positive reverse divergence.

    (C) A negative reverse divergence.

    (D) A mega overbought.

29. In order to spot a complex divergence:

    (A) It is first necessary to plot two different indicators using identical time spans.

    (B) Two indicators where the time spans are very similar in order to make sure that they confirm each other.

    (C) Three indicators plotted with widely differing time spans.

    (D) Two indicators plotted with widely differing time spans overlaid on each other.

30. Which phrase best describes the importance of extended momentum trendlines?

    (A) They reverse their support/resistance role after they have been violated.

    (B) They are not important because they have already been violated.

    (C) They gain their significance by their length and the number of times they have been touched or approached and reverse their support/resistance role when violated.

31. When you can construct a price pattern from a momentum indicator:

    (A) It means that when the pattern is completed, you should definitely take action in the markets.

    (B) You should expect an immediate reversal in the prevailing price trend.

    (C) Wait for confirmation by a trendbreak in the price itself.

    (D) Ignore the momentum price pattern and look for one in the security itself.

32. Price patterns in momentum oscillators:

    (A) Are very common and do not have much significance.

    (B) Are always important signals.

    (C) Are relatively rare and, therefore, have the potential to be an important technical event.

33. Which figure features an advance breakdown?

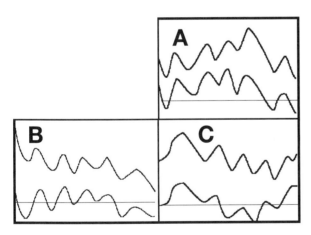

34. An extreme swing:

    (A) Can only develop after a major decline.

    (B) Can only develop after a bear market.

    (C) Can develop at the end of a bull or bear market.

    (D) Are always unreliable and should, therefore, be ignored.

35. Other things being equal, overbought and oversold crossovers and trendline breaks tend to be more reliable:

    (A) Using raw data like an RSI or ROC.

    (B) Using smoothed data.

    (C) Using smoothed data when previous crossovers or trendbreaks have been reliable indicators for that particular security.

36. Which event offers the strongest momentum buy signal?

    (A) A mega overbought is confirmed by a 2-year trendline break, the line has been touched on four occasions, and the breakout is accompanied by heavy volume.

    (B) An OCC is confirmed by a 3-year down trendline violation, and the line has been touched twice and volume is declining on the breakout.

    (C) An oversold crossover by a smoothed momentum indicator where the last five crossovers have worked.

    (D) Three positive divergences.

37. Which is the correct statement?

    (A) A mega oversold develops after a strong and powerful decline and is accompanied by heavy volume.

    (B) An OCC is more powerful than a mega oversold or mega overbought.

    (C) An extreme swing always contains a mega overbought or oversold.

    (D) A mega overbought develops after a one- or two-year decline and reaches a multi-year extreme. It should be confirmed by a trendbreak in the price and gains significance if accompanied by really heavy volume.

38. Momentum generally leads price. Which of the following represents an exception to that rule?

    (A) A reverse mega-oversold condition.

    (B) An extreme swing.

    (C) A reverse divergence.

    (D) An advanced breakdown.

KEY MOMENTUM INDICATORS (CHAPTERS 11–17)

1. A rate of change is normally constructed from:

    (A) The rate of change of two moving averages.

    (B) The relative strength of up days to down days.

    (C) Two changing rates of interest.

    (D) The price today divided by the closing price *n* periods ago.

2. The best momentum indicators are:

    (A) As complex as possible to take into account all possible variations.

    (B) Relatively simple and interpreted with a degree of common sense.

    (C) Always right.

    (D) A and C.

3. Which chart featuring the ROC indicator has the most reliable trendline?

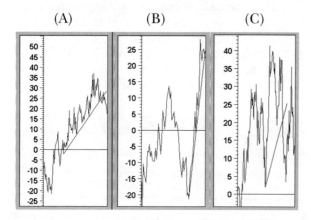

    (A)   (B)   (C)

4. Which indicator is *relatively* more suitable for overbought/oversold analysis?

    (A) Rate of change

    (B) RSI

    (C) MACD

    (D) Stochastics

5. The normal RSI defaults for overbought and oversold zones are 70 and 30. For time spans greater than 30 periods, you should:

    (A) Widen them.

    (B) Narrow them.

    (C) It doesn't matter.

    (D) Do nothing, but put in a line at the 50 for the equilibrium level.

6. Which circle flags an RSI failure swing in the following figure?

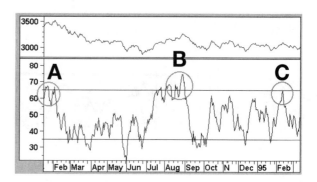

7. The MACD is constructed from:

    (A) Three moving averages.

    (B) Three rates of change.

    (C) Two EMAs.

    (D) None of the above.

8. Which arrow indicates the most reliable MACD signal once it has been confirmed by a trendbreak in the price?

(A)   (B)   (C)

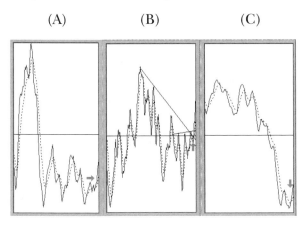

9. Which is the slower moving line, %K or %D?

(A) %K

(B) %D

(C) They both move at the same speed.

10. Which arrow points to a hinge in the stochastics interpretation?

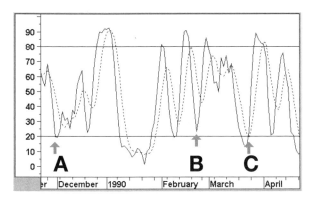

11. Which arrow in the following figure points to a bearish failure in the stochastics interpretation?

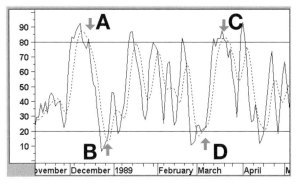

12. Which chart shows the strongest buy signal?

(A)   (B)   (C)

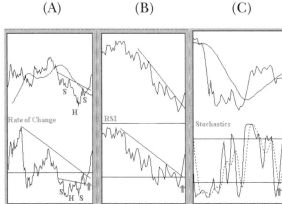

13. Looking at the following chart, what is the most likely outcome?

(A) The downtrend will continue because the ROC is overbought.

(B) A new bull market has begun because the ROC has experienced a mega overbought.

(C) This is an extreme swing and the price will rally.

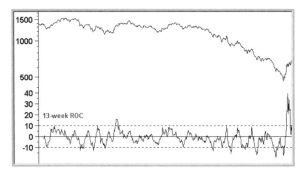

14. It is a good idea to place two or three ROC indicators on the same chart because:

   (A) They each reflect different time cycles and, therefore, give us a broader picture of what is going on.

   (B) The more things we look at, the better it is.

   (C) No, it is not, because we will get confused if we look at too much.

   (D) The ROC is the best oscillator; therefore, we should look at as many as possible.

15. Which statement best describes a complex divergence?

   (A) It consists of two oscillators with closely matched time spans, where the first experiences a mega overbought.

   (B) It consists of two oscillators with widely differing time spans.

   (C) It requires two oscillators with substantially different time spans. At the time the second is making an important peak or trough, the first is close to an equilibrium reading.

16. Which arrow is close to the complex divergence?

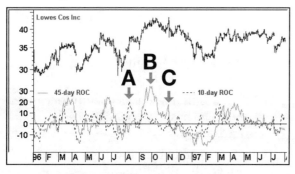

17. An RSI failure swing is similar to:

   (A) A stochastic warning.

   (B) A MACD reverse divergence.

   (C) A stochastic right-hand crossover.

   (D) None of the above.

18. Which rectangle contains a negative reverse divergence?

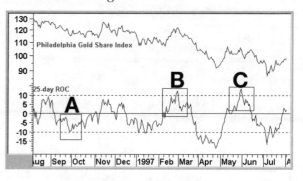

19. The MACD indicator is:

   (A Another form of trend deviation oscillator.

   (B) A smoothed rate of change.

   (C) Only used with the signal line.

   (D) Calculated from the least square fit of two exponential moving averages.

20. The RSI:

   (A) Stands for relative strength indicator, which is the same as comparative relative strength.

   (B) Can exceed a reading of 100 in a really strong bull market.

   (C) Stands for relative strength indicator, which is totally different from comparative relative strength.

   (D) Should always have its overbought and oversold bands drawn at 70 and 30.

21. What do the arrows in the following figure signal?

    (A) Negative divergences.

    (B) Reverse divergences.

    (C) Mega overboughts.

    (D) Overbought crossovers.

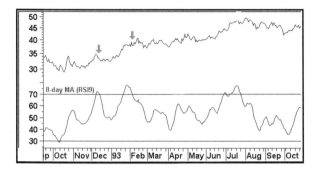

22. What is the technical phenomenon featured in the following chart?

    (A) A negative divergence.

    (B) A positive divergence.

    (C) A reverse negative divergence.

    (D) None of the above.

23. A trend deviation indicator calculated from a 2-day moving average divided by a 40-day moving average would be more suitable for:

    (A) Trendline analysis.

    (B) Failure swings.

    (C) Hinge analysis.

    (D) None of the above.

24. A trend deviation indicator constructed by dividing a 10-week moving average by a 25-week moving average would be suitable for:

    (A) Moving-average crossover analysis.

    (B) Trendline analysis.

    (C) Reverse divergences.

    (D) None of the above.

25. If you saw a stochastic %K move to a reading of 100, what would you expect to happen?

    (A) The price continues to rally.

    (B) The price retraces some of the previous rally and then goes on to make a new high.

    (C) The price immediately declines and does not reach the same level again.

    (D) A and B.

26. What is the most likely outcome, in the event that the two trendlines in the following chart are violated?

    (A) The price will decline.

    (B) There is no way of knowing until the moving average is violated.

    (C) The price will either decline or consolidate.

    (D) None of the above.

27. What is most likely to happen next in the following chart?

    (A) A small decline or consolidation.

    (B) A sharp decline.

    (C) A consolidation.

    (D) None of the above.

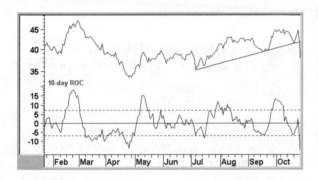

28. What is the technical phenomenon contained within the ellipses?

    (A) A negative reverse divergence.

    (B) A normal negative divergence.

    (C) A mega overbought.

    (D A positive reverse divergence.

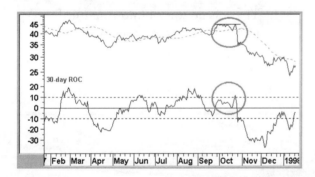

29. Which is the best indicator?

    (A) The ROC.

    (B) The RSI.

    (C) None of these indicators can be described "as the best"; each has its own strengths and weaknesses.

    (D) The stochastic and MACD.

The Definitive Guide to
MOMENTUM INDICATORS

PART II

18

Linear Regression Lines

INTRODUCTION

In recent years, some of the more mathematically inclined technical analysts have started to apply several well-known statistical techniques to the markets with the objective of trying to identify price trend reversals at a relatively early stage. One of these is linear regression. Indeed, linear regression forms the basis of several of these relatively new indicators. This section of the book explains some of these finer points, but to begin, I would like to briefly discuss the application of a simple linear regression line.

Technicians have worked for decades with the technique of smoothing data with various types of moving averages. The idea is to simply smooth the data to iron out random fluctuations. In this way, it is possible to gain a better understanding of the underlying trend. The linear regression line is another technique for obtaining this same objective.

The linear regression line, just like a moving average, is based on the trend of a security's price over a given time span. In many respects a linear regression line is really a statistically derived trendline and acts as a kind of equilibrium point for the prices included in its calculation.

LINEAR REGRESSION

The linear regression line, just like a moving average, is based on the trend of a security's price over a given time span. The trend is determined by calculating a linear regression, using the mathematical technique of least squares fit. To individuals not well versed in mathematics like me, that sounds a bit intimidating, but in reality it is not.

222

Essentially, this technique fits a trendline to the chart's data by minimizing the distance between the data points and the linear regression trendline. In effect, the line is drawn through the middle of the data, as shown in Chart 18-1. I have made a comparison between a linear regression line and a moving average, but as you can see, in many respects a linear regression line is really a statistically derived trendline. In a way, the linear regression line is a kind of equilibrium point for the prices included in its calculation. Consequently, the line acts as a rubber leash. If prices fluctuate too much from the line, they may be expected to be pulled back toward it before flying off in the other direction. In Chart 18-2, for instance, the linear regression line is bounded by two parallel lines that act as constraints on upward and downward price movements.

Linear regression lines are not particularly useful in their own right, but several very useful indicators have been derived from this basic calculation. They are the subject of the next few chapters of the book. Chapter 19 will begin this discussion with an explanation of the linear regression indicator.

Chart 18-1   McDonald's and a linear regression line

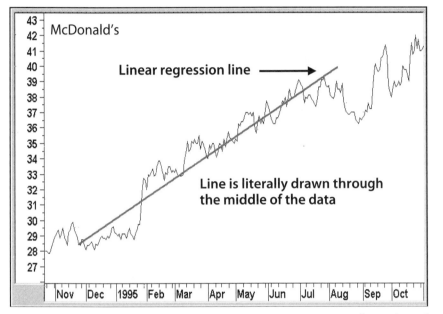

(Source: pring.com)

Chart 18-2   McDonald's and parallel linear regression lines

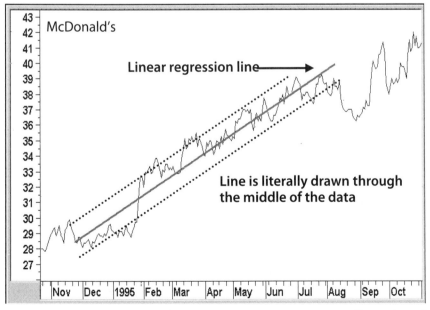

(Source: pring.com)

19

Linear Regression Indicator

INTRODUCTION

The *linear regression indicator* plots the last point of a linear regression line, but it does so continuously. Charts 19-1 and 19-2 feature three solid linear regression trendlines. Each has a length of two calendar months, which roughly corresponds with 40 trading periods. The smoother line is a 40-period linear regression indicator, which intersects the ends of each trendline. In a sense, the regression indicator is like a kind of moving average. The longer the time span, the slower it is to turn because it connects endpoints of linear regression trendlines that are much longer. This means that linear regression indicators based on longer lines (or timeframes) experience fewer whipsaws. If the time span is short, the line gives timelier buy-or-sell signals but many commensurately more false signals.

INTERPRETATION

The interpretation of linear regression indicators is similar to that of moving averages. The linear regression indicator, though, has two advantages. First, the regression method does not experience as much of a delay. This is because it is calculated by fitting the line to the data points, rather than by averaging them. In effect, the linear regression indicator is more responsive to price changes.

In Chart 19-3, the moving average has been plotted as a solid line and the linear regression indicator as a dashed one. Both have a 30-day time span. You can see how the regression line turns ahead of the simple average in every instance. Both have been plotted separately in the lower panel, where the leading characteristics of the linear regression indicator are more apparent. It is also possible to create an indicator based on the interrelationship between the two. The idea is to buy when the linear regression indicator crosses above or below the moving

Chart 19-1 American Century 2020 Fund and a linear regression indicator

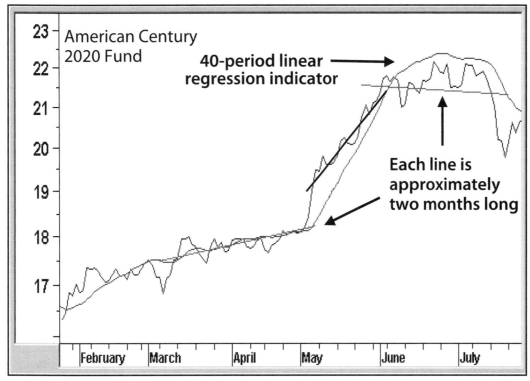

(Source: pring.com)

Chart 19-2 American Century 2020 Fund and a linear regression indicator

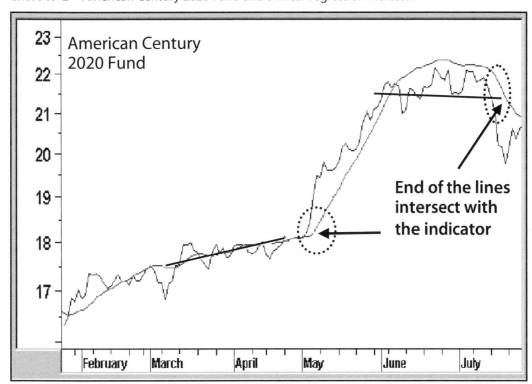

(Source: pring.com)

Chart 19-3   S & P Composite comparing an MA to a linear-regression indicator

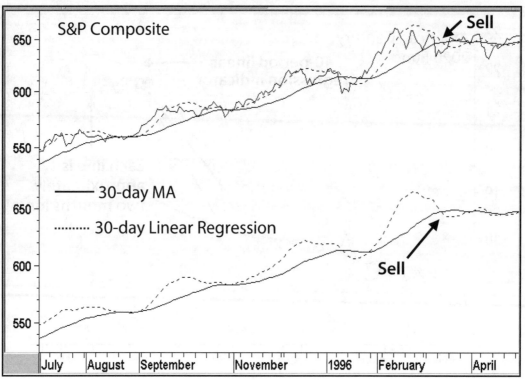

Chart 19-4   S & P Composite comparing an MA to a linear regression indicator

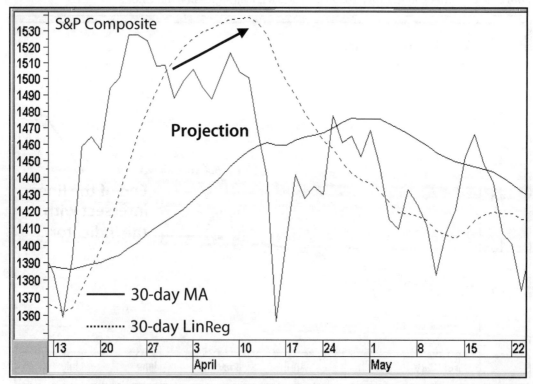

average, as in February 1996 in Chart 19-3. This is by no means a perfect indicator, but you might want to take some trouble researching it through your charting software's system tester optimization feature.

A second aspect of the linear regression indicator is that it is a rough forecast of the next period's price but plotted today (Chart 19-4). This occurs because the regression indicator is a statistical extension of the data included in the calculation. Only when the price itself changes direction for a couple of periods does the indicator reverse direction. However, since it is still moving in the direction of the prevailing trend, the regression line is able to experience a crossover more quickly than a simple, even exponential, moving average using the same time span. This is shown in Chart 19-5, where the initial crossover of the linear regression indicator takes place several days prior to that of the 30-day moving average (MA). Also note how the regression line

extends its upward trajectory well after the price peak.

Since the regression indicator is a very responsive type of moving average, a very useful approach is to plot one average with a relatively short-term time span in a separate window and use it as a basis for constructing trendlines. Chart 19-5 shows an example using the Benham 2020 Zero Coupon Fund. You can see that the trendline for the regression indicator, which is based on a 15-period time span, is violated well before that of the price. Most of the time this technique favors the regression

> The linear regression indicator has two key advantages: it does not experience much of a delay and it provides a rough forecast of the next period's price plotted today.

Chart 19-5   American Century 2020 Fund and linear regression trendline analysis

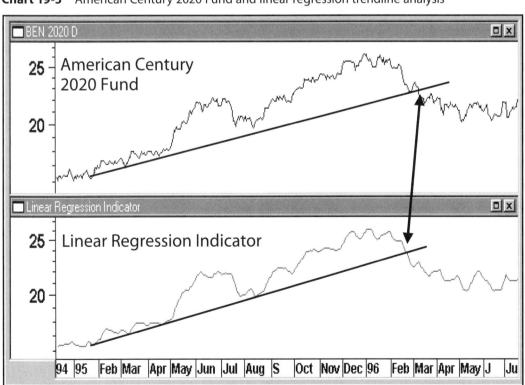

(Source: pring.com)

indicator, but occasionally the trend break is a little too fast, as shown in Chart 19-6 featuring Microsoft. See how the trendline for the regression line is only partially violated, but the trend break in the price never actually takes place.

If you look closely at the relationship between this indicator and the price, you can see that there are some fairly timely buy-or-sell signals. However, there are quite a few that we might call *inconvenient whipsaws* flagged in Chart 19-7. They do not look that serious on the chart, but if you are acting on every buy-or-sell signal in the expected, disciplined way, then such failures can add up to some costly losses. It is possible to set up a filter that implies one should only buy or sell if the price crosses the regression line for 2 or 3 consecutive days.

As an alternative, I tested for several combinations of time span and filtering mechanisms based on a percentage crossover. In other words, the rule might be "buy when the price crosses 1 percent above the linear regres-sion indicator, sell when it falls 1.5 percent below," and so forth. This was not a scientifi-cally based test because I only used five or six securities, each with about four years of his-tory. What I did find with this initial test was that crossovers of the 20- and 35-day time spans usually offered a profitable result when com-bined with a 1.5-percent filter for buy signals and a 2-percent filter for sell signals. In other words, when the close rallied 1.5 percent above the regression line, it qualified as a buy signal, and when it fell 2 percent below the line, it was a sell signal. What did surprise me about all the tests was that there was a very high persis-tence to create profits, whatever the combina-tion of time span and filtering. I am sure this was partly due to the fact that more than half of my sample consisted of stocks in a bull mar-ket, but even those that lost money on a buy-hold approach had a surprisingly small amount of losses in my test. The range of periods tested was 10 to 65 days.

Chart 19-6   Microsoft and linear regression trendline analysis

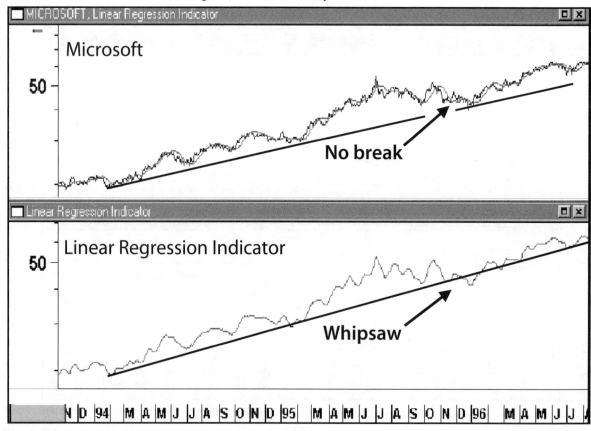

(Source: pring.com)

Chart 19-7 Microsoft and linear regression trendline analysis

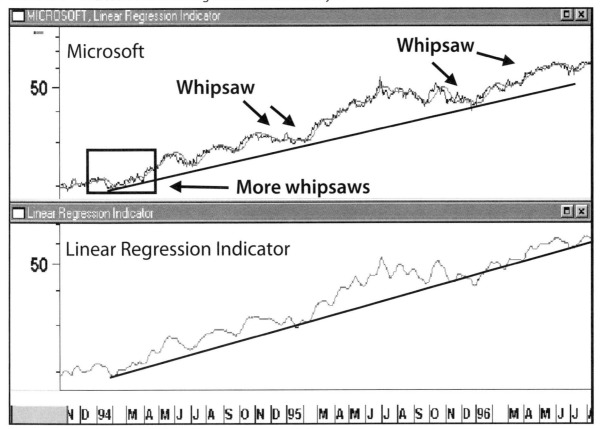

(Source: pring.com)

20

R-Square

REVERSALS FROM HIGH R-SQUARE READINGS

Since the r-square is used quite a lot of the time with the linear regression slope, it makes sense to discuss this concept first and then proceed with an explanation of the slope itself.

Moving averages offer us the basic ingredient for many other indicators, so, too, does the regression technique. One example is the r-square indicator. The objective of the r-square is to show the *strength* of a move, as opposed to its *direction*. The direction can be derived from overbought-or-oversold readings in the momentum indicators. There are also some methods for determining direction from the regression approach, as we shall later learn. Essentially, the r-square calculation tries to display the amount of a price trend that can be expressed purely as a trend factor and that part which is explained as random noise. *The higher the reading, the greater is the trend factor and the lower the random noise.* Also, the longer the time span from which the r-square is calculated, the lower the r-square value needed to determine if a trend is statistically significant. One of the things about rising and falling trends is that once they start to lose momentum, the price either consolidates or reverses. Since the r-square indicator can provide some useful information on when a trend is starting to lose momentum, it is possible to use peaks in this indicator as a signal that a trading range is about to start or that the trend itself is close to a reversal. Chart 20-1 features a 35-day r-square indicator. The arrows against the price indicate when it reverses direction from above its 0.9 overbought zone. The first one (A) signaled a temporary interruption of the strong uptrend that at B just touched the overbought line, but the result was similar. Finally, the overbought reversal at C signaled a loss of upside momentum quite close to the final peak. This indicator is not directionally biased, so it does not differentiate between an up- or downtrend. At point D, the overbought reversal developed after

Chart 20-1 The FTSE Index and a 35-day r-square

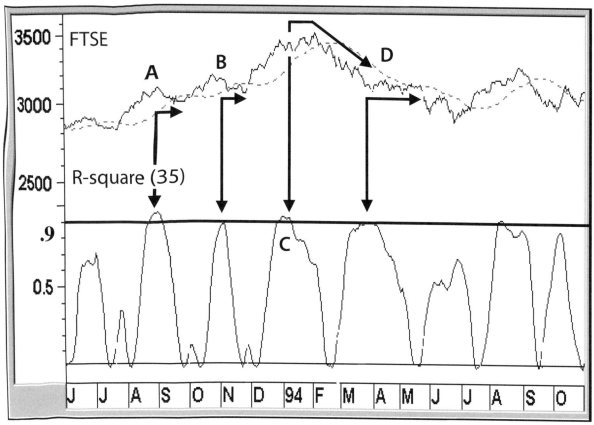

(Source: pring.com)

a strong downtrend, and it was followed by a sideways trend or a consolidation of losses.

REVERSALS FROM LOW R-SQUARE READINGS

The r-square can also be used to help determine when a trading range market is about to give way to a trending one. In Chart 20-2, the solid and dashed arrows indicate when the r-square indicator first touches the oversold, or I should say *trendless*, level. The concept revolves around the idea that if a market has been in a trading range and the r-square reverses direction to the upside from a low reading, this should indicate a trending market. I have drawn the arrows at those points

> The r-square calculation tries to display the amount of a price trend that can be expressed as either a trend factor or as random noise. The higher the reading, the greater is the trend factor and the lower the random noise.

where it is obvious that the r-square has bottomed. Quite often, this occurs as the price is breaking out from a consolidation, so two pieces of evidence of a potential trending market are given. Chart 20-3 shows some classic examples: first, at the February 1994 top, and

Chart 20-2   The FTSE Index and a 35-day r-square

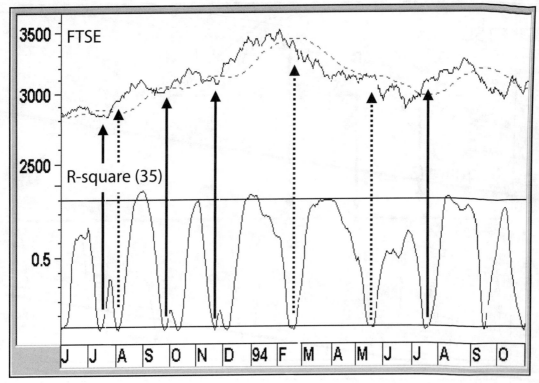

Chart 20-3   The FTSE Index and a 35-day r-square

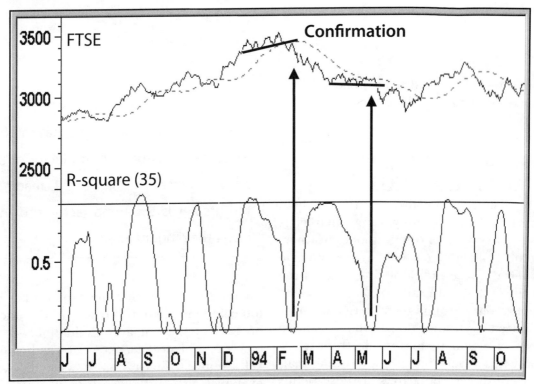

Chart 20-4   The FTSE Index and a 35-day r-square

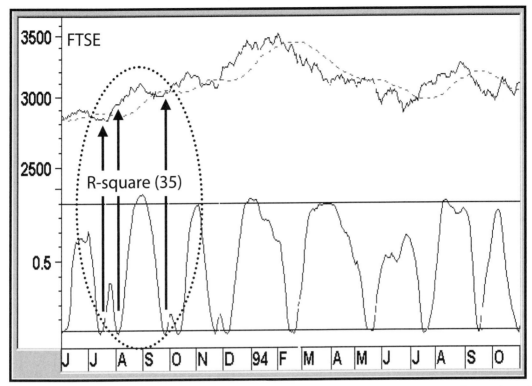

(Source: pring.com)

second, at the resumption of the downtrend in March 1994. The three examples between July and September in Chart 20-4 did not offer such obvious chart points, although the moving-average crossovers did trigger signals that the consolidation period was over. In this case, the average is a 25-day simple average that has been advanced by seven periods. In situations where a signal is triggered well after the price has reached its turning point, such as that in Chart 20-5, it is as well to move on to another situation. This example is shown with the benefit of hindsight, but what would we have done in the actual marketplace? After all, we did not know at the time how long the r-square was going to remain in the trendless zone. The answer lies in looking at the other indicators to see what they are doing. One should never buy and sell on r-square alone. In most of the examples shown in Chart 20-3, the price gave some good trend-reversal signals. However, it is as well to check out some momentum indicators to add additional weight to any trend-reversal possibilities.

R-SQUARE AND TRADING RANGES

Sometimes, the very fact that the r-square indicator does form a trading range can be especially useful. In Chart 20-6 we see it consolidate in the overbought region for several periods. The violation of the horizontal line

Chart 20-5   The FTSE Index and a 35-day r-square

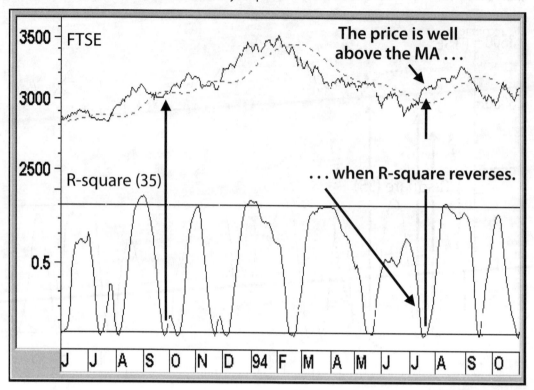

(Source: pring.com)

Chart 20-6   The Philadelphia Gold and Silver Share Index, FTSE Index, and a 35-day r-square

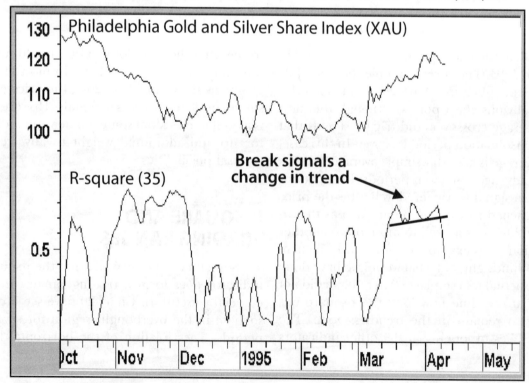

(Source: pring.com)

indicated that the period of trending was over. The top formation suggested that the price was about to experience a period of non-uptrending, that is, a change in the prevailing (up) trend. This could imply a new downtrend or a period of trading-range activity. Chart 20-7 shows that the price action in the box following this signal was indeed a trading range. Shortly after, we see another price pattern in the r-square (Chart 20-8), only this time it is a bottom. In effect, the r-square indicator is telling us that a trending market is now the most likely outcome. In this case, the three-week consolidation was followed by a two-week downtrend

(Chart 20-9). Again, it is important to use these signals in combination with other indicators, which can then help to determine the direction of the new trend.

Finally, Chart 20-10 shows an r-square indicator that experiences a smaller-and-smaller trading range. When it finally breaks out on the upside and is confirmed by the price, a very strong trending move results. In Chapter 21 we will learn how the r-square can be used in conjunction with the next linear regression indicator to be covered, the linear regression slope.

Chart 20-7   The Philadelphia Gold and Silver Share Index, FTSE Index, and a 35-day r-square

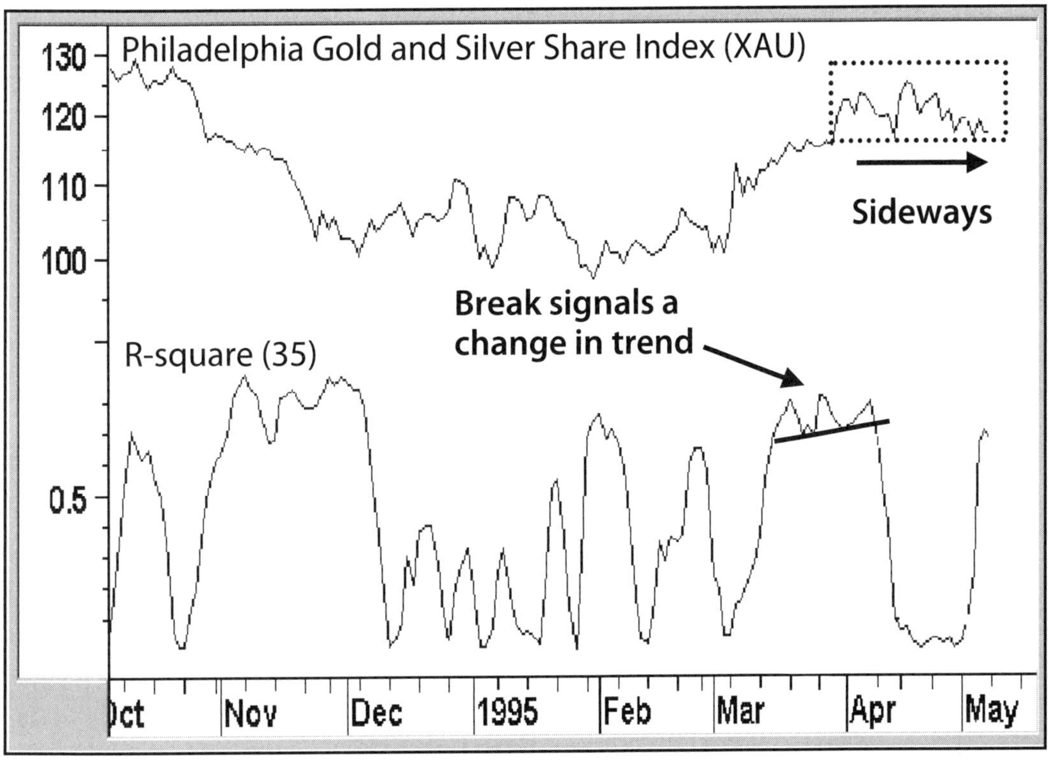

(Source: pring.com)

Chart 20-8   The Philadelphia Gold and Silver Share Index, FTSE Index, and a 35-day r-square

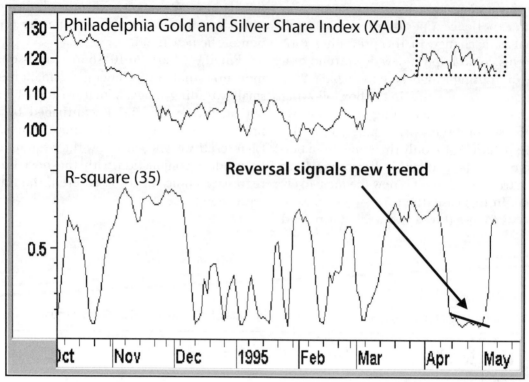

Chart 20-9   The Philadelphia Gold and Silver Share Index, FTSE Index, and a 35-day r-square

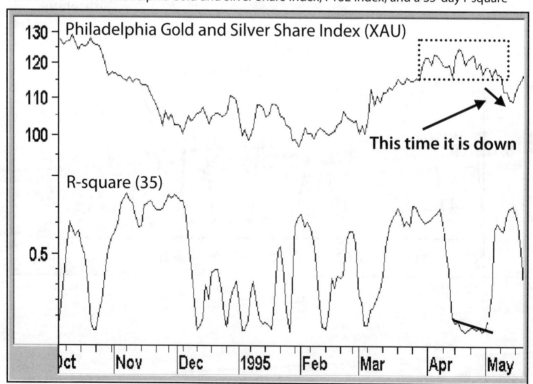

Chart 20-10   The FTSE Index and a 35-day r-square

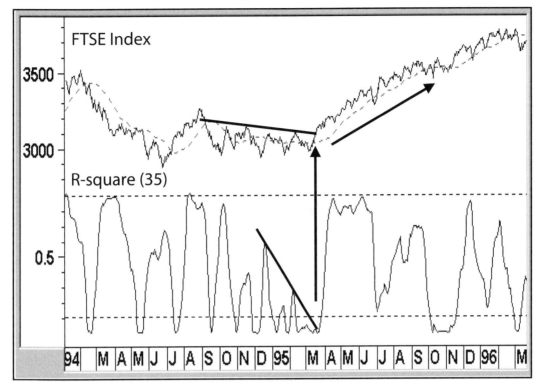

(Source: pring.com)

Linear Regression Slope

INTRODUCTION

The *linear regression slope* is a variation on the linear regression indicator. It is supposed to show how much prices are expected to change per unit of time, otherwise known as *rise over run.* Just think of the linear slope as a momentum indicator derived from the linear regression indicator. The dashed line in the upper panel in Chart 21-1 for General Motors features a 14-day linear regression indicator. The lower panel displays a 14-day linear slope. Chart 21-2 shows a variation by moving the linear regression indicator to the lower panel. It is evident that the fluctuations of both series are very similar. As with all momentum indicators, the linear slope has a tendency to lead the linear regression indicator itself. An example is shown at A.

We can even take it a little further. In Chart 21-3 the three series have been separated. Note how all three trendlines were all violated around the same time, thereby offering a very strong buy signal. Remember, the more indicators

pointing in the same direction, the greater the probability that the signal will be valid, and the greater the chances that a good trending move will follow. That was certainly true of the rally that followed this triple upside breakout. Then, in October, it was possible to reverse the procedure with the construction of three more trendlines. Again a worthwhile trend followed.

The interpretation of the linear regression slope is very similar to other momentum indicators, though it seems to work best with overbought-or-oversold lines. In Chart 21-4, a 14-period linear regression slope is featured. You can see that the overbought and oversold readings correspond with peaks and troughs quite well. The problem with this, as with all oscillators, is that occasionally you get what would normally be regarded as an extreme reading, indicating a top, only to be faced with another extreme reading a little later, such as the two early 1992 peaks. However, if you continue to look to the right of the chart you can see that there is a cluster of four extreme read-

Chart 21-1 General Motors and a 14 linear regression slope

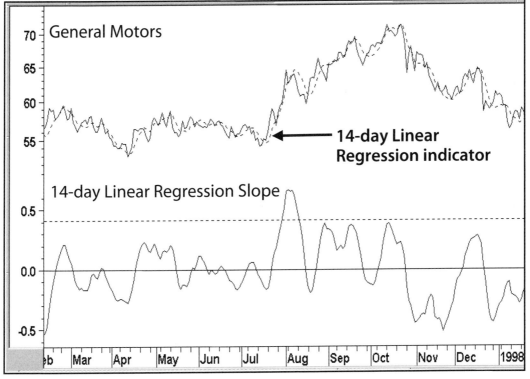

(Source: pring.com)

Chart 21-2 General Motors and a 14 linear regression slope

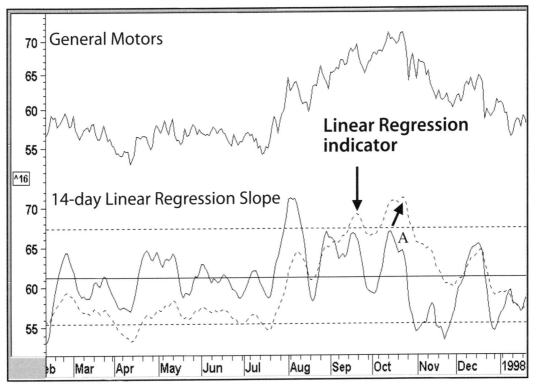

(Source: pring.com)

Chart 21-3   General Motors and two linear regression indicators

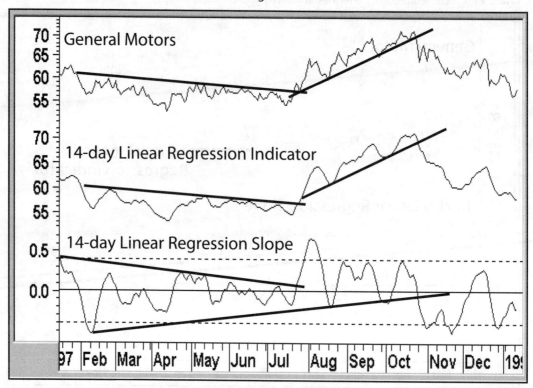

(Source: pring.com)

Chart 21-4   General Motors and a 14 linear regression slope

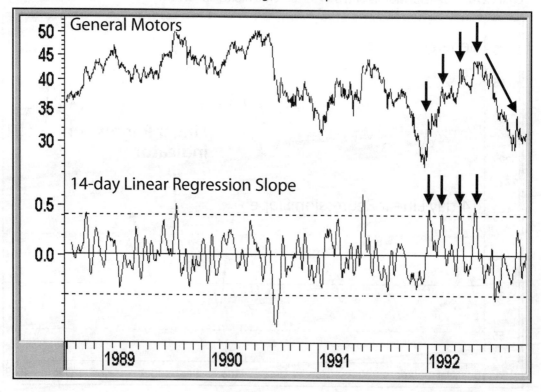

(Source: pring.com)

ings, only one of which is followed by a decline. This again points out the need to use several indicators at a time, not rely on one alone.

USING THE SLOPE WITH R-SQUARE

The regression slope is often used in conjunction with the r-square indicator. This is because the function of r-square is to tell you whether a market has trending ability or not, while the regression slope indicator tells you the general direction. This approach is by no means perfect, but it can offer you some good signals that alert you to the possibility of a trend change. You would then consult the other indicators to get confirmation.

Chart 21-5 features a 45-day regression slope and a 45-day r-square. It is then a good idea to look for those periods when the slope is either overbought-or-oversold and where the r-square indicator is also at an extreme high. If the slope is overbought and starting to decline, then the trend is about to reverse to the downside. Confirmation of this is given by the r-square also reaching an extreme, because this indicates that the trend is weakening.

Chart 21-5 features 45-day time spans on both indicators. The thick vertical arrows indicate where both series are rolling over from an overbought level. As a general rule, this type of time span, when used in conjunction with these indicators, appears to work reasonably well. The dashed arrow represents a bottoming signal, since the slope indicator was deeply oversold when the r-square was at an extreme. The slope indicator got too oversold during September 1992, but there was no extreme reading in the r-square. That is why the arrow is represented in a half signal or dashed format.

Chart 21-5 Ford, a linear regression slope, and an r-square

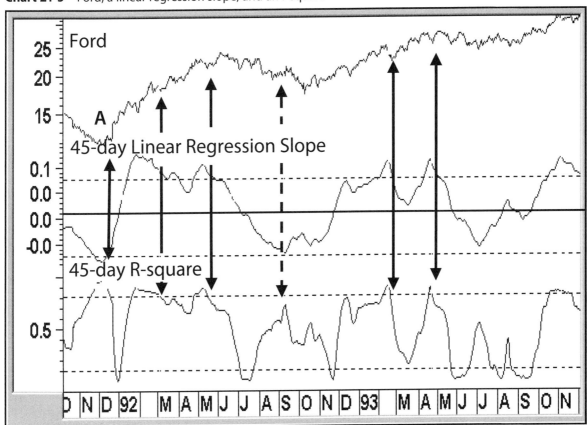

Chart 21-6 shows a 45-day period for the slope and a 30-day one for the r-square. Once again we are considering that the r-square indicates whether a security price is trending or not, while the slope tells you the direction of the trend and when it is overextended.

This means that you should look for an extreme in the slope that has begun to reverse and then for a high and reversal reading in the r-square. Remember, a high reading in the r-square indicates that the price trend has a high trending quotient and a low random noise factor. When r-square reverses, then it is telling us that the trend is also dissipating. This can mean that an actual reversal or a sideways trend is about to start.

The arrows flag when the r-square has retreated from an overextended reading, and this is confirmed by the slope crossing its 10-day linear regression indicator. You can see that the price also violated its trendline. In this

particular instance, the new trend was sideways rather than downward. See how the price moves in a slightly declining trading range in this area. Then, the r-square breaks out from a base. Remember, low r-square readings mean that there is no discernible trend, so a rally in r-square offers the probability that a new trend is beginning. The combination of the sell signal in the linear regression slope at this point, and the price trend break here, indicated that this new trend was most likely going to be negative.

In March 1996, charting r-square peaks and the slope gives a buy signal from an oversold condition (Chart 21-7). This should have indicated a rally. A small one did materialize, but it was never possible to construct a meaningful trendline for the price. Actually, what happened was a trading range between March and April. Then in late April, the r-square violates a downtrend (Chart 21-8), indicating a

Chart 21-6   CRB Composite, a linear regression slope, and an r-square

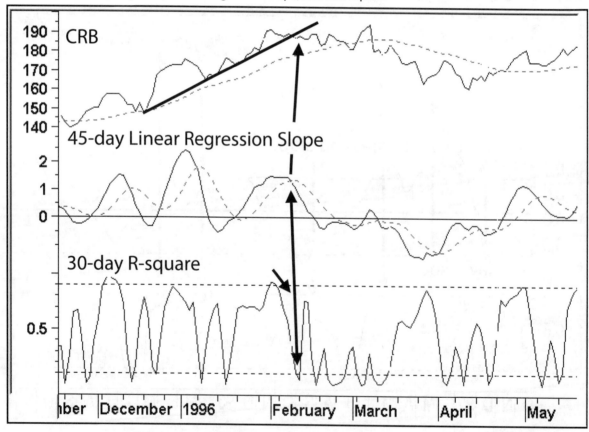

Chart 21-7   Chart 21-7   CRB Composite, a linear regression slope, and an r-square

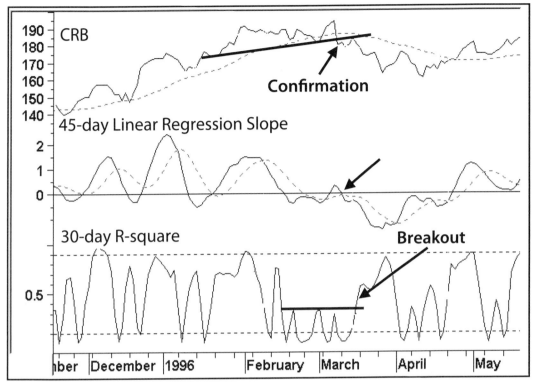

(Source: pring.com)

Chart 21-8   CRB Composite, a linear regression slope, and an r-square

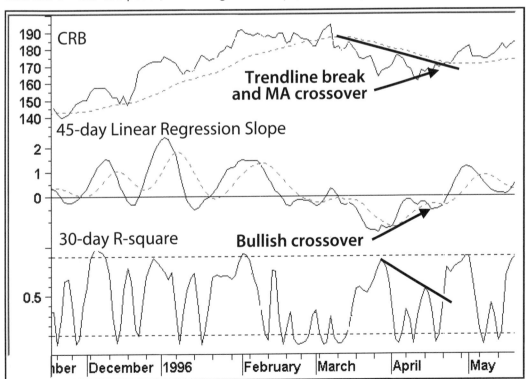

(Source: pring.com)

trending market; the slope diverges positively with the price and gives a buy signal, and finally the price violates a good downtrend, signaling that a new trend has begun. Notice that the price also violates its moving average at the same time the trendline is violated. This provides additional evidence that the trend has reversed.

One of the important points to note about this particular combination of indicators is that you have to hunt down specific situations, possibly using the other indicators, such as the smoothed RSI, as a filter. This is because the r-square does not give such clear-cut signals as many of the smoother series.

LINEAR SLOPE AND LONG-TERM MOMENTUM

There is no reason why the linear regression slope cannot be employed to monitor long-term, or primary, trends in momentum. That is precisely what Chart 21-9 tries to do. The trend's status is determined by the relationship of a 400-day linear slope to its 100-day simple moving average. If the indicator is above its average, and the price is above its 100-day moving average, the trend is regarded as bullish and the price is represented as a thin line. If the slope is positive but the price is below its 100-day MA, this downgrades the trend to neutral and the price plot is displayed in gray. A neutral trend is also called for when the price is above the 100-day moving average but the indicator is below its average, and a bearish trend occurs when both the price and the slope are below their moving averages and so is reflected by a thick line.

The price moving averages have been introduced as a fail-safe for those periods when the price moves too quickly for the slow-moving slope indicator to catch.

The neutral trend sometimes serves as an early warning that the primary trend is about to reverse, since the system will sometimes move into a neutral trend just prior to going bullish or bearish. A great deal will depend on the degree to which the slope is overbought or oversold. The more overextended it is, the greater the possibility that a neutral trend signal will begin a new primary trend.

In this example of the TSE Oil and Gas Index, the neutral trend preceded a bearish one in late 1993. But if you look at the position of the slope, you can see why: it was way overextended. A little later on, the trend moved back to neutral again. However, there was little chance of a reversal in the primary trend because the slope was still way overextended.

Chart 21-10 again plots a 400-day linear regression slope together with its 100-day moving average. The moving average has also been shifted to the right by 20 periods. This means that crossovers by the regression slope are delayed a little. However, this advancing approach eliminates some of the whipsaw signals, though it certainly will not eliminate them all. Fortunately, the delay in the moving average does not unduly impede the timeliness of the signals. The vertical lines represent the buy (thick) and sell (thin) signals.

The concept behind this indicator is that most markets revolve around the four-year business cycle. The cycle actually is a bit less than four years. The 400-day time span used in its construction is also a little under half of the four-year span, about 940 trading days, so it is able to pick up the four-year rhythms.

Once again, the basic rule is that when the slope is in a rising trend, the security is in a bull market, and vice versa. The moving-average crossovers are used as a triggering device to classify when the trend is bullish or bearish. Naturally, the security does not always oblige by experiencing a 4-year cycle. For example, the first signal totally misses the 1987 market crash. That in late 1988 captures a good part of the rally and then a sell signal is triggered in mid-1990. A consolidation rather than a decline follows. The next buy signal, in 1992, captures most of the rally and the late-1993 sell is followed by more consolidation. The final buy signal, in early 1995, captures a very worthwhile advance. Generally speaking, this indicator works quite well. However, it will never be

Chart 21-9 TSE Oil and Gas Index and a linear regression slope indicator

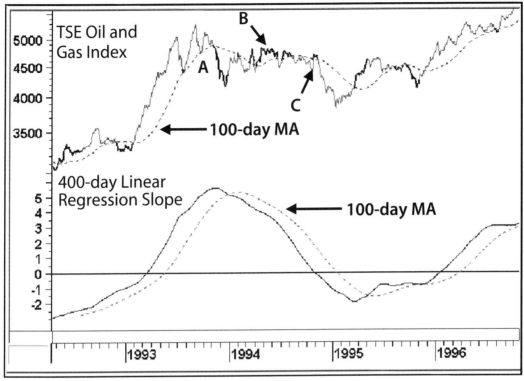

Chart 21-10 ASE Oil and Gas Index and a linear regression slope indicator

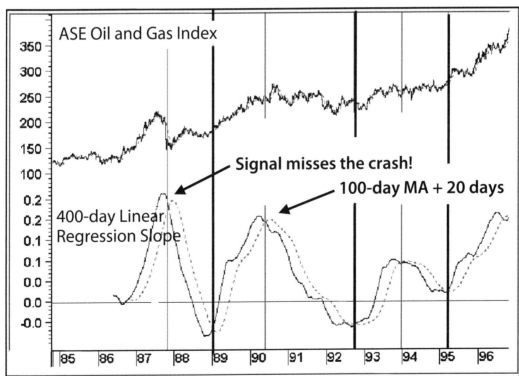

able to capture sharp up-and-down moves that do not relate to the business cycle, such as the 1987 crash. Nor will it be of much help in strong trending markets, such as the Japanese bull market of the 1980s or the bull market in the United States that began in 1990. One way in which it can be used effectively is to look for periods when it is at an extreme overbought or oversold level because at that point, the risk of a major reversal is that much higher. In 1987, for example, the indicator was clearly overextended, so it should not have been surprising that a sharp correction of some kind would develop. In a situation such as that, where the slope is overextended, be on the lookout for negative divergences in your short-term indicators that can be confirmed with a good trendline break in the price. Quite often, when the slope is overextended and starting to flatten,

the next short-term decline can act as the first trigger in a kind of domino effect.

LINEAR SLOPE AND WEEKLY DATA

When I first converted the 400-day time span to the weekly format, I found that the indicator did not experience the nice swings that are apparent on the daily chart. Consequently, I decided to expand the time span out to 104-weeks, or 2-years, and to use a 26-week, or 6-month, moving average (Chart 21-11). The triggering average for the price is 26-weeks.

The same bullish, bearish, and neutral trends are highlighted, and the principles of interpretation are the same as with the daily linear slope.

Chart 21-11   ASE Oil and Gas Index and a linear regression slope indicator

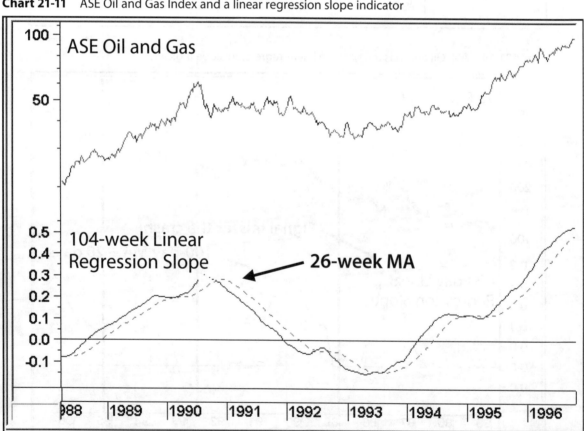

(Source: pring.com)

Chart 21-12 features a 10- and 52-week linear slope on the same chart. The 52-week series attempts to reflect the 4-year cycle and, therefore, serves as a proxy for the long-term trend. The effect is very similar to the 400-day series previously considered. The moving average is a 5-period one for the 10-week series and a 10-week one for the 52-week slope. The average plotted against the price is a 65-week Exponential Moving Average (EMA). The 10-week series is used to time short-term trends and the 52-week indicator to identify the direction and maturity of the long-term, or primary, trend. The 10-week slope can also be interpreted with positive and negative divergences, though these are rare relative to other oscillators.

Moving-average crossovers by the 10-week series can be used to time intermediate rallies and reactions. Some of these are highlighted with the upward- and downward-sloping

arrows. A positive divergence develops right at the bottom of the 1994 decline, and this is confirmed then by the price breaking above the dashed trendline in the early summer of 1994. Later on, the 52-week series crosses above its moving average and this is confirmed by the price completing a reverse head-and-shoulders pattern.

> The concept behind this indicator is that most markets follow a four-year business cycle. That being said, the indicator will not capture sharp moves that do not relate to the business cycle, like the 1987 crash.

Chat 21-12   American Electric Power and two linear regression slope indicators

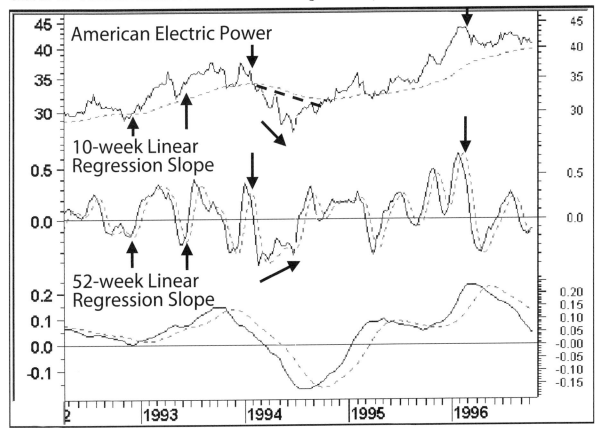

(Source: pring.com)

22

Volume Rate of Change

THE BASICS

The basic principles of volume interpretation are covered in our Introduction to *Technical Analysis CD-ROM Workbook Tutorial*, so it is assumed that you are already aware that it is normal for volume to go in the direction of the prevailing trend; that is, expanding on rallies and contracting on declines. It is also assumed that volume in an uptrend will usually lead price. In these next few chapters, we will be dealing with momentum indicators that are derived from volume alone or a combination of price and volume.

Normally, volume is displayed as a histogram underneath the price, as in Chart 22-1. A quick glance at any chart often reveals a noticeable increase in the size of the volume bars that are associated with breakouts, selling climaxes, and so forth. This is all well and good, but occasionally there are subtle shifts in the level of volume that are not easily detectable by this method. By massaging the volume data with an ROC calculation, it is possible to observe some new insights into the dynamics of volume interpretation. This is very important, since most of the indicators we deal with are a statistical variation on the price. However, an oscillator based purely on volume can give us a totally independent view of what is happening under the surface.

Chart 22-2 shows a 10-day ROC of volume, together with a regular volume histogram. As the price is breaking above the trendline in August, we do not get much of an impression that volume is expanding if we just look at the histogram. However, the ROC shows a definite jump over a period of several days, thereby confirming the breakout.

Chart 22-3 shows the opposite set of circumstances, where the ROC rallies sharply prior to the breakout. But when the breakout materializes, the ROC is at a much lower level. The volume histogram, alternately, shows that activity expanded a little on the breakout. However, this

248

Chart 22-1   DuPont 1999-2000 and a volume histogram

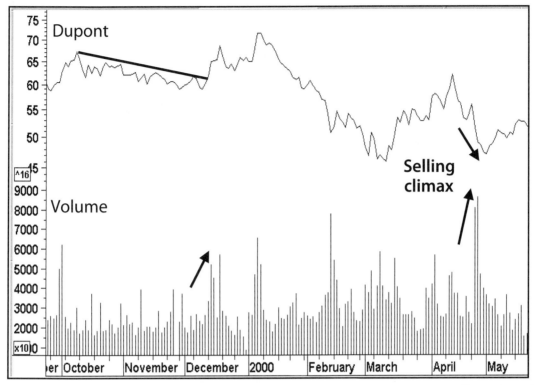

(Source: pring.com)

Chart 22-2   Briggs and Stratton volume histogram versus volume ROC

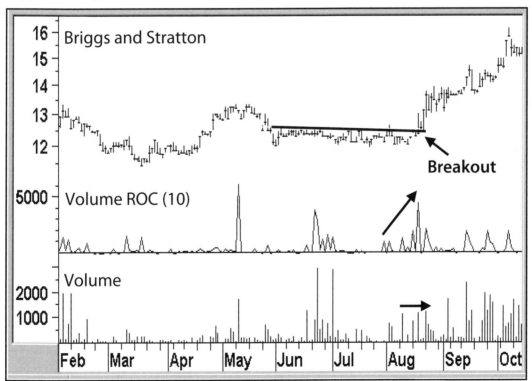

(Source: pring.com)

study shows us that it is the volume rate of change that is relatively more important, since the breakout proved to be a false one.

Sometimes, short-term trades can take advantage of overbought readings, since they often flag near-term turning points. For instance, the small arrows in Chart 22-4 of Abbott Labs show small selling climaxes by the upward-pointing arrows and rally turning points by the downward-pointing ones.

Divergences are sometimes flagged with this indicator. Look at the series of declining volume momentum peaks, as flagged by the two dashed arrows and the slightly rising peaks in the price in Chart 22-5. This pointed out potential weakness, and, sure enough, the price did experience a decline. Also, note how it is possible to construct a trendline joining a series of declining peaks in volume. When the line is violated, it indicates that the downtrend

in volume momentum has terminated and that we should expect a change. In this case, prices started to rally along with volume. This characteristic is flagged by the two diverging dashed arrows.

SMOOTHING THE VOLUME ROC

I prefer to run a moving average through a volume rate of change indicator because it smoothes out the jagged nature of the raw data. Chart 22-6 shows a 3-day simple moving average of a 15-day ROC of volume. I have drawn in an overbought line and flagged those periods when the indicator moves meaningfully above the overbought line. This does not happen very often (about once a year, in fact). However, you can see from the arrows that in the vast majority of cases, we are being warned

Chart 22-3   Briggs and Stratton volume histogram versus volume ROC

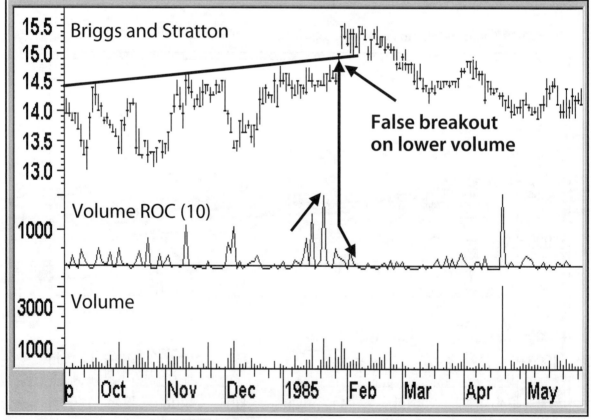

(Source: pring.com)

Chart 22-4 Abbott Labs and a 10-day volume ROC

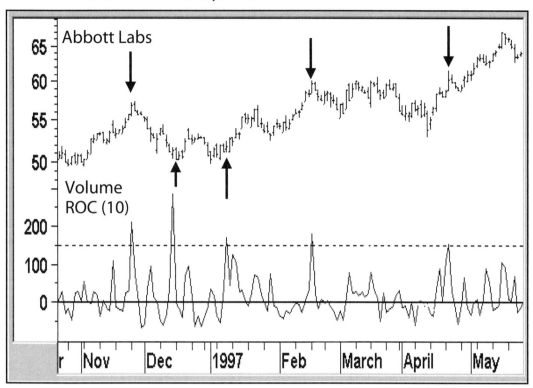

(Source: pring.com)

Chart 22-5 Abbott Labs and a 10-day volume ROC

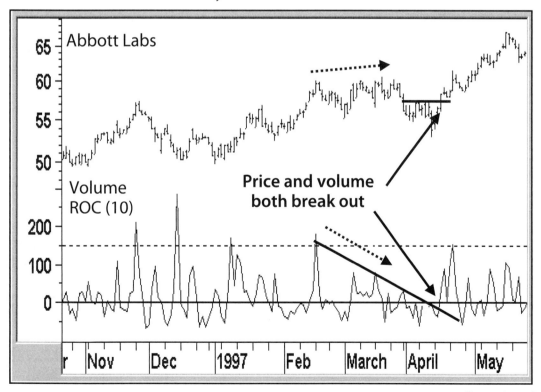

(Source: pring.com)

that something pretty important is happening with the price. It all depends on the previous trend. If it is down, then the arrows indicate a selling climax. If it follows a rally, then this is usually a top of some kind. Alternately, if it is a rally coming off a low, then the signal is bullish, as with the one at the extreme left-hand part of the chart.

The volume ROC in Chart 22-7 is based on a 10-day moving average divided by a 25-day MA. This series is a lot smoother than those we looked at so far. As you can see, it lends itself more readily to price pattern and trendline analysis. First, note that the overbought-or-oversold lines are not drawn on an equidistant basis. This is because the calculation treats the ROC as a percentage. And volume can expand, even on a smoothed basis, by 200 percent or 300 percent quite easily, yet can only fall by 100 percent. This means that downside action is far

more limited than upside potential. Later on, we will look at some alternative forms of plotting. At this point, there are two things to note. The first, in Chart 22-8, is a head-and-shoulders top in the volume ROC. The head represented a buying crescendo, so the violation of the neckline was merely a confirmation that the volume trend was down. Since the price was also declining, both were in gear and were not telling us anything significant, except that the technical position was weakening.

Later on, Chart 22-9 shows that both the price and volume violate important downtrend lines. Since both were reversing their direction, they were now in gear on the upside, which was a nice confirmation that the uptrend was healthy. The downtrend line for the oscillator actually represents the neckline of a reverse head-and-shoulders pattern. I did not display the S-H-S letters because the left shoul-

Chart 22-6   Snap-On and a 3/15 volume ROC

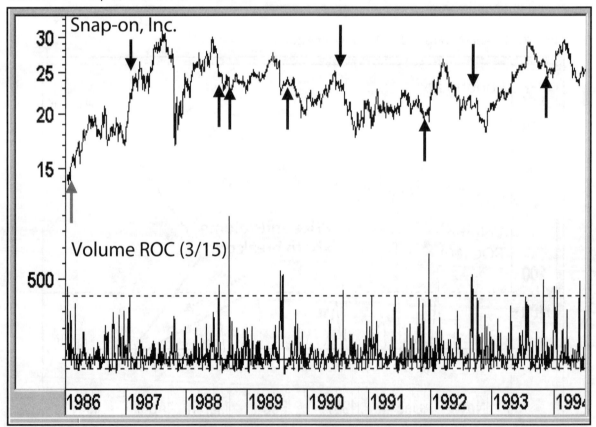

(Source: pring.com)

Chart 22-7 Snap-On and a 10/25 volume ROC

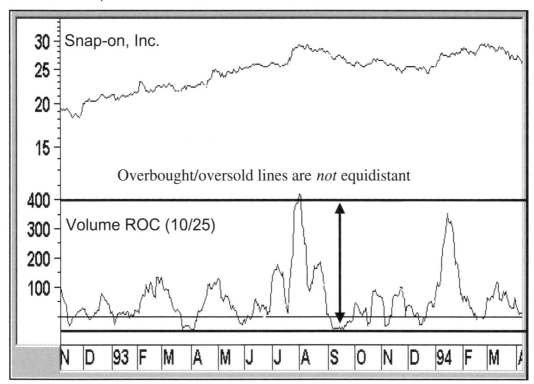

Chart 22-8 Snap-On and a 10/25 volume ROC

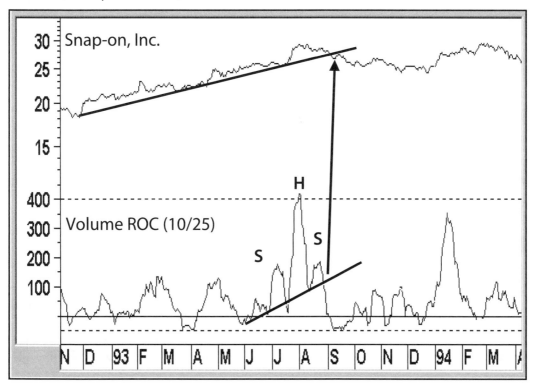

der was also the right shoulder of the previous upward-sloping head-and-shoulders top. And this would have complicated things.

TWO METHODS OF CALCULATION

I mentioned previously that the volume ROC indicator, when calculated with a percent method, does not lend itself to pointing out oversold volume conditions very well. One way around this is to calculate the ROC, substituting a subtraction, instead. An example is shown in the lower area of Chart 22-10. This series displays some nice oversold conditions that are not apparent using the percentage method. The disadvantage of the subtraction calculation is that volume momentum cannot be compared over long periods of time if the security

being monitored experiences a substantial increase in average daily volume. This is because the higher volume will distort the overall picture. For shorter-term charts, the subtraction method is a better technique, though it is important to remember that because the volume level for individual stocks and markets can vary tremendously, the over-bought/oversold lines will have to be adjusted accordingly. In this instance, the upper dashed horizontal line represents an overbought reading in both volume indicators. Since the price had been declining, this was a selling climax. The arrows in Chart 22-11 show that the sub-traction-based oscillator was deeply oversold at the next slightly lower bottom in December, hence, the indication that volume was totally drying up on the second slightly lower low, a classic double bottom characteristic. While you could see this taking place on the percent

Chart 22-9 Snap-On and a 10/25 volume ROC

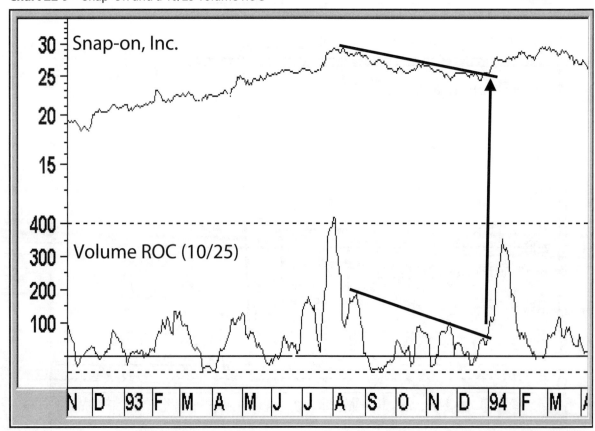

(Source: pring.com)

Chart 22-10   Snap-On comparing two 10/25 volume ROC calculations

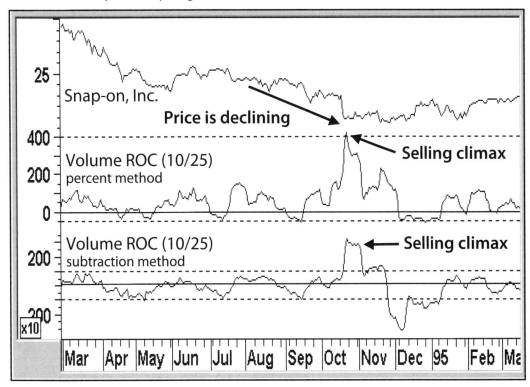

Snap-on, Inc.

Price is declining

Selling climax

Volume ROC (10/25)
percent method

Volume ROC (10/25)
subtraction method

Selling climax

Chart 22-11   Snap-On comparing two 10/25 volume ROC calculations

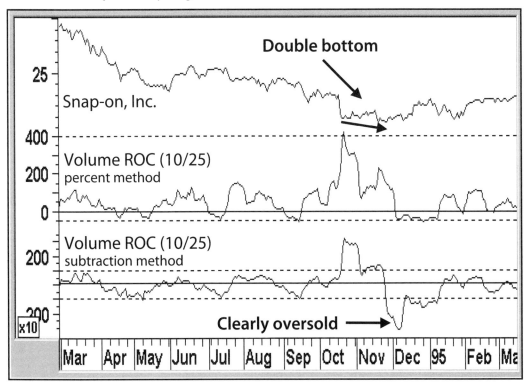

Double bottom

Snap-on, Inc.

Volume ROC (10/25)
percent method

Volume ROC (10/25)
subtraction method

Clearly oversold

Chart 22-12 Wausau Paper Mills and a 10/25 volume ROC

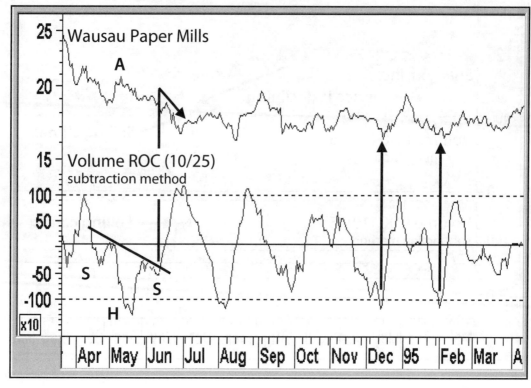

(Source: pring.com)

chart, it is much more apparent on the subtraction-based series. It is important to note that a high overextended reading in a volume oscillator does not necessarily mean that the price is overbought, merely that volume is overextended. Thus, a *high reading in the volume indicator can mean a top or a bottom*, depending on the previous price action. I will have more to say on that point a little later.

INTERPRETATION

There is an old Wall St. adage that says, "Never short a dull market." Basically, this means dull markets often reflect a sign that selling pressure has almost completely dried up. Chart 22-12, featuring the subtraction-based volume momentum, shows that extreme low readings are a sign that prices may be bottoming. We see two such instances in December

and February. Alternately, a market that rallies on low volume may also be considered dull. But in this case, it is usually bearish, since it indicates that prices may be rising but that there is not much enthusiasm for such a trend. When some selling comes out of the woodwork, prices are likely to decline.

The trough in volume in May 1994 at point A is a good example of this. Also, note how the oscillator traced out a reverse head-and-shoulders pattern. When the breakout (indicating a trend to higher volume) took place, this was associated with the final sell-off in the price.

A high reading in the volume indicator can mean a top or a bottom, depending on the previous price action.

Chart 22-13 Warner-Lambert and a 15/65 volume ROC

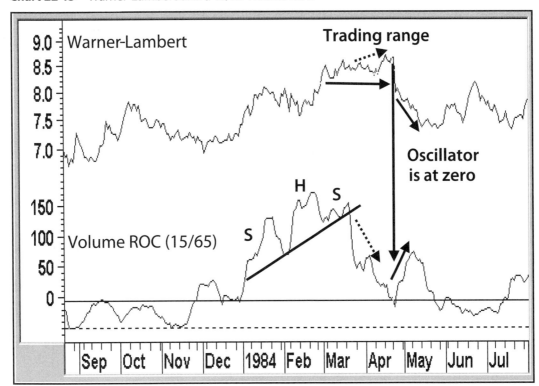

(Source: pring.com)

The decline then ended in June with a selling climax (a high-volume ROC reading).

Chart 22-13 features a 15-day MA of volume divided by a 65-day time span. The price was rising in the November 1983 to March 1984 period. Then it experienced some trading range activity, which ultimately turned out to be the high for the move. About halfway through this process, the volume indicator broke down from a head-and-shoulders top, which indicated that the volume trend was now downward. We then had a situation where the run-up to the final marginal new high was associated with declining volume, a bearish sign, which is flagged by the two diverging dashed arrows. In fact, the situation was even worse than this because the volume ROC was very close to a zero reading during the sessions when the price was recording its high for the move. This indicated that there was virtually no upside volume momentum, an extremely

bearish characteristic. Then, as the price began to slip, the volume oscillator started to rally, which is abnormal and bearish behavior.

Volume momentum can also be quite effective using weekly charts. Chart 22-14 of Family Dollar features an 8-week simple moving average of a 13-week volume ROC using the percent method. Note the very low volume, as the price was moving sideways in the summer of 1987. Then price started to slip and volume expanded—a deadly combination. At the October bottom, we see an overbought volume reading, indicating a selling climax. This is

> It is often a good idea to wait for the formation of a trading range after an overbought volume reading before taking any action.

shown in Chart 22-15. Whenever a volume ROC reaches an extreme overbought reading, one of three things usually happens. First, the price reverses on a dime; alternately, it experiences a trading range and then reverses direction; or third, it experiences a trading range and then resumes its trend prior to the overbought reading. In this third case, the price formed a classic bottom. After the selling climax, the volume ROC moves into negative territory, thereby indicating a definite contraction in the level of activity. Then the price breaks out of the trading range on expanding volume (Chart 22-15).

It is often a good idea to wait for the formation of a trading range after an overbought volume reading before taking any action. The next overbought condition in the April/May 1989 period looked like a selling climax and, therefore, a potential buying point (Chart 22-16). However, a trading range did not develop afterward. More to the point, as the price rallied in August of 1989, you can see that the volume oscillator remained well below

zero. This was certainly not a sign of a market wanting to take off on the upside. In actual fact, this event was followed by a decline to a new marginal low and then some indecisive trading action.

SUMMARY

The rate of change of volume

1. Often gives signs of subtle changes in the level of volume that are not apparent from volume data represented as a histogram.

2. Can be expressed as a percentage or subtraction format.

3. Can be used with overbought/oversold crossovers, trendline analysis, and price patterns.

4. Can be followed by declining or rising prices, in the case of overbought readings, depending on the nature of the previous trend.

Chart 22-14   Family Dollar and a 13/8 volume ROC

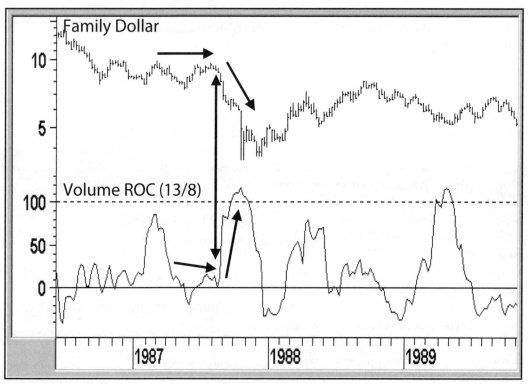

(Source: pring.com)

Chart 22-15 Family Dollar and a 13/8 volume ROC

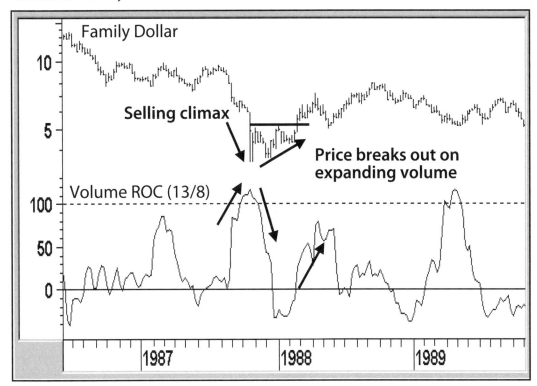

(Source: pring.com)

Chart 22-16 Family Dollar and a 13/8 volume ROC

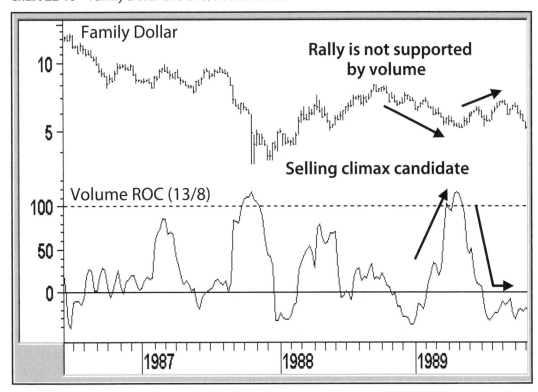

(Source: pring.com)

23

Volume Oscillator

THE CALCULATION

A method of expressing volume that sometimes works better than a rate-of-change calculation involves plotting the difference between two moving averages of volume. It is a trend deviation method in which the calculation substitutes volume for price. This technique also offers a way in which subtle changes in volume levels can be accentuated in a graphic manner.

As Chart 23-1 shows, the process involves the construction of two moving averages, the shorter being divided by the longer. It is also possible to subtract one average from the other, which, in some situations, is superior because it better reflects the contraction of volume in a similar way to that discussed previously for the volume ROC calculation. The upper area shows the volume together with its 10-day moving average. The center area then features this 10-day series together with a 25-day moving average. As you can see, they are continually crossing above and below each other. Finally, the lower area shows

the 10-period average divided by the 25-period series. This is the volume oscillator. The equilibrium line represents points where the two moving averages are at identical levels. Chart 23-2 eliminates the top area, where it is evident that movements above and below the horizontal line indicate that the two averages are crossing each other. The solid vertical lines signal upside crossover points and the dashed ones downside crossovers. The time spans of the averages can be varied to reflect short-, intermediate-, and long-term trends. For daily charts, I favor the combination of a 10-day divided by a 25-day simple moving average. This may be too long a span for very short-term traders, who may prefer a 5/20 EMA combination.

One advantage of the volume oscillator over the volume ROC calculated by the percentage method is that overbought-or-oversold lines can be constructed at equidistant levels from the zero line. The same principles of interpretation apply for both indicators. For example, the volume oscillator reflects overbought-or-oversold

Chart 23-1   Calculation of a volume oscillator I

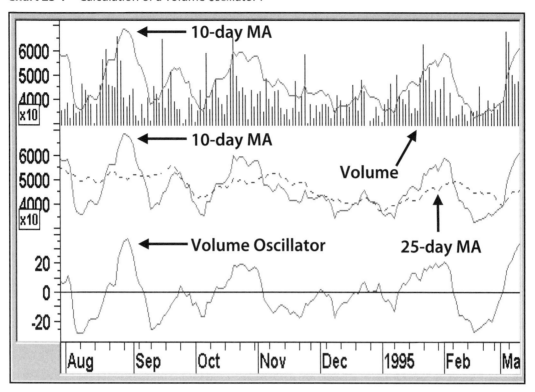

(Source: pring.com)

Chart 23-2   Calculation of a volume oscillator II

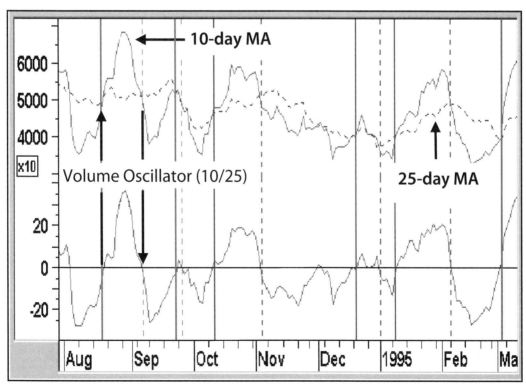

(Source: pring.com)

volume conditions. When it crosses back through one of these levels on its return toward the equilibrium level, a reversal in the trend of volume momentum is indicated. This is usually, though certainly not always, represented by a change in the price trend. Once again, we need to be alert to some kind of trend reversal in the price, which acts as confirmation. In a normal market environment, volume and price should move in roughly the same direction. For instance, in the case of a rally, the volume oscillator should rise. When it reverses from an overbought condition, this would typically signal that a correction of some kind is in the cards. Bottoms are often signaled by a selling climax. This type of condition existed in September 1996 for General Motors (Chart 23-3). The horizontal dashed arrow indicates an overbought oscillator following a decline, a classic sign of a selling climax. This is later

confirmed by a positive downtrend line break by the price.

Notice how the oscillator declines as the price is breaking above the line. This is not a cause for concern, since volume, by definition,

> In a normal market environment, volume and price should move in roughly the same direction. My suggestion is that once you see a reversal in an overbought volume indicator, look for a trading range to develop. Then watch very closely to see which way the price breaks out since this is usually a reliable signal of the direction of the next short-term trend.

Chart 23-3   General Motors and a 10/25 volume oscillator

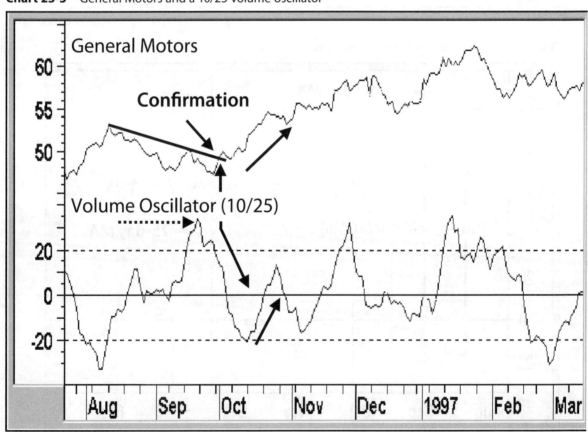

(Source: pring.com)

should decline after a selling climax. It is one of the few times when rising prices and falling volume are not bearish. Of course, if prices were to subsequently extend their rise on declining volume, this would be a negative factor. In this instance, though, the volume oscillator quickly moved to an oversold condition and reversed to the upside. The initial oscillator rally was not particularly impressive, since it was unable to move to its overbought level. However, the next one did manage to get there. The price then completed a small top, and a little decline followed (Chart 23-4). Once again, my suggestion is that once you see a reversal in an overbought volume indicator, look for a trading range to develop. Then watch very closely to see which way the price breaks out, since this is usually a reliable signal of the direction of the next short-term trend. In this case, the dashed lines indicate that the price traced out a small rectangle-type formation.

The decline did not last very long, and the volume oscillator and price both traced out a small pattern (Chart 23-5). The joint violation then indicated that the line of least resistance was upward. Once again, the volume oscillator rallied to the overbought level in January 1997. The price then experienced a sideways trading range, finally breaking to the downside. Do not forget that the oscillator was perfectly consistent with a decline in this instance because both price and volume were contracting.

SETTING PARAMETERS

Setting parameters for the volume oscillator is crucial. Obviously, the smaller the time span between the short moving average and the longer one, the greater the volatility. Chart 23-6 compares a one-day moving average against a 200-day series. Since the 200-day

Chart 23-4 General Motors and a 10/25 volume oscillator

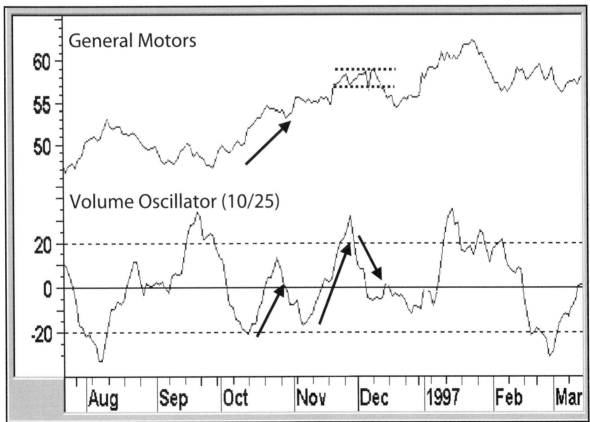

(Source: pring.com)

Chart 23-5   General Motors and a 10/25 volume oscillator

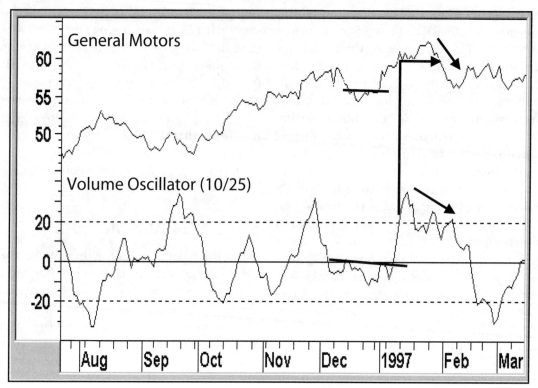

(Source: pring.com)

Chart 23-6   General Motors and a 1/200 volume oscillator

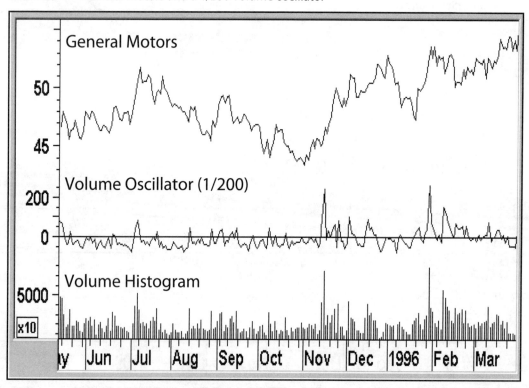

(Source: pring.com)

average is relatively flat, the result is not much different than displaying volume as a histogram, as is fairly evident by comparing the two lower areas.

Chart 23-7 shows the opposite extreme, where the oscillator is calculated from two moving averages that are very close in time. The curve is definitely smoother, but the turning points often develop in an unrelated way to the price. The key, then, is to use two moving averages that are fairly well separated. My personal preference when working with daily charts is a 10/25-day combination, although I freely admit there may well be a superior setting. Just remember not to look for perfection, but more for compromise. In other words, do not fit the data to make the past work for a specific market, try to find something that works reasonably well most of the time.

INTERPRETATION

Chart 23-8 for Daimler Chrysler features a 10/25 combination. I find that overbought/oversold readings, trendline breaks, and pattern completions work very well, in the sense that they provide relatively reliable signals that the trend of the volume oscillator has reversed. Once again, though, this does not always translate into a change in the actual price trend. Let me quickly run through this example. Both price and volume were expanding between May and early August, then the price moved sideways in a narrow band, as flagged by the dashed arrows. As is normal in a trading range environment, the level of volume subsided, since the trading range represents a period of evenhandedness between buyers and sellers. Volume reached an oversold level in early August, rallied, and then tested the oversold

Chart 23-7 General Motors and a 15/20 volume oscillator

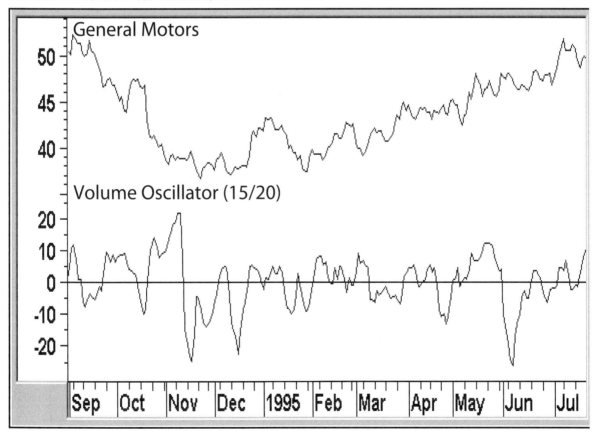

(Source: pring.com)

Chart 23-8   Daimler Chrysler and a 10/25 volume oscillator

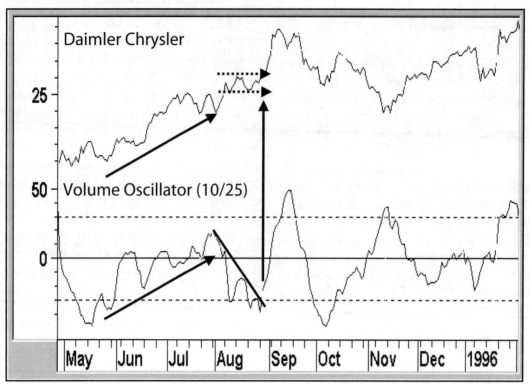

(Source: pring.com)

Chart 23-9   Daimler Chrysler and a 10/25 volume oscillator

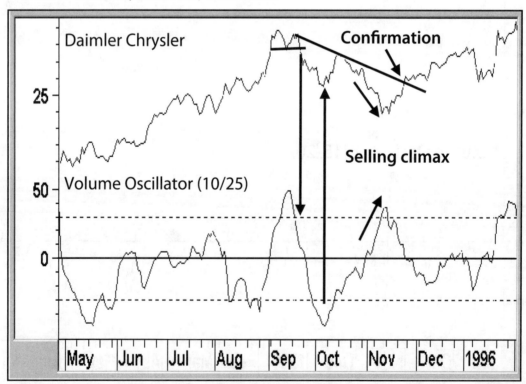

(Source: pring.com)

level later in the month. As it reversed from this low level, it also violated a downtrend line, as the price broke out from the trading range on the upside. Thus volume was expanding on the price breakout, which is a bullish combination. Then the volume oscillator quickly rallied to the overbought zone (Chart 23-9). As it crossed below this upper extreme zone on its way back toward zero, the price completed and broke down from a small double top.

The next oversold condition was followed by a small rally, but there was nothing in the price action that would have confirmed this brief trend change to the upside. Finally, volume expanded to a crescendo in November, and the selling climax was followed by a rally, which was signaled by a price trend break at the end of the month.

The rally itself was not particularly inspiring from a volume momentum point of view,

since the oscillator was barely able to rally above zero (Chart 23-10). This would have indicated that the advance was suspect. The actual signal came when the uptrend line was violated in early January. Needless to say, a sharp decline followed. The last event is shown in Chart 23-11, where mid-January saw the completion of a small base in the price and a breakout from a somewhat larger base in the volume oscillator.

Obviously, not all combinations of volume oscillator and trendline–price pattern analysis work out this well, but the explanation at least gives you a few pointers to watch out for. There is one final point. If you review all of the trend turning points in the volume oscillator, the overbought/oversold reversals, price patterns and trendline violations, and so on, you will appreciate that they had a very high degree of reliability in signaling a reversal in the prevailing volume momentum trend.

Chart 23-10   Daimler Chrysler and a 10/25 volume oscillator

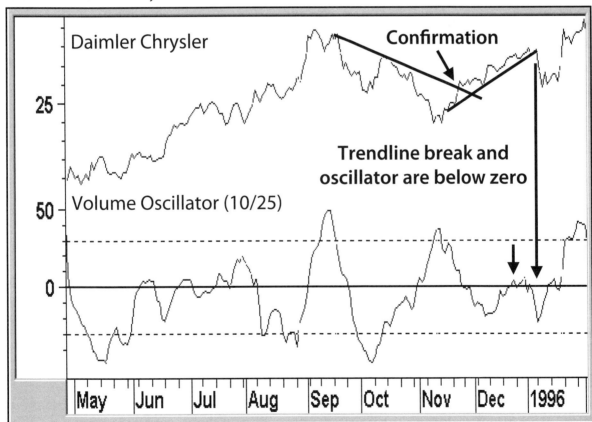

(Source: pring.com)

Chart 23-11   Daimler Chrysler and a 10/25 volume oscillator

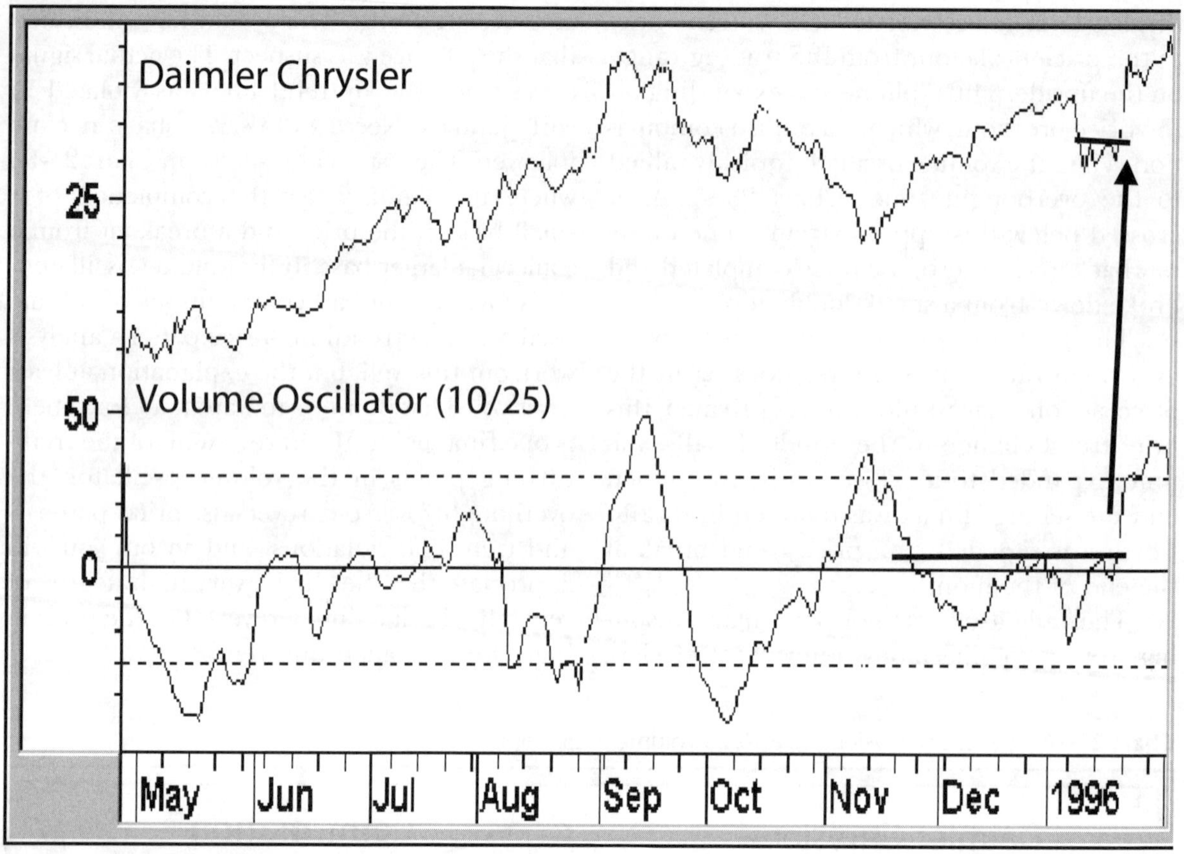

(Source: pring.com)

VOLUME VERSUS PRICE OSCILLATORS

Combining a volume and price oscillator on the same chart can offer a further dynamic to the analysis. This is because it then becomes easier to spot those situations where things are in gear and those where there are discrepancies. In this respect, it is vital to remember that the two series can move in opposite directions and remain consistent. For example, volume moves to an overbought condition during a selling climax, and the price oscillator falls to an oversold one. Alternately, a rally could see a price oscillator in an overbought position and a volume oscillator declining below zero. This would indicate weakness, since rising prices would be accompanied by declining volume. Chart 23-12, featuring Family Dollar Stores, is based on weekly data. The timeframe for the two oscillators reflect 10- and 25-week

trend deviations. The sell-off in early Fall 1994 is associated with a mini-selling climax, as you can see from the overbought reading in the volume oscillator. The price then breaks above a small downtrend line and the positive reading in the price oscillator sets the scene for a rally. Normally, I would have expected a larger rise than the one that took place because the price oscillator was at a fairly subdued level when it began. It would, of course, be normal for the volume oscillator to be declining on the first upward thrust in the price. However, as the declining trend of volume progressed, it would have become apparent that the rally was becoming suspect. The warning sign began to appear when the price was unable to cross above its 65-week EMA in early 1995 and the price oscillator reversed to the downside.

As it turned out, this was to be a test of the low. Then at the second vertical arrow in Chart 23-13, the price stabilizes, the two oscillators

Chart 23-12 Family Dollar and a price and volume oscillator

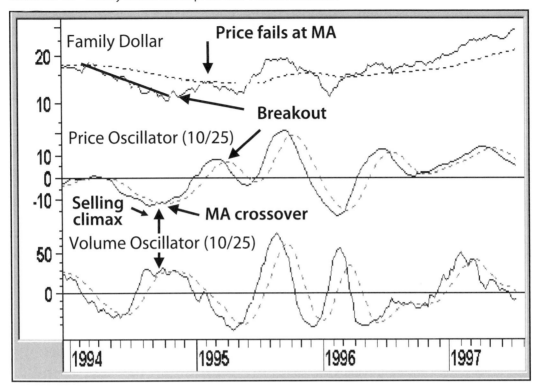

(Source: pring.com)

Chart 23-13 Family Dollar and a price and volume oscillator

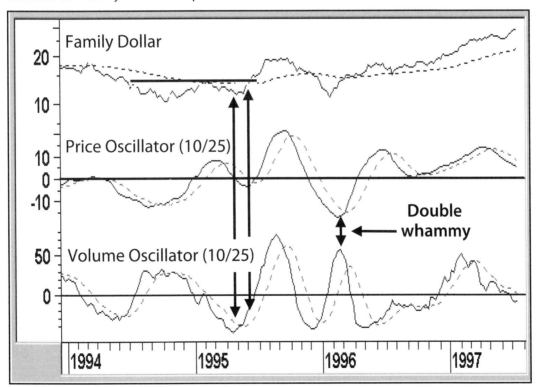

(Source: pring.com)

reverse to the upside, and the price breaks above the horizontal trendline and the 65-day EMA, a classic buy signal combination.

The rally does not last as long as I would have suspected from such a combination. However, the next event is what I call a *double whammy*. A double whammy develops when a volume oscillator is overbought and a price oscillator oversold. Both indicate that the decline in price is most probably over. You can recognize a double whammy because both series move toward each other:; obviously, the closer, the better.

Since volume is a totally independent variable from price, it makes sense to look at some more examples comparing a volume momentum indicator with a price momentum series.

Chart 23-14 shows an example of *churning*. That is a condition wherein, after a good rally, volume expands to very heavy levels, yet there is little response in the price. Such a situation developed for Hecla Mining in early 1996. The price rallied to a new recovery high, as the volume oscillator moved up to very overbought. However, at the time of the high (flagged by the vertical arrows), the price oscillator was still marginally below zero. It is true that it eventually rallied again, but this was more of a lagged statistical response, since the actual price was lower at this point. This type of

> A double whammy is an event that develops when a volume oscillator is overbought and a price oscillator is oversold.

Chart 23-14   Hecla and a price and volume oscillator

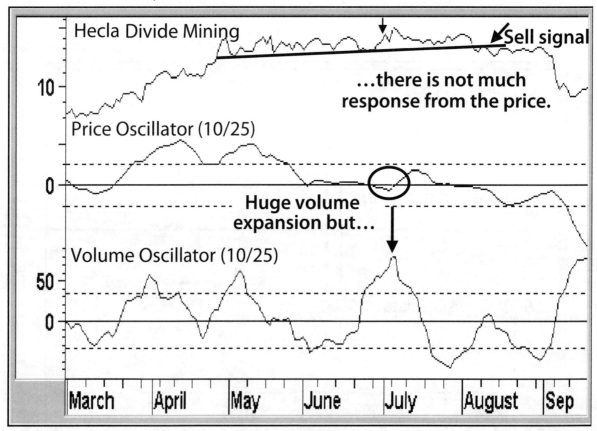

(Source: pring.com)

Chart 23-15   Federal National Mortgage and a price and volume oscillator

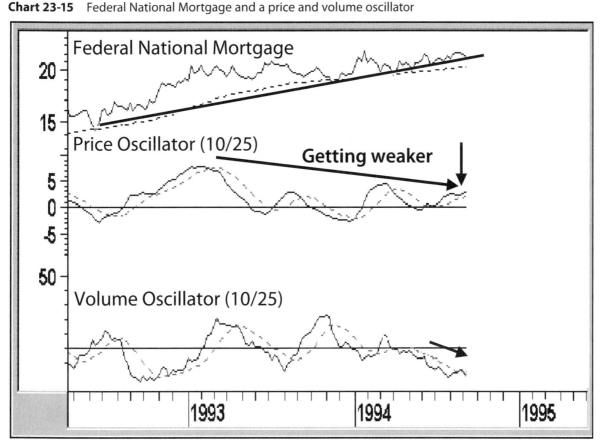

(Source: pring.com)

action would have warned that something was definitely very wrong. However, the actual sell signal would have come much later, when the price broke below the slightly upward-sloping trendline.

Federal National Mortgage (Chart 23-15) offers a great example of the interaction between price trends and price and volume oscillators. The chart shows that the price was able to remain above its 65-week EMA and uptrend line between 1992, right up until mid 1994. During this period, the peaks in the price oscillator were in a declining trend, so that by the time the price reached its final peak, the oscillator was barely above zero. This was bad enough, but look at the progress of the weekly volume oscillator. At the time of the final peak, it has actually been below zero for

some time. Since the price was not much above its previous high, it could be argued that the stock was in a trading range. This would mean that declining volume reflected a tight balance between buyers and sellers. A break to the upside on expanding volume would, therefore, resolve the dilemma in a bullish way. However, the weaker action of the price oscillator at the second 1994 peak, combined with the contracting volume, argued for a break in the opposite direction. When the break did occur (Chart 23-16), it was to the downside, and volume expanded tremendously. What we end up with is a double whammy effect, as the price and volume oscillators converge on each other for a classic selling climax.

Chart 23-16   Federal National Mortgage and a price and volume oscillator

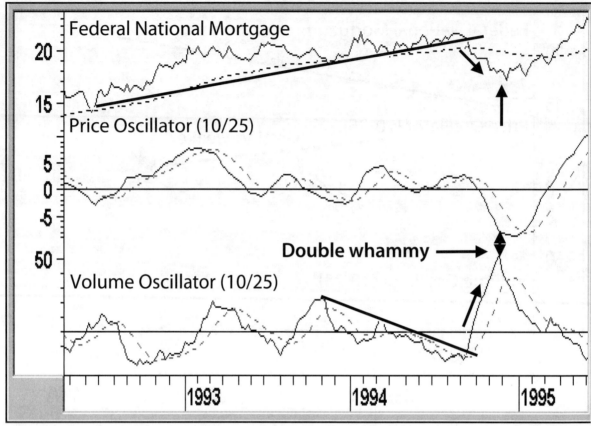

(Source: pring.com)

SUMMARY

The volume oscillator

1. Allows us to plot both overbought and over-sold zones.

2. Does not always translate into price trend reversals during volume trend reversals.

3. Adds depth to the analysis when combined with the price oscillator.

4. Can be calculated with any combination of time spans, but a good all-round combination is a 10-period divided by a 25-period moving average.

24

The Chaikin Money Flow Indicator

THE CONCEPT

The Chaikin money flow indicator (CMF) is based on the principle that rising prices should be accompanied by expanding volume, and vice versa. The formula emphasizes the fact that market strength is usually accompanied by prices closing in the upper half of their daily range with increasing volume. Likewise, market weakness is usually accompanied by prices closing in the lower half of their daily range with increasing volume. This indicator can be calculated with any time span: the longer the period, the more deliberate the swings. Money flow indicators calculated with a short-term timeframe, such as 10 periods, are, therefore, much more volatile.

When prices consistently close in the upper half of their daily high-low range on increased volume for the period under consideration, the indicator will be positive (that is, above the zero line). Conversely, if prices consistently close in the lower half of their daily high-low range on increased volume, the indicator will be negative (that is, below the zero line).

DIVERGENCE ANALYSIS

It is possible to construct overbought-or-oversold lines and use these as buy-and-sell alerts, but the indicator really comes into its own with divergence analysis. In Chart 24-1 of National Semiconductor, we can see some good examples in practice. In early 1994 (point A), the Chaikin was falling sharply as the price ran up to its final peak, and at the time of the actual high, it was barely above the equilibrium line. This showed that the quality of the last few weeks of the rally left a lot to be desired. In fall 1995 (point B), the divergence was more blatant, since the indicator was barely able to rise above the zero line at a time when the price was making a new high. Both these examples were followed by

Chart 24-1   National Semiconductor and CMF divergences

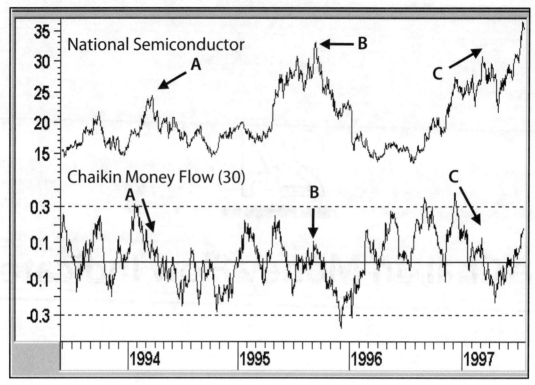

(Source: pring.com)

Chart 24-2   National Semiconductor and CMF divergences

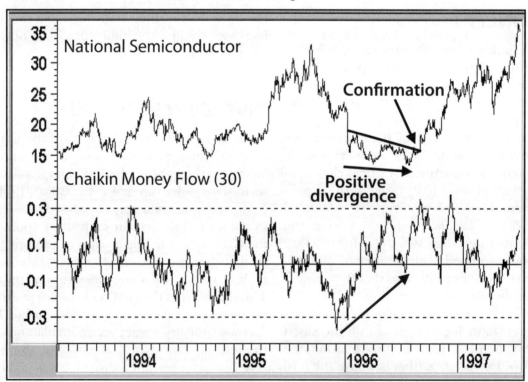

(Source: pring.com)

long downtrends. However, the negative divergence (C) that took place in early 1997 was followed by a quick, but sharp, sell-off.

Positive divergences also work quite well with the Chaikin indicator. Look at the early 1996 bottom in Chart 24-2. See how the price makes a marginal new low, but the oscillator is hardly below zero. This compares to the late-1995 bottom, where it was at an extremely oversold condition. Of course, this is merely a positive momentum characteristic; we still need to witness some kind of trend reversal in price to confirm this event. Divergences are not uncommon in momentum indicators. What sets the money flow indicator apart from the rest is that the divergences are usually far more blatant than, say, for the RSI or ROC. As a result, it can provide clues of probable trend reversals that may not be apparent elsewhere.

Chart 24-3 features a 20-week money flow. The indicator made a very low reading about halfway through the mid-1986 trading range. Then it shot up very sharply just prior to the point where the price took off on the upside. In fact, it was possible to construct a trendline marking the top of a small base for the price. The scene was then set for a worthwhile rally. Notice how the indicator gradually declined from early 1987 onward to the extent that by the time the final peak was seen, there was

> Divergences are not uncommon in momentum indicators. What sets the money flow indicator apart from the rest is that the divergences are usually far more blatant than, say, for the RSI or ROC.

Chart 24-3 Alexander and Baldwin and CMF divergences

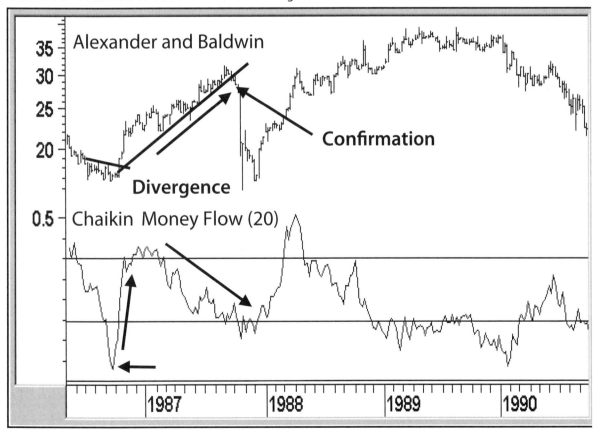

(Source: pring.com)

virtually no upside momentum. It was also possible to confirm this weak technical structure by observing a break below the 1986 to 1987 uptrend line prior to the market crash.

What I find incredible is that the 1987 low was slightly under that of 1986, yet the oscillator barely fell below zero (Chart 24-4). This indicated a very strong technical position. It was even possible to construct a downtrend line for the money flow indicator. The penetration of this line developed ahead of the decisive breakout in the price. The late 1988 to 1989 period was also associated with weak money flow (Chart 24-5). The price moved sideways while it traced out a head-and-shoulders top formation, but the oscillator spent a considerable amount of time below the zero line. When the actual breakdown in price took place, the money flow was well into negative territory. Sometimes the money flow indicator will give us an advanced warning that a pattern breakout may be imminent.

In Chart 24-6 of Merrill Lynch featuring a 20-period CMF, the spring 1992 lows experienced a small positive divergence with the price and this was confirmed by a trendline break. Later on, the price moved in a trading range.

The top at point A in Chart 24-7 was associated with some positive money flow, but look at the next one (point B); the indicator is at a much higher level, indicating substantial accumulation, but the price had not yet decisively broken above the horizontal trendline. In actual fact, the oscillator was still rising as the price started to decline. It was surprising, though, to see the price then experience a sharp setback. However, while the price fell below its previous low, the money flow did not. This divergence has been flagged by the two

Chart 24-4   Alexander and Baldwin and CMF divergences

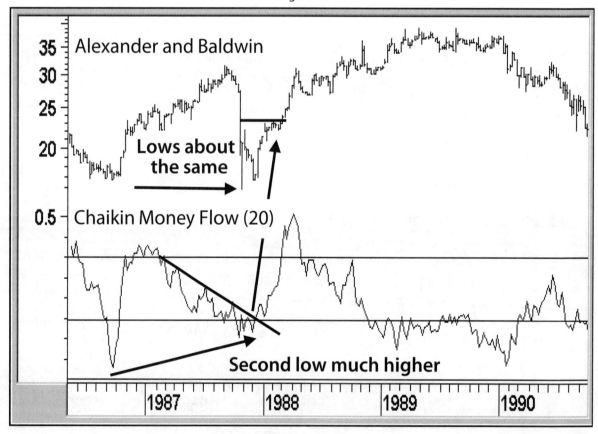

(Source: pring.com)

Chart 24-5 Alexander and Baldwin and CMF divergences

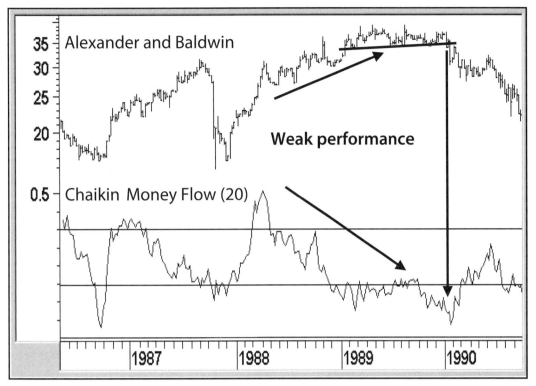

(Source: pring.com)

Chart 24-6 Merrill Lynch and CMF divergences.

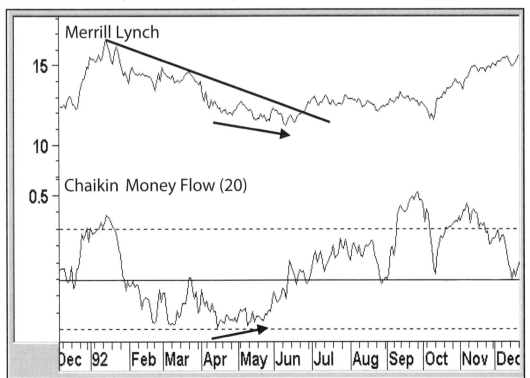

(Source: pring.com)

Chart 24-7 Merrill Lynch and CMF divergences

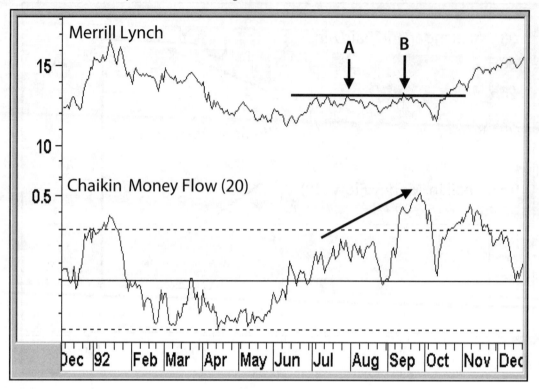

(Source: pring.com)

Chart 24-8 Merrill Lynch and CMF divergences

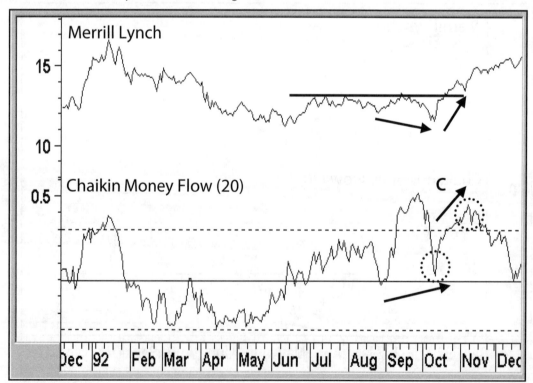

(Source: pring.com)

converging lines. Later on, in Chart 24-8, the oscillator rallied into overbought territory once again (point C) as the price broke above the solid horizontal trendline. This is the type of situation where the money flow can really be of help. On the surface, it looked as if the price weakness, once started, was likely to extend. However, the fact that the money flow indicator did not even cross below zero (at its October low) before it turned around indicated that selling pressure was really quite superficial. It is reasonable to have assumed that the neutral reading in the money flow in the ellipse would have indicated the potential for much further weakness. After all, the price could certainly have fallen quite a bit before the CMF would decline to an oversold level. The point is that the money flow is normally a leading indicator, so if it was going to register an oversold reading, it should have done this by now. Just

remember that the earlier examples demonstrated how the money flow was actually in negative territory when the price was at, or close to, a high.

This oscillator does not generally lend itself to trendline violations. However, Chart 24-9 offers an example in late 1993 wherein both the price and oscillator violate uptrend lines.

THE CHAIKIN MONEY FLOW INDICATOR AND TRADING RANGES

One of the ways in which I like to use the indicator is to study trading ranges and then compare the price action to the oscillator to see if it is giving a clue as to the direction of the eventual breakout. American Business Products was caught in a trading range in 1987

Chart 24-9   Merrill Lynch and CMF divergences

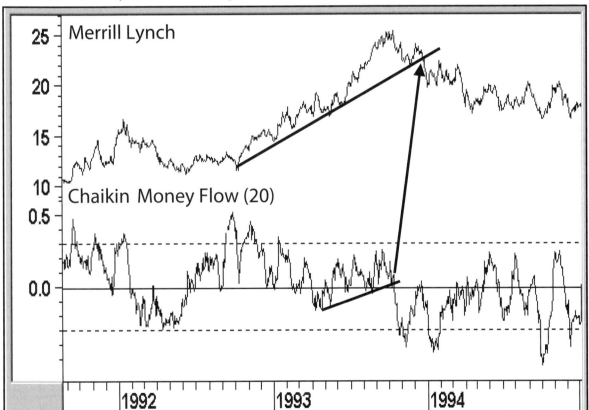

(Source: pring.com)

Chart 24-10   American Business Products and CMF divergences

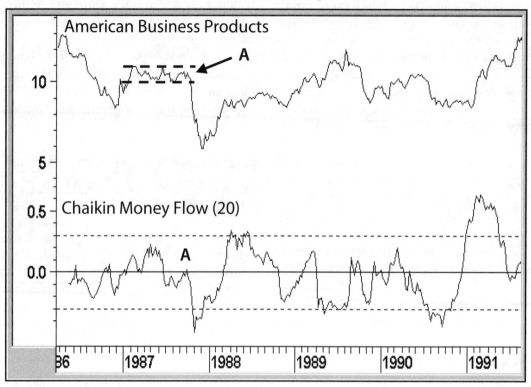

(Source: pring.com)

Chart 24-11   American Business Products and CMF divergences

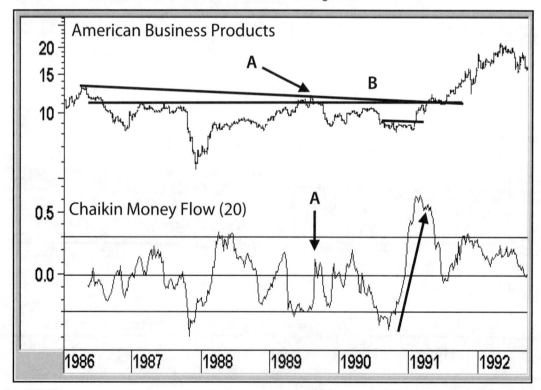

(Source: pring.com)

(Chart 24-10). Even though it held above the lower trendline, the 20-week CMF slipped quite decisively into negative territory. Then a rally followed at arrow A. The price came fairly close to the previous high, but the oscillator was well below it. This combination indicated vulnerability, so it was not surprising that the price experienced a nasty decline.

Chart 24-11 features the same stock, but the time span is greater. In 1989, the price broke above a multi-year resistance trendline at point A. On the surface, this looked pretty good. However, the money flow indicator was barely able to rally above zero. This indicated that the breakout was not supported by positive volume characteristics and that a whipsaw was likely.

The price tried to rally back to the line once more in 1990 at point B, but the money flow again was headed south, thereby indicat-

ing that the attempt, as far as money flow was concerned, would not end in a successful way.

Now compare the difference in the technical situation in early 1991, when the price did manage to break to the upside. First, during the basing formation that preceded the rally, the money flow was in a sharp uptrend. See how prices were essentially flat, yet the oscillator moved quickly off its oversold bottom. By the time the price eventually broke above the lower horizontal trendline, the money flow indicator was at its highest level in five years. This indicated a tremendous amount of upside momentum and buying power. Holders of the stock were not disappointed.

In Chart 24-12 of Newmont Mining, a resistance trendline forms in the $45 to $50 area. There was no real reason why the 1993 and 1994 sharp price rallies, accompanied by

Chart 24-12 Newmont Mining and CMF divergences

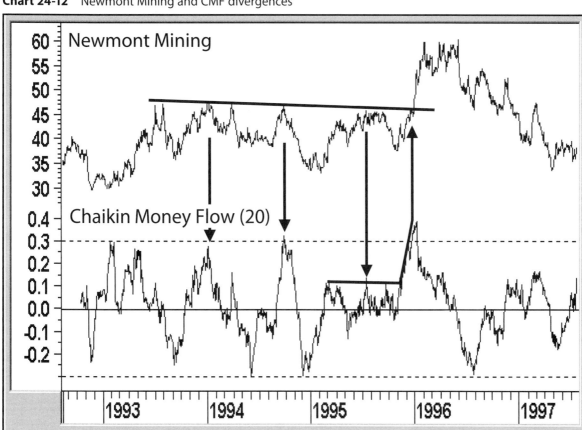

(Source: pring.com)

Chart 24-13   Newmont Mining and CMF divergences

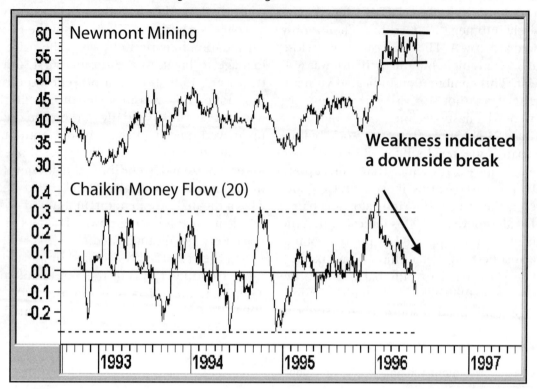

(Source: pring.com)

Chart 24-14   Newmont Mining and CMF divergences

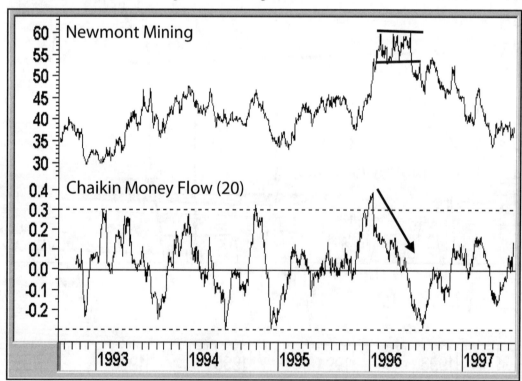

(Source: pring.com)

healthy readings in the money flow, should not have resulted in a breakout. However, the mid-1995 attempt was doomed to failure, according to the money flow indicator, since this series barely made it to the halfway over-bought zone. When the breakout did finally materialize, the oscillator was well above its previous high.

The top formation traced out in early 1996 was most instructive (Chart 24-13), since the price moved in a sideways trading range, which could have been resolved in either direction. However, the indicator started on a persistent declining trend that took it into negative territory just prior to the downside breakout, which is shown in Chart 24-14.

Chart 24-15 shows an unusual, but very powerful, combination of a double trendline break by the price and a 20-period CMF. This is a weekly chart, and the two lines extend back for several years. It was not surprising, therefore, that when the two breaks finally came, the price not only experienced a decline, but was unable to move to a new high for several years.

This same period also experienced a head-and-shoulders top in both series, as we can see in Chart 24-16. These two price pattern completions added greater weight to the two trendline violations, since they all developed around the same time.

Finally, Chart 24-17 shows the CMF in a less flattering light. In fall 1996, Western Deep, a South African gold mine, experienced a huge rally and a positive CMF. Then, in early November, the price also advanced and broke above a small secondary trendline. Taken on face value, this looked to be a solid combination that would be followed by a very worthwhile rally. However, Chart 24-18 indicates that the breakout was a whipsaw. This example was

Chart 24-15 Alcoa and CMF divergences.

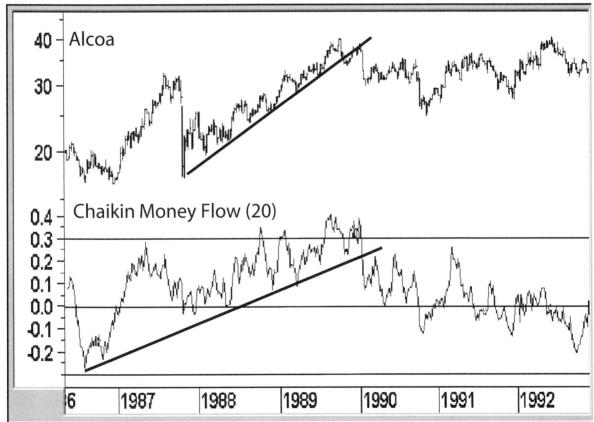

(Source: pring.com)

> Quite often, we find that if an otherwise very strong and reliable-looking signal fails, it is typically a countercyclical one, and countercyclical signals have an unfortunate habit of being false.

included to warn you that the CMF is not an infallible indicator and that even the best signals can sometimes fail to operate in the manner expected. All that can be said in the defense of this whipsaw is that the whole period covered by the chart was a bear market. Quite often, we find that if an otherwise very strong and reliable-looking signal fails, it is typically a countercyclical one, and countercyclical signals have an unfortunate habit of being false. That is exactly what happened here.

SUMMARY

1. The strength of the CMF indicator is its ability to throw out blatant divergences, which have a reasonable degree of accuracy.

2. During sideways trading ranges, the indicator will often move decisively in one direction or another. This provides a valuable clue as to the direction of the price breakout when it ultimately takes place.

3. When prices reach resistance, look to the money flow for a clue as to whether it will hold or be violated.

4. When prices reach support, look to the money flow for a clue as to whether it will hold or be violated.

Chart 24-16　Alcoa and CMF trendline violations

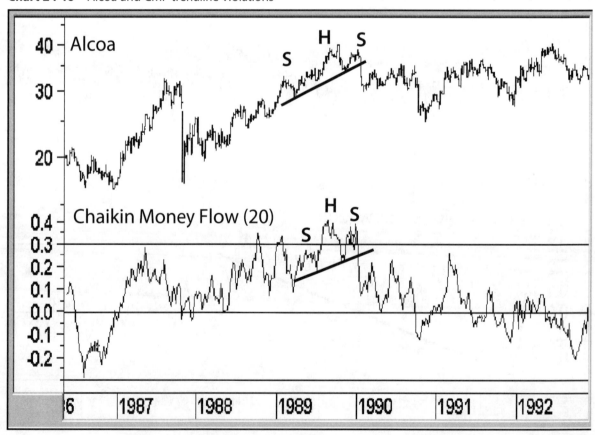

(Source: pring.com)

Chart 24-17 Western Deep and CMF price patterns

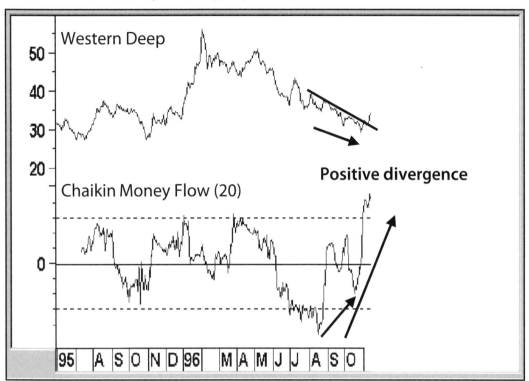

(Source: pring.com)

Chart 24-18 Western Deep and a false breakout

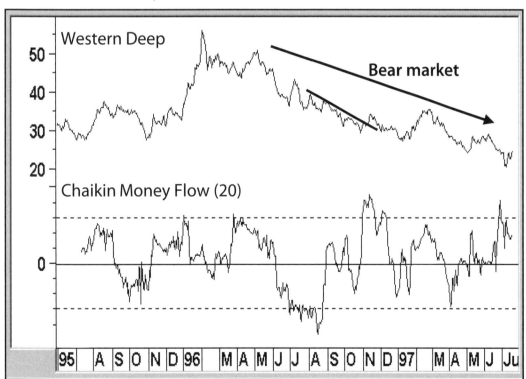

(Source: pring.com)

25

The Demand Index

THE INDICATOR

Technicians have always been fascinated by the possibility of being able to separate volume-initiated-buy buyers from sellers. The former is known as *upside volume* and the latter as *downside activity*. Unless you are in possession of tick-by-tick data where it is possible to appropriate volume associated with up-ticks or down-ticks, it is not possible to accomplish this analysis. The Chaikin money flow indicator described in the previous chapter tries to achieve this objective statistically, as does the demand index. It was developed by Jim Sibbet, editor of the *Let's Talk Silver and Gold* market letter, and combines price and volume into one indicator. The demand index is based on the premise that volume leads price. Consequently, the objective is to end up with an indicator that leads market turning points. It is included in many charting packages and is interpreted in the following ways.

SIX METHODS OF INTERPRETATION

1. *Divergences between the indicator and the price indicate underlying strength or weakness, depending on whether it is a positive or negative one.*

2. *A long-term divergence between the index and the price indicates a major top or bottom.*

3. *Zero crossovers represent a change in trend. Normally, this will occur after the fact, so it serves as a confirmatory indicator.*

4. *Constant fluctuations around the zero indicates a weak price trend that will soon reverse.*

5. *Overbought-or-oversold crossovers generate good buy and sell signals in some markets.* Since the level of the demand index is affected by the volatility of the security being monitored, optimum overbought-or-oversold levels will vary and should be

determined on a case-by-case basis. However, the ±25 levels appear to be a good compromise for most markets.

6. *The index sometimes forms price patterns and trendline violations.* They normally represent a reliable *advance* warning of an impending price trend reversal.

Let us consider each of these interpretive principles in turn.

DIVERGENCES

The interpretation of divergences between the price and the demand index is essentially the same as any other indicator. In Chart 25-1 you can see a positive and negative scenario.

When the price makes its final peak in early March, the demand index has already started to decline fairly precipitously. This, of course, just warns that the underlying technical structure is not as good as it looks on the surface. However, it is still necessary to observe some kind of trend-reversal signal in the price to confirm the probability that a new trend is underway. This signal comes when the uptrend line is violated.

The example on the right develops at the September 1985 bottom. See how the price makes its final low for the move there, but the demand index actually bottomed in June. The confirmation of this improving technical picture came later on, when the downtrend line was violated on the upside.

In Chart 25-2 the price makes a secondary peak at the end of 1992 (point A) that is ever

Chart 25-1 DuPont and demand index divergences

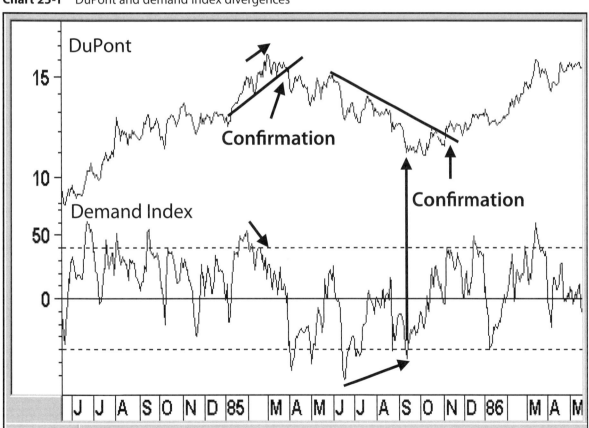

(Source: pring.com)

so slightly below the first one. It's not, strictly speaking, a divergence, but in technical analysis, we are dealing as much in common sense as mechanical interpretation. The point being that the second peak was for all intents and purposes at the same level as the first one. However, momentum, in this case the demand index, was barely able to rally above zero. Consequently, the enthusiasm was just not there at the second peak. Ordinarily, when momentum is barely able to rally above zero at a time when the price makes a marginal new high or comes very close to it, this is usually followed by a sharp decline, once confirmed by a price trendbreak. That was certainly true in this particular case.

LONG-TERM DIVERGENCES

The divergences that we saw in the previous example were of relatively short-term duration. In Chart 25-3 we see that the demand index bottomed in April, eight months prior to the December rally off the bottom formation. In the intervening period, it diverged several times in a positive manner with the price. Note that although the demand index did experience a series of higher bottoms between April and June, this occurred within the overall March-to-December downtrend. That is why we are able to count the April demand index low as part of the overall long-term divergence in this case.

A final point worthy of attention comes from the fact that the December low in the demand index was barely below the zero level (Chart 25-4), yet the price was within a whisker

Chart 25-2   Rite Aid and demand index divergences

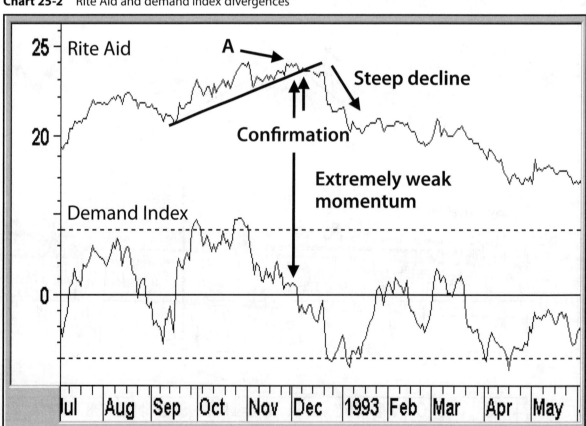

Chart 25-3 Rite Aid and demand index divergences

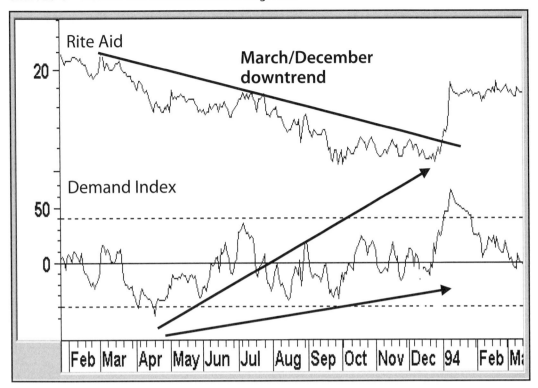

(Source: pring.com)

Chart 25-4 Rite Aid and demand index divergences

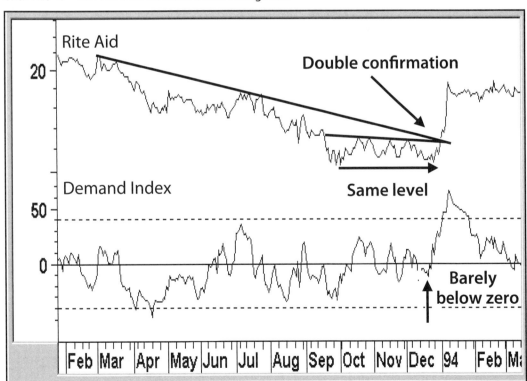

(Source: pring.com)

Chart 25-5   Rohm and Haas and demand index zero crossovers

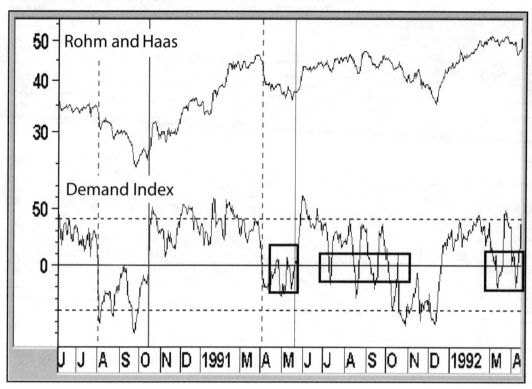

Chart 25-6   Royal Dutch Petroleum and demand index zero crossovers

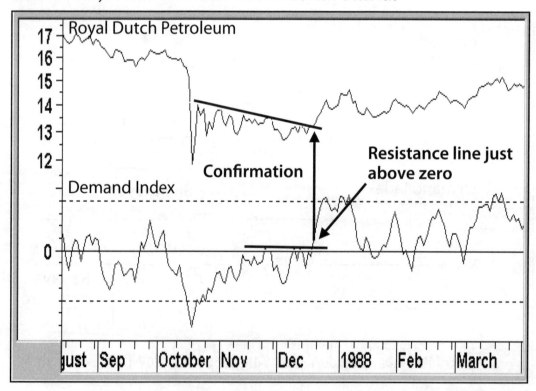

of the early October low. Hence, we have the exact opposite set of circumstances to that in Chart 25-2, where a demand index that was barely able to rally above zero was followed by a sharp decline. In this case, the inability of the demand index to fall much below zero was followed by a spectacular rally.

ZERO CROSSOVERS

Some people use zero crossovers by the demand index to generate buy-or-sell signals. Sometimes this can work quite well, as you can see from the position of the solid and dashed vertical lines in Chart 25-5. The solid lines represent buy signals when the demand crosses above zero and the dashed ones sell signals, when it crosses below. In these particular instances, this approach was very profitable. But what about the period between the two lines in April and May for Rohm and Haas? Here we see that the index whipped above zero on two occasions. Had we been following the zero crossover religiously, losses would have been incurred. Indeed, if you cast your eyes to the right, you will see several other examples of false signals contained in the boxes. This chart is not an isolated example because this is a fairly common occurrence. Therefore, my advice is to ignore zero crossovers unless you can spot instances when they turn out to be a good support or resistance point. Under such circumstances, the zero crossover will represent a form of support-or-resistance penetration and, therefore, it has a tendency to be more reliable.

> My advice is to ignore zero crossovers unless you can spot instances when they turn out to be a good support or resistance point.

CONSTANT FLUCTUATIONS AROUND ZERO

I had to search several charts and countless years of data to find the example in Chart 25-6 of what we might call a *zero-resistance crossover*. Even then, the horizontal trendline is slightly above zero, so it does not really count. If I have to do a lot of digging to find an example for an interpretive point that I am trying to make, it really means that this interpretive characteristic is not particularly useful. Consequently, I am not really sold on Rule 4, which states that if the index waffles closely around the zero level, it indicates a weak price trend that will soon reverse. In this case, I ask myself the question, What constitutes "around" the zero level? After studying countless charts, I still cannot answer that question to my satisfaction, probably because it is often very difficult to determine when the indicator has moved sufficiently away from the zero level to constitute a change in trend. Most of the time, when you can identify such situations, the horse has bolted from the barn, anyway.

I have drawn two circles in Chart 25-7, featuring Royal Dutch Petroleum. Both indicate what I would regard as indecisive price action around zero. The first was followed by a break to the upside, and the one on the right, a break to the downside. However, in both cases, the new price trend was already well underway by the time it became obvious that the index had moved away from its relatively narrow zero-based trading range.

OVERBOUGHT-OR-OVERSOLD CROSSOVERS

I mentioned earlier that the construction of the demand index is such that overbought-or-oversold levels will differ with the volatility of the security being monitored. As you may have noticed, most of the examples used so far have placed the lines at ±40. That seems to work out quite well in a lot of situations. But it is very important to examine the security being ana-

Chart 25-7   Royal Dutch Petroleum and demand index constant zero crossovers

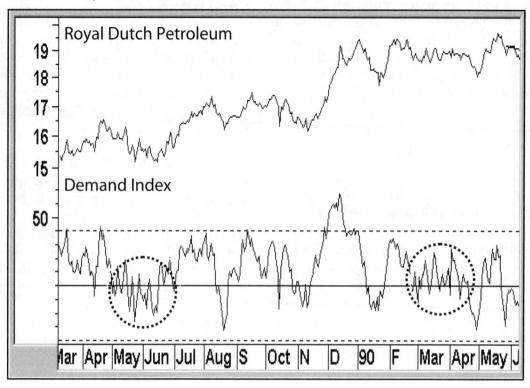

(Source: pring.com)

Chart 25-8   Royal Dutch Petroleum and demand index overbought/oversold crossovers

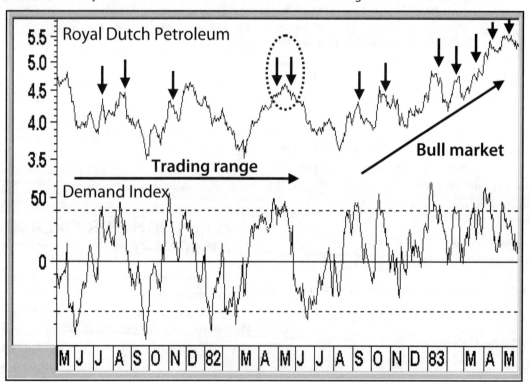

(Source: pring.com)

lyzed on a case-by-case basis to make sure that the price history of that particular one is consistent with where the lines have been placed.

In Chart 25-8, the downward-pointing arrows indicate the price where the index crossed below its overbought level. Two types of market activity are covered. The first was between May 1981 and May 1982. This was a trading-range environment. During this phase, the overbought crossovers, with the exception of the first one contained within the ellipse, worked reasonably well. The period following this was an uptrend, or bull market. In this environment, the demand index gave a couple of reasonable signals. However, in other instances, the price only experienced a small decline prior to resuming the uptrend.

There were really two signals in the area of the ellipse. The first had absolutely no effect on the price because it still continued to run up. The second was followed by a pretty nasty decline. Had someone sold on the first ellipse signal, the benefit of hindsight would have called this particular one a fairly good signal.

Obviously, it is not possible to know at the time whether the sell signal from an overbought crossover will be followed by a small or a large decline. We need to look at other indicators to obtain clues. Is the long-term KST in a bearish or bullish mode? Has the price recently completed a major head-and-shoulders top, indicating a bear market? And so on. However, I think that it is fair to say that when the demand index does cross below its overbought zone, the odds of at least a small decline are pretty high. This is the place where you might want to take at least partial profits, depending on your interpretation of the direction and maturity of the main trend.

The opposite is also true of oversold crossovers. In the vast majority of the charts that I

have studied, these observations appear to hold true.

PRICE PATTERNS AND TRENDLINES

My own feeling is that the demand index really comes into its own when it is possible to identify price patterns and trendline violations. In Chart 25-9 we see a head-and-shoulders violation in September 1995. The break develops a little bit below the zero line, so the downside potential was partially limited. However, the nice neckline break combined with the violation of the up trendline in the price offered a fairly timely signal. The next one that developed in May 1996 was not. See how the demand index breaks out from a reverse head-and-shoulders pattern. This was confirmed by a break in the price above its early-1996 trading range. The problem was that the head-and-shoulders momentum break came very close to the overbought level and was, therefore, suspect.

Chart 25-10 shows that it could have been better used as an opportunity to watch for additional weakness and a sell signal, not as a buy signal. Ironically, the day after the peak was an outside day, although that is not apparent from this line chart. The rule, then, is to look for a pattern completion from an overextended level, which is subsequently confirmed with a price break in the opposite direction to that of the breakout. This whipsaw activity can then be used as a basis from which a short position may be placed. This is because whipsaw signals are almost invariably followed by a very strong move in the opposite direction to that indicated by the original break.

Speaking of false breaks, look at the trendline on the extreme left-hand part of Chart 25-11. It marks the neckline of a head-and-shoulders pattern that did not "work." Once again, we have a form of whipsaw, but this time the indicated direction was downward, so when the pattern was not completed and the price confirmed by rallying above the down trendline, the price literally exploded on the upside.

> When the demand index does cross below its zone, the odds of at least a small decline are pretty high.

Chart 25-9   Newmont Mining and demand index price patterns

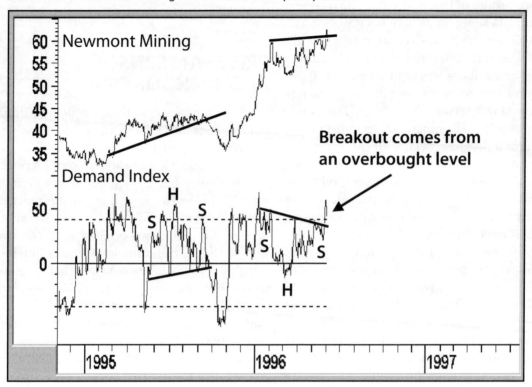

(Source: pring.com)

Chart 25-10   Newmont Mining and demand index price patterns

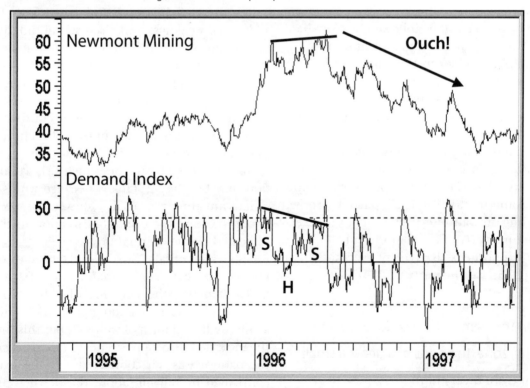

(Source: pring.com)

Since this is a momentum indicator based partially on volume, we can interpret this situation in another way. See how the index was down at an oversold condition in November at arrow A. This indicated severe selling pressure. However, by the start of the new year, this downside pressure had abated until there was virtually none at the February bottom, as the right shoulder was being formed—this, despite the fact that the price was testing its December low. Little wonder that when the buyers began to come back, there was very little selling pressure and the price rose very sharply.

The patterns that seem to work best are the head-and-shoulders variety at both tops and bottoms. In Chart 25-12 a small top develops in the demand index. It was then confirmed by a break in the price in September. The decline does not amount to much, but that

is not surprising, given the relatively small size of the two patterns. The next example on the right also coincided with a major uptrend line break in the demand index. The decline following this break was far more substantial. It represents a classic example of the neckline and trendline breaks in the demand index reinforcing each other in confirmation of a reversal in trend. One of the reasons trendline and pattern completions seem to work so well with the demand index, as opposed to a momentum indicator based solely on price, is that a trend break in the demand index reflects changes in the volume as well. So in a sense, there are two pieces of evidence pointing to a trend reversal. This same data (in Chart 25-13) also features several overbought/oversold crossovers that generate timely buy-or-sell signals. Indeed, the head of the head-and-shoulders

Chart 25-11   Newmont Mining and demand index price patterns

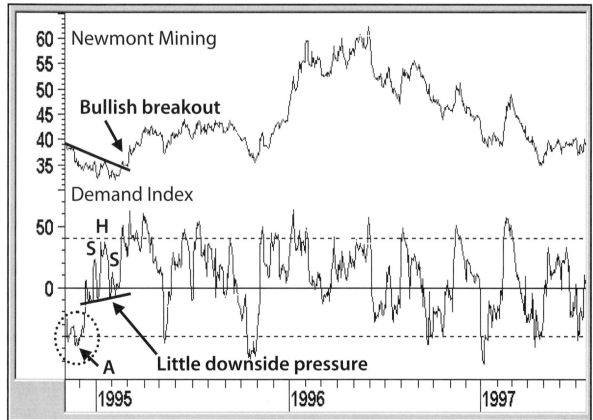

(Source: pring.com)

Chart 25-12   Schlumberger and demand index price patterns

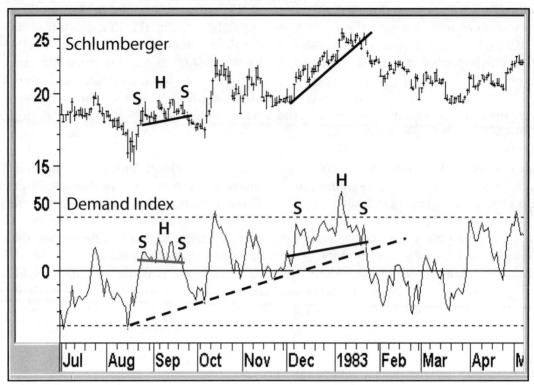

(Source: pring.com)

Chart 25-13   Schlumberger and demand index price patterns

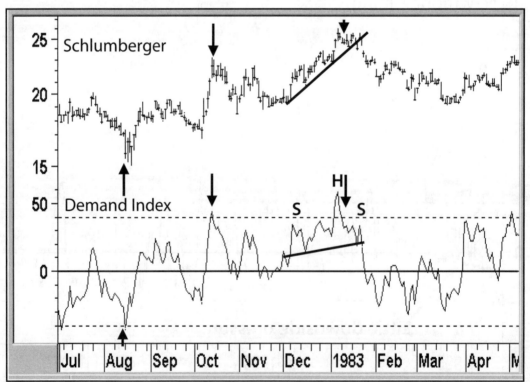

(Source: pring.com)

Chart 25-14 Schlumberger and demand index price patterns

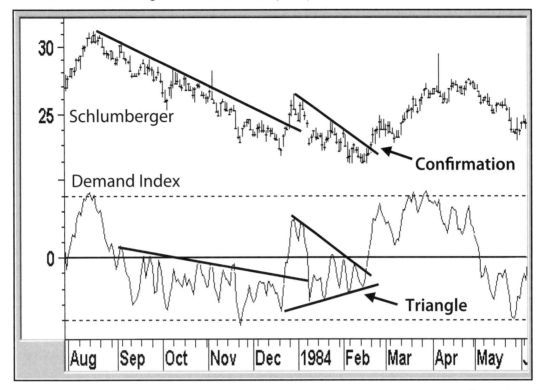

(Source: pring.com)

top on the right is associated with an over-bought crossover that develops right at the top of the rally.

Chart 25-14 offers some bullish examples. I would have thought that the rally following the breakout from the first set of downtrend lines would have been larger. After all, these are quite long and well-tested lines. However, in retrospect it is evident that this was a bear market rally. The thrust off the February bottom was indicated by the demand index breaking out from a small triangle formation. This was then confirmed by a price break.

You may have noticed that I drew the first trendline in the demand index, so that it was violated by the late November rally (see Chart 25-15). Some may say that this is not a legitimate line because of the break. However, I

believe that a good trendline reflects the underlying trend and should represent strong resistance in a downtrend and support in an uptrend. In this instance, the line is a very good reflection of the downtrend, because despite the false break, it is touched or approached on no less than nine occasions.

You can see a similar break earlier on in the trendline for the price. The same principle holds here, as well. Had I constructed the line to intersect with the intraday high, it would actually have been briefly whipped during the subsequent rally. In actual fact, the one-day break above this particular line that I drew was an exhaustion move; once the price fell back below the line, it was unable to mount a rally for about two months. In retrospect, this exhaustion break shows that the line was indeed a better reflection of the underlying trend.

Before we leave Schlumberger, there are two other points to cover. First, in Chart 25-16, notice how the demand index reached its low in November, and by the time the price reached the end of its decline, the oscillator had diverged positively with it on several occasions.

Finally, note the head-and-shoulders top in the demand index that signaled the end of the rally and the trendline break in the price that confirmed it. In actual fact, this is the neckline of an upward-sloping head-and-shoulders formation.

Chart 25-17 shows Schlumberger in a different period. This time we see a giant reverse head-and-shoulders pattern in the index. There was also a positive divergence with the price (flagged by the converging arrows), and after the breakout, we see a normal retrace-

ment move back to the extended trendline. This is classic stuff, but where is the strong rally that should have followed the retracement? It just was not there. Later on, we get a clue as to what may have happened, because the demand index is unable to reach the overbought level on either the first or second rally following the breakout. This throws up a cautionary signal because momentum indicators that cannot reach an overbought reading are either indicating a trading range or, more likely, a bear market environment. This action is particularly suspect because of the two very nice trendline breaks in the price and demand index that took place in October.

Chart 25-18 shows that this period was part of an overall downtrend, so the action was typical of what we should expect in a bear market environment.

Chart 25-15   Schlumberger and demand index price patterns

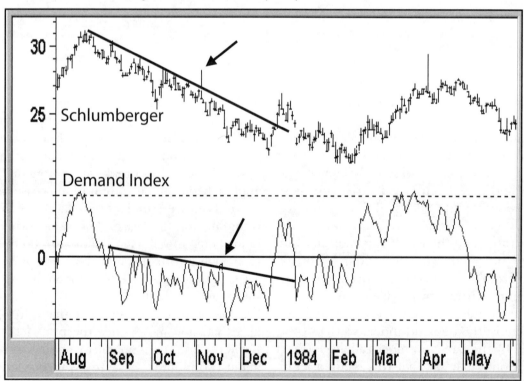

(Source: pring.com)

Chart 25-16 Schlumberger and demand index price patterns

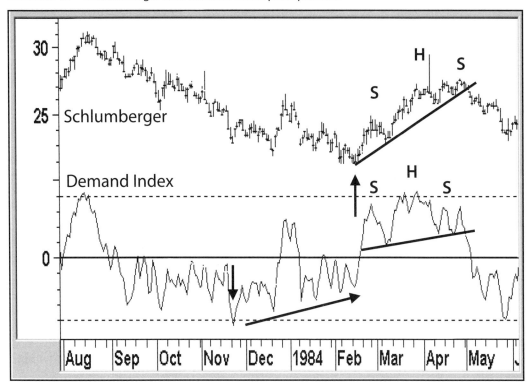

(Source: pring.com)

Chart 25-17 Schlumberger and demand index price patterns

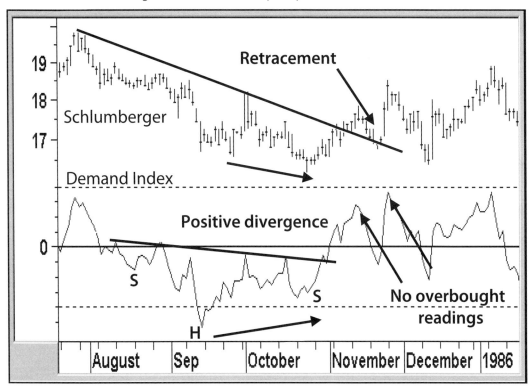

(Source: pring.com)

Chart 25-18   Schlumberger and demand index price patterns

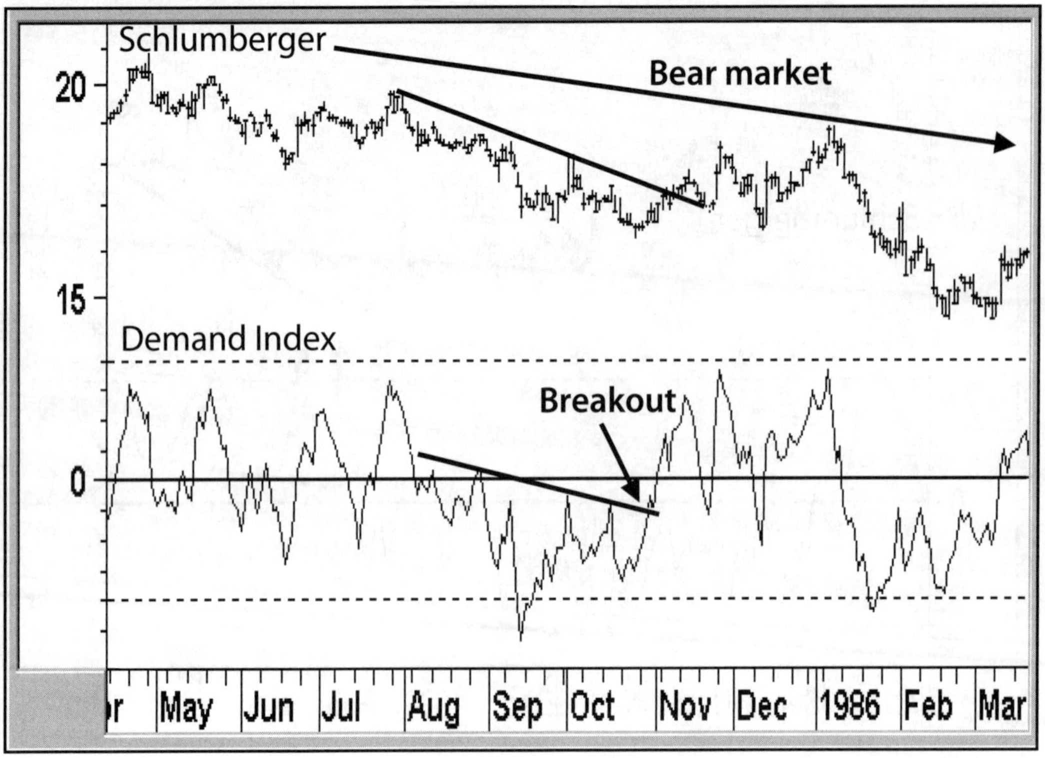

(Source: pring.com)

SUMMARY

The demand index:

1. Is constructed from both price and volume data.

2. Experiences divergences with the price.

3. Is better used with overbought-or-oversold crossovers.

4. Is best used with trendline breaks and price pattern completions.

26

The Chande Momentum Oscillator

COMPARISON WITH THE RELATIVE STRENGTH INDICATOR

The Chande momentum oscillator (CMO), named after its inventor Dr. Tushar Chande, is a variation on the relative strength indicator (RSI), yet it is uniquely different. The CMO has three characteristics. First, the calculations are based on data that have not been smoothed. This means that extreme short-term movements are not hidden. Second, the scale is confined within the -100 to +100 range. This means that the zero level becomes the equilibrium point. With the RSI 50, one is the equilibrium point and is not always readily identifiable. With zero as the pivotal point, it is easier to see those periods when momentum is positive and those when it is negative. The zero equilibrium also makes comparisons between different securities that much easier. Finally, the calculation also uses both up and down days.

Although a variation on the RSI, the Chande momentum oscillator differs in that 1) the calculations are based on data that have not been smoothed, 2) the calculation uses both up and down days, and 3) the scale is confined between -100 and +100.

The CMO, as it is sometimes called, is interpreted in a similar way to other oscillators. Chart 26-1 compares the CMO with a 20-day RSI and a 20-day ROC. The 20-day period has been selected because it is the default for the CMO. What is striking is that the performance of all three (in terms of the swings) is very similar.

The three-wave advance between October and December 1995 is reflected in all three indicators. The January/February 1995 decline is also apparent.

Chart 26-2 limits the comparison to the RSI. The first thing that becomes apparent is that the RSI is much smoother. The November/December 1995 rally for the RSI is a zigzag ascending affair, but for the CMO, it is more of a spike. The April and June 1996 declines are also represented by spikes in the CMO, but not in the RSI. In fact, it is readily apparent that while the CMO does diverge from the price, the diverging characteristics of the RSI are much stronger in this instance.

Alternately, the CMO lends itself to trendline construction better than the RSI. Look at the rally between October and November 1995 in Chart 26-3. It was possible to construct a good uptrend line for the CMO, but not for the RSI. Similarly, in the March/April 1996 period, it was possible to draw a line only for the CMO. In this particular instance, it was not of much use, since the price had already peaked.

However, the important point is the establishment of the principle that it is easier to construct trendlines for the CMO.

COMPARISON WITH THE ROC

In Chart 26-4 the CMO is compared to the ROC. The individual swings are almost identical. Look at the fall 1995 rally and the February/March 1996 decline contained in the rectangles; the peaks are also very similar.

I have also drawn several trendlines for each indicator in Chart 26-5, and once again they are extremely close. It would be possible to say that the CMO is no better than the ROC. However, there is one very important point that should be taken into consideration and that is that the CMO is constrained by its calculation within the -50 or +50 zone. This means

Chart 26-1   ASA comparing the CMO, RSI, and ROC

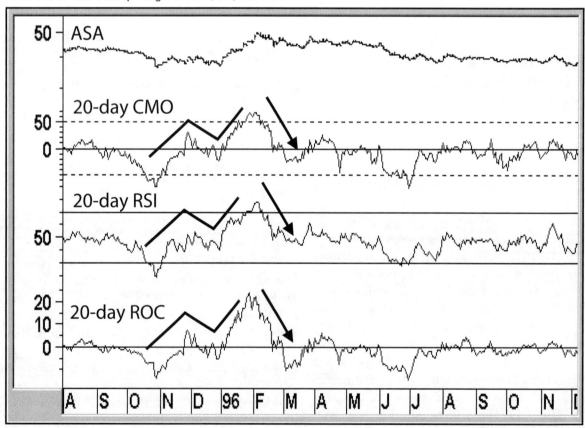

Chart 26-2   ASA comparing the CMO and the RSI

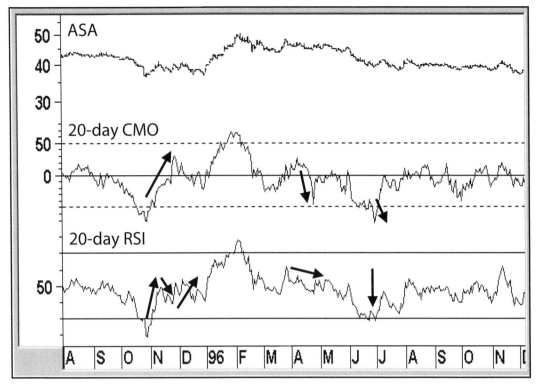

(Source: pring.com)

Chart 26-3   ASA comparing the CMO and the RSI

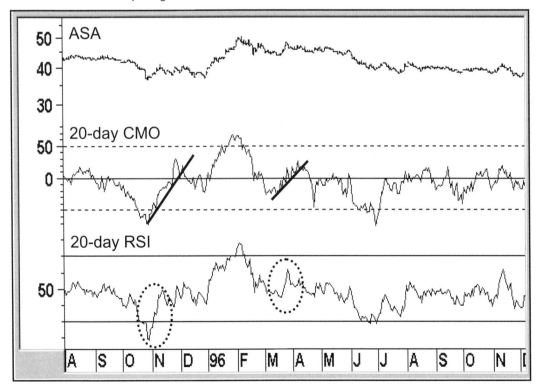

(Source: pring.com)

Chart 26-4   ASA comparing the CMO and the ROC

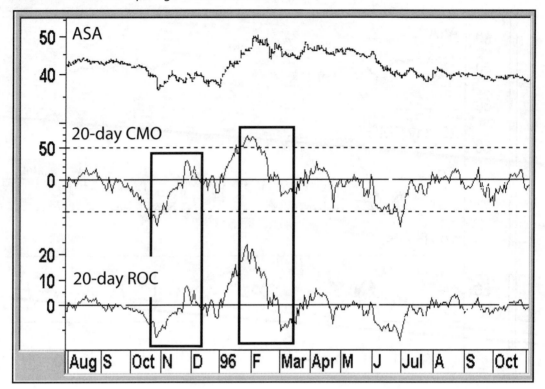

(Source: pring.com)

Chart 26-5   ASA comparing the CMO and the ROC

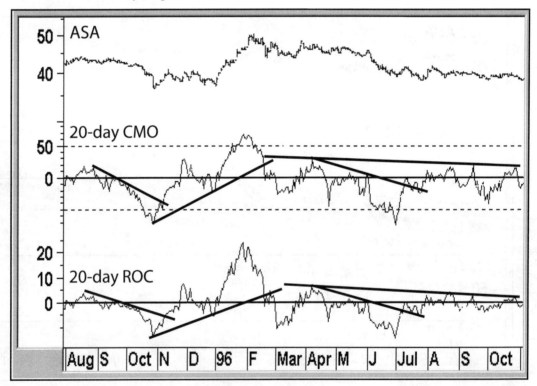

(Source: pring.com)

that it is possible to construct some standard overbought-or-oversold lines, that is, ones adaptable for all securities. This is not possible with the ROC because the volatility factor differs from security to security. With the CMO, it is possible to compare one security with another if the same timeframe is adopted. In other words, compare a 14-day CMO of security A with that of security B. What cannot be done is to compare a 14-day CMO for one security against a 30-day period for another.

For example, Chart 26-6 displays the 20-day ROC of two different securities on the left and the 20-day CMO of the same securities on the right. It is quite clear that while the swings in both oscillators differ from time to time, the scaling is much closer and the comparison much easier to make on the CMO side.

INTERPRETING THE CMO WITH TRENDLINES

One approach that I often use with the ROC indicator is to construct trendlines. When the trendline is violated, I then look around for a trend confirmation from the price itself. In Chart 26-7 several buy signals using this approach with the CMO have been highlighted. In late 1996, the CMO experiences a downtrend break, which is followed a little time later by one in the price. More than one vertical line marks the spot. The July 1996 trend break combination on the right also worked out well. It is also flagged by a vertical line.

I have displayed the February/May 1996 downtrend line as a dashed line because it was only half a signal, since the price of IBM was never able to rally above its downtrend line.

Chart 26-6 Comparing two securities — the CMO versus the ROC

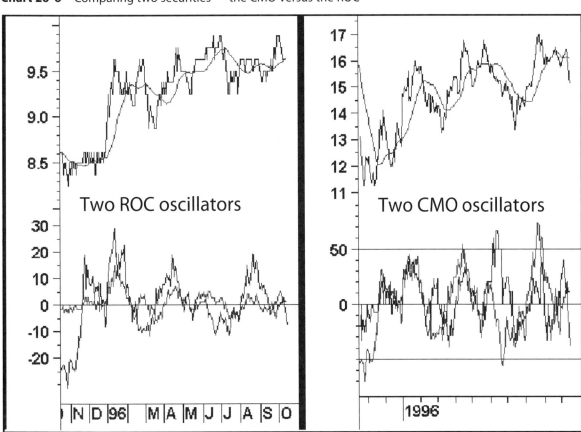

(Source: pring.com)

Chart 26-8 goes through the same exercise but from the point of view of sell signals. This time a 45-day CMO is being used. Note that the oversold line is barely visible. This is because swings in the CMO become less pronounced the longer the time span is used in the calculation. The RSI has exactly the same characteristic. Therefore, it is appropriate to narrow the overbought-or-oversold lines with longer-term time spans. In this case, there are two sell signals. The one on the left, in March 1993, is almost immediately confirmed by the price. Alternately, the one on the right, in February 1994, is not confirmed until just over a month later. At the time of the trendline break in the price, we actually get another trend break in the oscillator. If you look carefully, you will see that this was a breakdown from a head-and-shoulders top. At the time of the break there were several pieces of evidence suggesting that the trend had reversed; that is, the two trendline breaks and the CMO head-and-shoulders completion.

It is important to note that these joint trend breaks do not occur that often. This chart, for instance, covers about two years. Consequently, patience is definitely a requirement in searching out this type of opportunity. Not every trend break results in a worthwhile move, but most generally do. It is best to wait for a fairly lengthy trendline that has been touched or approached on at least three or four occasions, and if a similar setup in the price is observed, it is even better.

SMOOTHING THE CMO

One approach that I have found helpful is to create a custom indicator of the CMO,

Chart 26-7   IBM showing CMO trendline breaks

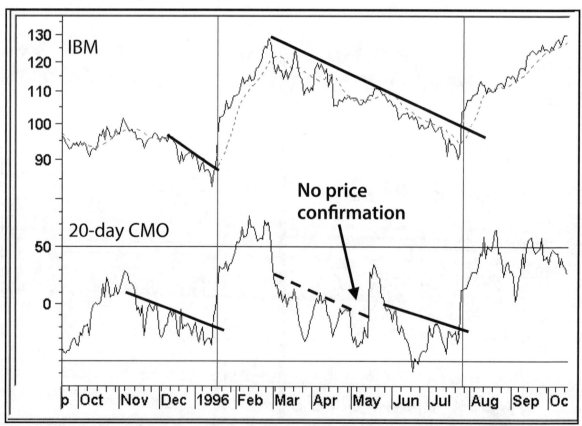

(Source: pring.com)

smoothing, say, a 20-day CMO with a 10-day simple moving average. An example is shown in Chart 26-9. The dashed line plotted against the CMO is a 10-day exponential moving average. EMA crossovers are then used to generate buy or sell alerts. If these signals can be augmented with trend breaks in the price itself, then it makes sense to take some action. Since there are a lot of moving-average crossovers, it is important to filter out those that are not likely to work out. For example, a buy signal that is triggered when the indicator is overbought greatly reduces the odds of success, so do not use them. Generally speaking, though, even when you get broad swings in the oscillator, it is rare that you can rely solely on the EMA crossovers. A more accurate approach is to draw a trendline on the smoothed CMO, just as we did earlier with the CMO, using raw

data. The upside breakout (Chart 26-9) in mid 1994 represented an excellent signal when it was finally confirmed by the price.

In March 1995 we have an EMA crossover from an oversold condition. Then the price breaks a trendline confirming the momentum trend reversal (Chart 26-10). But look at the smoothed CMO; it, too, is violating a downtrend line, thereby offering a third piece of evidence that the trend is reversing. You can see the wisdom of waiting for a price trend reversal from the oscillator EMA crossover in early 1996. At the time, it would have looked pretty impressive, since the CMO has just terminated a long downswing and was extremely oversold. It also broke a downtrend line. However, within a few trading sessions, the price had once again reversed to the downside. It was never possible to construct a meaningful

Chart 26-8   Philippine Fund and CMO trendline breaks

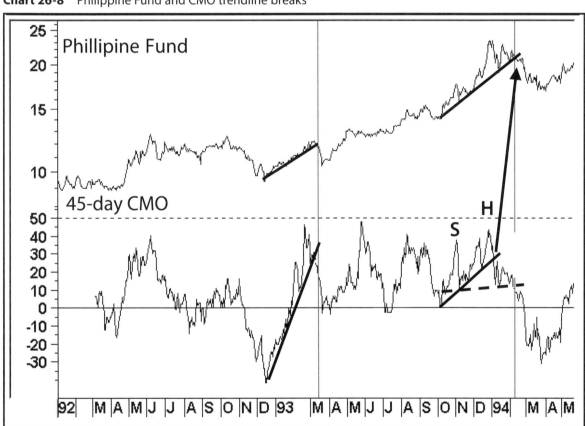

Chart 26-9   Echo Bay and a smoothed CMO

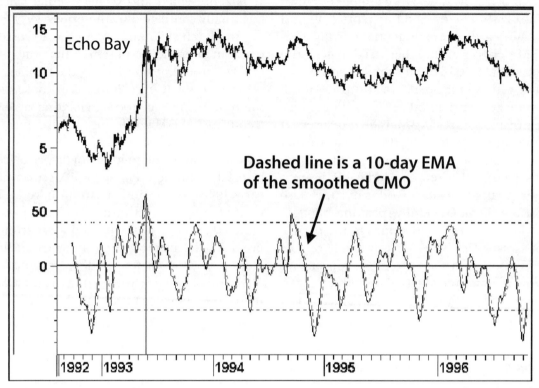

(Source: pring.com)

Chart 26-10   Echo Bay and a smoothed CMO

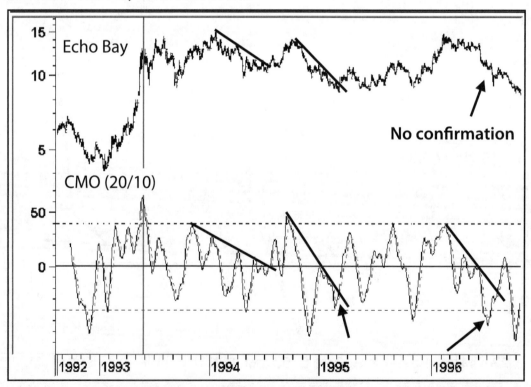

(Source: pring.com)

downtrend line for the price, so in this case there was no double signal.

One final way in which I like to use the CMO is to plot a smoothed CMO above an r-square indicator (Chart 26-11). When the 30-day r-square moves above 0.9 and then starts to reverse, this indicates that the trending factor has begun to dissipate and the random factor increase, causing a possible trend reversal. Reference to the smoothed CMO indicates the direction of the reversal. However, it has to come from an oversold-or-overbought condition. In other words, both the CMO and r-square have to be at an extreme reading before we can have a high degree of confidence that the trend is about to reverse.

In this chart, which covers 4 1/2 years, we do not get many such signals. But when they do appear, they result in some very interesting situations. The buy signal in late 1992 met all the principles I have outlined. However, it cannot be considered successful because the price subsequently made a new low. The sell signal in the spring of 1993 caught the top of the rally, which was pretty close to the final top. The next buy signal in December 1994 was not confirmed by a price trend break. However, that in November 1995 was followed by a very worthwhile rally.

DOUBLE CHANDE

The arrangement in Chart 26-12 features two Chande momentum oscillators, with 14- and 45-day time spans. The objective is to spot

Chart 26-11 Echo Bay, a smoothed CMO, and an r-square

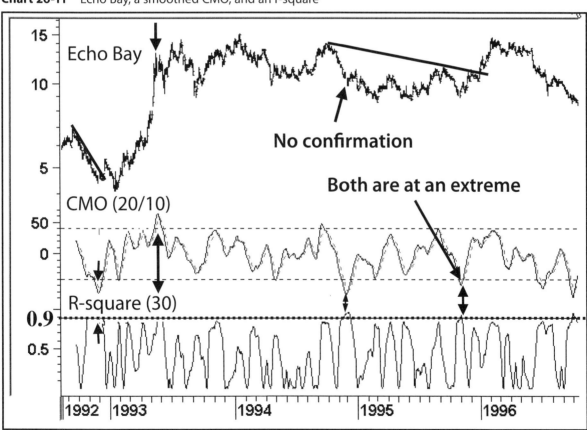

(Source: pring.com)

those periods where both series are overbought or oversold, since this often corresponds with turning points. We see an example of a double overbought by the two arrows in February 1996. There was no possibility to draw a trendline or witness a price pattern completion in this instance, although the price did decline sharply. While the conditions for a short sale did not, therefore, materialize, this kind of joint overbought condition by the two oscillators is certainly a great place to take profits or write options, for while the price may not go down much, it usually experiences at least a small drop or consolidation. This then offers enough time for the option premium burn-off. There is a good example of a joint trend break in July 1996. See how both CMOs and the price violate downtrend lines simultaneously. This

> Both the CMO and r-square have to be at an extreme reading before we can have a high degree of confidence that the trend is about to reverse.

combination does not happen that often, but when it does, it is usually followed by a worthwhile move.

Chart 26-12   IBM comparing two CMOs

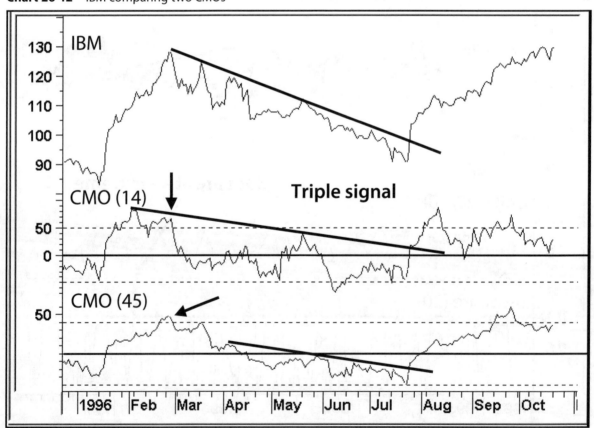

27

The Relative Momentum Index

BASIC CONCEPTS

The *relative momentum index*, or RMI as it is known, is a variation on the RSI. In the calculation of the RMI, the standard formula for the RSI is modified to allow for a momentum factor. This modification has two effects. First, it smoothes the indicator, and second, it accentuates the degree of the fluctuation. The result is a less jagged oscillator that experiences more rhythmic fluctuations. The effect is that more overbought-or-oversold crossovers are generated. The RMI requires two parameters. The first, as with the RSI, is the timeframe. The second is the momentum factor.

Chart 27-1 shows a 20-day RMI and a 20-day RSI. The two are identical, since the RMI contains a momentum factor of 1, which makes it identical to the RSI.

In Chart 27-2, the RMI momentum factor has been changed to 5, which results in a substantial difference. The RMI is far smoother. Note also that the overbought-or-oversold lines

have been drawn at 25 and 75 for both series, but you can see that the RSI reaches the overbought zone on far fewer occasions than the RMI.

Chart 27-3 substitutes a 30-period RMI with a momentum factor of 10 for the RSI. As you can see, this series is even smoother than the 20/5 combination.

Chart 27-4 shows the 30/10 combination on its own. The downward-pointing arrows indicate those points where the RMI crosses below the overbought line on its way toward the neutral 50 level. The upward-pointing ones indicate the opposite set of conditions, where the RMI is crossing above its oversold zone. By and large, these signals provide a timely warning of an impending change in the intermediate-term trend. The chart reveals the fact that this versatile indicator also traces out price patterns, though this is quite rare when the momentum factor is as large as it is in this instance. A head-and-shoulders top is completed in early 1997, just as the bond price starts to break in a major way.

Chart 27-1   Heinz comparing an RMI with an RSI

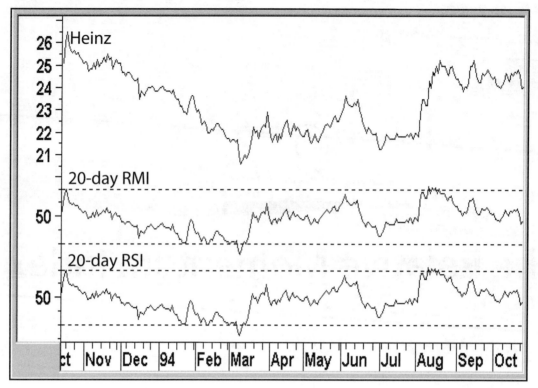

Chart 27-2   Heinz comparing an RMI with an RSI

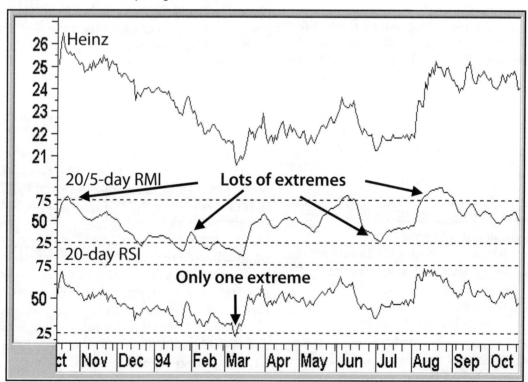

Chart 27-3   Italian Government Bonds two RMIs

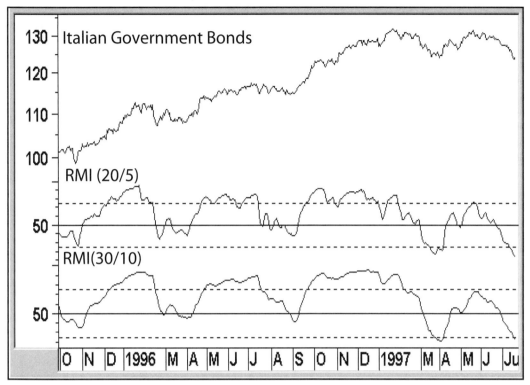

(Source: pring.com)

Chart 27-4   Italian Government Bonds with a 30/10 RMI

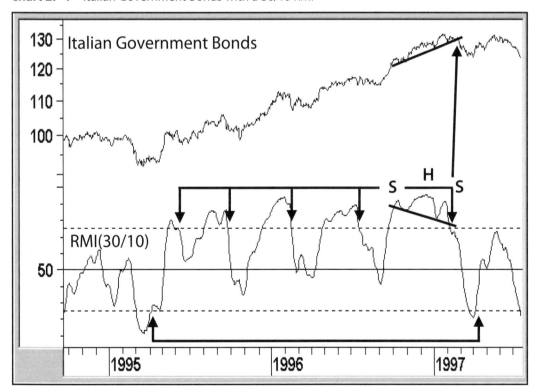

(Source: pring.com)

CHARACTERISTICS IN BULL AND BEAR MARKETS

No momentum indicator, however well-devised, is able to generate timely buy-or-sell alerts in a market undergoing a linear up- or downtrend. The RMI is no exception. In Chart 27-5, we see it with the S & P Composite. Some negative overbought crossovers are followed by a sideways trend, or even a small decline. But for the most part, they offer false signals of implied weakness. This again goes to emphasize the fact that it is of paramount importance for momentum signals to be confirmed by some kind of trend-reversal signal in the price.

Chart 27-6 of the Japanese Topix Index can be roughly divided into two bear and one bull periods. The first bearish environment developed between 1994 and 1995: the bullish

No momentum indicator, however well-devised, is able to generate timely buy-or-sell alerts in a market undergoing a linear up- or downtrend. This is why it is so important to wait for confirmation in price before acting on any signal.

one between mid 1995 and early 1996, and the second bear in early 1997.

Now look at the performance of this 30/10 RMI. During the bear phase, it is rarely able to rise above zero but spends a lot of time in the oversold area. This is indicative of the kind of characteristic we should expect from a momentum indicator in a bear market. Note that none

Chart 27-5 S & P Composite with a 30/10 RMI

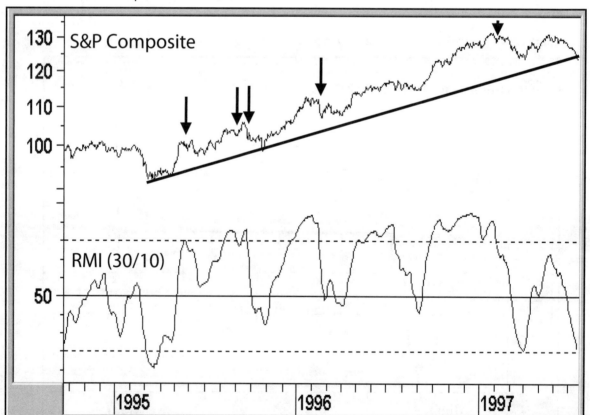

(Source: pring.com)

of the oversold conditions are able to trigger very much in the way of a rally. Then, in mid 1995, the situation changes dramatically, as the indicator moves to an overbought condition. But during the whole rise it is unable to slip back into oversold territory. This is the way we would normally expect a momentum indicator to act during a bull market. In effect, its action is providing us with a vital clue as to whether the Topix is in a primary bull or bear market.

Then, in early August of 1996, the RMI falls back into the oversold zone for the first time in over a year. Not every oversold condition following a long uptrend in the price signals a bear market, but quite often when a short-term momentum indicator reaches an oversold reading that surpasses anything seen in the previous 12 months or so, this increases the odds that a bear trend is underway. In this case, a new primary trend was in force and the

RMI entered a period when it did not experience an overbought reading yet fell into oversold territory three times. Look also at how the price rallies after this second attempt to fall into oversold territory fails. The character of the rally gives us two clues that the bear market is still alive at this point. I am now going to focus on the bear market consolidation contained in the rectangle.

First, the momentum indicator peaks from a fairly low level (Chart 27-7). This failure to reach an overbought condition, especially following the small positive momentum divergence in September 1996, is indicative once again of tired bear market activity. The second clue came from the fact that the price rallied above this trading range and then fell back below it again. False breakouts are unusual and are, again, a characteristic of a negative primary trend.

Chart 27-6 Topix Index with a 30/10 RMI

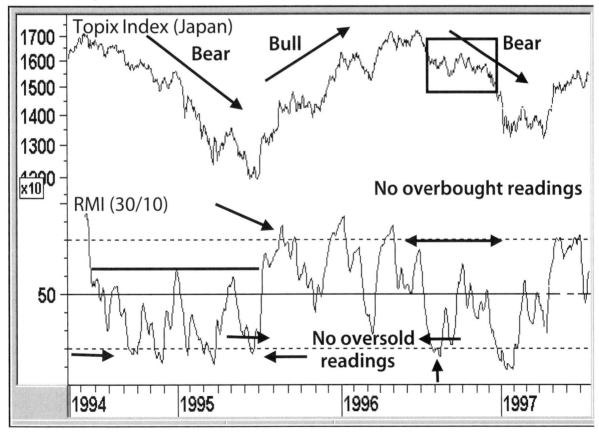

RMI AND TRENDLINE CONSTRUCTION

Chart 27-8 shows us how the RMI occasionally lends itself to trendline construction and analysis. See how it was possible to construct a good downtrend line for the RMI. Just shortly after its penetration, the price experiences a double trendline violation. Not surprisingly, a very nice rally followed.

THE RMI VERSUS THE RSI

Chart 27-9 compares the performance of a simple 30-day RSI with that of an RMI with a 10-day momentum factor. First of all, the overbought-or-oversold zones are set at different parameters. The RSI is at a fairly narrow 65/35, whereas the RMI is at 75/25. The action

of the RMI is much smoother and gives clearer signals. For instance, the arrows point out those periods in 1996 when the RMI falls to its oversold zone and then crosses the dashed horizontal line on its way back to the equilibrium point. Given the neutral/bearish environment, these are reasonably good signals. However, the RSI, despite the narrower bands, does not reach the oversold zone on any of these occasions and is, therefore, relatively useless from the point of view of offering a momentum buy signal. Even if I had narrowed the overbought-or-oversold zones still further, the jagged price action of the RSI would still have been less decisive as a signal generator than the RMI.

A second point comes from the fact that the reverse head and shoulders for the RMI was much easier to spot than that for the RSI at the end of 1995. Alternately, the trendline

Chart 27-7   Topix Index with a 30/10 RMI

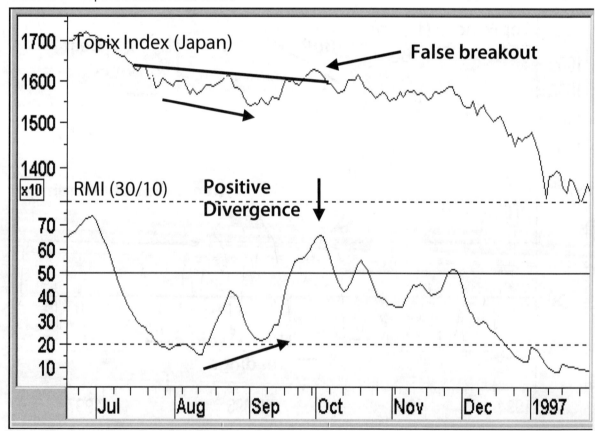

(Source: pring.com)

Chart 27-8   Topix Index with a 30/10 RMI

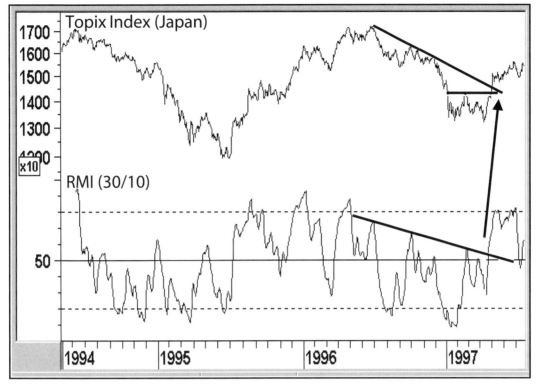

(Source: pring.com)

Chart 27-9   TVX Gold with an RMI and an RSI

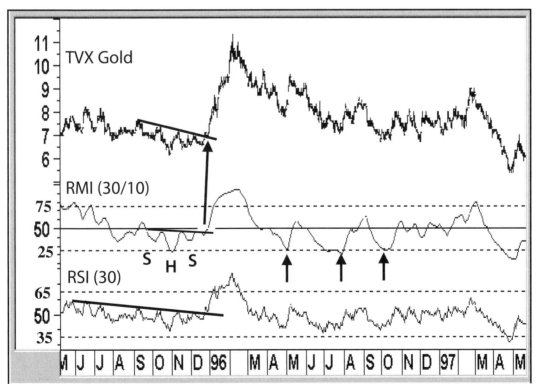

(Source: pring.com)

for the RSI was certainly a lot longer. This underpins the point that it is often a good idea to compare two or more indicators on the same chart, thereby letting one reinforce the other. One advantage that an RMI with a relatively large momentum quotient appears to have over the RSI is that the smoothed nature of the index is less prone to whipsaws. Yet the time-lines of buy-or-sell momentum signals are not unduly affected. Look at the RSI in January of 1996 (Chart 27-10). See how it moves down below its overbought zone and then quickly rallies back above it, resulting in a false signal. Alternately, the 30/10 RMI gives no hint whatsoever of a decline and goes on to smoothly roll over and cross its overbought zone at roughly the same time as the RSI.

On the right-hand part of the chart, we see a good example of a momentum breakout from an overextended level. Normally, this kind of thing does not work, since a momentum breakout that develops close to an overbought zone indicates that the price is already overextended by the time the breakout takes place. This example was no exception, as Chart 27-11 shows the price experienced a false breakout.

RMI VARIATIONS AND ARRANGEMENTS

The RMI lends itself nicely to short-term trends when used with a smaller time span. Chart 27-12 features an RMI with a 10-period time span and a 5-period momentum factor. As the time span is shifted to a smaller number of periods, so the indicator becomes increasingly volatile. As a result, it is less suitable for

Chart 27-10   TVX Gold with an RMI and an RSI

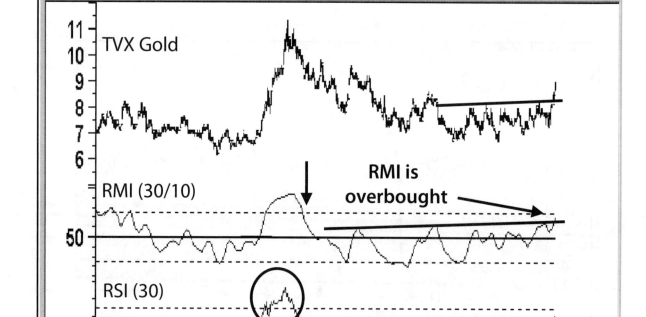

(Source: pring.com)

Chart 27-11 TVX Gold with an RMI and an RSI

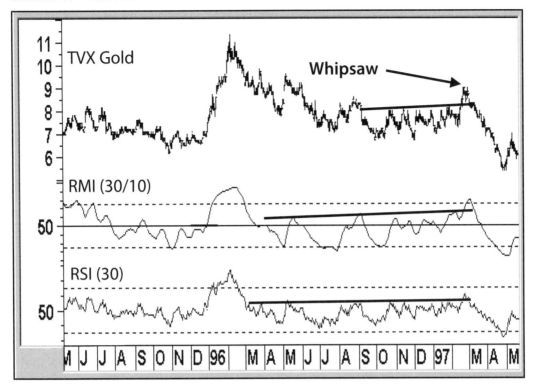

Chart 27-12 Homestake and two RMIs

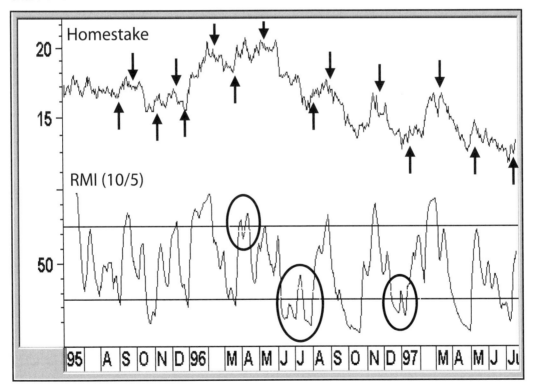

Chart 27-13   Homestake and two RMIs

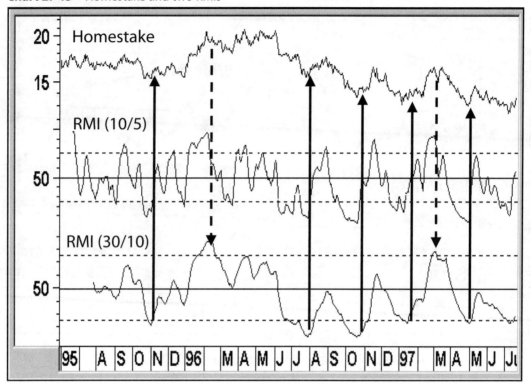

Chart 27-14   Homestake and two RMIs

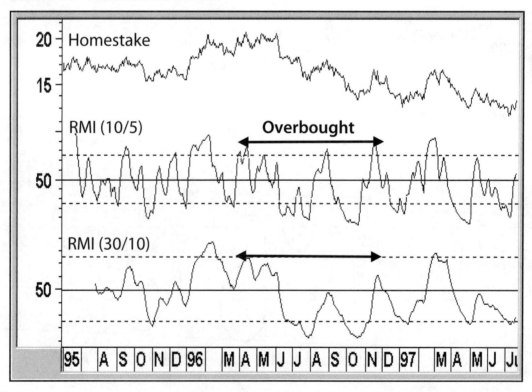

the construction of trendlines or the formation of price patterns. However, this disadvantage is partly offset by the fact that the movements between overbought-or-oversold zones become far more pronounced. The upward- and downward-pointing arrows indicate those periods when the RMI reaches an extreme and then turns back toward the equilibrium level. By and large, these signals are fairly good. However, the arrows were placed with the benefit of hindsight. In the three cases flagged by the ellipses, the RMI would have left us in doubt on a real-time basis, since it whipped above and below the overbought-or-oversold line on several occasions.

One solution for this problem is to plot an RMI with a longer time span and momentum factor on the same chart. In this way, it's possible to get a better perspective of what is really going on (Chart 27-13). The longer-term RMI

is much smoother in nature. As a result, it is possible to use a more conservative interpretation by waiting for the smoothed RMI to reverse direction before taking any action. In most cases, this will delay the signal by a few sessions but will not substantially affect the result adversely.

You can also see that the short-term RMI in the center area is not very helpful from the point of view of interpreting whether the current primary trend is bullish or bearish (Chart 27-14). Note how the lower series fails to reach an overbought reading in the March/December period in 1996, yet its short-term counterpart

> The RMI lends itself nicely to short-term trends when used with a smaller time span.

Chart 27-15   Merrill Lynch and two RMIs

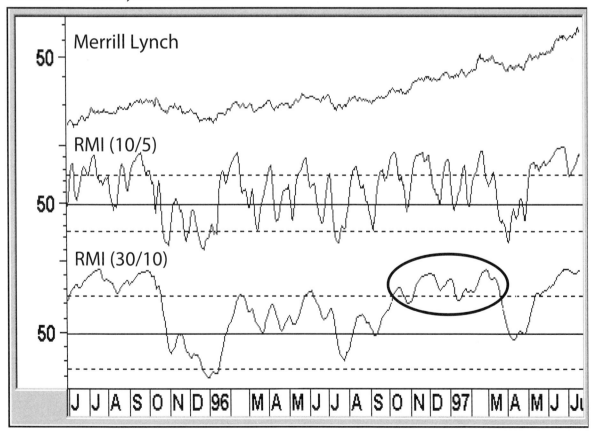

(Source: pring.com)

did. This is because the RMI is calculated from a short time span, and with a small momentum factor, it has a tendency to move to an extreme on virtually every move. Consequently, they are of little help in trying to characterize whether a market is in a bull or bear primary trend.

We have to remember, though, that in a linear trend such as this one, no momentum overbought/oversold system will work. Look at the longer-term RMI contained in the ellipse in Chart 27-15. There are numerous changes in direction that would have given a false signal of extended weakness during this period.

SUMMARY

The RMI:

1. Is a modification of the RSI indicator.

2. Has a tendency to exaggerate oscillations and generate overbought-or-oversold signals more often than other indicators.

3. Becomes smoother when the momentum and time factors are increased. In this format, it lends itself to trendline construction.

28

The Dynamic Momentum Index

THE DMI VERSUS THE RSI

The *dynamic momentum index*, or DMI, is a variation on the RSI index. The principle difference is that the period of calculation is fixed with the RSI, but in the case of the DMI, it is not. This is because the DMI controls the periods in the calculation based on the volatility of recent price changes. Consequently, during quiet trading periods, the DMI will use a smaller time span in the calculation than when things are more volatile. The index can use as many as 30, and as little as 3, periods.

For those who are mathematically inclined, the DMI is based on a calculation that uses a 5-period standard deviation and a 10-period average standard deviation.

The index is justified on the grounds that the variable time lengths enhance short-term movements that are often obscured by the regular RSI calculation. This enables it to turn faster than the regular RSI. Both indicators have been plotted in Chart 28-1. There is no question that

the DMI is more volatile and turns ahead of the RSI. However, if you look very carefully, you will find that there is very little difference between the two, as each little rally and reaction in the RSI is reflected in the DMI.

The big difference is in the volatility. In Chart 28-2 the DMI has been overlaid on the RSI. The DMI is the dashed line. There is no doubt that the DMI reaches an overbought-or-oversold reading ahead of the RSI. It also touches extreme levels when the RSI does not, as in December 1983 and again in May 1984. Indeed, the DMI warns us of a possible trend reversal when the RSI does not. This leads us to arguably the best occasion for this index, and that is when it diverges with the RSI.

Chart 28-3 features the same two indicators, but this time I have introduced some additional overbought-or-oversold lines at 80 and 20. These are for the more volatile DMI. Now you can see the DMI cross the 80 level in May 1984 and then reverse direction. But the RSI fails to reach its overbought zone, and a divergence is set up.

Chart 28-1   Dow Jones Bond Index comparing an RSI with a DMI

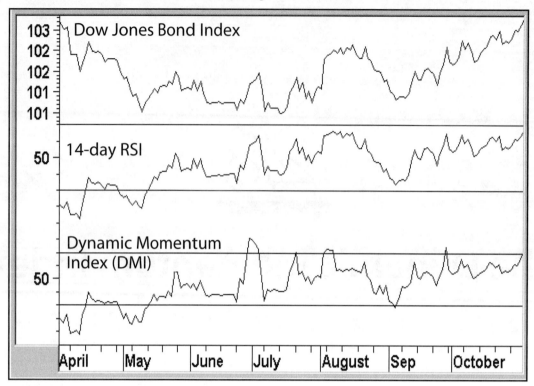

(Source: pring.com)

Chart 28-2   Dow Jones Transports comparing an RSI with a DMI

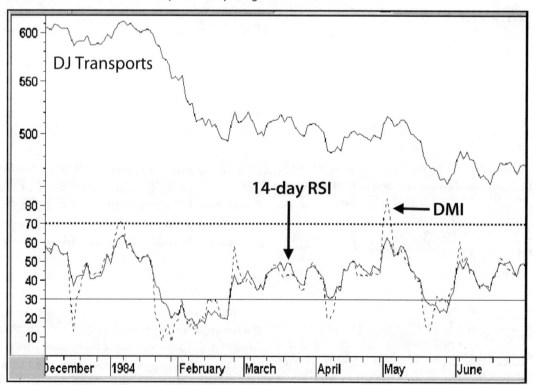

(Source: pring.com)

Chart 28-3 Dow Jones Transports RSI/DMI divergences

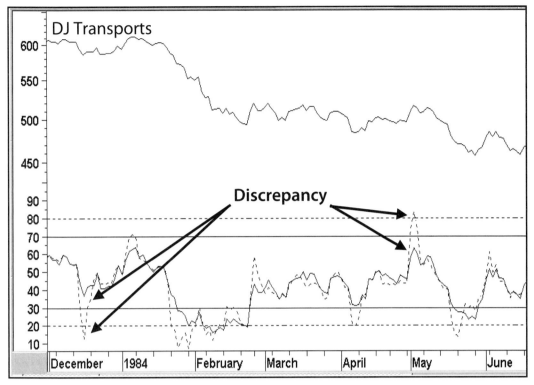

(Source: pring.com)

Chart 28-4 Dow Jones Transports RSI/DMI divergences

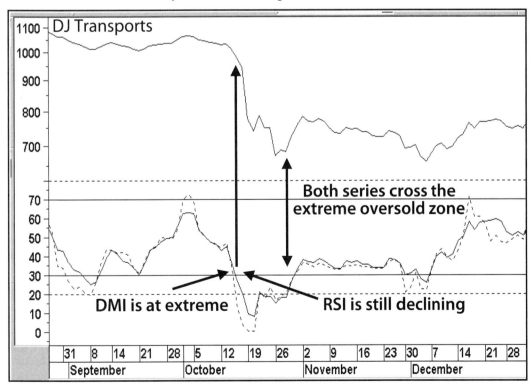

(Source: pring.com)

Another example develops in December 1983, where the dashed DMI crosses below its extreme, yet the RSI fails to make the 30 oversold level.

There is one important caveat: you must make sure that both the RSI and the DMI reverse direction. This is usually not a problem for the sensitive DMI, but for the slower-moving RSI, it can be critical. For example, in October 1987 (Chart 28-4) we see the DMI for the Dow Jones Transportation Index at an extreme, yet the RSI is right at its oversold zone. This is clearly an example of when it would have paid to wait for the RSI to reverse, since the price still had some way to decline before hitting bottom. Eventually, the RSI joined the DMI in oversold territory, so there was no divergence at all. In this particular instance, the DMI was not telling us anything we did not already know from an examination

of the RSI or any other short-term index: that the transports were deeply oversold. This approach works well most of the time. But as with all signals, it is important to check out the situation with other indicators to make sure that they agree.

THE CLUSTER RULE

There is another way in which I like to use the DMI, and that is with the cluster rule. The cluster rule states that if, after an advance or decline, the DMI makes three peaks or troughs above the extreme overbought level or below the oversold zone within a period of roughly 90 days, then a reversal of the prevailing trend is expected. A peak is defined as a rally that takes the index above 80, where this is followed by a reaction below the extreme level, as shown

Chart 28-5   Dow Jones Transports and a DMI

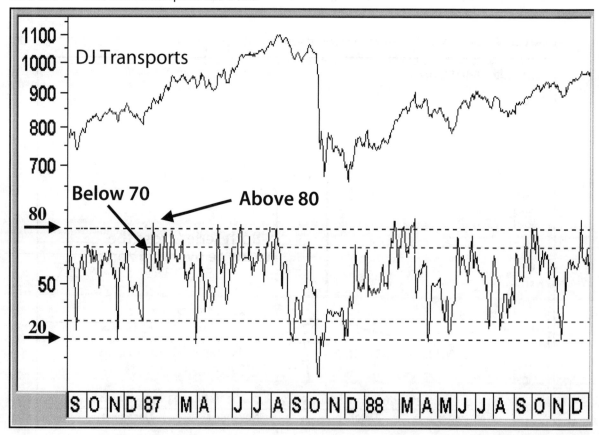

in Chart 28-5. Then, when the index rises above the 80 zone again, a new peak is formed. However, one or more of the two reactions must push the indicator below the normal overbought parameter at 70. In effect, the second and third peaks will be separated by two valleys, at least one of which will find its bottom somewhere below the regular overbought zone. The condition for a bottom will be exactly the reverse.

Chart 28-6 shows a far longer period, and you can see several instances that have been highlighted with the boxes. Each was followed by an important advance, decline, or consolidation. Now let us take a closer look at one such situation.

Chart 28-7 focuses on the period contained in the large box in the 1992 to 1993 period. The three peaks in January, February, and April 1993 are flagged by the downward-pointing arrows. Each one is separated by a reaction, where the DMI registers a low below the regular overbought condition. These are flagged by the upward-pointing arrows. Then, when the third peak crosses below the extreme zone, the indicator triggers a three-cluster sell signal. You can

> The cluster rule states that if, after an advance or decline, the DMI makes three peaks or troughs above the extreme overbought level or below the oversold zone within a period of roughly 90 days, then a reversal of the prevailing trend is expected.

Chart 28-6 Dow Jones Transports and the three-cluster rule

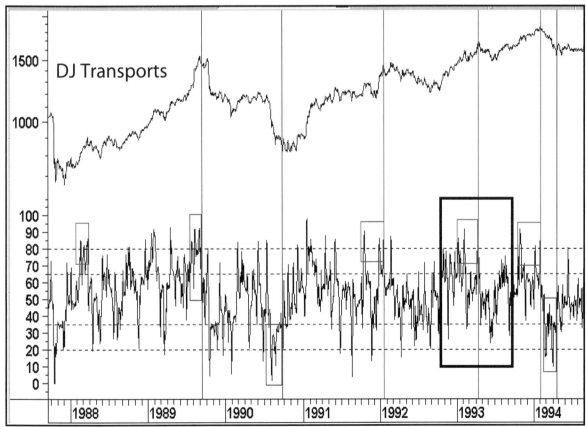

(Source: pring.com)

Chart 28-7 Dow Jones Transports and the three-cluster rule

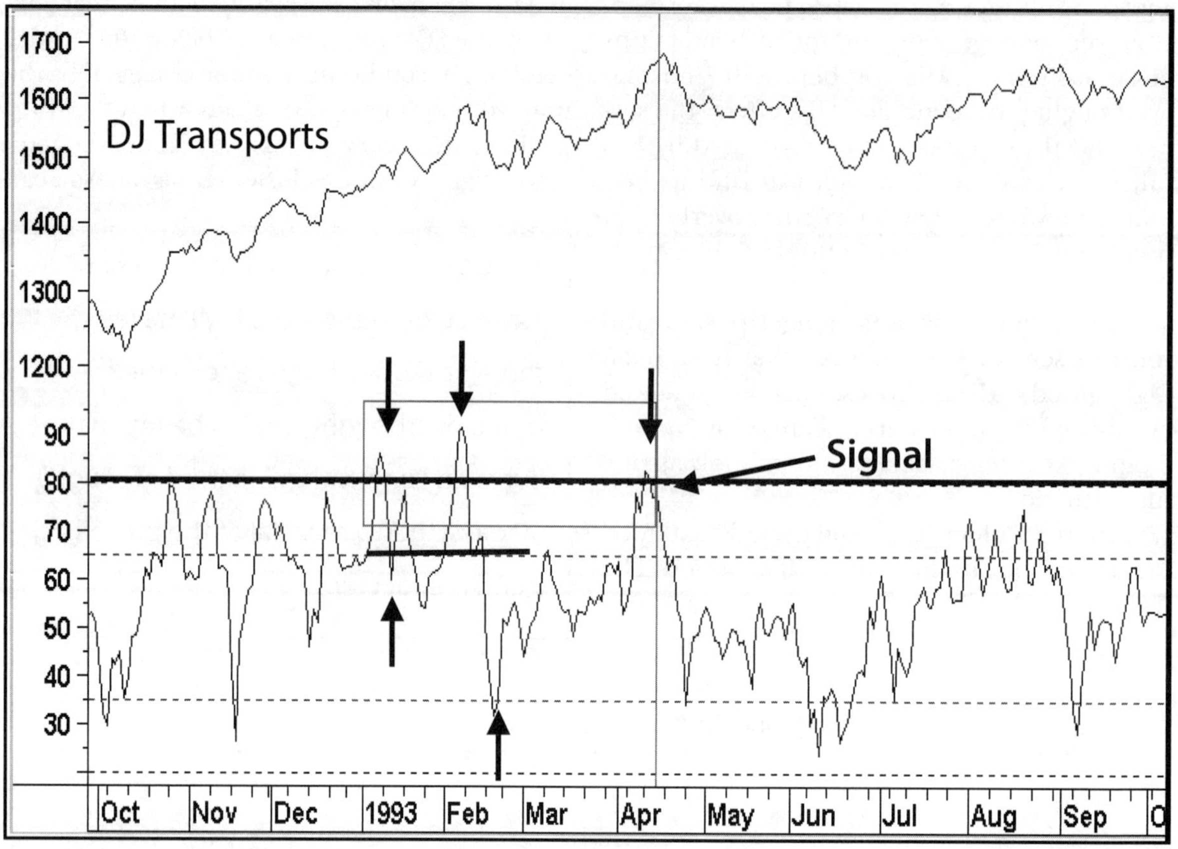

(Source: pring.com)

see that the first and third peaks are separated by just a little over 3 months. I do not like to see a separation greater than 3 1/2 months as a general rule. The idea behind the 3-months-or-less rule is that after a rally, three overbought extremes within a 90-day period indicate exhaustion. If the peaks are separated by 5 or 6 months, this means that the price trend has had time to take a rest and recuperate. Consequently, there will be less chance of a reaction. The opposite set of principles applies to a reversal from a downtrend to an uptrend.

If you look at the July to August period in Chart 28-8, you may come to the conclusion that this is another cluster sell signal. However, while the DMI does move into overbought territory, it never reaches an extreme position. Therefore, it is not a valid signal.

Chart 28-9 shows buy and sell signals that are very close to each other. In this case, the

sell signal in February 1994 is followed by relatively short-lived decline. The three bottoms in early 1994 are separated by less than 3 months. Both rallies separating the bottoms are halted well above the oversold zone. In this instance, the cluster buy signal was not followed by a rally, but by a 3-month consolidation.

SMOOTHING THE DMI

Another idea is to plot two exponential moving averages and use overbought-or-oversold crossovers as buy-or-sell points. In Chart 28-10, I have plotted an 8-day EMA and a 25-day EMA of the DMI. When the 8-day series moves into the extreme overbought-or-oversold zone, this puts me on the alert that the trend in the price may be about to reverse. As you can see, there are not many instances, but when these

Chart 28-8 Dow Jones Transports and the three-cluster rule

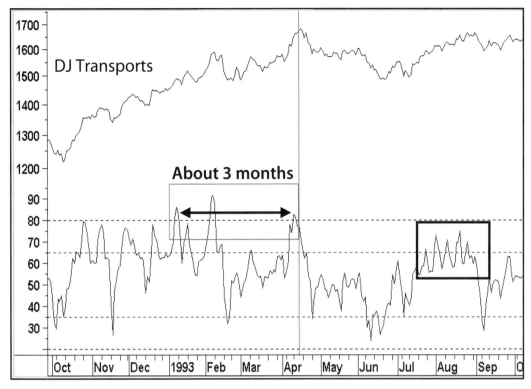

(Source: pring.com)

Chart 28-9 Dow Jones Transports and the three-cluster rule

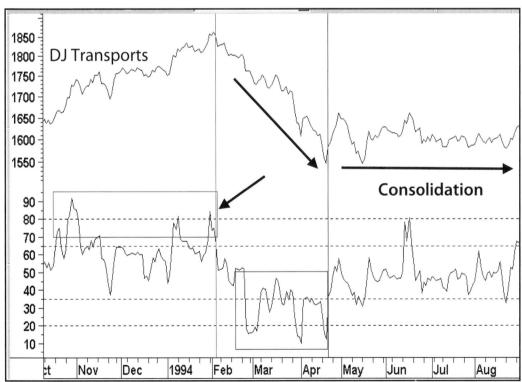

(Source: pring.com)

momentum buy-or-sell signals are triggered, the price itself usually undergoes an important trend reversal. Narrowing the zones a little will increase the number of signals, but some of them are likely to be less reliable. It is really a matter of trial and error with each security to see which might fit the best. Remember to plot as much data as possible in your experimentation, so that your chart encompasses different market situations. The fall 1994 sell signal is a bit of a stretch because the indicator never quite made the overbought level.

In Chart 28-11, the overbought-or-oversold zones are not quite as extreme as the previous ones. They have been narrowed from an 80/20 zone to a 75/25 zone. The reason for this is that we are now dealing with a smoothing of the data rather than the raw series itself. The technique is to wait for the 8-day EMA to move to the extreme zone above 75 or below 25 and

cross the 25-day series. It is the crossing that generates the signal. Examples are flagged with the vertical lines. They are not triggered very often, but when they are, there is a good chance that the prevailing trend is about to reverse. Of course, this is only a momentum sell signal, so then it is necessary to look around to see what price trend-reversal signals may be in the offing. This could be a crossover of a reliable moving average, a trendline break, a price pattern completion, and so forth.

Chart 28-11 shows several years of trading for the ASE Biotech index. There are not many occasions when the 8-day EMA moves into the extreme overbought-or-oversold zone. But nearly all of them trigger some kind of trend change. Chart 28-12 offers a closer look at some of these signals. In January 1994, the 8-day series did not make it to the extreme zone, but the crossover did confirm the second

Chart 28-10   ASE Biotech Index and two smoothed DMIs

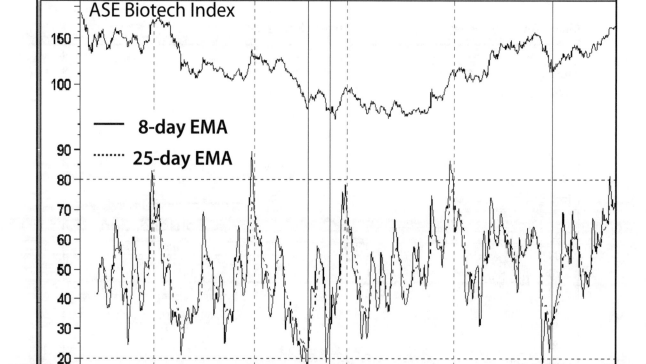

Chart 28-11   ASE Biotech Index and two smoothed DMIs

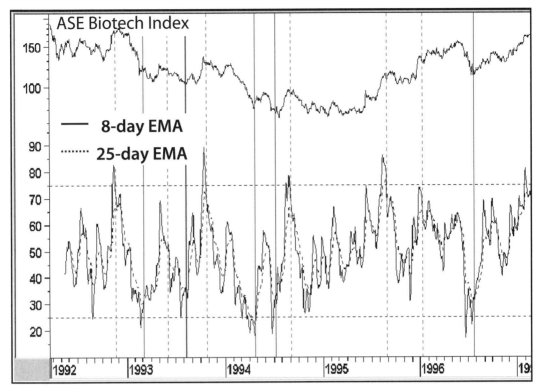

(Source: pring.com)

Chart 28-12   ASE Biotech Index and two smoothed DMIs

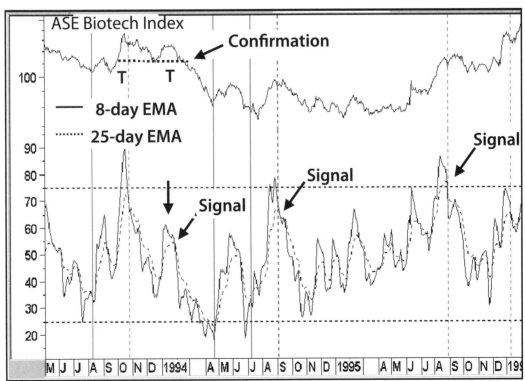

(Source: pring.com)

Chart 28-13   Nolose and two DMIs

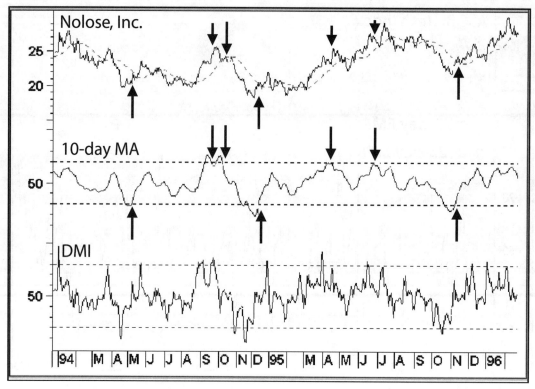

Chart 28-14   Nolose and two DMIs

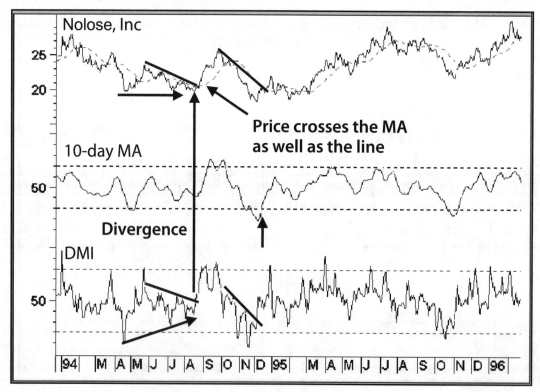

top in a double top formation. The actual momentum signal would have been given at point A, where the solid DMI crossed the dashed one. The signal in August 1994 was followed by a decline. Though there was no way in which a trendline could be constructed for the price, it did experience a small top. The final sell signal on the chart in August 1995 was followed by a 3-month consolidation.

DYNAMIC MOMENTUM INDEX AND 10-DAY MOVING AVERAGE

Chart 28-13 features a dynamic momentum indicator in the bottom area and its 10-day moving average in the center. The DMI itself is useful for flagging overbought-or-oversold conditions. However, the 10-day moving average offers a more stable indication of these extreme reversals, which are indicated in the chart with the upward- and downward-pointing arrows.

The DMI sometimes lends itself to trendline construction. Chart 28-14 shows a couple of examples. The trendline on the left experiences a trend break for both the DMI and the price. Note that it was not confirmed by an oversold reading in the smoothed DMI, but that does not really matter, since this indicator is diverging for a second time in a positive way with the price. Note also that this action was also confirmed by the price crossing its moving average. The second example, in early 1995, was confirmed with a trend break in the DMI and price, as well as a positive crossover of the oversold line by the smoothed DMI.

29

The Klinger Oscillator

BASIC CONCEPTS

The *Klinger oscillator* was developed by Stephen J. Klinger with two objectives. The first is to have an indicator that is sensitive enough to signal short-term price reversals and the second is to reflect the long-term flow of money in and out of a specific security. This oscillator uses both price and volume. The price range is the measure of movement and the volume reflects the force behind the movement. Price is defined as the high minus the low for a specific period. If this number is larger than the previous period, then the formula treats it as accumulation. And if it is lower, the formula treats it as distribution.

Volume is then introduced into the calculation as a positive or negative force, depending on whether the price is classified as being in an accumulation or distribution phase. It is a general technical principle that volume leads price. This means that the Klinger oscillator should peak ahead of price in uptrends and bottom out ahead of prices during downtrends.

The indicator is represented in the chart as the difference between a 39- and 55-period exponential moving average of the resulting volume-price calculation. A trigger line, somewhat along the lines of the MACD trigger line, is also part of the approach.

This indicator seems to have its definite strong and weak points. First of all, the signal line is not of much help. Crossovers by the oscillator are so frequent that many whipsaw signals are generated (Chart 29-1). Zero crossovers by the signal line are also of little help in identifying trend reversals, as can be seen from Chart 29-2 of Coca-Cola around the year's end, 1992.

RELATING KLINGER SIGNALS TO AN 89-PERIOD EMA

It is recommended that the oscillator be compared to the price in relationship to its 89-period EMA. The idea is that when the price is above its 89-period EMA, it is in a bull trend,

Chart 29-1   Coca-Cola and a 13-day Klinger

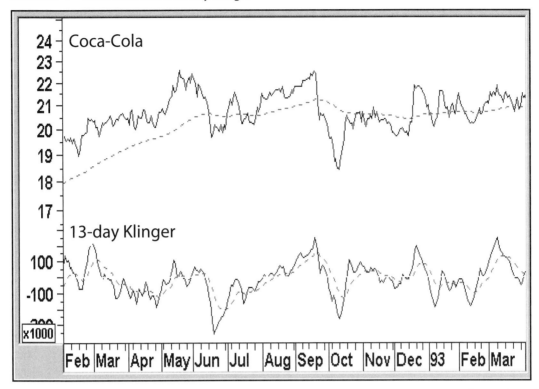

(Source: pring.com)

Chart 29-2   Coca-Cola and 13-day Klinger zero crossovers

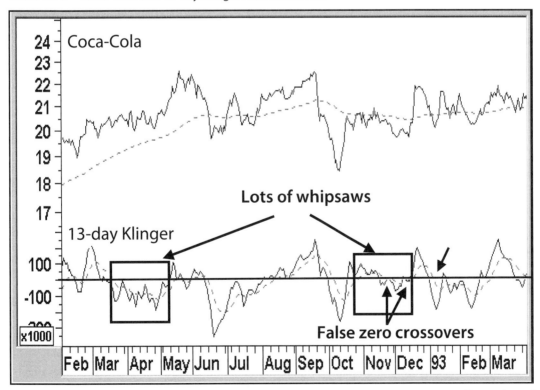

(Source: pring.com)

and when it is below, this indicates that the trend is down. One interpretive rule states that when the price is above its EMA and the Klinger oscillator falls to an unusually low level, this is a buying opportunity. Chart 29-3 contains an oversold line for the oscillator. The vertical lines indicate where the price is above its EMA and the oscillator falls decisively below the oversold line. They all seem to work quite well, but remember this was a strongly trending market, so they should do so. In effect, what we are saying is buy on a short-term oversold in a bull market, and vice versa. The best situations seem to occur when the price experiences a decline that takes it close to the EMA, but not through it. Of course, you do not know at the time that the decline will halt at the average, but that is where the extreme reading in the Klinger oscillator comes in.

Chart 29-4 focuses on the two signals contained in the rectangle in Chart 29-3. The first one in late May turns out to be okay, but only

after a little decline takes place. Then in September, the price declines close to the EMA and the oscillator moves well into extreme oversold territory and actually rises, as the price touches its EMA. A good rally follows. This is an interesting approach, but by and large, I do not find it to be any better than a lot of other indicators. The choice of 89 periods for the EMA is interesting, though I have never found the period to test particularly well. Innovative readers might wish to experiment with other timeframes, such as a 200-day MA, for the purposes of defining the long-term trend.

DIVERGENCES

The strongest point I can find in favor of the oscillator is its ability to diverge from the price during both uptrends and downtrends. Chart 29-5 shows an example using Heinz, where a double top formation develops between

Chart 29-3   Coca-Cola relating Klinger signals to an 89-day EMA

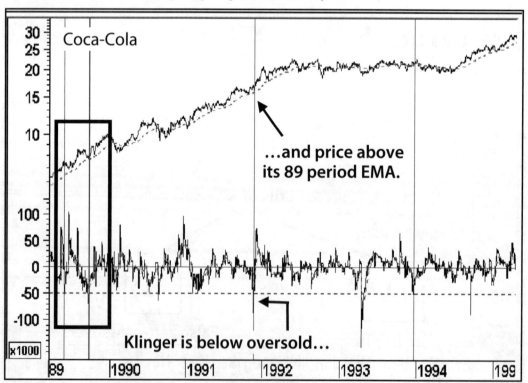

(Source: pring.com)

December 1992 and March 1993. It is fairly evident that the second top is accompanied by a very weak reading in the oscillator. This warned of potential underlying technical weakness, and sure enough, the price did decline quite sharply. Note that up to the time of the first top, the indicator was in gear, because it makes a series of ascending peaks. Only later did it diverge in a serious way.

One final idea is to construct a 10-day EMA of the Klinger oscillator and observe at what point it becomes overbought. In Chart 29-6, you can see that the smoothed oscillator rallies up to the overbought zone on three occasions. The first one developed during an extremely powerful advance in early 1993. Consequently, the overbought reading was not followed by a significant decline but by something more resembling a short-term consolidation. A more typical reaction developed after the second signal in mid-1994, which marked the top of a rally. The third overbought smoothed Klinger

was also associated with a peak. You can also use this smoothed version to time reactions in uptrends. Quite often you will find that the smoothed Klinger will decline sharply in countercyclical bull market reactions, as volume literally dries up. An example developed in November 1993 and another one in April 1995. When the indictor declines sharply like this, look for a reversal in direction and to some short-term indicators for a better sense of timing.

> The strongest point I can find in favor of the Klinger oscillator is its ability to diverge from the price during both up-trends and downtrends.

Chart 29-4   Coca-Cola relating Klinger signals to an 89-day EMA

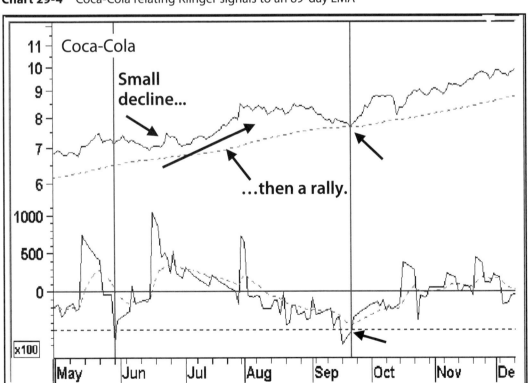

(Source: pring.com)

Chart 29-5   Heinz relating and a 10-day Klinger

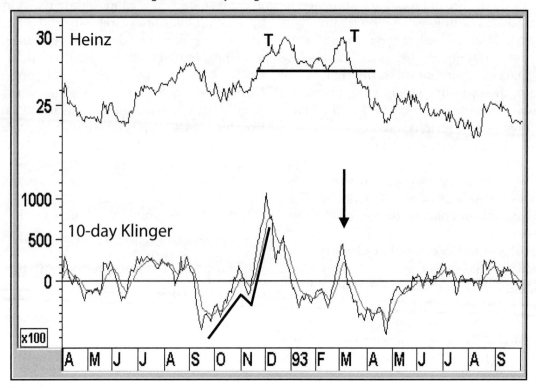

Chart 29-6   American Barrick and a 10-day EMA Klinger

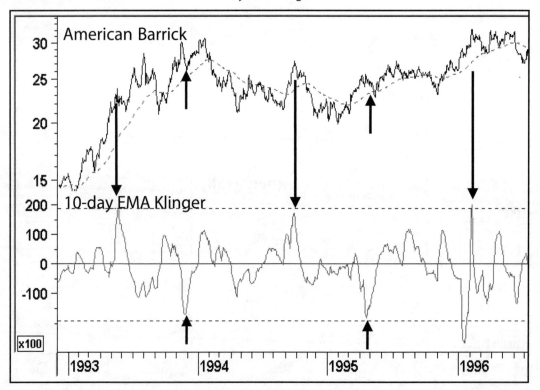

30

The Herrick Payoff Index

THE CONCEPT

The *Herrick payoff index* tries to measure money flowing into, and out of, a security. It does this by incorporating open interest into the formula by calculating the difference between the current period (usually a day) to the previous period's open interest. The formula is as follows.

$$HPI = (Ky + (K1 - Ky)S/100{,}000$$

Ky is yesterday's HPI, S is the user-entered smoothing factor (0.1 is the default), y is yesterday's value, and K1 (wait for it) is $CV(M - My)[1 \pm 2I/g]$.

In this case, M represents the mean and is calculated as half the value of the high plus the low. C is the value of a 1c move, V is the volume, and I is the absolute value of today's open interest.

The plus sign in the right-hand part of the formula occurs if M is greater than My (yesterday's mean). It would be a minus sign if yesterday's mean was below today's mean, that is, My < M.

Since the formula incorporates open interest, *this indicator can only be applied to the futures markets where open interest data are available.*

There are two variables that can be set by the user. The first is an exponential smoothing factor. As you might expect, the greater the smoothing factor, the smoother the oscillator. Chart 30-1 features a payoff index with a 2-day smoothing in the middle area and a 75-day smoothing in the lower one. As you can see, there is a tremendous difference in the volatility of the two series. The second user-determined variable is the value of a 1c move for the futures contract being monitored (for example, $400 for cattle, $50 for soybeans, and so on). This does not affect the shape of the index and has no bearing on the signals and interpretation.

339

One problem in the calculation of the index results from the fact that most data services only provide data for the total volume and open interest on all contracts. This causes a predicament for many agricultural commodities, where for seasonal reasons, price movements in the nearby contracts can differ considerably from more distant ones. This dilemma is not so acute for financial futures, because their price movements are more interrelated between the various contract months, generally fluctuating due to changes in interest rate differentials. Where commodities are subject to such seasonal differences, a single contract system is recommended. In other words, use the volume and open interest pertaining to that specific contract.

This can be quite an onerous task unless the data can be conveniently downloaded electronically from a data vendor. If that is not possible, it is probably better to limit payoff analysis to financial futures and other markets not seriously affected by seasonal variations. Except when it comes close to expiration, the nearby contract typically attracts the majority of the trading volume. For most futures contracts where there is little or no seasonal variation, a 3-month perpetual contact will provide a satisfactory compromise. The perpetual contract is a continuous contract with a theoretical

> If data cannot be conveniently downloaded electronically, it is probably better to limit payoff analysis to financial futures and other markets not seriously affected by seasonal variations.

Chart 30-1   London Copper and two Herrick payoff indexes

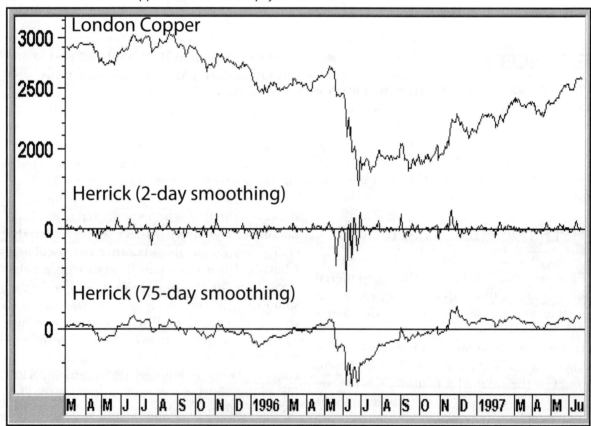

(Source: pring.com)

life for a specific period, say, 3, 6, or 9 months, with a theoretical life of 3 months. Carrying costs and other differentials are calculated with reference to more distant contract months. It offers the best compromise of obtaining a continuous series for contracts that would otherwise expire every 3 months. Data for these contracts are provided by CSI Data of Boca Raton, Florida (csidata.com).

Finally, one should always be on the lookout for contracts that often undergo a sharp reduction in open interest purely because of quarterly contract expiration. An example is shown in Chart 30-2, featuring the Euroyen contract. See how the open interest takes a sharp drop every quarter.

INTERPRETATION

Zero Crossovers

The first step is to determine whether the payoff indicator is above or below zero, as this gives a good indication of whether money is flowing into, or out of, the market. Readings above zero indicate that interest is growing, and they are regarded as a positive sign. Readings below zero indicate a contraction of activity, and they are bearish. The choice of time span for the smoothing factor is obviously quite critical; the shorter the span, the greater the number of zero crossovers. In Chart 30-3, featuring Comex Silver, the payoff index is calculated with a 30-day span. The idea is that when the indicator experiences a decisive zero

Chart 30-2 3-month Euroyen and open interest

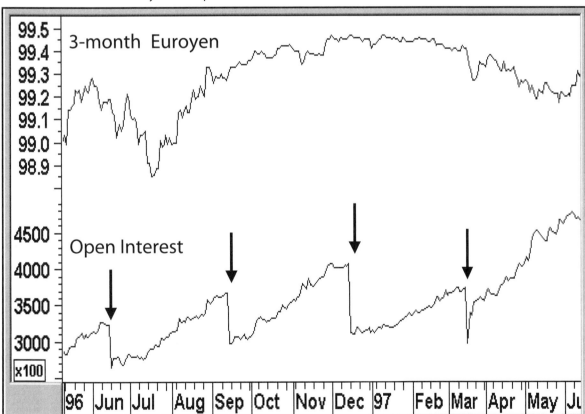

(Source: pring.com)

Chart 30-3   Comex Silver and a Herrick payoff index

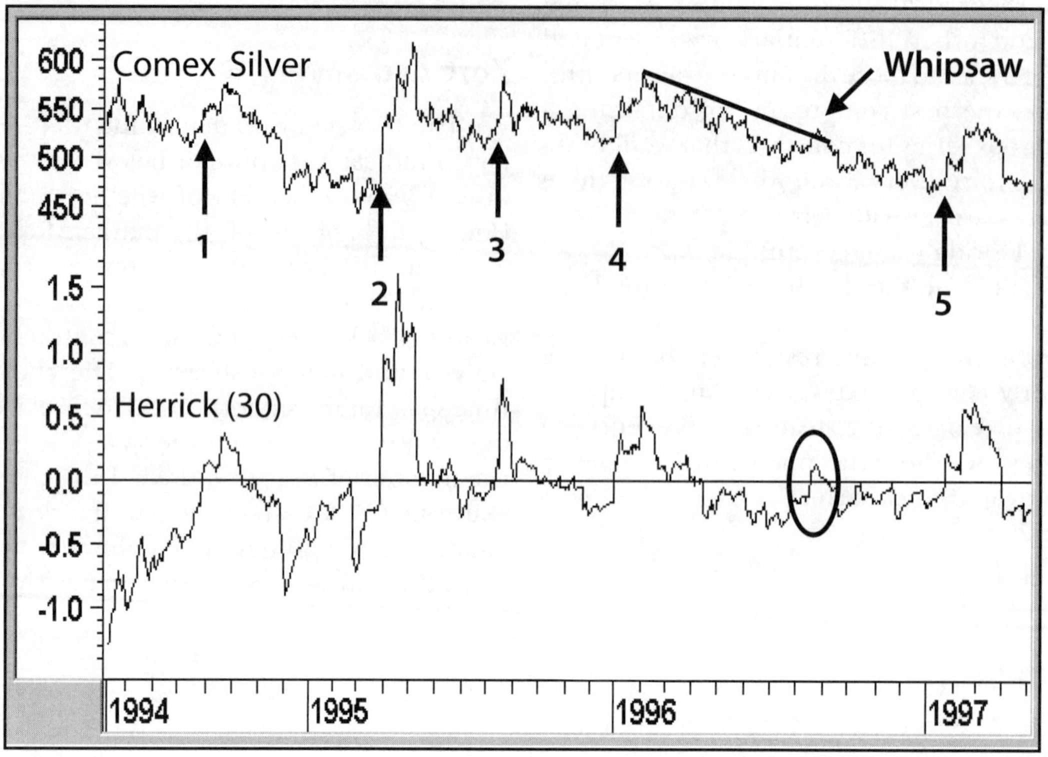

(Source: pring.com)

crossover, this often signals that a new sustainable short or intermediate trend is under way. There are several good buy signals labeled 1 to 5. When I say "decisive," I am just considering those signals that come from below zero and cross it in an almost vertical fashion. In a fast-moving market, it is possible, when the rally turns out to be sub par, for a substantial part of the move to have already been seen by the time it is realized that a sharp zero crossover has been achieved. For this reason, it seems that the best signals come from a situation where the index has been below zero for a while, say, 2 or 3 months.

You may have noticed that the August 1996 crossover has been flagged with an ellipse. This is because it was a failure. See how the signal was given right at the top of a whipsaw downtrend line break.

Generally speaking, decisive zero crossovers tend to give long-term signals relative to the timeframe under consideration. For exam-

ple, if the average short-term rally lasts for 3 weeks and gains 5 percent, a good Herrick zero crossover might be expected to signal, say, a 5-week rally with a gain of 10 percent. Having said that, it is important to analyze each security on its own merit from the point of view of the reliability and timeliness of zero crossovers. If a particular time span or market proves undependable, then disregard or significantly downplay the zero crossover concept. While I regard zero crossovers in many securities to be a useful concept, it should be noted that the innovator of the payoff system, John Herrick, has discounted their importance.

Overbought/Oversold Crossovers

An alternative approach is to construct overbought-or-oversold lines for the payoff index, using those periods when it crosses these extreme levels on its way back to zero as buy-or-sell alerts. Chart 30-4 features Live

Hogs. I have drawn overbought-or-oversold lines at +3 or -3, respectively. This is by no means a perfect approach, but it is amazing how often it warns of probable trend-reversal points. I have labeled all the sell signals, using this method. You can see that most of them came early. The second signal, for instance, was triggered about three-quarters of the way up. After the signal, the price lost a lot of upside momentum, but eventually went on to reach a new high. The third was far too early; the fourth came too far off the top. The fifth and sixth were spot on, and the seventh was early again.

The buy signals in Chart 30-5 (numbered 8 through 12) were far more timely as a group. All of them were triggered fairly close to the lows. Why is this? Well, the answer probably lies in two areas. First, there is a general tendency in markets for prices to appreciate at a slower pace than they retreat. Remember, it takes a lot longer to construct a building than to tear it

down. The same is true of markets. This means that momentum indicators have a greater tendency to lead during uptrends. Second and perhaps more to the point, this chart covers what we might term a bullish period, since the price moves from a November/December 1994 low of about 27c to a 1997 high more than double that amount. As explained previously, short-term indicators in a bull market have a tendency to move to higher levels and stay there longer than in a bear market. Oversold conditions are rarer in a bull market, as prices are much more sensitive to them.

Recognizing this fact, one way to improve the results is to use the Herrick payoff extreme signals as an alert and then use some kind of moving average crossover as an actual sell signal. This is not going to improve every signal, but it will definitely help. Also, you may find that some signals are less profitable because they are delayed too long. What I have done in Chart 30-6 is to display dashed vertical lines

Chart 30-4   Live Hogs and a Herrick payoff index

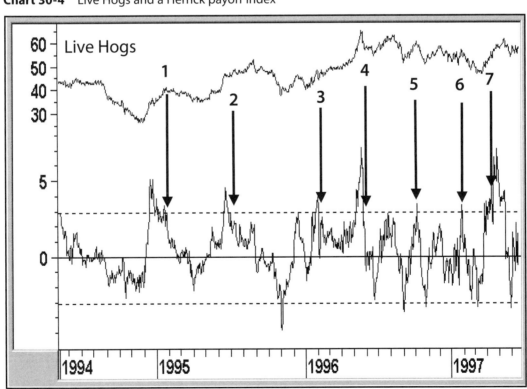

(Source: pring.com)

where the payoff index crosses its overbought line and solid ones where this is later confirmed by an MA crossover in the price. You can see that there is a substantial difference. While the MA crossovers all come after the peaks, they are still sufficiently timely to enable participation in the majority of the up-move that follows the Herrick extreme signal. Where the arrows are close together, the MA filtering approach would not have worked so well. However, in most instances, they are quite far apart, indicating that the filtering approach was more profitable.

Chart 30-7 shows the December 1994 to October 1995 period in greater detail. See how the 12-period payoff index breaks below its overbought zone in January 1995, thereby triggering a premature sell signal. Only in February, a little time after the peak, does the hog price

cross below its moving average. We see a similar set of circumstances later on in the June to August 1995 period.

Trendlines and Divergences

Supplementary analysis should look for positive and negative divergences, as well as trendline violations and price configurations. It is also possible to look for moving-average crossovers. In this respect, a lot will depend on the smoothing factor used in the formula.

As discussed previously, payoff indexes calculated over a longer time span are much smoother and more deliberate than those based on a shorter one. You can see this by comparing the difference in characteristics between the two lower areas in Chart 30-8, where payoff indexes have been plotted using

Chart 30-5   Live Hogs and a Herrick payoff index

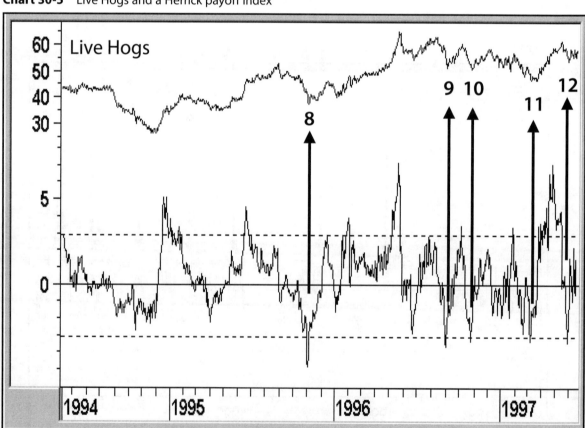

(Source: pring.com)

Chart 30-6 Live Hogs and a Herrick payoff index

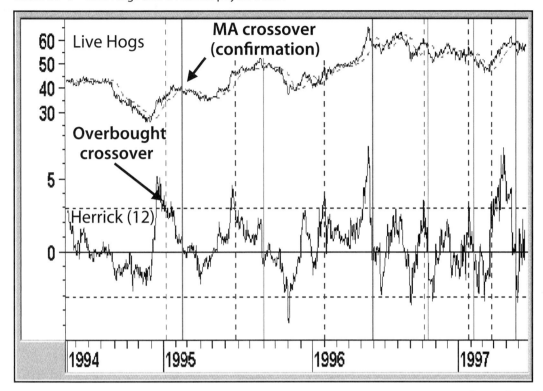

(Source: pring.com)

Chart 30-7 Live Hogs and a Herrick payoff index

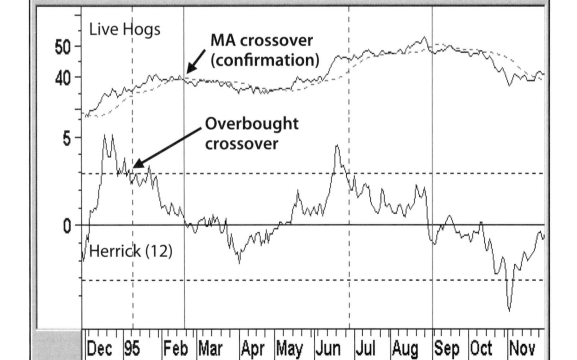

(Source: pring.com)

2- and 10-week smoothings, respectively. See how it was possible to construct a trendline for both the price and the 2-period smoothing in March 1995. It was not possible to do this for the 10-period smoothing at the bottom.

There are a couple of examples of divergences. See how the final March low in the silver price was not confirmed by either of the indexes. Later on, we see a negative divergence, as the February 1996 high was not confirmed by the August 1995 high in either of the indexes. Note also how this rally was signaled by a price and payoff trendline break. The natures of the two payoff trend breaks were different, but the results were still valid.

Extreme Swings

One other important characteristic of the payoff index that appears to be very useful from a short-term trading aspect is the fact that from time to time, the index moves to an extreme, often reversing quite sharply. An

example is shown in Chart 30-9, which features two payoff indexes. See how the 2-day series reaches extreme readings on the upside on three different occasions. The first two reverse simultaneously with the price and the third one is followed by some sideways trading action before the price continues on the last leg of its rally. These are also confirmed by an extreme reading in the 10-day series. The only buy signal on the chart using this approach is triggered in May 1995, but this is not confirmed by the 10-day series.

Chart 30-10 features Euro deutsche marks. The vertical lines indicate when the index reverses from an extreme reading. Solid ones indicate good signals and dashed ones indicate poor or questionable signals. In this case, the reliable ones beat the poor signals on a two-to-one basis. However, it is important to note that this is basically a bull market and that all the bad signals develop on the sell side. This only goes to underscore the importance of making an attempt not only to understand the direc-

Chart 30-8   Comex Silver and two Herrick payoffs indexes

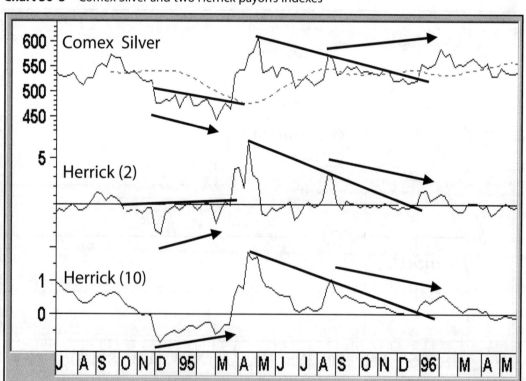

Chart 30-9 German deutsche mark and two Herrick payoff indexes

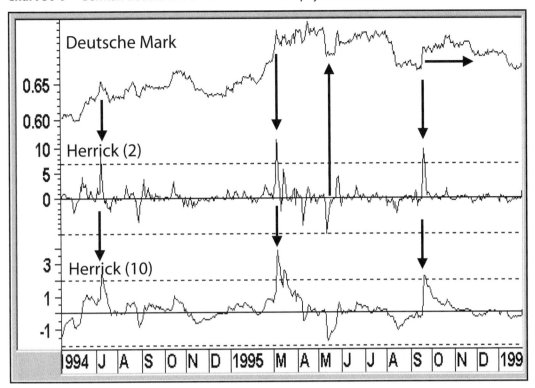

(Source: pring.com)

Chart 30-10 Euro deutsche mark and a Herrick payoff index

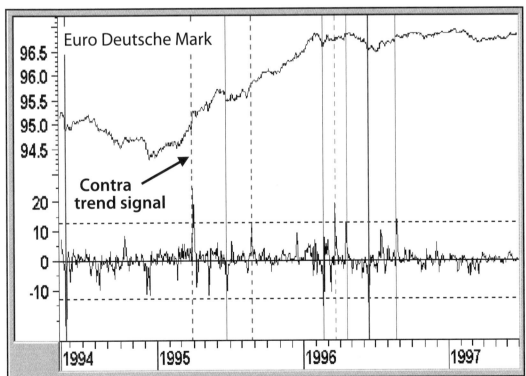

(Source: pring.com)

Chart 30-11   German Bunds and a Herrick payoff index

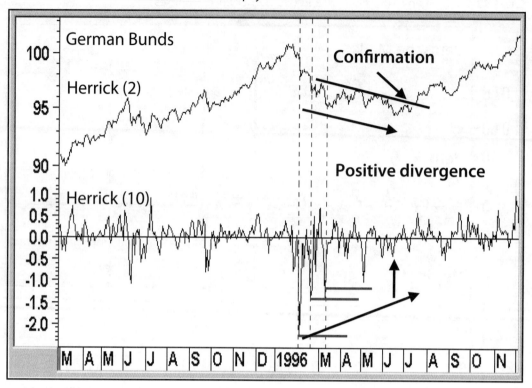

Chart 30-12   Topix Index and two smoothed Herrick payoff indexes

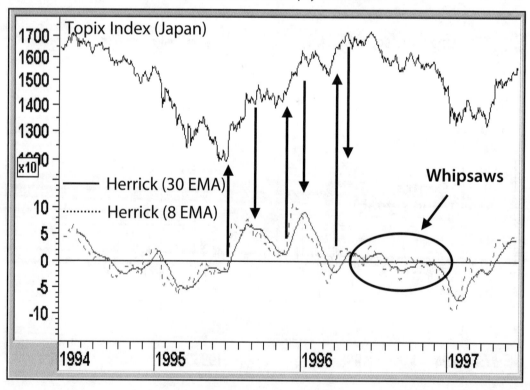

tion of the main trend, but also whether it possesses a lot of momentum. Typically, short-term signals that go against the main or primary trend run a far greater risk of being false.

When a market does not respond to an extreme reading in the way that it should, a strong warning is given that a powerful trend is under way. The false signal in early 1995 is a classic example. The price should have moved down or at least sideways, following this extreme reading. Instead, it just kept on barreling upward, thereby indicating that this was a very strong trend, indeed. Problems with this false signal could have been avoided, had we waited for some kind of confirmation of a trend reversal by the price itself. In this particular case, it was not possible to identify a price pattern, construct a trendline, or even witness a moving-average crossover, so no such confirmation was given.

Chart 30-11 shows an example of an extreme oversold reading in January 1996, following a strong advance. The first thing to note is that this is by far the most extreme oversold in the previous year. In fact, my data go back to 1994, and nothing surpasses this reading on the downside. This clearly indicates a major reversal in sentiment. And under the rules set out in Part I, this characteristic is indicative of a bear market. Consequently, it would be reasonable to expect that any rally developing from this extreme reading would be countercyclical. The odds of a worthwhile move on the upside would, therefore, be relatively low. That certainly turned out to be the case even at the next signal, indicated by the second vertical line. The extreme reading at the third line was also followed by weak action in the form of a trading range. Note how the final low in June was associated with a relatively mild reading in the index, as it diverged positively with the price for the sixth time. Then, when the price violated a nice downtrend line, a buy signal was given.

Moving Averages

The payoff index can also be used with moving averages. Chart 30-12 features a 30-day simple moving average (the solid line) and an 8-day EMA (the dashed line). This combination has not been selected on an optimized basis, so I am sure you could come up with a better combination. However, I am showing it here to indicate that it is possible to use moving-average crossovers as a basis for interpreting the payoff index. The idea is that when the shorter-term average is above the longer one, this represents a bullish environment, and vice versa. This approach certainly worked well for the Topix in the second half of 1995 and the first half of 1996. However, this was a good trending environment, so in the latter half of 1996, this technique was very disappointing. It really does not matter what combination of averages you use. I am sure that a trading-range whipsaw-inspired period such as this will defeat even the most intelligently designed systems. That is why I prefer to study the averages themselves and then use trendline breaks in combination with those of the price to filter out good buy-or-sell signals.

Chart 30-13 also shows some more signals using trendlines as confirmation. This time we are rewarded with a good buy in 1995 and a good sell in late 1996.

Chart 30-14 shows the same period, but this time a false sell signal has been indicated. The two trendlines are perfectly legitimate using the technique that I have described. Why, then, do we get a false signal? First of all, it is important to understand that technical analysis is concerned with probabilities. While the probabilities favor a combination, such as this being followed by a worthwhile trend reversal, they by no means guarantee it. In this particular case, though, you can see that the solid 30-day moving average of the payoff index did not diverge negatively with the price. Since a divergence is the norm, a small clue that the subsequent joint break might fail was given—not a strong discrepancy, but one that definitely lowered the odds of a reliable signal.

Chart 30-13   Topix Index and two smoothed Herrick payoff indexes

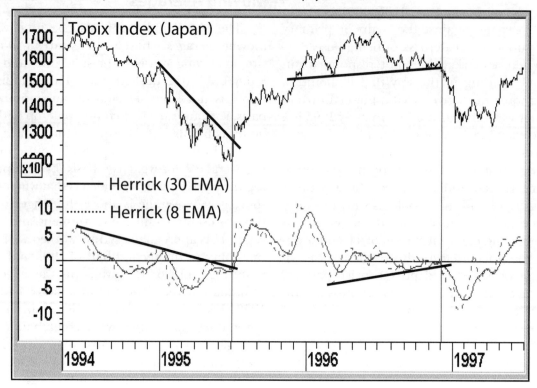

(Source: pring.com)

Chart 30-14   Topix Index and two smoothed Herrick payoff indexes

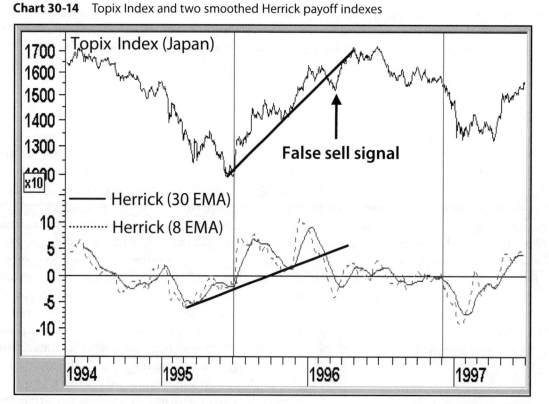

(Source: pring.com)

31

The TRIX Index

THE CALCULATION

The TRIX index is a rate of change of a closing price smoothed by a triple exponentially smoothed moving average. That sounds like a big mouthful, but it is really quite simple. The process merely requires calculating an EMA of a 1-period rate of change, then smoothing the result with another EMA, then a second, and finally smoothing it again with a third EMA. The result is an EMA of an EMA of an EMA.

Chart 31-1 features the price in the top area, along with a 1-day rate of change in the lower one. This thicker line is a 12-day EMA of the ROC. Now, when I extend this a little further, Chart 31-2 includes an additional panel. The smoother dashed line in the lower panel (A) is a 12-day exponential smoothing of the first EMA (B). The dashed line in the lower panel is a 12-day EMA of the thick line in the middle and lower panels.

Finally, in Chart 31-3, we see B again. It is smoothed again by another 12-day EMA, which is the thick line in the bottom panel. This is the TRIX indicator.

The result is a very smooth curve. Indicators always represent a trade-off between sensitivity (reliability) and timeliness. One would think that the triple EMA smoothing would give the indicator good characteristics so far as reliability is concerned but would leave it lacking in the timeliness department. Obviously, the longer the time span, the less timely an indicator will be. Nevertheless, it is surprising how well the TRIX, though far from perfect, can balance these two different characteristics.

Chart 31-4 shows three time spans for a 2-, 12-, and 45-day TRIX. You can see that the shorter 2-day span is almost as volatile as a short-spanned RSI or ROC indicator. The 12-day series is certainly a lot smoother but still suffers a significant amount of whipsaw directional changes, as highlighted in this box. The 45-day series captures the flavor of the intermediate moves but definitely lacks the timing capabilities of the 12-day TRIX.

Chart 31-1   DuPont and two indicators

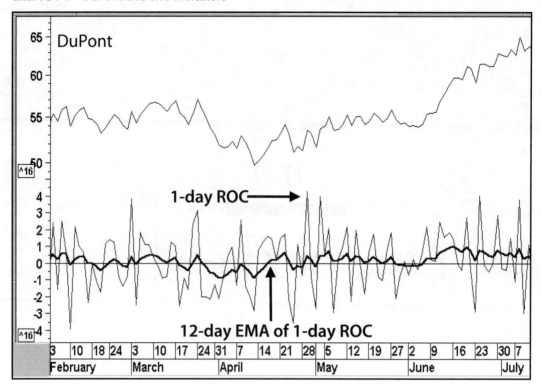

Chart 31-2   DuPont: Some exponential smoothings

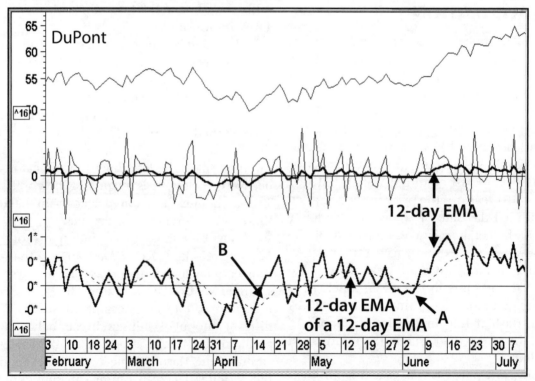

Chart 31-3   DuPont and a TRIX Indicator

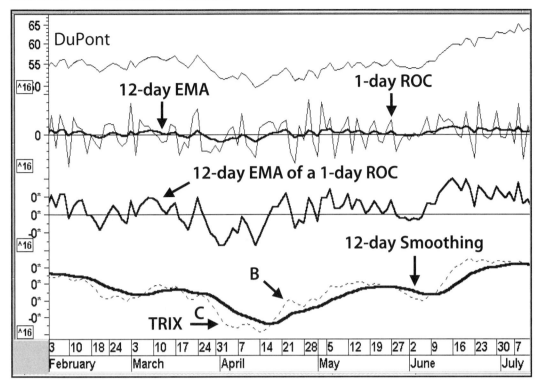

(Source: pring.com)

Chart 31-4   National Semiconductor and three TRIX Indicators

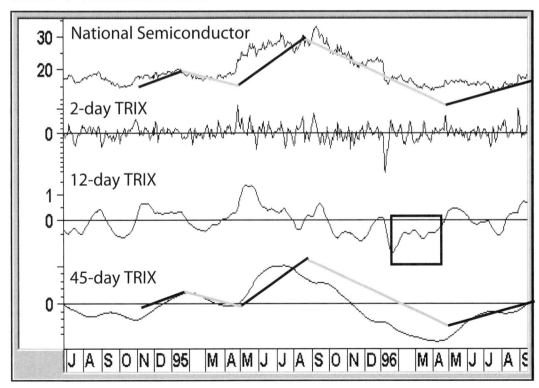

(Source: pring.com)

When considering what is often regarded as the default time span of 12-periods, it is apparent that changes in direction are not particularly helpful for triggering consistently accurate buy-or-sell signals. An alternative approach is to run a moving average for the TRIX and use these as buy-or-sell alerts.

In Chart 31-5, I have used a 9-day EMA. It is still far from perfect, but it does eliminate a substantial amount of whipsaws. If you look closely at this spring 1995 period, you will see several false signals of weakness as the TRIX reverses direction to the downside. However, during this phase, the EMA is never penetrated on the downside. Use of the EMA crossover as a filtering system does not appear to adversely affect the sensitivity or timing of the signals. However, there are some notable failures, such as the three bullish signals that took place just before a nasty decline. They have been flagged with the upward-pointing arrows. Even so, it is important to note, first, that two of these sig-

nals developed when the TRIX was close to an overbought reading and, second, that none of these signals were confirmed by a meaningful trend break in the price of National Semiconductor, such as a trendline break, pattern completion, or MA crossover. The moral of the story, as with all momentum interpretation, is to use the analysis first as a filtering approach, which is later confirmed by actual trend analysis in the price, before any serious action is taken.

DIVERGENCE AND OVERBOUGHT/OVERSOLD ANALYSIS

The TRIX indicator also lends itself to divergence and overbought/oversold analysis. Chart 31-6, for instance, contains some overbought-or-oversold lines. Movements that re-

Chart 31-5   National Semiconductor and a 9-day TRIX

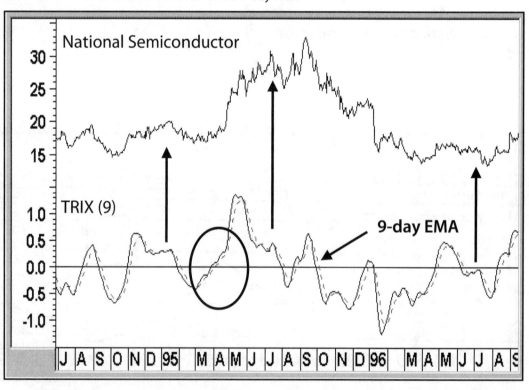

(Source: pring.com)

Chart 31-6 National Semiconductor and a 12-day TRIX

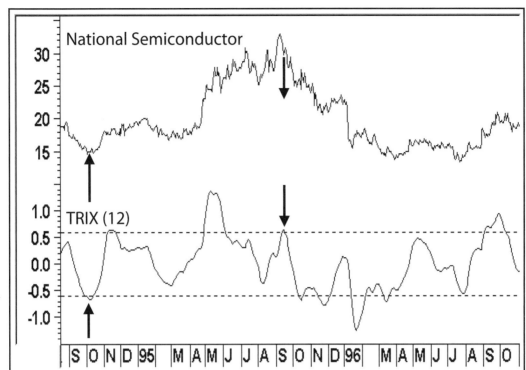

(Source: pring.com)

cross the lines on their way back to equilibrium are indicated by the arrows. The buy signal in October 1994 and the sell signal almost a year later catch the bottom and top on a very timely basis. In Chart 31-7, the sells in November 1994 (point A) and summer 1995 (point B) were also associated with a change in trend, but this time it was a sideways movement. However, the buy signals later in October and November 1995 were far too premature to be of much help, since they developed in a pervasive downtrend. Let us take a closer look at them, since the overall technical position of the TRIX in this period is quite instructive.

First, notice that the period between 1994 and fall 1995 was a bull market environment (Chart 31-8). You can see that the TRIX spent quite a bit of time in an overbought condition and not that much time in oversold territory, again a characteristic of a bull market environment. The fact that it was able to reach an extreme overbought reading in May 1995 offers additional evidence. Note what happens in September 1995: the TRIX experiences a neg-

ative divergence as the price reaches a new high (Chart 31-9). This is a bearish sign, but not in-and-of-itself a signal that a bear market had begun. Later on, the price completes a 6-month top, which does suggest that something more serious is in the air. Now look at the TRIX: it falls to an oversold reading (point A) for the first time in well over a year. The failure of the price to bounce and the previous top completion both indicate that the odds of a bear market have increased substantially. Any doubt in this regard would be erased when the TRIX rally reversed, quickly sending it back to an oversold condition once again (point B). Remembering the principle that oversold conditions often fail to trigger rallies in a bear market, the action of the TRIX would have warned a trader that he would need much stronger evidence than an oversold TRIX crossover to take a position from the long side.

I do not wish to leave you with the idea that this type of interpretation will work perfectly well at all times because it certainly does not.

Chart 31-7   National Semiconductor and a 12-day TRIX

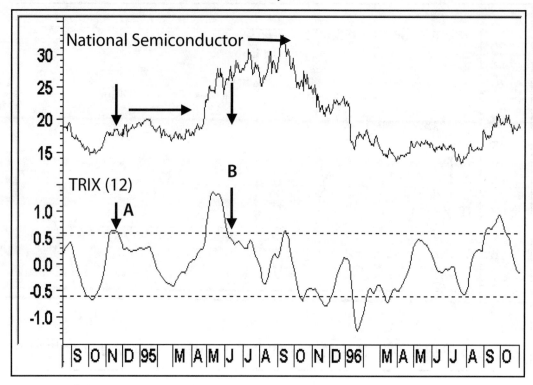

(Source: pring.com)

Chart 31-8   National Semiconductor and a 12-day TRIX

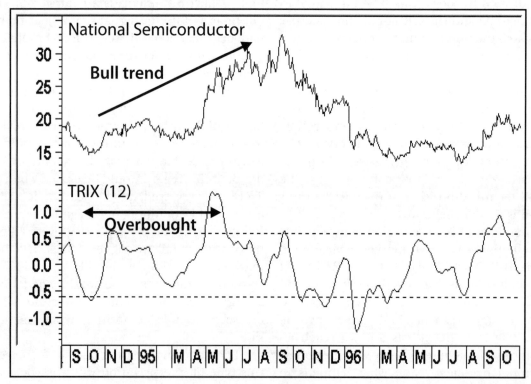

(Source: pring.com)

In Chart 31-10, National Semiconductor experiences an almost identical replay in the 1996–1997 period. The TRIX traces out a negative divergence in March 1997, a top is completed, and the momentum series moves into oversold territory for the first time in a year. Yet the price rallies to a new high (Chart 31-11). However, I would say that this is very much the exception and certainly not the rule. Not to make excuses for this approach, but summer 1997 happened to be one of the strongest periods for market breadth on record. So it was not surprising that a normal bearish condition failed to operate.

APPLIED TO WEEKLY AND MONTHLY CHARTS

The TRIX indicator can, of course, be applied to weekly or monthly data. In Chart 31-12, we see the monthly copper price together with a 9-month TRIX. The dashed moving average for the TRIX itself is a 9-month EMA. The price of copper is very sensitive to the business cycle and, therefore, experiences a substantial amount of cyclicality. Sometimes great buy-or-sell signals are triggered when the TRIX reverses direction from an extreme condition beyond either of the two overbought-or-oversold zones. Even when they are late, they still serve as a reasonably reliable confirmation that the primary trend has reversed. Incidentally, since volatility differs between markets and

Chart 31-9 National Semiconductor and a 12-day TRIX

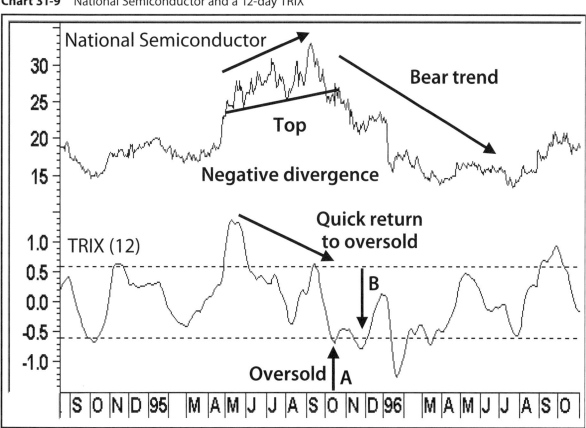

(Source: pring.com)

Chart 31-10   National Semiconductor and a 12-day TRIX

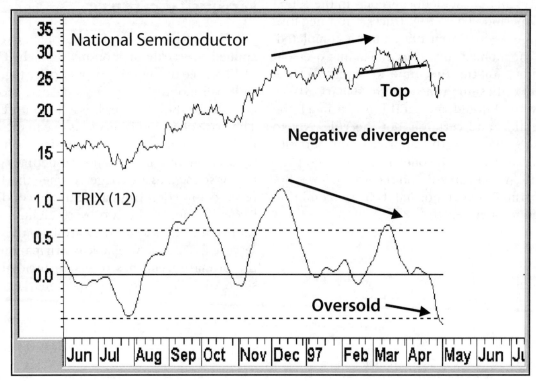

(Source: pring.com)

Chart 31-11   National Semiconductor and a 12-day TRIX

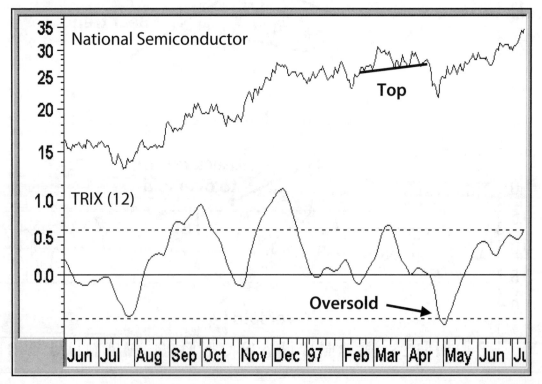

(Source: pring.com)

Chart 31-12   Copper and a 9-month TRIX

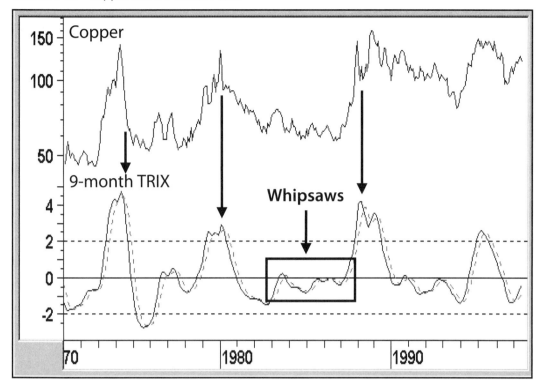

(Source: pring.com)

Chart 31-13   Copper and a 9-month TRIX

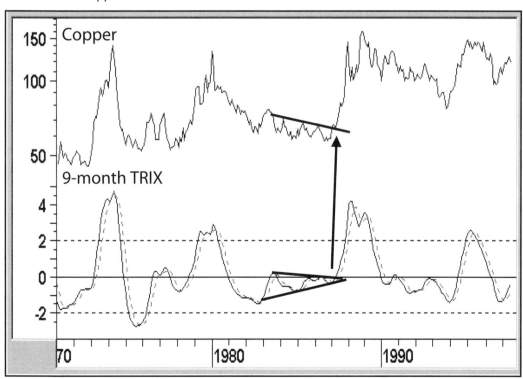

(Source: pring.com)

stocks, the optimum place for drawing over-bought-or-oversold zones will also vary.

In some very unusual circumstances, the TRIX will become extremely subdued in its fluctuations, and such action will trigger whipsaws. This type of thing happened between 1982 and 1987. These environments are very frustrating from the point of view of playing the MA crossovers. However, when it is possible to observe trend breaks in both the TRIX and price, a very powerful move almost always follows. That was certainly the case in 1987 (Chart 31-13). The subdued and indecisive action of the TRIX indicates a very fine balance between buyers and sellers, as neither is strong enough to gain control. However, when this battle is eventually resolved, the defeated parties are usually far too weak to put up a fight, and the victors run away with the honors.

Sometimes great buy-or-sell signals are triggered when the TRIX reverses direction from an extreme condition beyond either of the two overbought-or-oversold zones.

32

Aroon

THE INDICATOR

The *Aroon indicator* has a very different appearance than the other items covered in this book. It was developed by Tushar Chande and the indicator's name is a Sanskrit word meaning *dawn's early light,* or the change from night to day. The objective of Aroon is to warn the trader when market action is going to change from a trading range to a trending condition.

The Aroon measures two conditions. The first is the number of days that have passed since the last high. The period in question is determined by the user. Thus a 10-period Aroon will measure the number of days that have elapsed when the price did not make a 10-day high. That is displayed by the solid line in Chart 32-1. The dashed line measures the number of days that have passed since the price made a 10-day low. The solid line is known as the *Aroon up* and the dashed line as the *Aroon down.* The range for this indicator is 0 to 100. A reading of 100 in the Aroon up means that the security has just made a new high over the time span specified in the calculation. Thus a reading of 100 in this 10-day Aroon means that the price has registered a 10-day high. A reading of 0 in the Aroon up means that the price has not recorded a high for 10 days, and vice versa, for the Aroon down.

INTERPRETATION

There are three principal methods of interpretation. First, look for extremes when the indicators are at 100 or 0. In theory, when the Aroon up is at 100, strength is indicated. A persistent reading between 70 and 100 means that a new uptrend has been signaled. And a strong uptrend is indicated when the Aroon up remains above the 70 level and the Aroon down stays below the 30 level.

The problem I have with this approach is that the trend is usually well under way by the time you realize that the up and down indicators are persistently at an extreme, that is, above 70

Chart 32-1   IBM and a 10-day Aroon

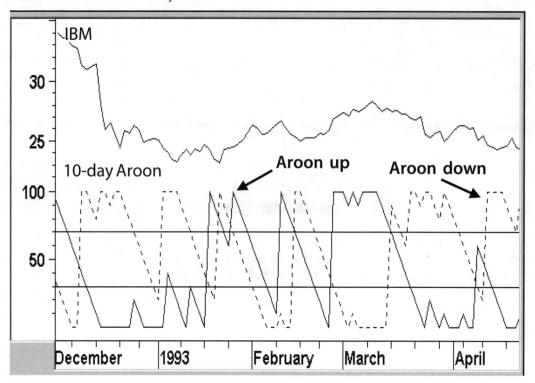

(Source: pring.com)

Chart 32-2   IBM and a 14-day Aroon

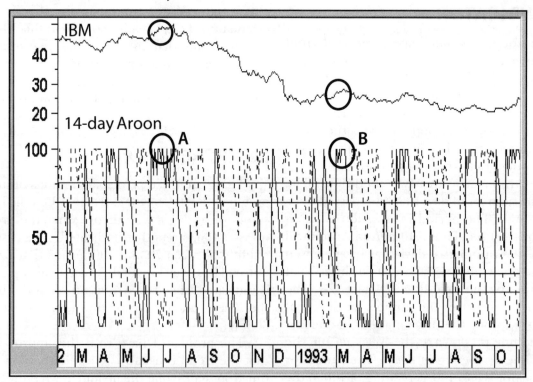

(Source: pring.com)

for the up and below 30 for the down. Look at Chart 32-2 of IBM in early 1993. See how the Aroon is trading up in the 100 zone in ellipse A. However, once it appears that it is persistently hovering in the 100 zone, at about this point, the trend is more or less over. The same could be said of the rally here in 1993 at ellipse B. When it is obvious that the indicator has been persistently above 70, the rally falters once again.

The second rule of interpretation is that when the up and down lines move in a parallel manner with each other, expect a consolidation. In Chart 32-3 we see the two lines in a parallel formation in the ellipse, and this is followed by a small trading range. Unfortunately, in my experience with the indicator (and I have to say that it is a fairly limited experience), this does not always occur. Chart 32-4 shows another situation in September 1989. The two

lines in the ellipse are parallel, so we should expect to see a trading range. You can see that the price fell dramatically later on.

The third interpretive rule is that when the down line crosses the up line, expect potential weakness, and when the up line crosses above the down line, look for a rally. The problem here is that this system generates far too many whipsaws. Look at Chart 32-5. The indicators are far too volatile to generate any consistent results.

USING MOVING AVERAGES

One way that I have found the Aroon to be of practical help is to smooth the up and down series with a 30-day EMA. In Chart 32-6, the smoothed version of the Aroon up is displayed as a dashed line and the Aroon down as the

Chart 32-3   Biomet and a 12-day Aroon

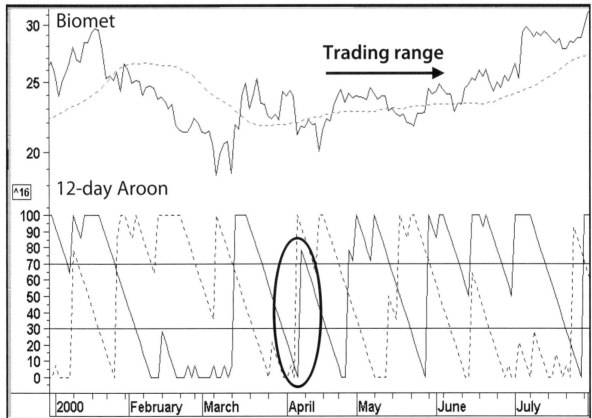

(Source: pring.com)

Chart 32-4   IBM and a 10-day Aroon

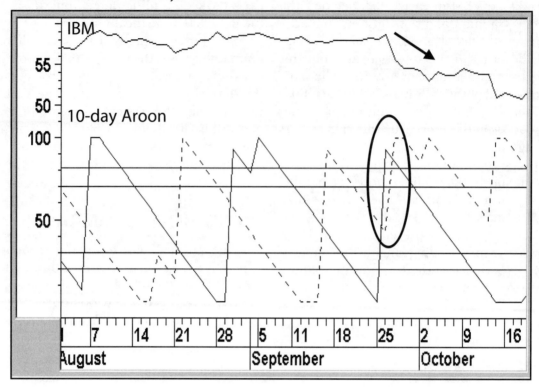

Chart 32-5   IBM and a 10-day Aroon

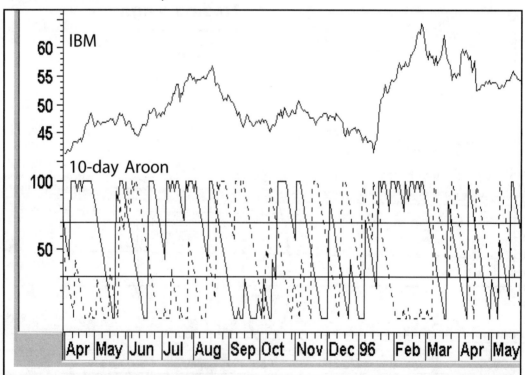

Chart 32-6 IBM and a smoothed 10-day Aroon

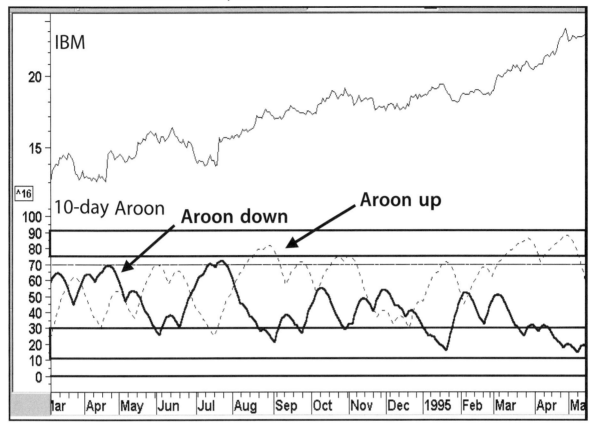

(Source: pring.com)

thick solid one. I have also put in an overbought reading at 80 and an oversold one at 20. The idea is that when the dashed (up) series moves below 20 and then rises above it, a buy signal is triggered. When it rallies above 80 and then reverses direction, a sell signal is triggered. You can also use the Aroon down for confirmation. When the two are juxtaposed, the situation becomes clearer than if just one indicator is positioned at an extreme. Unfortunately, this approach will not work in a persistent up- or downtrend and, as with any oscillator, it will give premature buy-or-sell signals.

As you may gather, I do not find the established interpretive rules to be very helpful. However, when used with this MA approach, its seems to work reasonably well—which is good because I believe that the basic concept is sound and builds on a form of peak-and-

trough analysis, a basic building block of technical analysis. Incidentally, I am suggesting a 30-day EMA, but this was established on a quick trial-and-error basis. If you like this approach, I encourage you to experiment with other possibilities.

33

Qstick

THE CONCEPT

The *Qstick indicator* is a momentum series that uses a basic concept incorporated in candlestick charting: that the open and close are the two pivotal points in any trading period. The important point concerning these data points is whether the closing price is higher or lower than the opening. If it is lower, then this is generally regarded as a bullish factor. If the opening is higher than the close, then in a general sense, a bearish interpretation is given. The Qstick indicator essentially calculates a simple MA of the difference between the open and closing prices. The result is displayed as an oscillator. In Chart 33-1, I have shown the price in candlestick format. Qstick is often used with divergence analysis. We see here, for instance, that the indicator makes a peak in late April, and by the time the price itself reaches its high, the Qstick diverges from it in a negative way. Then, when the price violates the trendline in mid May, a sell signal is triggered.

Chart 33-2 shows the same indicator, only this time I have constructed an overbought-or-oversold line. In this case, the lines are at ±0.6. Positioning of these lines is done on a trial-and-error basis, so the levels chosen will depend a great deal on the volatility of the security being monitored. The idea is that when the Qstick touches, or goes through, the overbought-or-oversold zones and then reverses direction, a buy-or-sell alert is triggered. I have highlighted these points with arrows. I deliberately use the word alert because it is usually a good idea to make sure that these types of momentum signals are confirmed by some kind of price reversal. That is not much of a problem if you were already long, because you could have taken profits in early December 1995. However, if you were considering entering a short position at the first peak in December 1995, you would have had to undergo a scary-looking rally. Better to have gone short when the Qstick was being confirmed by a price trend break, which in this case would have been a penetration of the horizontal trendline in late December.

Chart 33-1 JP Morgan and an 8-day Qstick

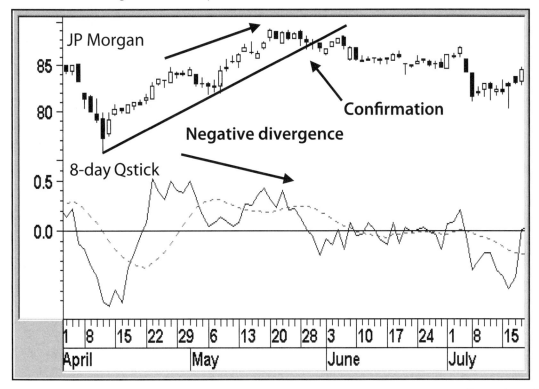

(Source: pring.com)

Chart 33-2 JP Morgan and an 8-day Qstick

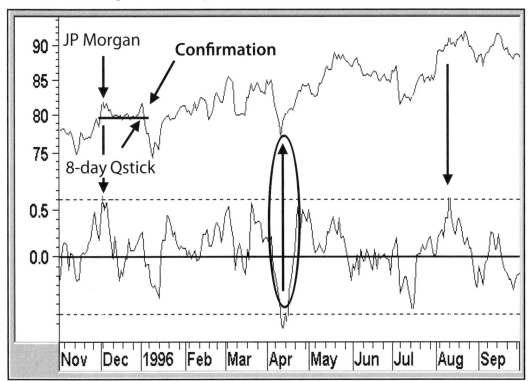

(Source: pring.com)

A buy alert developed in April, but there was no meaningful trend-reversal signal by the price. However, had a trader been lucky enough to be short at this point, then it would have represented a great covering point (reasonably close to the day of the low).

> The Qstick indicator lends itself better to trendline and other types of analysis when longer timeframes are calculated.

PRICE PATTERNS AND MOVING AVERAGES

The two examples of Qstick shown so far have been plotted with an 8-day time span. However, the indicator lends itself better to trendline and other types of analysis when longer timeframes are calculated.

For instance, Chart 33-3 uses a 25-day span. Now it is easier to construct a trendline and, when the line is violated, to wait for a confirmation by the price. A buy signal is then triggered.

The Qstick often forms price patterns when the time span is extended. In Chart 33-4, using a 25-period series, I have been able to mark quite a few tops. There is a broadening formation with a flat bottom in the September/October 1995 period. The trendline break in the price confirms this at around the same time; a small decline follows. In December 1995, a head-and-shoulders top is formed, and a trendline break in the price also takes place. Finally, a good uptrend line in the Qstick is confirmed by a trend break in the price in April 1996. Normally, I would have expected a somewhat larger price decline than the one that developed, since the Qstick trendline was quite long and had been touched or approached on numerous occasions. However, the price

Chart 33-3   General Motors and a 25-day Qstick

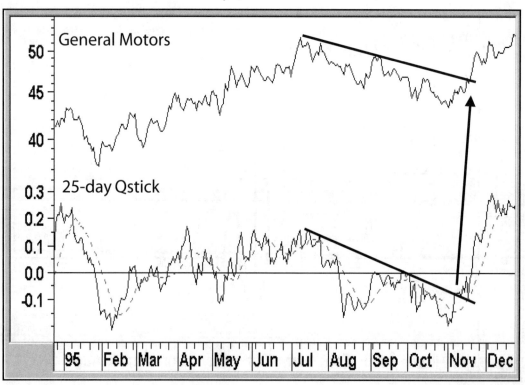

(Source: pring.com)

Chart 33-4 JP Morgan and a 25-day Qstick

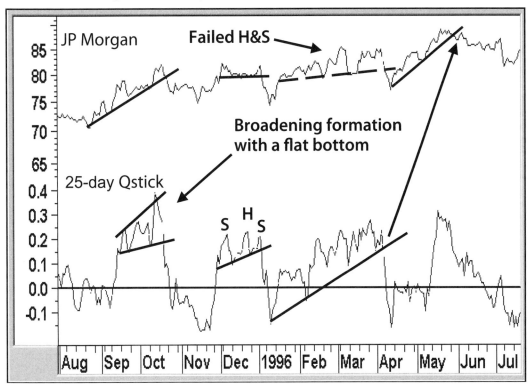

(Source: pring.com)

experienced a failed head-and-shoulders top. Normally, failed price patterns are followed by a powerful move in the opposite direction to that indicated by the formation. That was certainly the situation here.

Chart 33-5 shows another example using the Philadelphia Gold and Silver Share Index. The 30-day Qstick time span again offers some useful price pattern examples. I have not labeled the one on the left in the March/April 1995 period, but it is a small head-and-shoulders top that was subsequently confirmed by a trend break. Later in May/June, we see an upward-sloping head-and-shoulders top, which was subsequently confirmed by a penetration of the neckline in July. Finally, the late 1995 to early 1996 top in the price was not immediately confirmed but was so confirmed later on by a penetration of the dashed uptrend line. The price moved sideways for about a month and then broke below the solid line. Note also how the Qstick traced out a small head-and-shoulders top and its completion occurred just about four weeks before the final price breakdown.

One final way in which I find the Qstick to be of help is to calculate an MA and to use the average to trigger buy-or-sell alerts as it crosses an overbought-or-oversold zone on its way toward equilibrium. The vertical arrows in Chart 33-6 flag such instances. The solid ones are relatively timely signals and the dashed ones are less timely. In all these instances, the signals flagged by the solid lines were followed by a rising trend of some kind. The only exception was that triggered in August 1994, which was followed by a consolidation and then a sharp decline. This, however, is one of the faults of all momentum indicators, for in a persistent up- or downtrend, nothing works. That is why it makes sense to wait for some kind of trend reversal in the price itself. Even this does not always work out, but it certainly improves your odds of success.

Chart 33-5   Philadelphia Gold and Silver Share Index and a 30-day Qstick

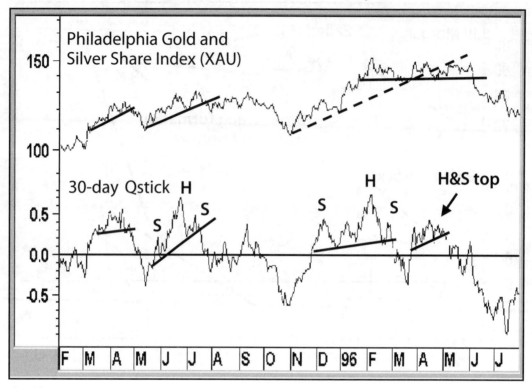

Chart 33-6   General Motors and a 25-day MA of a 25-day Qstick

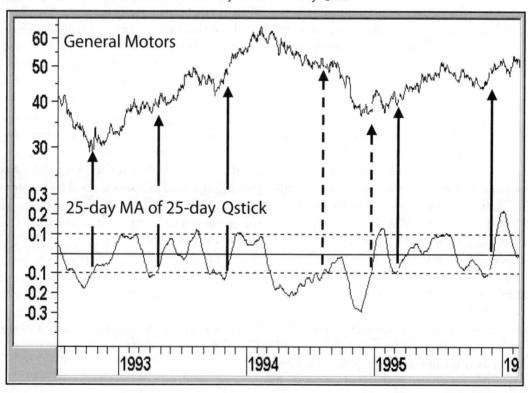

34

The Relative Volatility Index

THE CONCEPT

The *Relative Volatility Index* (or *RVI* for short) was introduced by Donald Dorsey. It is used to measure the direction of volatility. The calculation is very similar to the RSI, except that the RVI incorporates the standard deviation of price changes instead of absolute price changes. The indicator is used to enhance the results from MA crossover systems. The following are the rules devised by Dorsey.

The first rule is: only act on positive MA crossovers when the RVI is above 50. Chart 34-1 features a 25-day simple MA, which has been advanced by 5 days. The upward-pointing arrows indicate when these two conditions have been met. The dashed arrow indicates a poor signal. The two dotted arrows indicate when the MA crossover occurred, but the RVI was still below 50. The one on the left (point A) in November 1989 was very successful. The one in February (point B) was a more or less breakeven situation. The April signal (point C) was a definite disas-

ter. The signal in July 1990 (point D) experienced a small rally, but by the time the price re-crossed below the average, the trade would have barely broken even. Unfortunately, the November 1990 buy signal was followed by a worthwhile rally but did not qualify, because the RVI was below 50. The signal in late 1991 (point E) was followed by a small rally but then whipsawed. Finally, the last signal developed when the indicator was below 50 and was not, therefore, a valid one.

Chart 34-2 shows the sell signals, where the rules are reversed. The October 1990 sell was followed by a small decline. The next couple of signals in 1990 did not qualify because the RVI was just above, or at, 50 during the time of the MA violation. The next sell in April 1990 did so but was only followed by a short-term decline. The June signal did not qualify, which is just as well, since the price did not decline by very much. The August 1990 sell was a very timely one, unlike the October signal, which was a total failure. Finally, the sell signal in March 1991 was

371

372

Part II: The Definitive Guide to Momentum Indicators

Chart 34-1   DuPont and a 14-day RVI

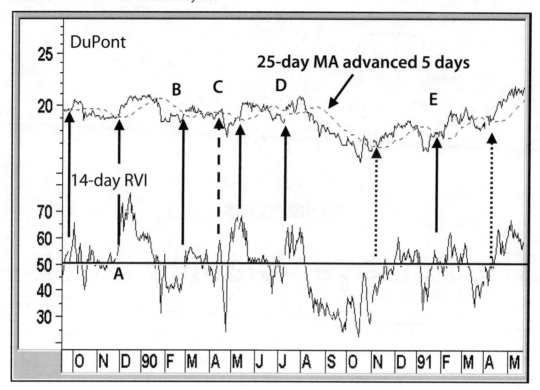

(Source: pring.com)

Chart 34-2   DuPont and a 14-day RVI

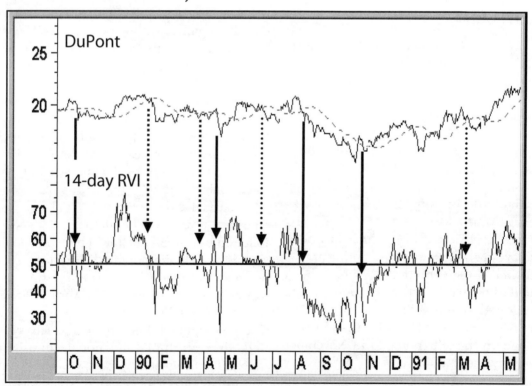

(Source: pring.com)

Chart 34-3 Heinz and a 14-day RVI

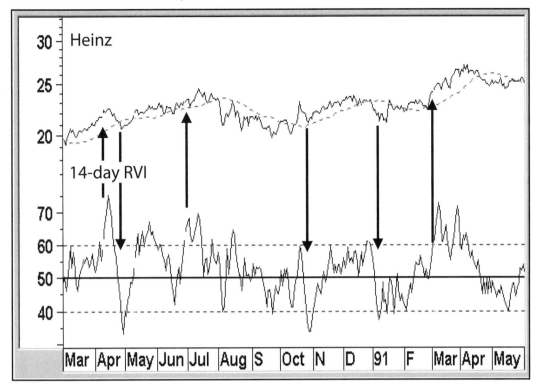

(Source: pring.com)

Chart 34-4 Heinz and a 14-day RVI

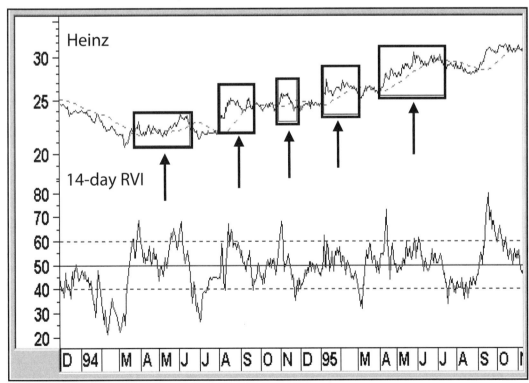

(Source: pring.com)

filtered out. As you can see, the RVI 50 rule has its plusses and minuses. Obviously, you cannot judge the performance of an indicator based on one chart, but by and large, the results generally appear to be as mixed as this one. Sometimes, the filtering method using the RVI helps; at other times, it does not. In my view, there is a mild advange to using it, but I feel there are other approaches that are more consistently profitable.

The second rule states that if a buy signal is ignored, enter long; if the RVI moves above 60 or if a sell signal is ignored, short when the RVI moves below 40. The buy-or-sell signals using these rules are shown in Chart 34-3. I am not sure that this does anything to improve on those based on rule one, but this was a trading-range market. Chart 34-4 alternately features a trending one. I have drawn boxes around the price where this rule was in force. The result was that two instances barely broke even and three made a profit.

35

The Inertia Indicator

THE CONCEPT

The *inertia indicator* was developed by Donald Dorsey and is an outgrowth of Dorsey's relative volatility index (see Chapter 34). The name *inertia* was chosen because of his definition of a trend. He states that a trend is simply the "outward result of inertia." It takes significantly more energy for a market to reverse direction than to continue along the same path. Therefore, a trend is a measurement of market inertia. Dorsey asserts that volatility may be the simplest and most accurate measurement of inertia. The inertia indicator is simply a smoothed RVI. The smoothing mechanism is a linear-regression indicator.

Chart 35-1 features a 14-day RVI setting for the inertia. At the bottom is a 21-day inertia overlaid on a 21-period linear-regression indicator of the RVI. As you can see, both indicators are identical.

The trend is considered bullish when this indicator is over 50 and bearish when below 50. In Chart 35-2, the bullish periods have been highlighted with the thin line and bearish ones with the thick line. Most of the time, this approach appears to work quite well. However, it is good to bear in mind that this is a trending market.

Chart 35-3, alternately, shows a trading-range market, and you can see that the approach was far from satisfactory, since there were several periods, such as September/October 1992 and April/May 1993, when the price declined sharply and persistently in a bullish period. Conversely, in the bearish October/November period, the price rallied. This is not typical, though. In this regard, Chart 35-4 shows the trading range for Newmont Gold. You can see that the indicator, while far from perfect, certainly performed adequately. There are a few transgressions (such as the failed bullish period in mid 1996), but by and large it captures the bulk of the important rallies (such as that in early 1993 and again in early 1996). With a lot of indicators, we have the inclination to look for the holy grail. And if a new one fails its initial test, we move on to something far more promising, but which in reality is probably just as flawed. With the inertia index, we may be tempted to discard it due to these whipsaws, but I think it deserves additional experimentation with different time spans and smoothings, and so forth. It is certainly far from perfect, but it does show some promise.

Chart 35-1   Heinz comparing the inertia to a linear regression of the RVI

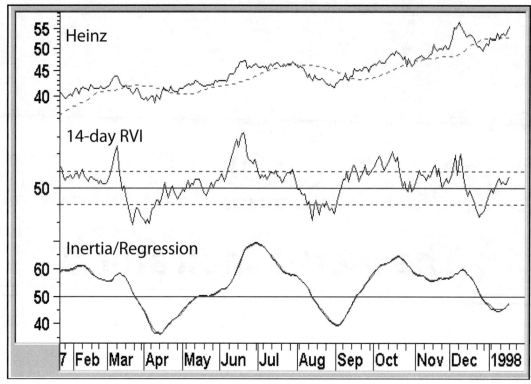

Chart 35-2   Newmont Mining and a 45/21 inertia

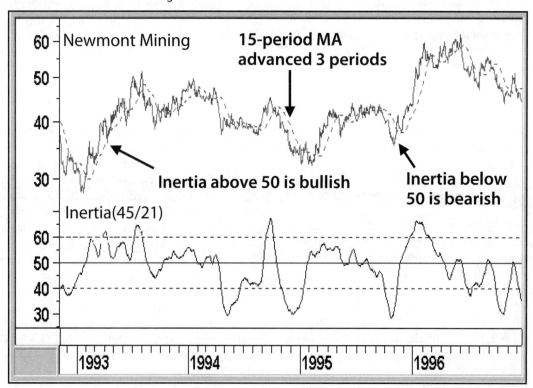

Chart 35-3   Coca-Cola and a 21/14 inertia

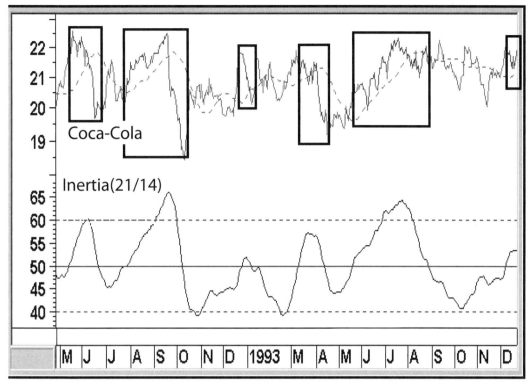

(Source: pring.com)

Chart 35-4   Newmont Mining and a 45/21 inertia

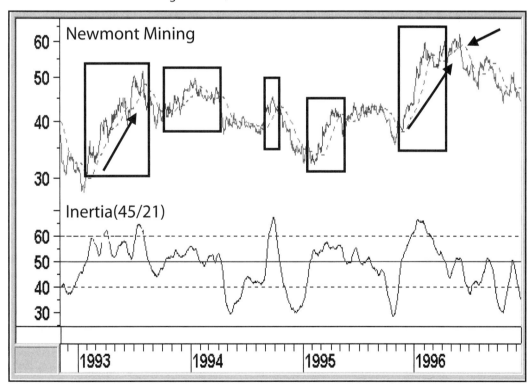

(Source: pring.com)

36

The Directional Movement System

THE OBJECTIVE

One of the key problems faced by all traders is to determine whether the future characteristics of the market in which they are involved are going to be of the trending or trading-range variety. This is very important, since a trading-range market should be attacked by selling into an overbought reading and buying into an oversold one. Short positions would be initiated with an overbought condition and covered with an oversold one. Alternately, if it is known ahead of time that a market is likely to trend, greater emphasis would be placed on trend-following devices such as moving averages, trendlines, and so on, and less on oscillators.

After all, if you believe that a market will continue to rally, why take decisions based on a momentum indicator that is likely to undergo several negative divergences with the price before the final peak?

There is, of course, no precise way in which this task can consistently be achieved. However,

in *New Concepts in Technical Trading*, Wells Wilder outlines an approach that tries to identify when a market is likely to break out of a trading range. He called it the *directional movement system.*

Most of the techniques described here deal with a description of technical systems, but the directional movement approach tries to fit a system relative to the likely market action. In other words, if we apply a particular system to a market, it's rather like trying to ski regardless of whether it is summer or winter, which is really like putting the cart before the horse. The directional movement system, alternately, tells us what the prevailing season is likely to be so we can decide whether to use momentum indicators that are suitable to trading range environments or MAs, which work more profitably in trending markets. In my experience, the approach does not do a very good job in discriminating between these two key trading environments. However, there are some useful and practical twists to its application, as we shall learn later.

WHAT IS THE DIRECTIONAL MOVEMENT?

In order to measure directional movement, two periods are required so that a comparison can be made. In short-term trading, these would be represented by days, but there is no reason why weekly, or even monthly, data could not be used. Taken to the other extreme, the comparison could be made between hourly bars in an intraday chart, and so forth.

In this explanation I will use days, but please remember that these principles can be applied to any period. In essence, the directional movement is defined as the difference between the extreme part of the current period (today) that falls outside the previous period's (yesterday) range. Let us consider some examples.

In Fig. 36-1 the range of day 1 is AB and day 2 is ED. Part of the price range in day 2, namely, the distance between C and D, retraces some of the ground covered in day 1. It is the distance between C and E in day 2 that really earmarks the directional movement. The difference between point E in day 2 (that is, the high and point A in day 1, meaning the high) is called *plus DM (+DM)* because the movement is an upward one.

Minus DM (-DM) would occur when the price declined between the two periods, as in Fig. 36-2. In effect, the distance between the low today and the low yesterday would represent the -DM.

There are some other possibilities to consider. The first is shown in Fig. 36-3, where the trading range in day 2 is so great that

Figure 36-1 Plus directional movement

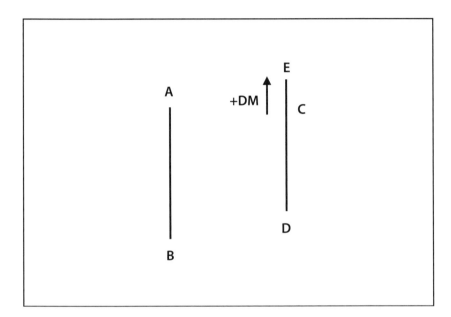

Figure 36-2 Minus directional movement

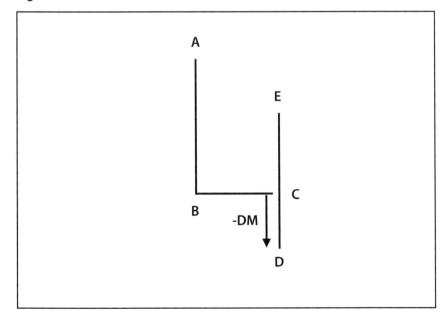

Figure 36-3 Plus directional movement variation

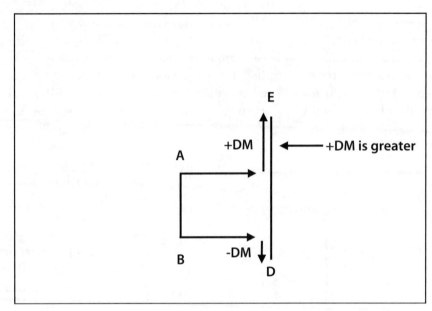

Please note that the +DM is *not* the extent of the limit, that is, the distance between day 1's close and the limit. Rather, it is the difference between day 1's high (that is, point A) and the limit itself. In this example, it is assumed that the price never comes off "limit up" all day. Finally, Fig. 36-7 shows an example of a -DM in which we are looking at a limit move on the downside.

it encompasses all of day 1 and then some. How should this example be treated? In effect, this situation offers both a +DM and a -DM, but for the purposes of calculation, we take the *greater* of the two. In this example, this would be recorded as a +DM, because the distance between A and E is greater than that between B and D. Figure 36-4 shows the same idea, but this time day 1 encompasses day 2, so there is no directional movement.

Alternately, we might get an example where the two trading ranges are identical, as in Fig. 36-5. Again, the directional movement would be nonexistent.

In futures trading, many contracts are subject to limit moves, which must also be addressed. Figure 36-6 shows a limit up day.

> The directional movement system tells us what the prevailing market environment is likely to be so we can decide whether to use momentum indicators, which are suitable to trading-range environments, or MAs, which are more profitable in trending markets.

TRUE RANGE*

Price movement is best measured in proportion rather than in arithmetic numbers. This enables a more realistic comparison to be made between two periods or two securities of differing price magnitudes. For example, a $1 +DM measurement for a stock trading at $100 would have a very different implication than a $1 move for a $2 stock, since the former would represent a 1 percent move and the latter a 50 percent one.

Wilder deals with this problem by comparing the +DM and -DM to what he calls the "true range." This is defined as *the maximum range that the price has moved, either during the day or from yesterday's close to the extreme point reached during the day.* This means, in effect, that the true range is the greatest of the following:

1. The distance between today's high and today's low.

2. The distance between yesterday's close to today's high.

3. The distance between yesterday's close to today's low.

---

*For a full discussion on this concept, please refer to N*ew Concepts in Technical Trading* by Wells Wilder (Trend Research).

Figure 36-4   No directional movement

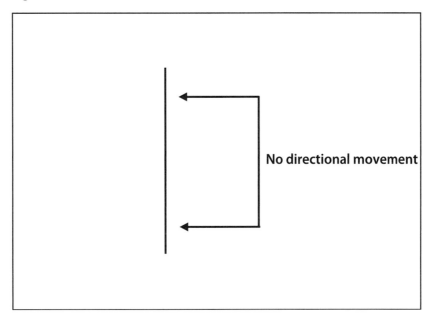

Figure 36-5   No directional movement variation

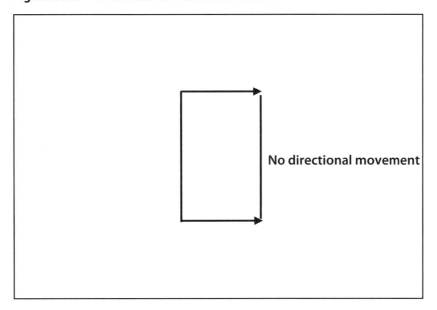

Figure 36-6   Limit up move

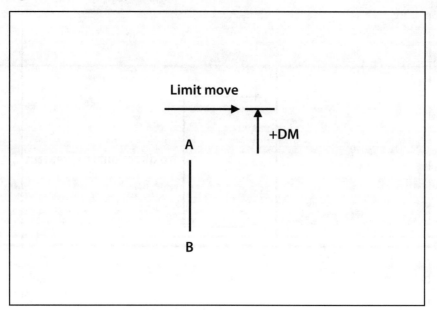

Figure 36-7   Limit down move

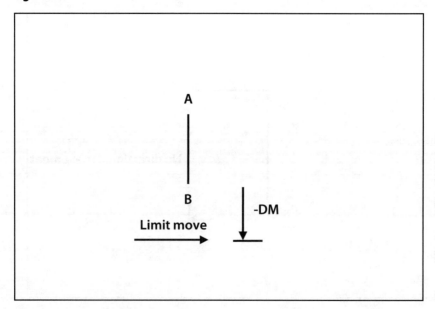

INTRODUCING THE DIRECTIONAL INDICATORS (DIS)

When the directional movement is related to the true range, two indicators, the plus and minus DIs, are born. Since the resultant series is unduly volatile, they are each calculated as an average over a specific time period, and the result is plotted on a chart. Normally, they are overlaid in the same panel, so that it is possible to observe when they cross each other. The standard, or default, time span for the DIs is 14 periods. Chart 36-1 shows the two DIs using a 14-day span. Crossovers of the DIs are then used as buy-or-sell signals, but we will discuss that later.

INTRODUCING THE ADX

There is one other important indicator incorporated in this system, and that is the *Average Directional Index (ADX).* The ADX is simply an average of the +DI and -DI over a specific period. In effect, it subtracts the days of negative directional movement from the positive ones. However, when the -DI is greater than the +DI, the negative sign is ignored. This means that ADX only tells us whether the security in question is experiencing directional movement or not. Again, the normal default time span is 14 days.

The ADX is calculated in such a way that the plot is always contained within the scale of 0 to 100. High readings indicate that the security is in a trending mode (that is, has a lot of directional movement), and low readings indicate a lack of directional movement and are more indicative of trading range markets.

Chart 36-1 Singapore Fund and two DIs

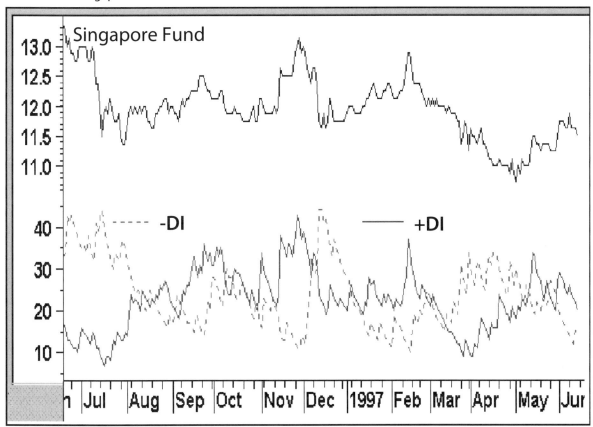

(Source: pring.com)

Unlike other oscillators, the ADX tells us nothing about the direction in which a price is moving, only its trending or non-trending characteristics. We need to use other oscillators for this task.

In this respect, note that the two highs in the index at points A and B in Chart 36-2 are each associated with a top and bottom, respectively. For example, if the price moves down sharply and then stabilizes, the ADX will move from a high number, as it did between points B and C. Then as the price continues to rally

> The ADX only tells us whether the security in question is experiencing directional movement or not; it does not tell us the specific direction.

or starts to decline again, as it did in this example, the ADX rallies once again. The low ADX numbers between points C and D indicate low directional movement. Only after prices resume their decline does the ADX rally again. This low reading between C and D arises because the difference between +DI14 and -DI14 is decreasing, occasionally touching zero.

A high ADX reading does not tell us then that the market is overbought and about to go down. What it does do is inform us that when the indicator is at a high reading and starts to reverse, the prevailing trend has probably run its course. From here on in, we should expect a *change* in trend. This is different from a reversal in trend, since a change in trend can either be from up to down or up to sideways. Similarly, a downtrend could change to a trading-range or to an uptrend.

Chart 36-2   JP Morgan and a 14-period ADX

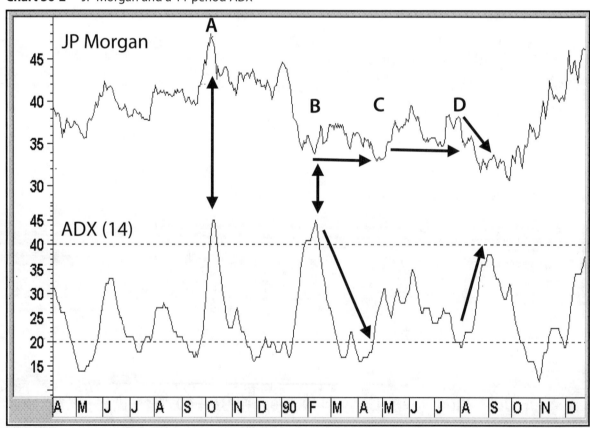

(Source: pring.com)

I mentioned earlier that the ADX is normally calculated with a 14-day span. However, it is possible to vary this number in the same way you might for an MA or other oscillator. Chart 36-3 features a 32-day ADX in the lower area. You can see that this is a more smoothed version, compared to the 14-period variety featured in the middle area. Because of the smoothing effect, longer-term time spans or averaging also experience lower levels of volatility. The overbought level for the 14-day series has been drawn at 40, for example, yet the 32-day series in the lower area never reaches 40. In fact, it is only able to register a 30 reading once in 8 years! You can also appreciate from this chart that an ADX calculated from a longer time span is also much more step-like in nature, compared to the 14-day series, which is more jagged.

> The actual reversal point in the ADX tells us when the security in question has become tired of moving in an up or down direction and is ready for a change in trend.

The other principal point to grasp is that reversals in the ADX that develop from an extremely high reading indicate an exhausted price trend. The actual reversal point in this indicator tells us when the security in question has become tired of moving in an up or down direction and is ready for a *change* in trend. Since the reversals, when they come, are usually pretty deliberate, a peaking-out action usually indicates that the ADX has begun a move to a far lower reading. This compares to many

Chart 36-3 JP Morgan and two ADX indicators

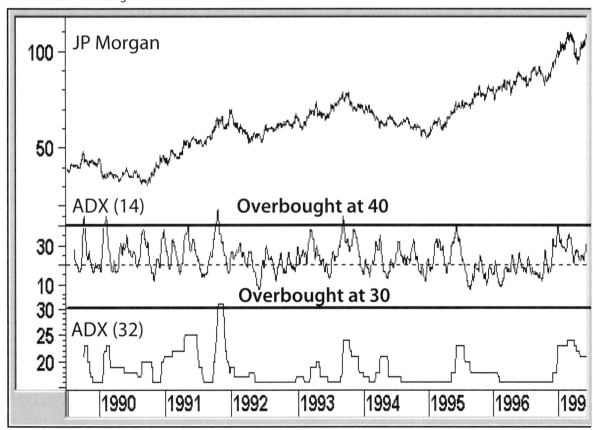

(Source: pring.com)

oscillators, whereby a reversal from a high level can often result in a double or even triple top formation. Since the ADX is far less prone to such misleading signals, a reversal in its direction is usually a reliable signal that the ADX has peaked. As a general rule, I would say that the higher the level at which the reversal takes place, the more reliable the signal is likely to be.

37

Interpreting the ADX and the Directional Indicators

HIGH AND LOW ADX READINGS

Since the ADX only tells us about the trending qualities of the price and not its direction, we need some system to warn us of which way a price is likely to trend once a directional signal has been given. One possibility would be to compare the ADX with a regular oscillator, as in Chart 37-1, where I have compared an ADX with a smoothed 9-day RSI. See how the 14-day ADX for JP Morgan reverses from a peak trend reading in October 1989 at roughly the same time that the smoothed RSI crosses below its overbought zone. Then a little later on, the reverse set of circumstances develop as the ADX once again peaks out, but this time when the RSI is crossing above its oversold zone. In this instance, the trend reversal was from down to sideways. This, then, is a sharp reminder that a trend change does not have to be a 180-degree turn from up to down, or from down to up, but can also be a 90-degree one from up to sideways, or from down to sideways.

Low readings in the ADX indicate a trendless market. This can also be used to some advantage. For example, if the ADX slips to an unusually low reading, as in Chart 37-2, it is then possible to construct a trendline for the ADX. The subsequent break above the line indicates that the market is likely to trend again. This type of signal needs to be confirmed by some kind of breakout in the price itself. In Chart 37-2, the oversold reading for the ADX has been set at 20. You can also see that it was possible to draw a trendline for both the ADX and the price. The signal to buy would have developed after both lines had been violated.

It is not always possible to draw lines for the ADX. In Chart 37-3, for instance, the ADX reaches a low reading, but there is no convenient series of peaks against which a line could be plotted. In this instance, the trend break in the price would be used to confirm that the period of relatively trendless price activity is over. A quick glance at the chart may give the impression that the price was not trendless, but declin-

Chart 37-1   JP Morgan, an ADX, and an RSI

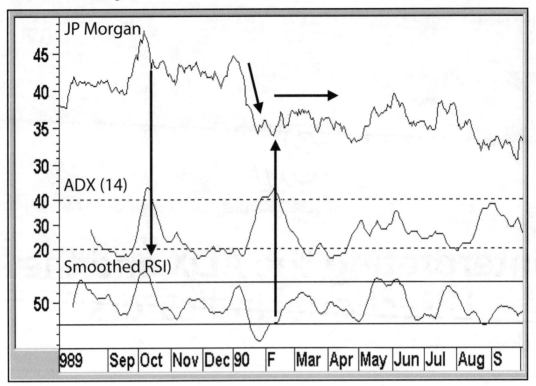

(Source: pring.com)

Chart 37-2   JP Morgan and a 14-period ADX

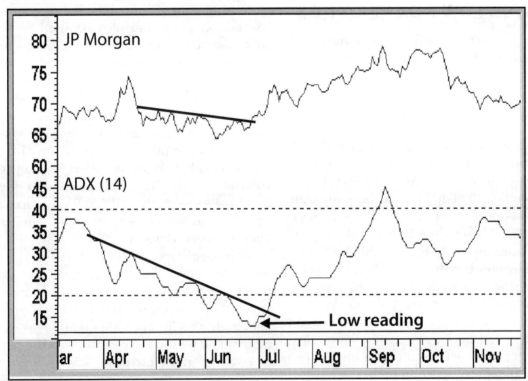

(Source: pring.com)

ing. This is true, but at the point where the ADX makes its low, you can look back and see that the previous period was essentially flat. This has been flagged on the chart with the two horizontal arrows.

The other point to bear in mind is that these signals are relatively short-term in nature. The first one (on the left) was followed by a one-month rally after the breakout. The second was followed by a more sustainable 3-month advance. The reason the first was so anemic was because this whole period was one within the confines of a bear market. This once again underscores the idea that it is very important to make an attempt at discovering the direction of the primary trend, whether you are a trader or an investor. A rising tide lifts all boats, but a falling one takes them all down again.

On balance, I find that the reversals from a high reading in the ADX are far stronger and

more reliable than reversals from low, nontrending readings.

> I find that the reversals from a high reading in the ADX are far stronger and more reliable than reversals from low, nontrending readings.

DI CROSSOVERS

Another way in which the directional movement concept can be used is to compare the progress of the plus and minus directional indexes, or DIs. Remember the 14-day +DI measures the average of the directional movement when the price is rallying and the -DI

Chart 37-3   JP Morgan and a 14-period ADX

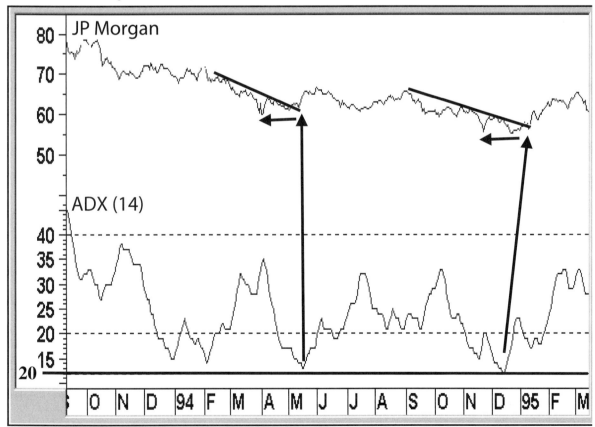

(Source: pring.com)

measures the average directional movement when the price is declining. The average in this case will depend on the time period over which the calculation is made, the default or norm being 14 days. When the two are overlaid, as we see in Chart 37-4, the crossovers act as buy-or-sell signals.

In Fig. 37-1, points A, B, and C represent the equilibrium points, that is, the places where the DIs cross. This example shows that there is a fair degree of volatility, but unfortunately, the profit potential from buying at A, and selling at B, is not very great (Fig. 37-2). According to Wilder, this type of market would have a *low* ADX rating. Figure 37-3 shows a small profit from a short sale between B and C.

Alternately, Fig. 37-4 illustrates a situation where the profit between the equilibrium points is quite good. In this instance, the ADX is assumed to have a *high* reading. In other

words, the high ADX reading not only indicates that a market is volatile but that there is a tradable direction to this volatility.

Figure 37-5 shows the best situation of all. This occurs in a strong trending market where the two DIs are continually moving toward each other, but rarely cross. At W, X, Y, and Z, they almost cross, but at the last moment they diverge once again, so that the position is maintained. According to Wilder, this type of market condition has a very high ADX rating.

Figure 37-6 shows an example of a volatile but unprofitable market. The A–B long trade breaks even, but even the B–C short sale loses money. In *New Concepts*, Wilder points out that this type of market action is reflective of a situation in which the ADX is less than 20. He argues that when the ADX rallies above the 25 level, the equilibrium points widen out.

Chart 37-4   Singapore Fund and two 14-day DIs

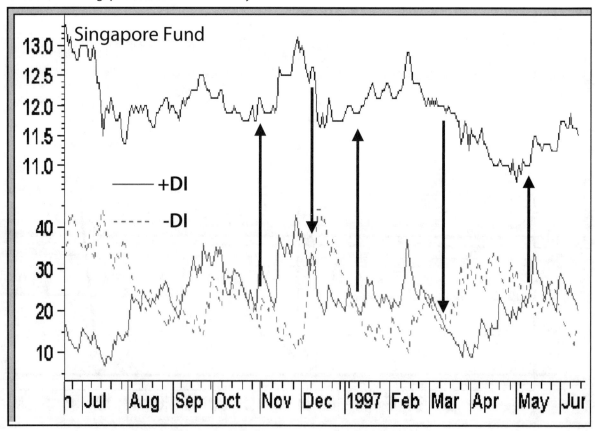

Figure 37-1   DI crossover

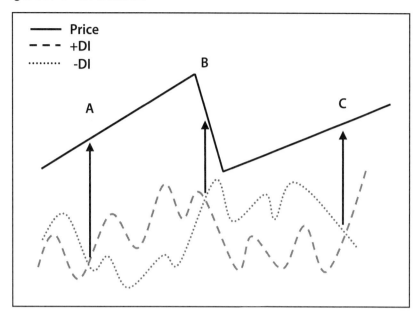

Figure 37-2   DI crossover and small long profits

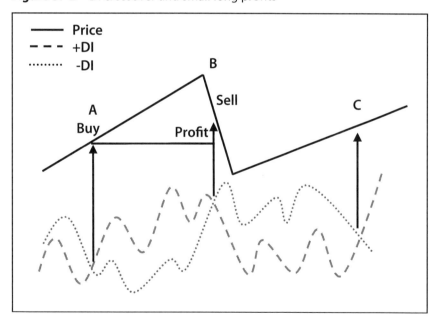

Figure 37-3   DI crossover and small short sale profits

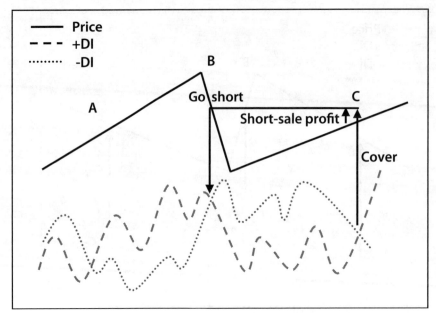

Figure 37-4   DI crossover and large profits

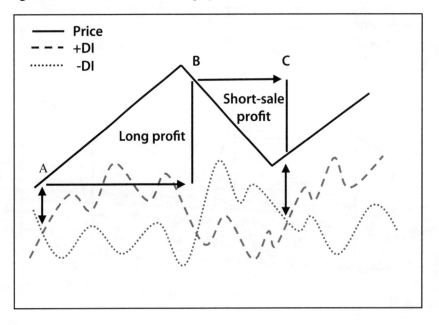

RELATING THE DIS TO THE ADX

The question, then, is how we select trades from crossovers where the probability of making a good profit is high. According to Wilder, the first step is to select a security with a high ADX reading. This indicates that directional movement will be sufficient to make tradable profits from trend-following signals. In my own research, I have found the *opposite* to be truer. In fact, when the ADX has been rallying and is at a high level, the two DIs are usually far apart and do not cross each other. The best signals appear to come when the ADX is at an unusually low reading.

In Chart 37-5, the first buy signal comes in

Figure 37-5   DI crossovers in a very bullish market

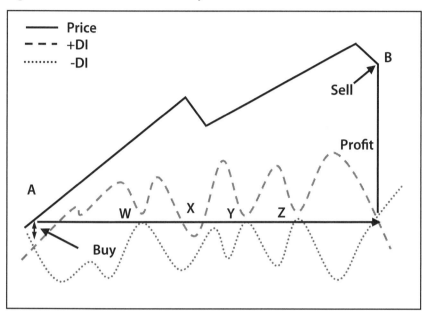

November 1992, as flagged by the arrow. At this time, the ADX is below its solid oversold line. This is followed by a good rally, and then a sell signal is triggered at the first vertical line. This one, too, comes when the ADX is at a low reading. However, it turns out to be a slightly unprofitable trade, even though the right condition (that is, a low ADX reading) is in force. Then, at the next vertical line, a new crossover and buy signal are given. The chart clearly indicates that by July 1993 the directional movement was very strong indeed as the ADX rallies above its "overbought" zone. Because of this, the next DI crossover (point A) comes at a high, but falling, ADX reading. As we discovered earlier, this can either mean a consolidation or an actual reversal in trend. In this instance, the dashed -DI crosses above the solid positive one and a sell indication is triggered. I

Figure 37-6   DI crossovers and breakeven trades

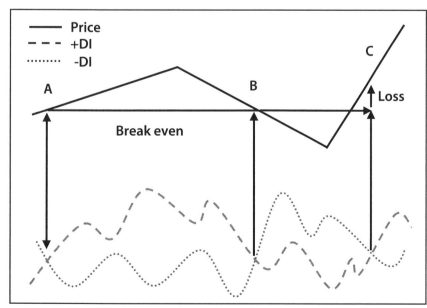

would have used this as a signal to liquidate a long position, but not necessarily to put on a short. As it happened, the price declined, so a profit would have been made. However, there was no guarantee at that point that the price was not about to enter an unprofitable trading range. Indeed, if you look at the two DIs between August and September, you can see that they came very close to a crossover on two occasions.

The next buy crossover developed in mid October. However, it was not triggered at a time when the ADX was at a particularly low reading. This was then followed by a quick whipsaw crossover, which can hardly be detected on this chart. What is interesting is that the ADX subsequently fell back to its oversold reading, and when the DIs crossed again, a powerful rally ensued (point B). The last sell signal in February 1994 (point C) developed at a fairly high ADX reading. This, too, proved to be unprofitable as a buy signal was given right at the end of the chart.

This example featured both good and bad signals, but by and large, the best ones came when the ADX was at an unusually low reading. I will not deny that some good signals are triggered just as, or just after, the ADX has peaked at a high ADX reading. However, this system does not tell us whether a trading range or trend reversal is going to take place, so it is a

> Use reversals from low readings in the ADX to identify securities that are likely to trend and then use the DIs and trend signals in the price to actually time the move.

Chart 37-5   General Motors, an ADX, and two 14-day DIs

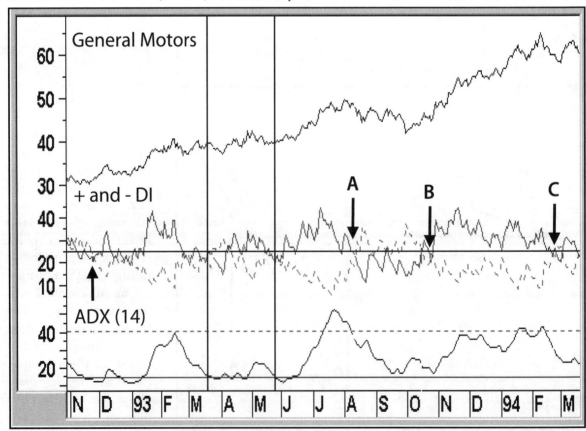

(Source: pring.com)

bit like rolling the dice unless we can get some pointers from other indicators. Of course, if you are writing or selling options, you do not care whether the trend changes to a sideways or downward one, because you are interested in seeing that time premium erode away.

To sum up our findings, use reversals from low readings in the ADX to identify securities that are likely to trend and then use the DIs and trend signals in the price to actually time the move.

EXTREME POINT RULE

There is one more feature of the directional movement system that we should cover, and that is the *extreme point rule*. The extreme point rule is concerned with the best level to place a stop once a trade has been entered. This principle states that on the day that the DIs cross, use the extreme price made that day as the reversal point. Long positions would use the low of the day, short positions the high, as shown in Fig. 37-7. These, then, become the stop points that should be used for the next couple of days or so, *even if the DIs signal that the position should be liquidated by re-crossing each other.*

Wilder rationalizes this on the basis that the initial equilibrium or crossover day tends to be an important one, regardless of whether or not a market is going to reverse. As a result, the extreme price point reached on that day is psychologically important to market participants. For this reason, it is not normally breached, but if it is, then this typically indicates that the DI crossover was a whipsaw.

Figure 37-7 Extreme point rules

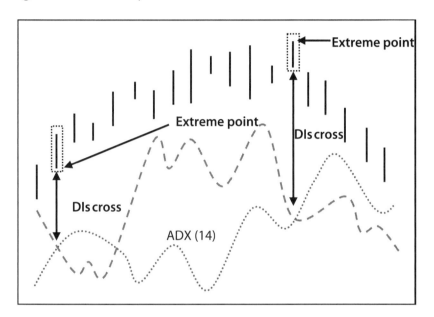

Figure 37-8 Relating the ADX to DI crossovers

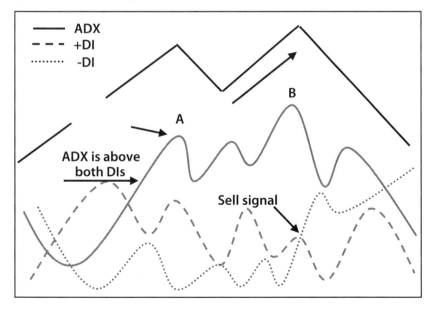

OVERLAYING THE ADX ON THE DIS

One approach that is sometimes used for enhancing the interpretation of the directional movement system is to overlay the ADX on the two DIs. Important turns are indicated when the ADX reverses direction *after it has moved above both DIs*. In Fig. 37-8, the ADX reverses direction at point A, and after one more rally, the price also peaks. The actual signal would have occurred when the +DI14 crossed below the -DI14, but it would not have been a bad idea to take some profits at A, since the timing was better. In a really strong market, similar to that indicated in this example, the ADX will reverse direction from a high level, decline, and then move back up. Yet the DIs don't cross until much later, as at point B in this instance. Conversely, when the ADX line moves below both DIs, Wilder recommends staying away from trend-following systems.

SUMMARY

It is possible to set out a series of rules as explicitly proposed by Wilder.

1. *Only trade trend-following systems with securities that have a high ADX rating.* The ADX level reflects the degree of directional movement, not the direction itself.

2. *Use crossovers of the +DI14 and -DI14 as timing points for entering and exiting the markets.*

3. *The principal exception to rule 2 occurs when the extreme point trading rule takes effect.* It states that on the day of the DI crossover, use the extreme price point in the opposite direction to your position as a stop point. Long positions should use the low of the day, and short ones the high. This becomes the stop point regardless of whether the DIs subsequently and temporarily re-cross again.

4. *When the ADX moves above both DIs and reverses direction, this represents an early indication that a trend reversal is about to take place.* Some profit-taking is in order. Final liquidation would occur with a DI crossover or an extreme point violation. If the +DI14 is above the -DI14 at the time of the ADX reversal, this would mean a change in trend from up to down, and vice versa.

5. *If the ADX is above both DIs and it is at an extreme reading, this means that the trend has been in force for some time and it is not a good point for entering new trades in the event that the DIs re-cross in the direction of the prevailing trend.* In other words, the high reading in the ADX is a form of overbought-or-oversold reading where new trades in the direction of the prevailing trend are not usually profitable.

6. *When the ADX is below both DIs, avoid trend-following systems as little directional movement is indicated.*

7. *When the ADX is below the 20-25 area regardless of its position to the DIs, avoid trend-following systems since little or no directional movement is indicated.*

Extremes in the ADX

PRING ALTERNATIVE INTERPRETATION

Technical analysis is an art rather than a science, so it would not be surprising if other methods of interpretation of the directional movement system were to evolve. In my own research, I have found different ways in which the directional movement system can be used. These comments are in no way intended to denigrate Mr. Wilder's contribution; rather, they are meant to elaborate and expand on his ideas. You are free, of course, to choose whatever principles you find most useful.

In Chart 38-1, we move back to the DI arrangement. The idea is that buy signals are generated when the solid +DI crosses above the dashed -DI, and vice versa. In some market environments, this works very well. However, in others, a substantial number of whipsaws can be generated. In this example of the Singapore Fund, you can see that numerous whipsaws were, in fact, triggered.

One way around this is to smooth the DIs. In this respect, Chart 38-2 is presented as an example. You can see that most of the whipsaws have been filtered out. In this instance, the trading action is so volatile that these smoothed crossovers would (in most instances) have occurred well after the turning points. So what was gained from fewer whipsaws was lost in tardy signals. However, since we know that these signals were more reliable, it is possible to pick and choose entry points. In other words, if a signal is given well after a turning point, ignore it and either wait for another one or look for another security.

This approach works better in a trending market, where the price stalls sufficiently to trigger a quick whipsaw with the simple DI crossover approach but does not with the smoothed variety. Chart 38-3 of IBM displays two whipsaws with the DI crossover approach.

In Chart 38-4, though, the DIs have been smoothed. Consequently, a great deal of this whipsaw activity has been filtered out. Now it is true that the sell signal for IBM in January 1997 comes right at the bottom of the first down leg. However, the overall performance, allowing for slippage, commissions, and so forth, still beats the two whipsaws that developed in the ellipse using the raw DIs. Also, the actual DI crossover sell signal developed about halfway down the decline. So not much was lost overall with the smoothing approach, but a great deal was gained.

> To avoid the whipsaws associated with Welder's DI crossovers, I recommend smoothing the DIs. This approach is particularly helpful in trending markets.

MORE ON THE ADX

These simple crossovers form only part of the system, of course, and should be related to the ADX. From my own observations, I have not found the concept of a high ADX rating as a selection tool for securities with a strong directional movement to be particularly helpful. Any momentum indicator in an overbought-or-oversold extreme can tell you that a market has been trending. It is a fact that once a market has had a good run, the chances are that it will subsequently consolidate its gains or losses. In most cases, I find that a reversal in the ADX from an extreme high level is often followed by a change in trend. Sometimes this is an actual reversal; at other times it is a consolidation. In this respect, such reversals can be of invaluable help if you are selling options. This is because the price of an option declines over time if there is no price movement or if the trend reverses direction.

Chart 38-1   Singapore Fund and two 14-day DIs

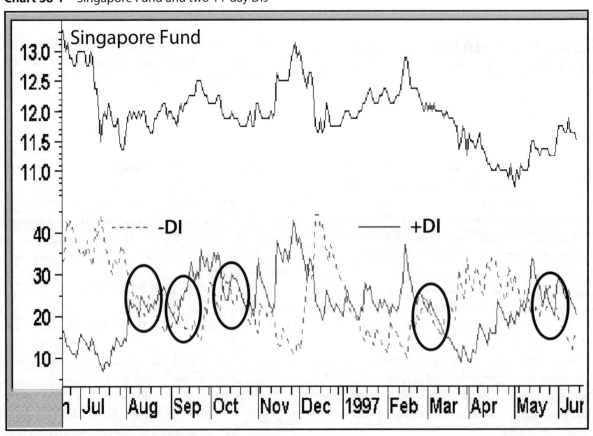

(Source: pring.com)

Chart 38-2 Singapore Fund and two smoothed 14-day DIs

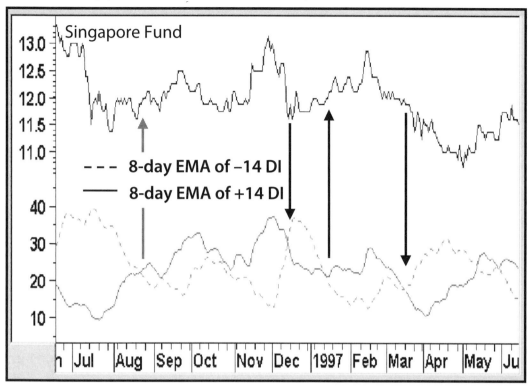

Chart 38-3 IBM and two 14-day DIs

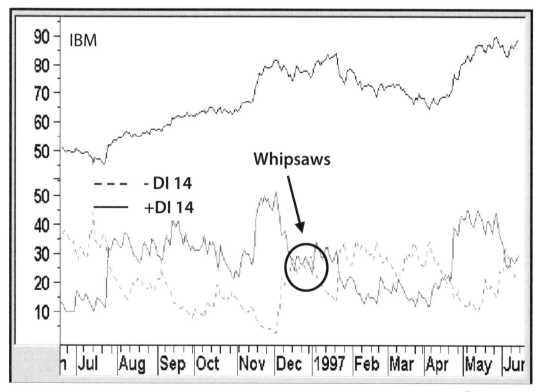

Chart 38-4   IBM and two smoothed 14-day DIs

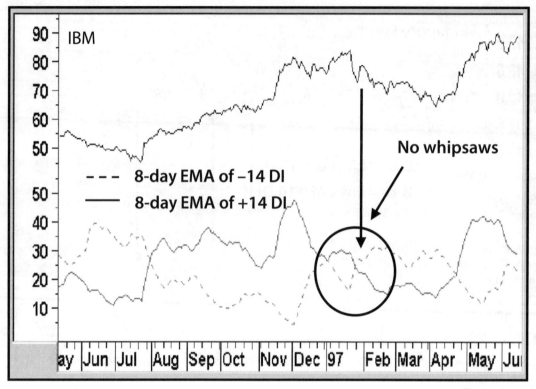

(Source: pring.com)

Chart 38-5   JP Morgan and Newmont Mining ADX indicators

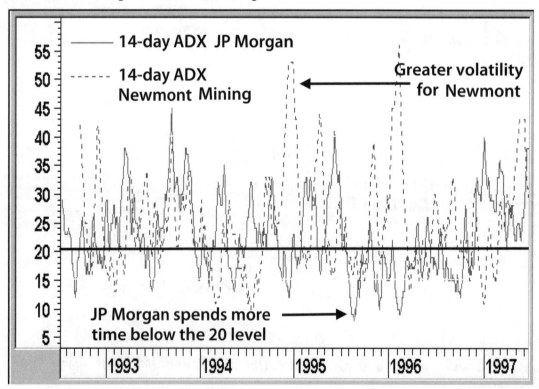

(Source: pring.com)

First of all, it is important to note that not all securities are created equal. By this I mean that what may be regarded as a high ADX reading for one price series may not be high for another, and vice versa. Chart 38-5 features two ADX series plotted on the same scale. The dashed line reflects a 14-day ADX for Newmont Mining. See how the volatility for this series is generally much greater than for the JP Morgan solid ADX. JP Morgan also spends a lot more time under the horizontal line, indicating very little directional movement. If finding a security with a substantial amount of directional movement is your objective, then a visual comparison such as this, or a statistical one using your favorite charting software, makes good sense. In this case, though, my point is that we should be judging the ADX performance of a specific security relative to its past. This way, we can establish the extreme points or over-

> We should judge the ADX performance of a specific security relative to its past.

bought levels in the ADX. Then when the ADX reverses direction, it is time to anticipate a reversal in trend or the start of some trading range action.

Chart 38-6 shows International Paper at the end of the 1980s and the start of the 1990s. The dashed line is an 8-day MA of the 14-day ADX. I have placed the extended zone for the ADX at 40. The vertical lines show those periods when the ADX, having crossed above the overbought zone, then crosses below the 8-day MA. On each occasion, the price reverses trend. The first signal in 1989 is followed by a small decline, but the ensuing price action is really an extended trading range. The next

Chart 38-6   International Paper and an 8-day MA of a 14-day ADX

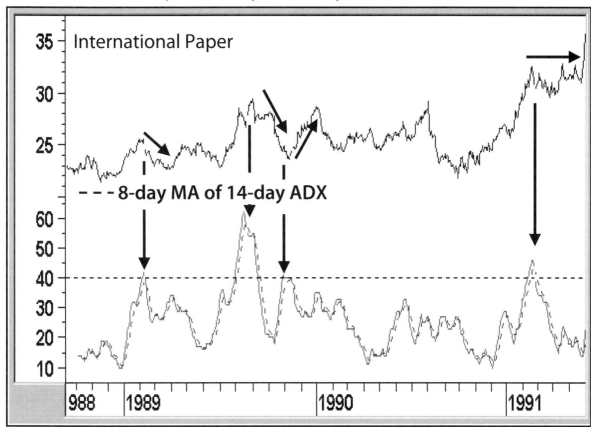

(Source: pring.com)

signal develops just before the August 1989 peak. Note how the end of the decline is signaled by another instance in which the ADX moves above its overbought zone and then crosses below its average. Finally, the whole of 1990, despite some volatile action, is totally devoid of any extreme directional movement. We have to wait until 1991 for the ADX to give us another signal. This time it is followed by a relatively short 3-month consolidation.

Chart 38-7 features DuPont. The detail is not so good because I wanted to show you the perspective over a long period. The vertical lines again signal the 8-day MA crossovers after the ADX reached an extreme. The solid horizontal lines indicate that almost all of the signals were followed by a consolidation. The two dashed vertical arrows in 1995 point up to those periods when nothing much happened. In fact, after a small decline, both signals were followed

by an extension of the previous advance. What is interesting is the fact that the next signals were not long in coming, and once they occurred, they were followed by an extensive consolidation. The other two dashed arrows in 1989 and 1994 also point up to failures. These examples all used a 14-day time span. There is, of course, no reason why a different span cannot be used. However, in my experience, 14 days seems to work as well as any.

LOW ADX READINGS

I have found that some of the best trend-following moves begin when the ADX is at a low number and *starts to reverse* to the upside. In Chart 38-8, we can see that several major trending moves are all signaled by a DI crossover that occurs *when the ADX is at a low 20 reading.*

Chart 38-7   DuPont and an ADX

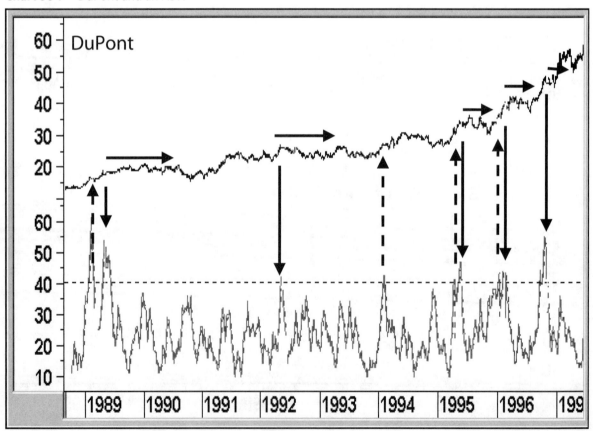

(Source: pring.com)

Low readings are very useful, since they tell us in a fairly graphic way those times when a market has *not* been trending. For other oscillators, such as an RSI, directionless markets are reflected in dull activity around the 50 level, which is relatively difficult to spot. In the case of the ADX, it is easier to detect, since the indicator falls to a low reading of 20 or less. Again, the actual level for a specific security can best be obtained by a quick historical review to discover what is the norm for a trendless market. When the ADX starts to rally, it warns us that a directional move is on the way. The nature of the direction can be obtained from a review of other momentum series. The problem that I have found is that by the time the ADX starts to rally, the move is often well underway.

One way around this is to look for an abnormally low ADX reading and then wait to see if it is possible to construct a trendline for the price itself. Then, when the price violates the line (provided the ADX is still at a subdued reading), use the trendline break as a buy signal. It is even better if you can see a strong DI crossover or even a DI trend break. In Chart 38-9 of the Philadelphia Gold and Silver Share Index (XAU), I have plotted the lower ADX extreme at 20. The bottom area features a 14-period +/-DI. In any situation it is always best to have as many indicators offering signals as possible. This, then, increases the odds that they will work. In the example on the left-hand part of the chart in October 1993, we see that the ADX moves below the 20 level in August. However, we do not see a trendline violation in the price until October. At that time, the ADX and +DI also violate trendlines for a very strong buy signal. Later on (January 1994), the ADX once again slips below the 20 zone. In March

Chart 38-8   The XAU, two DIs, and an ADX

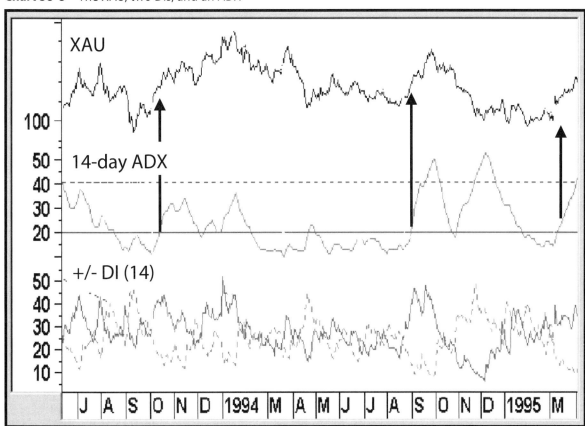

(Source: pring.com)

the price breaks above a nice downtrend line. It actually takes place when the ADX makes its low for the move. The price then rallies sharply. However, the advance is very short-lived and the signal is a bit of a failure. Based on our rules, it was quite legitimate, but we need to realize that not every situation is going to work out in a profitable way. In this particular instance, we could point to the fact that neither the ADX nor the two DIs violated a trendline. But even so, the result was a disappointment.

The next signal (in August 1994) was followed by a pretty good rally, but note how the ADX and +DI both broke above downtrend lines.

Chart 38-10 shows the same arrangement, but for a later time period. See how the ADX was below 20 in May and June 1995. Then we see a trend break in the price. This time it was followed by a small rally and consolidation—not a disaster, but certainly disappointing. Note also that neither the ADX nor the DIs violated trendlines in this instance, as in the previous weak signal.

Finally, look at the situation in October. The ADX had been in a nontrending mode below 20 for over 2 1/2 months. Then the price completed a top and the ADX violated a trendline. Following this, the price fell quite sharply. Note how the bottom was signaled by the ADX crossing below the 40 extreme.

The directional movement system should always be used in conjunction with other momentum indicators. In this way it is possible to gain some valuable clues as to the nature of the forthcoming trend. For example, we would expect to see a far stronger trend develop after a momentum indicator had reached an oversold condition and perhaps diverged positively with the price a couple of times. A low and reversing ADX in combination with a positive DI crossover would then be more likely to be followed by a fairly good advance.

There is no doubt that the directional movement system can offer some quite good trading signals. However, as with all technical indicators, this approach is best used in conjunction with others.

Chart 38-9   The XAU, two DIs, and an ADX

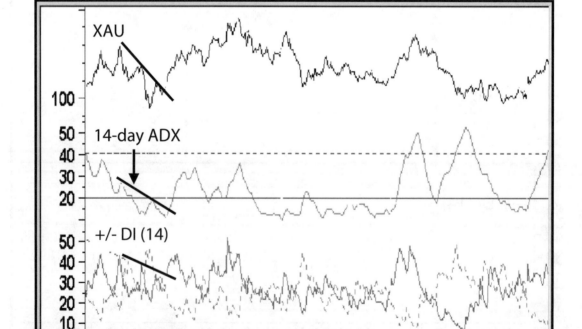

(Source: pring.com)

Chart 38-10 The XAU, two DIs, and an ADX

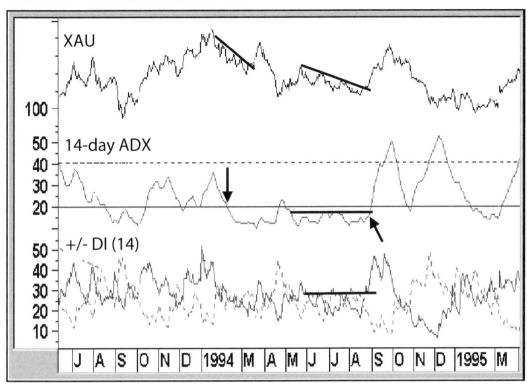

(Source: pring.com)

Chart 38-11 The XAU, two DIs, and an ADX

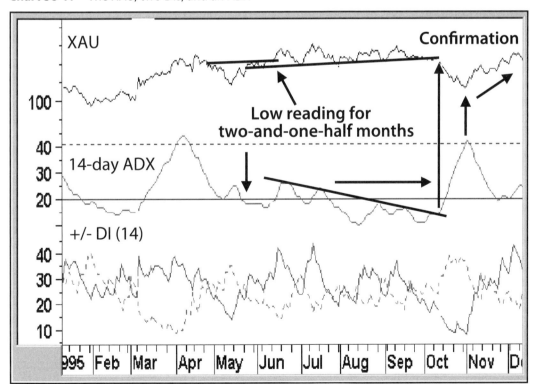

(Source: pring.com)

39

The Commodity Selection Index

The *commodity selection index* (CSI) is another Wells Wilder innovation. It was originally named the commodity selection index, but this oscillator can really be applied to any security for any timeframe.

The objective is to identify which securities are likely to give the trader the greatest bang for the buck. The characteristics measured by this oscillator are directional in nature. It also takes into consideration volatility, margin requirements, and commission costs. The result in theory is an indicator that allows for comparison and selection, the idea being to select the security with the greatest directional movement.

The CSI is not designed as a timing device in its own right but more as a method for finding out where the most leverage can be obtained relative to the implied volatility and trending characteristics of various contracts.

My own view is that this is a poor method for selecting potential trades since it places emphasis on the greed factor, that is, how quickly and easily someone can make money. Anyone who has studied the psychology of trading or who has learned from his or her own errors in the markets knows without a shadow of doubt that one of most important psychological attributes is objectivity. Any hint of the greed factor substantially increases the odds of failure. Patience and discipline, not greed and speed, are the order of the day. Having said that, I have noticed that in some cases, when the selection index reaches an extreme and reverses, it can often warn of an important change in trend. In this sense, I am assuming that there are three trends: up, down, and sideways. A change in trend does not, therefore, mean the same thing as a reversal in trend. The CSI is not interpreted in the usual

> One of most important psychological attributes is objectivity; any hint of the greed factor substantially increases the odds of failure.

way in that a high reading indicates an over-bought condition, and a low one an oversold. This is because it indicates the degree of direction. Thus a high reading indicates lots of directional movement, and vice versa. When the CSI reaches an extreme and reverses, as it does in early 1996 (Chart 39-1), it indicates that the prevailing trend is likely to change. In this instance, it is from up to down. However, it might easily have been from up to sideways. Two other extremes (in September and December 1994) indicate reversals, one from an up to a down and one from a downtrend to a sideways congestion.

The question naturally arises as to what is an extreme. The answer is that it can really only be determined on a trial-and-error basis for a particular security. For this you will need a lot of historical data. I would suggest more than five years' worth. In Chart 39-2 featuring the U.S. dollar index I have placed the overextended extreme line at 200, since this appears to catch most of the sharp rallies in the CSI.

The chart covers a 12-year period in which there were roughly nine extreme CSI movements: of the nine, six were followed by a change of trend lasting about three months or more, and three were failures (flagged by the dashed arrows). In some instances, especially when a price is in a linear up- or downtrend, the CSI does not work as well.

Chart 39-3 of Abbott Labs illustrates an example. This long-term uptrend in the CSI is a function of the calculation. I have tried various methods of detrending the data, but none seems to work satisfactorily from a practical aspect.

Even though it has many deficiencies, the extreme reading interpretation can be useful at times. However, since it can be unreliable, this approach should most definitely be used as a filter. Use the extreme readings as an alert that a change of trend may be in the wind, but use other indicators as a backup. Never rely on one indicator alone, especially the CSI.

Chart 39-1   ASA and a 14-day CSI

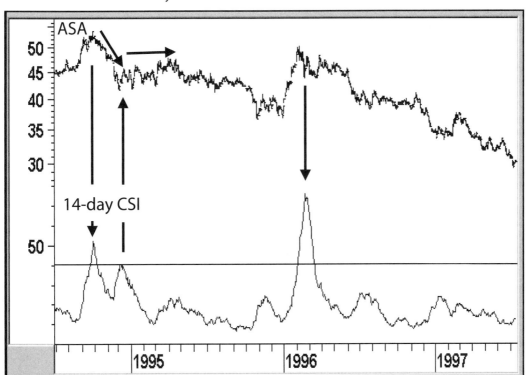

(Source: pring.com)

Chart 39-2   U.S. dollar index and a 14-day CSI

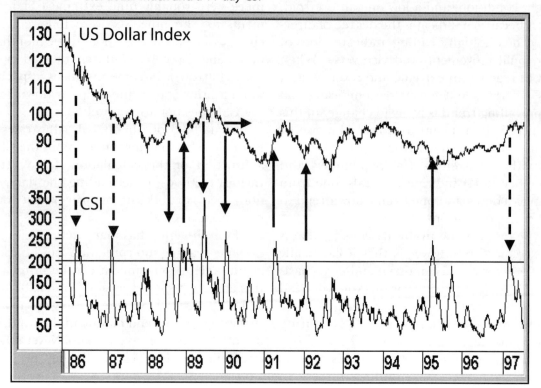

(Source: pring.com)

Chart 39-3   Abbott Labs and a 14-day CSI

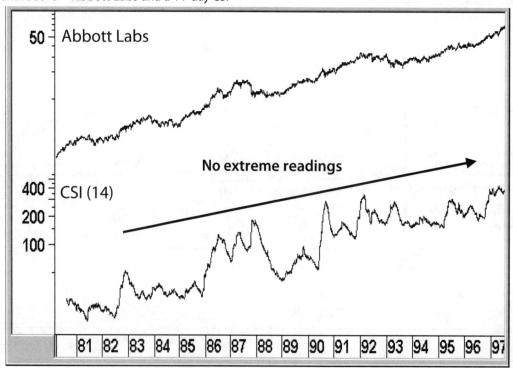

(Source: pring.com)

40

The Parabolic Indicator

INTRODUCTION

The *parabolic indicator*, devised by Wells Wilder, is not a momentum indicator and so, strictly speaking, does not fall within the scope of this book. However, it is being mentioned briefly, since it has become a very popular trading mechanism and can be used with momentum indicators to generate timely stop-loss signals.

One of the most valid criticisms of trend following systems is that the implied lags between the turning points and the trend reversal signals obliterate a significant amount of the potential profitability of a trade. The parabolic system is designed to address this problem by increasing the speed of the trend, so far as stops are concerned, whenever prices reach new profitable levels. The concept draws on the idea that time is an enemy, and unless a trade or investment can continue to generate more profits over time, it should be liquidated. Since it is a stop-loss system, it can be used with any momentum series, once that indicator has been used to filter out a good entry point for a trade. It is also a trailing stop-loss system, which means that the stop is continually being moved in the direction of the position, that is, up for a long position and down for a short.

The parabolic stop reversal system is a trailing stop technique. The formula is designed so that the stop is constantly being tightened as the market moves in your favor. The disadvantage is that when the position is first initiated, it is given a relatively long leash, so to speak. Then as time passes and the price increases, the stop is gradu-

> The parabolic indicator is a trailing stop-loss system, which means that the stop is continually being moved in the direction of the position, that is, up for a long position and down for a short.

ally tightened. The expression *parabolic* derives from the shape of the curve of the stops as it appears on the chart. In a rising market, the stop is continually being raised, never lowered. In a declining market, the opposite will hold true.

HOW DOES IT WORK?

The parabolic shows up on the chart as a parabolic-shaped curve that is plotted above and below the price (Chart 40-1). This curve is often referred to as the SAR, which stands for "stop and reversal system." This is because the parabolic, when triggered, is often used not only to stop out a position, but to actually reverse it. Thus a parabolic would simultaneously trigger the liquidation of a long position and the entering of a short one.

The parabolic indicator is automatically calculated for us by the major charting software packages, but Fig. 40-1 shows how the dynamics of this method operate. The first step involves the establishment of a reference point. Wilder instructs us to take the extreme high or low from the previous trade. For exam-

ple, if you had earlier been short and are now long, the reference point would be the extreme low for the previous (down) move. However, every trade has to start somewhere, so if this is your first trade in this particular security, the logical point ought to be the previous minor low. In this example that would be at point X on the fourth day.

For the sake of argument, our trade is initiated on day 8. The SAR would then be placed at the previous minor low established on day 4. The SAR for the next day (meaning day 9) will be the high experienced on day 8 less the SAR multiplied by an *acceleration factor*. Wilder stated that the acceleration factor should begin at 0.2 on the first day of the trade (Fig. 40-2). This is gradually increased by 0.2 *each day that a new high from the trade is recorded* until the position is either stopped out or the maximum acceleration factor of 2.0 is reached. After that, the acceleration factor remains constant at 2.0. This means that if the price continues to make new highs, the acceleration factor rises to 0.4 on day 10 (Fig. 40-3), 0.6 on day 11 (Fig. 40-4), and finally 0.8 on day 12 (Fig. 40-5). If a new high for the trade is not recorded between, say, days 8 and 12, the acceleration factor would remain unchanged. In effect, the system is saying that if a security records a new high, this is reflective of improving momentum and that it is then appropriate to raise the stop a little more aggressively, for when momentum starts to deteriorate again, the price trend is likely to reverse quickly.

There are really two steps to using this approach. First, find and execute an entry point either from the long or short side using your favorite set

Figure 40-1   Initiating the trade

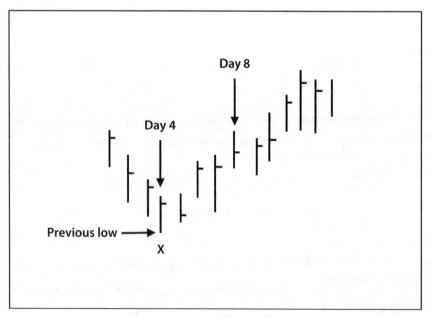

(Source: pring.com)

Figure 40-2 Starting the parabolic

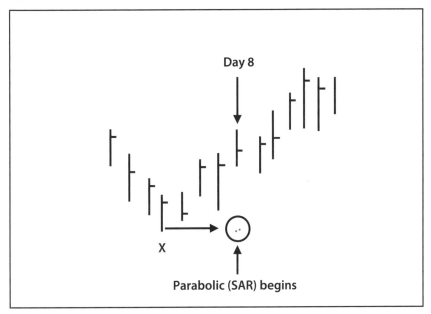

(Source: pring.com)

Figure 40-3 The acceleration factor kicks in

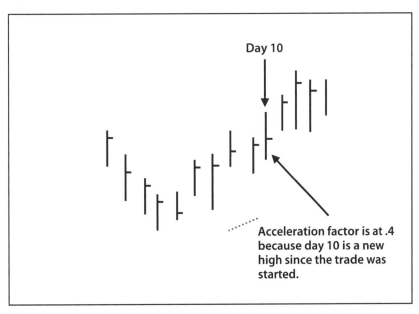

(Source: pring.com)

Figure 40-4   The acceleration factor moves to 0.6

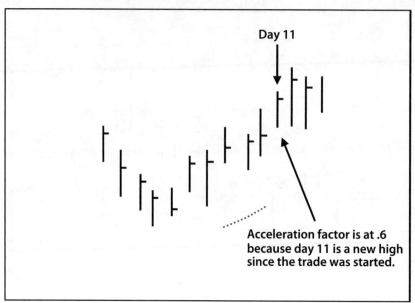

(Source: pring.com)

Figure 40-5   The acceleration factor moves to 0.8

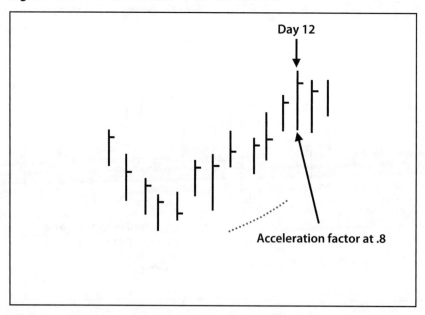

(Source: pring.com)

of technical indicators. Then place a stop using the parabolic system.

There are really three ways in which these stops or SARs can be set. Since most of us are now able to use charting software packages, this is automatically calculated for us, so we do not have to concern ourselves with the actual methodology. For those who do not use software or who wish to understand the system more fully, I will briefly cover the three points. Actually, the first two have already been explained. The initial stop is set at the extreme

point for the previous trade. Then the stop is moved in the direction of the trade with reference to the extreme price for the new trade and the acceleration factor. The final rule for positions states that you should never move the SAR for tomorrow above the previous day's or today's low. In the event that the calculation calls for the SAR to be plotted above the previous day's or today's low, then use the lower of today's or the previous day's. The next day's calculation should then be based on this SAR. The reverse would be true for short positions.

The parabolic system is sometimes termed a *stop and reverse* system because it assumes that you are always in the market. Every sell stop, for instance, is expected to produce a long position when activated, and each long stop induces a short trade. Personally, I prefer to select an entry point and use the parabolic system for the purposes of setting the stop,

> I prefer to select an entry point and use the parabolic system for the purposes of setting the stop, rather than continually reversing positions.

Chart 40-1   eBay and a parabolic indicator

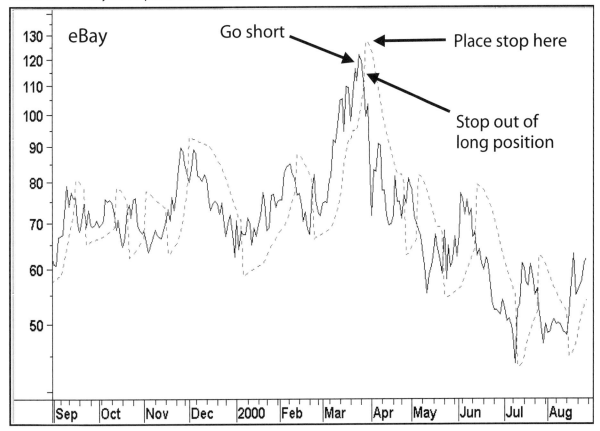

(Source: pring.com)

rather than continually reversing positions. Remember, most losing trades develop when you go against the direction of the main trend. Chart 40-2 demonstrates that quite clearly. In the period under consideration, the dollar index is in a bear market. The solid ellipses indicate bear market rallies that would have resulted in losses, and the dashed ellipses indicate the two sole instances when a profit would have been realized from the long side. This is an extreme example, I grant you, but research has confirmed that if losses are to occur, they will almost always develop in positions that run contrary to the main trend. Working on the assumption that most markets in most periods are either in a primary up- or downtrend, half the signals developed by the SAR approach will be countercyclical in nature. That is why I prefer to use the parabolic system as a stop system only, and not as a stop and reverse system.

AS A SIGNALING DEVICE

I would now like to take a look at how the parabolic indicator can be used in the marketplace. Chart 40-3 shows the price of the Iberia First Fund, a closed-end fund of Spanish and Portuguese stocks listed on the NYSE, together with the stop points as calculated by the parabolic system. The first entry point would be made on day 10 of the chart (by the arrow) as the price rallies above the dotted line. The initial stop is placed at the new dotted line. Since the price declines for the first few sessions, the parabola only rallies by the amount of the initial acceleration factor, which in this case is 0.2. Then on about September 26 the price makes a new high, so you can see that the parabola starts to accelerate a bit to the upside. This is because the acceleration factor is now being increased. In early November, the price

Chart 40-2   U.S. dollar index and a parabolic indicator

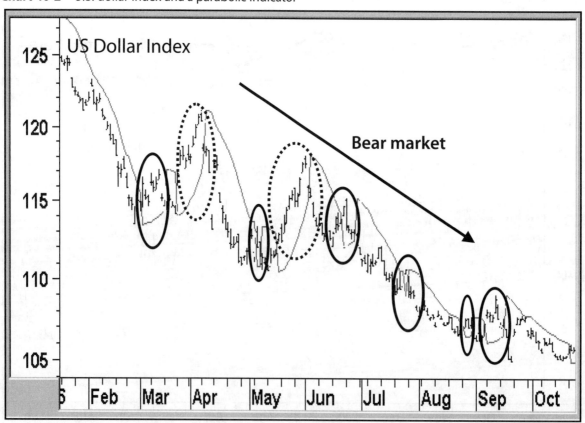

(Source: pring.com)

nearly slips below the stop line. However, the line itself is not increased because of rule 3 stated earlier: that the stop cannot be raised above today's or the previous day's low. In effect, you cannot get stopped out because the stop line rises above the price only when the price declines below the line. If on the next day the price had fallen, this would have represented a valid stop-loss sale. As we move on, you can see that the stop line accelerates because the price consistently makes new highs. Then in early December (Chart 40-4) the price does fall below the stop level. However, this is a countercyclical move and a new buy signal is quickly generated. Had a trader gone short at this point, the trade would have resulted in a loss, because the next buy signal occurred at a higher level than the short sale. Having established that fact, let us take a quick look at how we might go about determining the two variables, the acceleration factor and the maximum acceleration factor.

ACCELERATION FACTORS

The level of the acceleration factor is critical when setting stops. With MAs there is always a trade-off between timeliness and sensitivity. A short-term MA gives very timely signals but is so sensitive that it also generates numerous whipsaws. Alternately, a long-term term average has fewer whipsaws, but crossovers are less timely. The parabolic system works in the same way, but in this case, the lower the acceleration factor, the less timely the signal, and the higher the acceleration factor, the more sensitive and timely the signals. However, they result in more whipsaws. In Chart 40-5, the upper area features an acceleration factor of 0.01 with a maximum of 0.1, whereas the lower area shows a

Chart 40-3 First Iberia Fund applying the parabolic

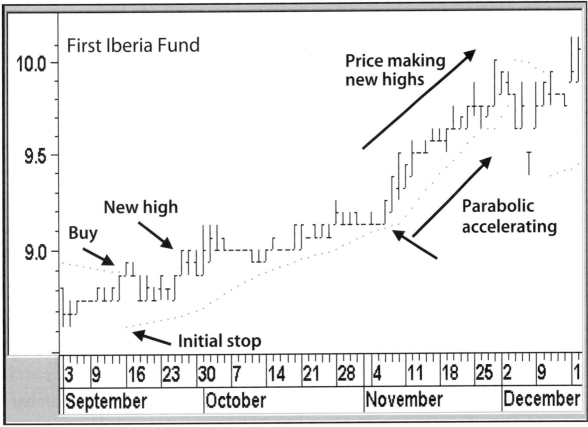

Part II: The Definitive Guide to Momentum Indicators

more aggressive 0.08 acceleration with a 0.8 maximum. The difference is very clear. The smaller acceleration factor featured in the top area results in far fewer whipsaws than the one featured in the lower. In this instance the smaller acceleration factor would have won hands down, but this is because of the strong-trending quality of the market. Setting levels for the accelerating factor is a trial-and-error process, just as with the process of determining the optimum span for an MA. In this case, though, we have two variables, the initial acceleration factor and the maximum.

Of the two, the initial acceleration factor has by far the largest influence. Chart 40-6 shows two parabolas using the same 0.01 initial factor. The dashed line has a maximum of 0.1 and the solid line has a 0.8 maximum. As you can see, both lines are identical until the price really begins to accelerate in mid June.

Wells Wilder, the innovator of this approach, recommends a 0.02 acceleration factor with a maximum of 0.2.

INTERPRETATION

The interpretation of the parabolic system is purely mechanical. On the whole, this approach has a lot of merit. However, one of the principal problems that I have found is that the initial stop point can often occur a long way from the entry point. In the example of the Swiss franc in Chart 40-7, there is a shorting possibility as the price violates the trendline. The first opportunity to initiate the trade was at the opening, since the price gapped down on the day and the opening was at 70.7 cents. However, the stop would have been placed above the extreme point of the rally at

Chart 40-4 First Iberia Fund applying the parabolic

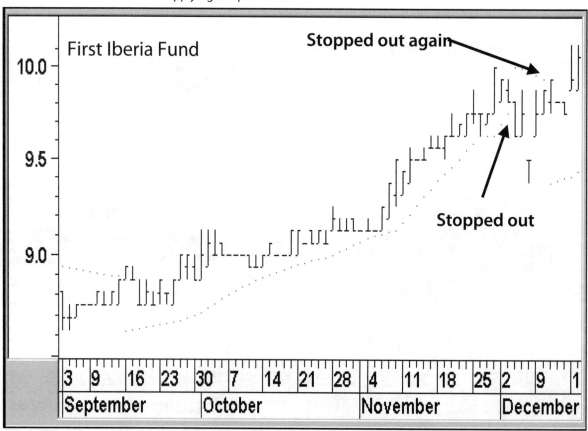

Chart 40-5 First Iberia Fund comparing two acceleration factors

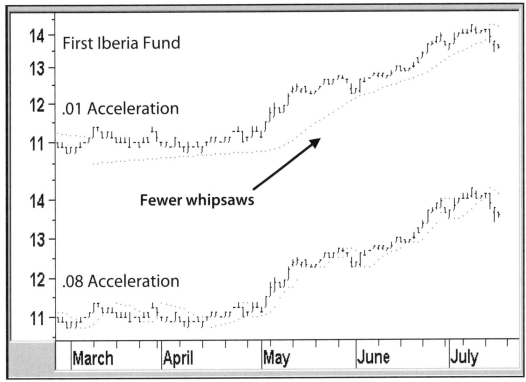

(Source: pring.com)

Chart 40-6 First Iberia Fund comparing two maximum acceleration factors

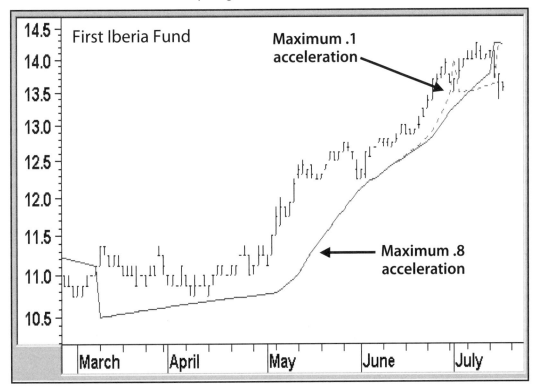

(Source: pring.com)

73.3 cents. This is quite a huge potential loss of 2.6 cents, especially when it is considered that this is a highly leveraged futures market. As it turned out, the trade was stopped out for a small loss (Chart 40-8). This was a lucky outcome, but really the best thing to do under this kind of situation is not to put on the trade in the first place because the risk, relative to the reward, was just too high.

Chart 40-9 shows another example just using the parabolic signal as a basis for trading. A short signal develops around February 18 and the initial stop point offers a fairly substantial risk, since the short was made at about $53 1/2 and the stop is at $57. As luck would have it, the stop moved down slightly, but the price rallied up to meet it. And the short would have been covered at about $56 1/2 for a loss. Ironically, had a long position been initiated

on the stop reversal principle, the trader would have gone home with another loss. This trade started off quite well and the price actually rallied to a new high. This meant that the stop point was progressively raised higher but not fast enough to have stopped another whipsaw resulting in a small loss. The next short trade (Chart 40-10) is a disaster, as the stop is just clipped at pretty well the high tick for the move. The long trade entails a great risk, since the stop is down at the previous low, and sure enough, the trade is once again stopped for a nasty loss. I could have shown you lots of examples wherein this approach would have done well in trending markets. However, I deliberately presented these examples because this type of false signal occurs far more often than we would like.

Chart 40-7   Swiss franc assessing risk using the parabolic

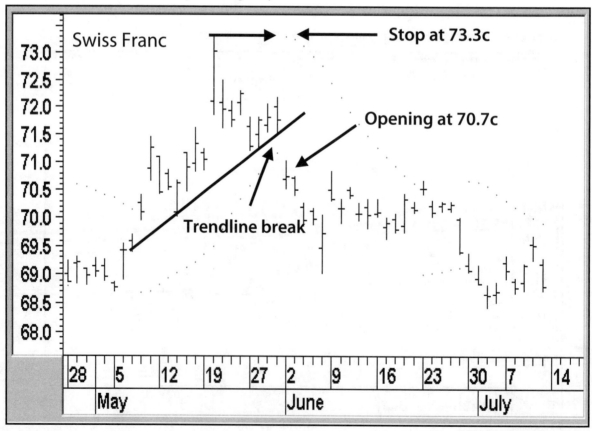

(Source: pring.com)

Chart 40-8   Swiss franc assessing risk using the parabolic

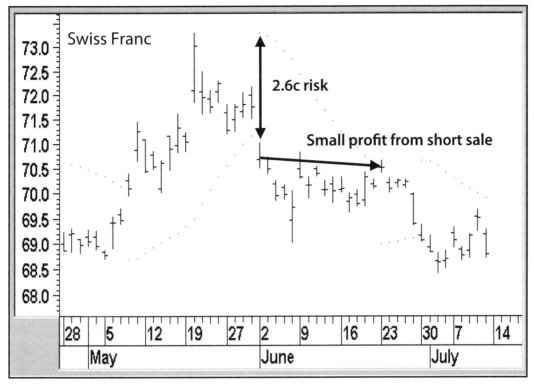

(Source: pring.com)

Chart 40-9   DuPont assessing risk using the parabolic

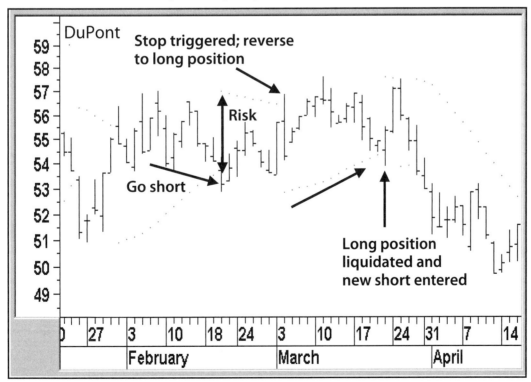

(Source: pring.com)

PLAYING PARABOLIC GUERILLA

There are two good ways around this problem. The first is to play parabolic guerilla. In other words, do not operate on every parabolic signal, but wait until you can see a situation where the price is close to a stop and an intelligent support-or-resistance point. Take the shorting signal flagged in Chart 40-11, for instance. At the time when the parabolic sell signal for International Paper was triggered, the risk was fairly high, all the way up to the top of the vertical arrow. Now, had we played guerilla and waited for the market to come to us, it would have been possible to short at the arrow just below the stop. There was even a second chance when the price rallied back to the trendline in Chart 40-12 and the parabolic line. Remember, it was only after the price had

> It is best not to operate on every parabolic signal, but to wait until you can see a situation where the price is close to a stop and an intelligent support-or-resistance point.

rallied back to the parabolic line 4 days earlier that it was possible to construct the trendline, since a valid line requires two points that need to be joined. As you can see, this combination of shorting close to the stop point and close to a resistance level would have resulted in a worthwhile profit. Incidentally, this particular parabolic line was set at 0.01 with a maximum acceleration factor of 0.2. It was, therefore, less sensitive than the others that we have been studying so far.

Chart 40-10   DuPont assessing risk using the parabolic

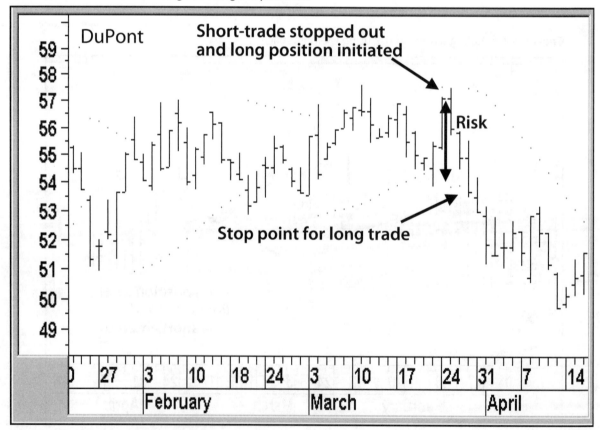

Chart 40-13 offers a sell signal at point A. Once again the risk is pretty large since the short would be covered at the first dot. Also, the brief intraday penetration of the stop line at point A indicated a whipsaw possibility. However, had we waited for a more opportune time using patience and discipline, a far less risky trade could have been initiated. There were two possibilities. The first would be in the ellipse, for it would have been obvious at this point that the tops of these 1-day rallies represented resistance. Thus a short could have been initiated from the same parabolic signal but at a higher price. Also, the stop line was gradually declining, further reducing the margin of risk. The second possibility came at the breakdown point as the triangle was completed. Now it is certainly true that the level of risk was higher than shorting into resistance at the upper trendline of the triangle. However, the odds of a successful trade were higher at the breakdown point (Chart 40-14), since it indicated that the period of consolidation was over. Also, the implied decline from the break would have meant that the parabolic line would accelerate on the downside, so the stop would soon move progressively lower.

USING THE PARABOLIC AS A STOP SYSTEM ONLY

The second useful approach is to enter a trade based on signals from other indicators and use the parabolic as a way of exiting the position. Even in this instance, sound money management principles would involve the setting of a stop loss at a reasonable level. In effect, if the trade seems well backed by the weight of the evidence, but the initial parabolic

Chart 40-11 International Paper playing guerilla parabolic

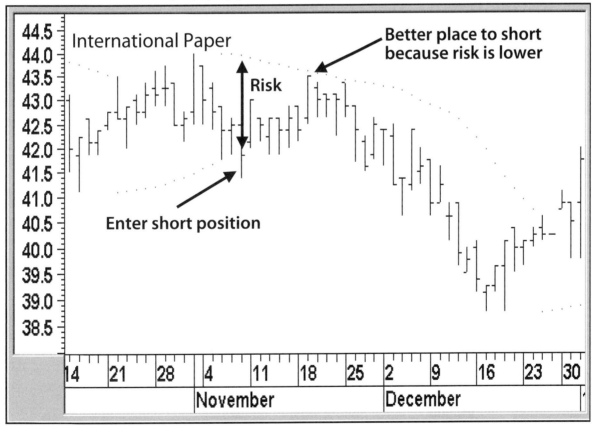

(Source: pring.com)

Chart 40-12   International Paper playing guerilla parabolic

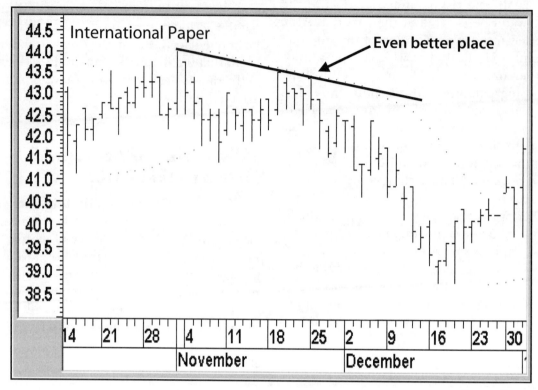

(Source: pring.com)

Chart 40-13   International Paper playing guerilla parabolic

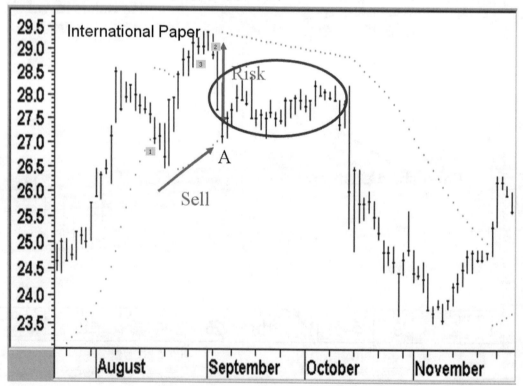

(Source: pring.com)

stop has to be set a long way from the entry point, the best thing to do would be to look for another trade.

Chart 40-15 using December 1997 gold indicates that using the parabolic stop at the entry point in May 1997 would have risked $10. Apart from the fact that this was a pretty emotional outside day, there was not much technical evidence to justify a short-term trade. After all, no trendline or serious MA breaks had taken place. Later on, we see a trendline violation in the 30-day ROC. This warned that the price could be vulnerable, but we still needed a trend signal from the price. That came on June 27, as the price crashed through the support trendline. At the time of the break, the parabolic was still in a sell mode, but now the distance between the stop point and the entry

point was much less. Also, because of the break in price, the acceleration factor had begun to increase, so the stop was being progressively lowered at a faster and faster rate right from day 1. The trade ended in a profit, as the next parabolic buy developed at a lower level.

Chart 40-16 shows a classic example using JP Morgan. The parabolic had signaled a buy signal at point A. Since the price did not fall very much, the buy signal was still in force when it reversed to the upside with a breakout at point B. The breakout was well supported by the buy signal in the short-term KST and the 45-day ROC. However, the great thing was that the parabolic stop line had already begun to move up, so the risk was not only being reduced, but continually being reduced as time progressed, and the line started to accelerate.

Chart 40-14   International Paper playing guerilla parabolic

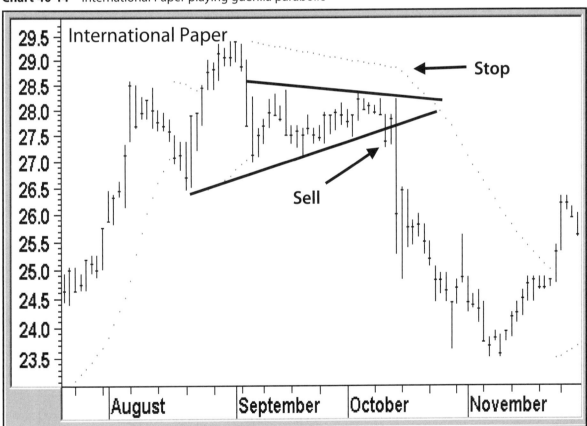

Chart 40-15   December 1997 Gold and two indicators

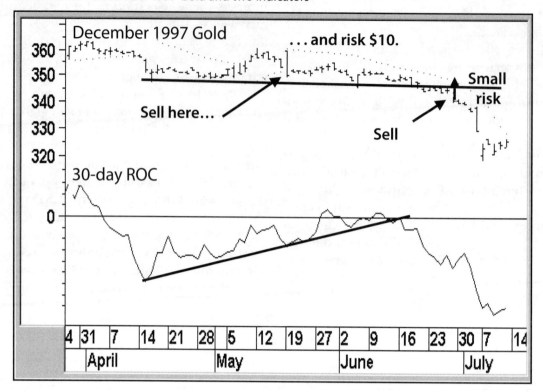

(Source: pring.com)

Chart 40-16   JP Morgan combining momentum signals with the parabolic

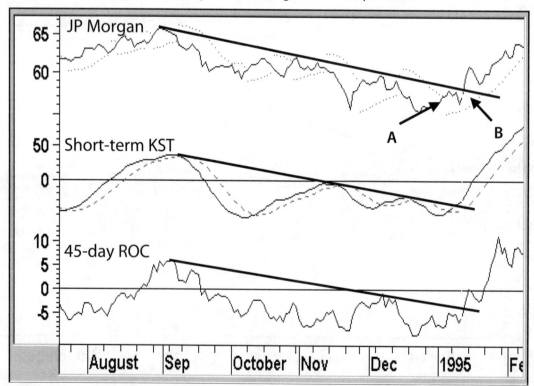

(Source: pring.com)

41

Price Projection Bands

THE CONCEPT

Price projection bands are similar in nature to envelope analysis and Bollinger bands. *These* bands also have some of the characteristics of channel lines, such as the Raff regression line. The projection band is not a momentum indicator. However, I have included a discussion of it here because it forms the basis for the calculation of the price projection oscillator, or PPO, which is our final topic.

Projection bands are calculated by finding the maximum and minimum prices over a specified time span; the longer the time, the wider the bands, and vice versa. These extreme values are then projected forward, parallel to a linear regression line. The indicator is then displayed as two elastic bands representing the minimum and maximum price over the specified time span. An example is shown in Chart 41-1. However, unlike the Raff regression channel and Bollinger bands, the price will always be contained by projection bands. This is because

> Projection bands are calculated by finding the maximum and minimum prices over a specified time span; the longer the time, the wider the bands, and vice versa.

the last plot of the projection band is the high or low for the period. If the latest data are at a new high or a new low, they will, by definition, be plotted at the same level.

The bands are interpreted in much the same way as any envelope. Look for prices to find resistance at the upper band and reverse trend. The lower band should find support, and so forth.

I have noticed that in a very strong market the price will hug the band for a considerable period of time. Then when it moves away from the upper band, it indicates a dissipation of upside momentum. Chart 41-2 shows that this is either immediately followed by a price decline (such as that in December 1995) or one is delayed a few periods as the price reaches a new high and then declines (such as the situation that developed in February 1996). In this instance, the price hugged the line for several sessions before moving away from it. A consolidation, rather than an actual trend reversal, followed. It really does not matter that much because once the price moves away from the band, most of the profit from a move usually has been captured.

The same principle applies in reverse. Sometimes it is only necessary for the price to touch the line for one or two periods. The main point is that when it moves away from the band, a signal of a possible trend reversal is given. This approach is far from perfect. In late June 1996, we see an example of the price pulling away from the line (Chart 41-3), but this only proves to be temporary, as it rallies for a

couple of days and then resumes its downtrend with a vengeance.

THE PROJECTION BANDS AND R-SQUARE

One way of filtering these whipsaws is to combine the projection band with the r-squared indicator. Chart 41-4 features a 14-period projection band with a 10-period r-square. Now if you look at the false signal in October 1995, you can see that the r-square was not at an extreme and was not, therefore, indicating a potential reversal in the downtrend. Alternately, the price starts to move away from the band in December 1995 and the r-square is at an extreme, so in this instance, an important bottom was registered. Not every extreme r-square reading results in a reversal, but that should

Chart 41-1   Morgan Stanley Cyclical Index and price projection bands

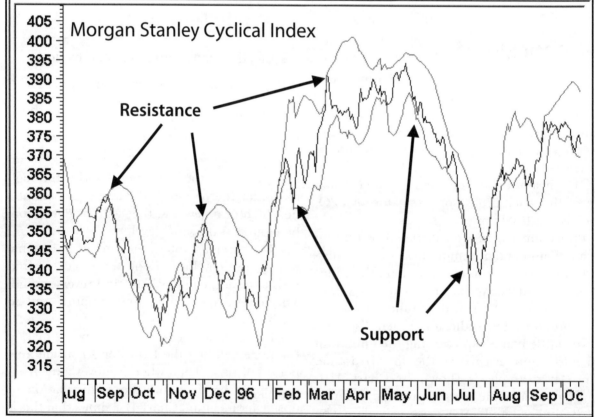

(Source: pring.com)

Chart 41-2   Morgan Stanley Cyclical Index and price projection bands

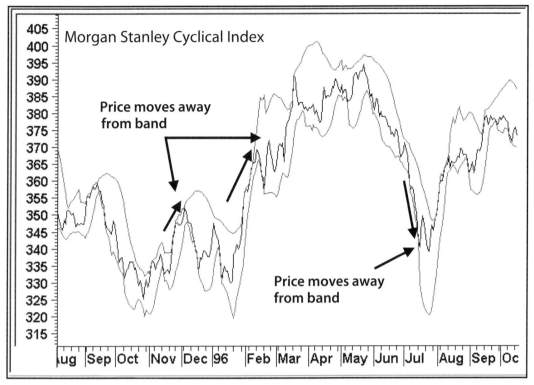

Morgan Stanley Cyclical Index

Price moves away from band

Price moves away from band

(Source: pring.com)

Chart 41-3   Morgan Stanley Cyclical Index and price projection bands

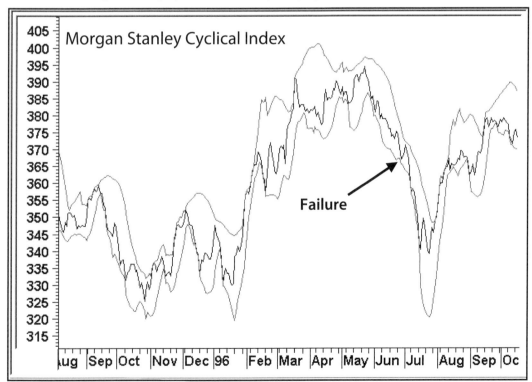

Morgan Stanley Cyclical Index

Failure

(Source: pring.com)

Chart 41-4   Mexico Index, price projection bands, and a 10-day r-square

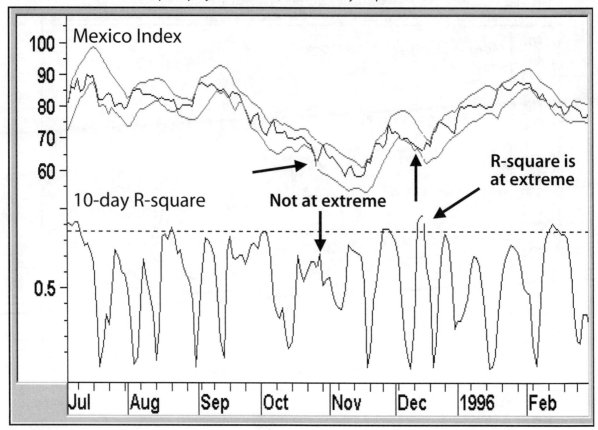

(Source: pring.com)

not be surprising because the price may not be at a projection band extreme. The early October 1995 r-square extreme represents an example wherein the price fails to confirm with a price projection signal.

As a general rule, whenever the price touches one of the bands for an extended period and then moves sharply away from it, we get a strong signal that the prevailing trend is vulnerable. For instance, Chart 41-5 (using a 30-day projection band) shows that for a lot of the time, the more vertical the up move as the price touches the band, the greater the odds of an important reversal. An example develops at the August 1995 peak in the Nikkei at point A and another one in July 1996 at point B. In both situations, the fact that the line is being continually touched means that the price is making a new 30-day high each time, because 30 days is the time span for this projection band. When it fails to make a new high after

> As a general rule, whenever the price touches one of the bands for an extended period and then moves sharply away from it, we get a strong signal that the prevailing trend is vulnerable.

consistently achieving new closing highs for 5, 6, or 10 days in a row, it indicates that the period of urgent buying is over. The longer the period it can cling to the upper band, the greater the swing in sentiment to the bullish side (then the greater the need for a swing to the other side).

The same principle works in reverse, so in June 1995 at point C, we see an example of the price hugging the band on the downside for a few days. Then the gap between the two rapidly increases.

Chart 41-5 The Nikkei Index and a 30-day price projection band

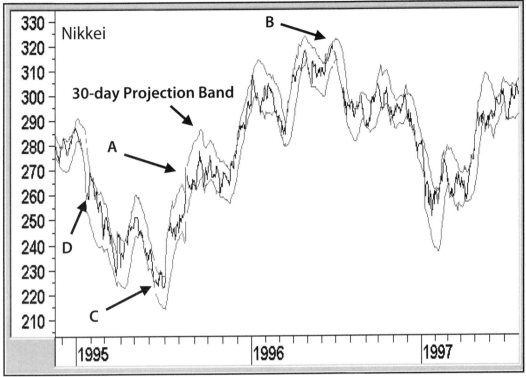

(Source: pring.com)

Chart 41-6 Price Company, price projection bands, and a 13-week r-square

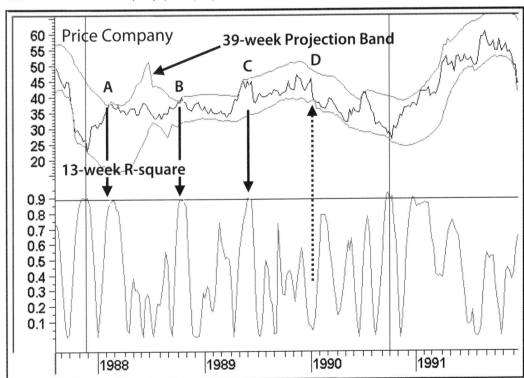

(Source: pring.com)

PROJECTION BANDS WITH WEEKLY CHARTS

Both the projection band and r-square work quite well with weekly charts, though I have found that it is crucial to experiment with different combinations with different securities. Chart 41-6 displays a 39-week projection band together with a 13-week r-square. The vertical lines show the points where the price, having hugged or touched the outer boundary of the projection band, then reverses away from it. At the same time, the r-square indicator reaches an overextended reading and then reverses. The late 1987 buy signal was followed by a sharp rally. The countervailing sell signal was triggered a few months later in mid February (point A), as the price touches the band and quickly reverses and the r-square peaks out from its overbought line. The trend reversal was far less dramatic, although prices did con-

solidate for 6 months. Do not forget that this chart covers a far greater period than the others we have been looking at. The next two sell signals in late 1988 (point B) and mid 1989 (point C) are also followed by consolidations. Finally, the late-1990 buy signal at the second vertical line was a classic: a sharp down move in which the price touches the band, followed by a quick reversal as the projection band declines. But look at the r-square; it is also at an extreme. This combination differs from the January 1990 low (point D), when the r-square had not reached an extreme reading.

Chart 41-7 shows a weekly chart of the coffee market using the same 39-week projection band and 13-week r-square combination. There were three periods when the r-square indicator reached an extreme reading. The December 1992 signal (point A) represented a textbook sell, since the price had been hugging the projection band for a while. Later on in December

Chart 41-7   Coffee, price projection bands, and a 13-week r-square

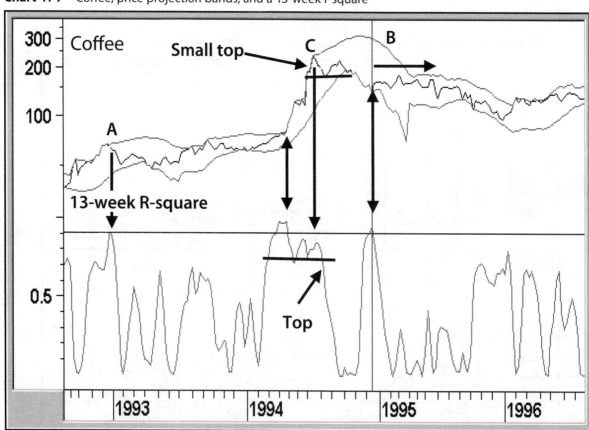

(Source: pring.com)

1994 (point B), all the conditions for a rally were in place, but the price consolidated instead. This is a reminder that a high reading in the r-square just indicates that the prevailing trend is likely to terminate, in this case, from up to sideways, not up to down. Finally, the mid-1994 peak in the r-square (point C) deserves closer scrutiny. This is because it occurred when the price rallied right to the upper band; the r-square then reversed direction, indicating that the price was losing its trending qualities. But it continued to rally sharply, still holding right on the band. When the final top did develop and the price moved away from the band, the r-square was overextended but below the extreme line. However, it still generated a sell indication because it completed a small top. In effect, the result was the same as if it had reversed from an extreme reading above the dashed line.

42

The Price Projection Oscillator

THE BAND VERSUS THE OSCILLATOR

The *price projection oscillator* is a variation on the stochastic. The stochastic assumes that prices close at, or near to, their high during an uptrend and close to or at their low in a downtrend. It is when the price starts to close away from these extreme points that momentum slows and the prevailing trend starts to reverse. The calculation of the stochastic, therefore, takes this concept into consideration. The price projection oscillator, alternately, does the same thing but adjusts the maximum and minimum prices up and down by a linear regression of the price. In plain English, this means that the price projection oscillator is more sensitive to short-term price swings.

Chart 42-1 shows a 45-day price projection oscillator together with a 45-day price projection band. If you look closely, you will see that there is a connection, because the price projection oscillator is really displaying the same infor-

mation, but in an oscillator format. See how the oscillator moves to 100 in August 1996 (point A) at the same time that the price touches the outer band. Then when the oscillator dips toward zero in October at point B, this occurs at the same time that the price moves to the lower band. In effect, we are seeing the same thing in a different way. This is similar to a comparison between a price envelope and a trend deviation oscillator based on the same timeframe.

There are several methods of interpretation. The first is to spot those periods when the oscillator is at, or extremely close to, the 0 and 100 readings and use those as a filter for seeing if other indicators are pointing to a peak or trough. That would have worked quite well at the May

> The price projection oscillator is more sensitive to short-term price swings than the stochastic.

Chart 42-1   Merrill Lynch and a 45-day PPO

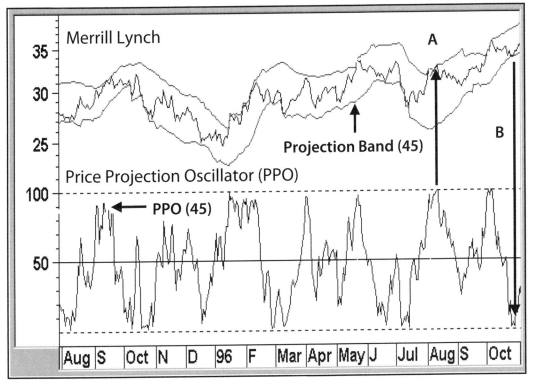

Chart 42-2   Merrill Lynch and a 45-day PPO

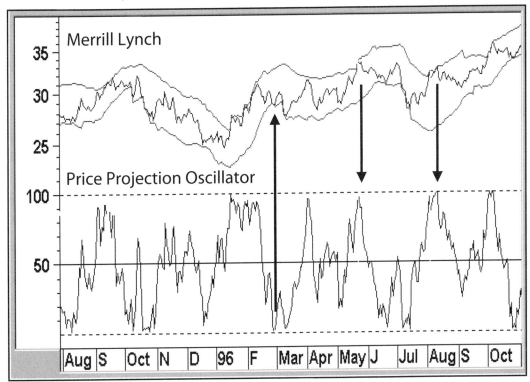

and August 1996 highs in Chart 42-2, but not at the February low; hence the need to check out the situation with other indicators.

Another possibility is to place the over-bought-or-oversold zones at less extreme numbers, say, 80 and 20 (Chart 42-3), and then wait and see when the indicator re-crosses these levels on its way back toward zero. That, too, has its limitations because there are quite a few occasions when the price whipsaws above and below the lines, as it did in January 1996 and later on in the late February to early March period. Both examples are contained within the ellipses. This type of situation will leave you in doubt as to what is really going on. Again, the price projection oscillator acts as a filter, and it is necessary to refer to some other indicator based on trend to confirm these signals.

OVERLAYING THE TWO OSCILLATORS

Another alternative is to overlay one oscillator on another, using two widely separated time spans. In Chart 42-4, I have plotted a 14-day period with a solid line and a 45-day one with a dashed line. The idea is that when both are simultaneously overbought-or-oversold and then start to move in the same direction, this places higher odds on the prevailing trend reversal. The reason for doing this is based on the assumption that prices at any one point are determined by the interaction of many different time cycles. Considering one oscillator only takes into consideration a limited number of cycles. However, if you look at two oscillators, the amount of cycles taken into consideration doubles.

Chart 42-3   Merrill Lynch and a 45-day PPO

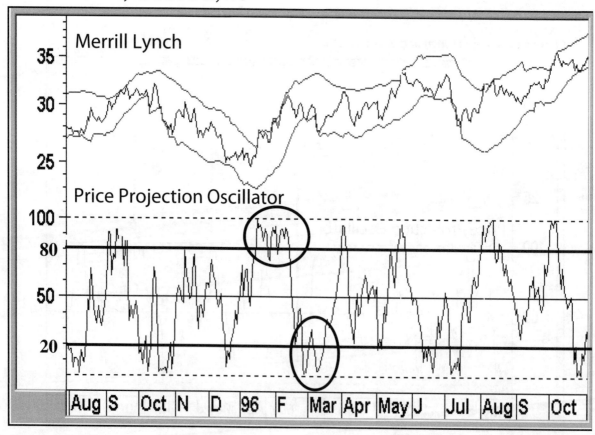

Chart 42-4 Merrill Lynch and two PPOs

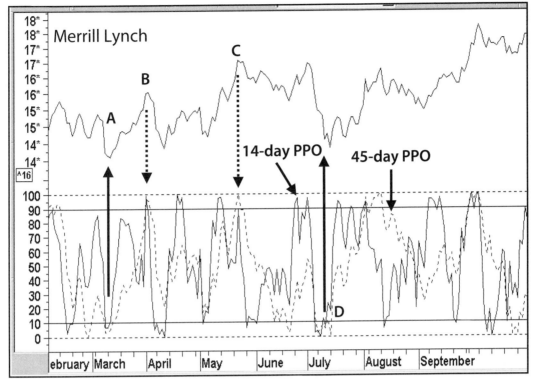

Chart 42-5 Merrill Lynch and a 45-day PPO

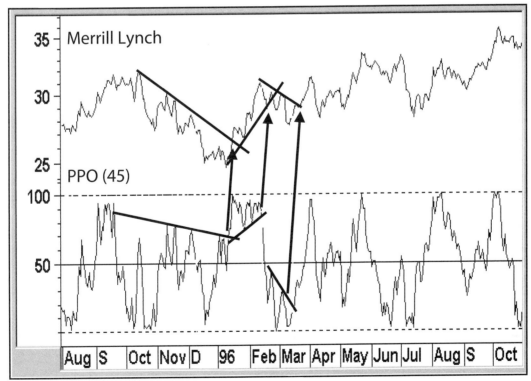

Chart 42-6   Merrill Lynch and a 45-day PPO

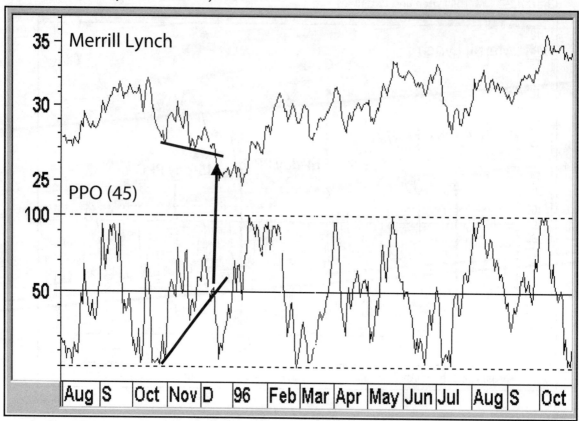

(Source: pring.com)

Chart 42-4 highlights those occasions when both series are at extremes. In March 1996 (point A), both series bottom at the same time and then rise in tandem. Then in April (point B), the reverse set of circumstances set in. In May (point C) both series peak again, but this was not a genuine signal because the 14-day indicator did not reach an extreme. Finally, both series did so in early July, but the price continued on its last leg down. It was not until they both rallied that a bottom was experienced (point D). For this approach to be effective, it is necessary to use timeframes that are fairly well separated. A 14- and 17-day comparison would not be very helpful, but a 14- and 45-period comparison is. Generally speaking, it is best to use a combination of time spans, where the second is at least double the first.

That is why I prefer the joint trendline approach that we have discussed with other indicators. This appears to work quite well with the projection oscillator. Chart 42-5 features a 45-day oscillator on its own. You can see how we got some useful buy-or-sell signals in March 1996, December 1995, and February 1996, respectively. In February 1996, the PPO breaks down from a one-month top. This is also confirmed by a trendline break in the oscillator, followed by one in the price. Finally, a small buy signal in early March develops as a double trendline break– one for the oscillator and one for the price take place.

Chart 42-6 shows that in December 1995 the price projection oscillator violates an uptrend line just as the price is taking out its October and November lows.

TWO PRICE PROJECTION OSCILLATORS

Chart 42-7 features two price projection oscillators. This arrangement again reflects the concept that price at any one particular point in time is determined by the interaction of several time cycles. Here we have two indicators that reflect cycles some distance from each other. The dashed line is a 45-day PPO and the solid one a 17-day series. Look for periods when both price projection oscillators are at an extreme. This is because the differing cycles that these two indicators represent are topping or bottoming simultaneously and therefore the odds of a trend reversal become greater. Obviously, there are a lot more cycles at work, but by displaying two indicators, instead of one, the odds of a valid reversal are increased.

The bottom area displays an MA of the two indicators. In this case, the 17-period series has been smoothed with a 5-day MA and the 45-day series with a 10-day average. I find this arrangement to be much more useful than just looking at the raw data. There are several rules of engagement. First, look for periods when both MAs are at an extreme and then start to reverse. An example develops in Chart 42-7 in July 1994. Rule 2 is a little more reliable. It looks for crossovers of the longer-term dashed average by the shorter-term solid one. If this crossover comes at an extreme level, the signal is usually, though not always, more powerful. July 1994 offered a good sell signal. In all of these inter-

> Look for periods when both price projection oscillators are at an extreme.

Chart 42-7   ASE Oil Index and PPO variations

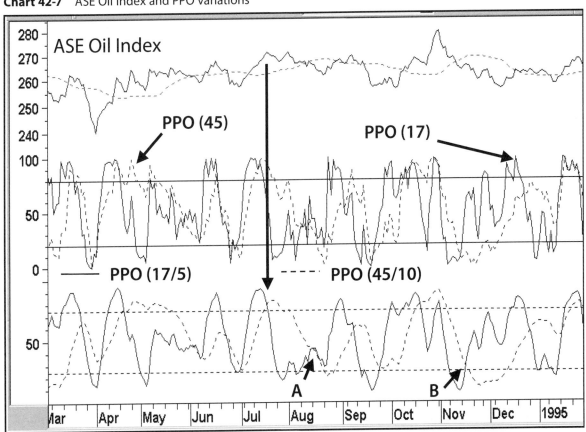

(Source: pring.com)

Chart 42-8   ASE Oil Index and PPO variations

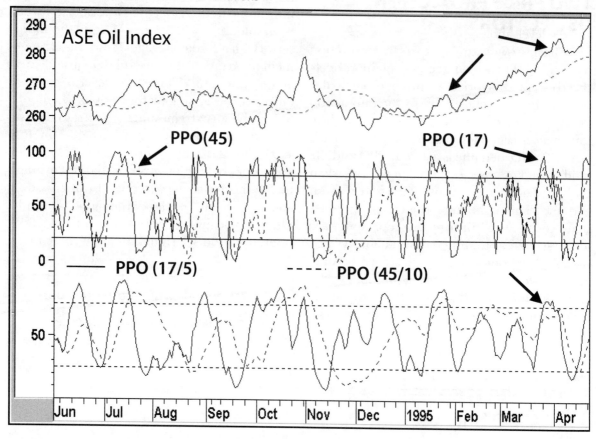

(Source: pring.com)

pretations, we are really trying to establish the point at which both series reverse direction. A crossover in and of itself does not guarantee this. Consider the situation in August 1994 (point A). The solid line crosses the dashed line and then starts to decline again. Only when they both bottom at the very end of the month does the price reach its low. Then in November (point B), another crossover develops. The price is clearly oversold but continues down anyway. The bottom is reached as the 45-day PPO MA bottoms. However, the rally does not really get underway until the dashed 45/10 PPO line actually crosses above its extreme oversold level in mid December.

In a srongly trending market, nothing in the oscillator department will work. The arrows in Chart 42-8 show that both reversals from an extreme in the 45-day series fail to signal much of a decline. I show you this example not

because I have no faith in this arrangement, but because I do. It is done more because it is important to offer a balanced presentation and not leave you with the opinion that this or any of the other arrangements and indicators is perfect.

PRICE PROJECTION OSCILLATOR AND R-SQUARE

Chart 42-9 features a 45-day r-square along with a 65/25 PPO. One useful technique is to look for extreme readings in the PPO and see when this indicator crosses above or below its MA. Then look for a trend reversal in the price to confirm. The inclusion of r-square offers an additional filter. In March 1995, an extreme in the r-square develops and a sell signal by the PPO is triggered. However, there was no meaningful trend reversal signaled by the price. Later on, though, the r-square touches its overbought level and starts to decline. The price subsequently violates a trendline. Since the PPO gave a bear signal by penetrating its average, there are lots of pieces of evidence indicating a trend change. In this case, the change was from up to sideways, not up to down. By late November it was possible to draw a trendline for both the r-square and price. The violation of the r-square trendline did not indicate a rally, merely that the sideways trend had probably come to an end. It was the bullish MA crossover by the PPO, combined with the price break, which indicated the trend was to be a positive one.

The rally did not last very long, and its termination in early January 1996 was signaled by the arrows in Chart 42-10, where the price breaks an uptrend line, the PPO goes negative,

and the r-square crosses below the 0.9 area, indicating the probability that the uptrend was over. Actually, it ushered in a relatively long period of a slightly up-sloping consolidation. The termination of this trading range was signaled by the completion of an r-square base (Chart 42-11) combined with a PPO buy signal and price breakout to the upside.

> One useful technique is to look for extreme readings in the PPO and see when this indicator crosses above or below its MA. Then look for a trend reversal in the price to confirm.

Chart 42-9   ASE Oil Index, a PPO, and r-square

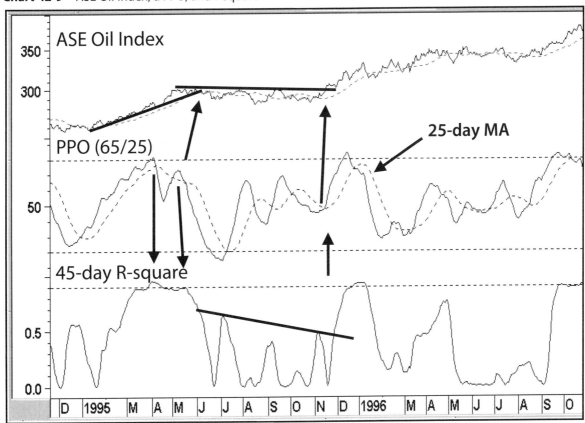

(Source: pring.com)

Chart 42-10   ASE Oil Index, a PPO, and r-square

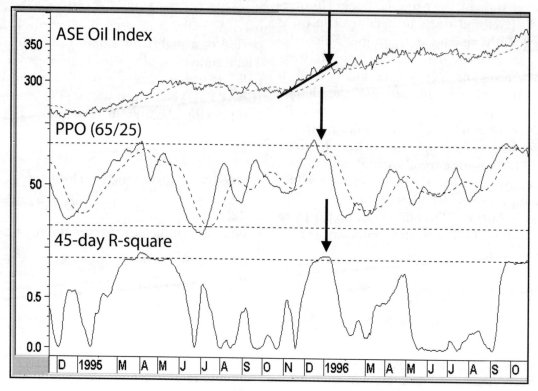

Chart 42-11   ASE Oil Index, a PPO, and r-square

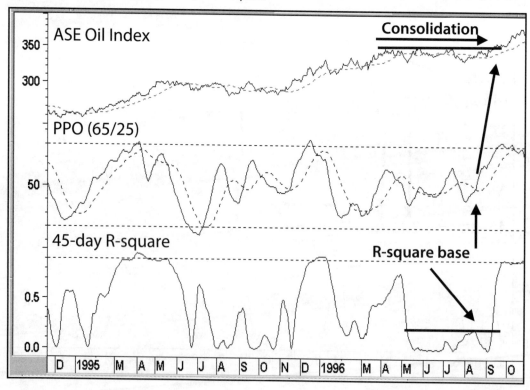

Part II Quiz

**For answers, go to
www.traderslibrary.com/TLEcorner.**

QUIZ CHAPTERS 18–29

1. The linear regression indicator turns:

   (A) More quickly than a simple moving average.

   (B) More slowly than a simple moving average.

2. The linear regression slope is a direct derivative of:

   (A) A linear regression line.

   (B) A Raff regression line.

   (C) The r-square indicator.

   (D) A linear regression indicator.

3. In looking at this chart, it is:

   (A) A bull market correction.

   (B) The start of a new bear market.

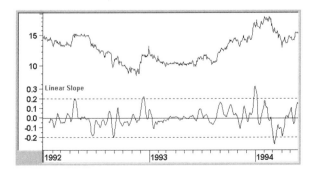

4. Looking at this chart, at the time of the vertical line, is there anything major in the linear slope that suggests that a top is at hand?

   (A) No.

   (B) Yes.

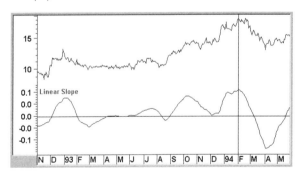

441

5. A high reading in the r-square indicates:

   (A) That a market has strong trending characteristics.

   (B) That a market has strong trending characteristics and is overbought.

   (C) That a market has strong trending characteristics and is oversold.

   (D) None of the above.

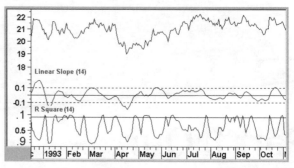

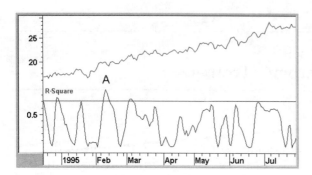

6. At point A, what is the r-square telling us?

   (A) That the price is in a bull market and unlikely to respond to overextended r-square readings.

   (B) That the odds favor that the strong directional movement to the upside is in the process of terminating.

   (C) That you should sell everything, but this turned out to be a false signal.

7. What is wrong with the following chart?

   (A) The linear slope overbought/oversold lines are plotted too closely together.

   (B) The linear slope overbought/oversold lines are plotted too closely together, but there is also another problem not covered by these answers.

   (C) It is not appropriate to plot a linear slope and an r-square on the same chart because they are both derivatives of the same thing.

8. When the r-square reverses trend from a low level this represents:

   (A) A buy signal.

   (B) A sell signal.

   (C) That the odds favor the price starting a new trend which could be up or down.

9. The Chaikin formula works on the assumption that:

   (A) Market strength is derived from prices closing near the middle of the trading session.

   (B) Market weakness is characterized by prices closing close to the session low.

   (C) Market strength is characterized by prices closing near the session high.

   (D) Both B and C.

10. The Chaikin money flow cannot be calculated without volume.

    (A) True.

    (B) False.

11. One of the most useful interpretive characteristics of the Chaikin money flow is:

    (A) Its ability to forecast prices in the next session.

    (B) Its ability to flag strong directional price movement.

    (C) Its strong diverging characteristics.

    (D) None of the above.

12. Which letter represents the best example of a positive divergence.

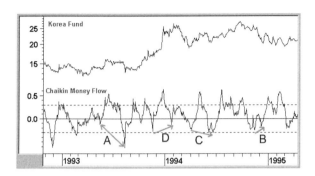

13. The principal difference between an oscillator constructed from volume and one of price is:

   (A) Volume does not reach to such extremes as price.

   (B) Price is smoother than volume.

   (C) Overbought readings in volume can come after a price decline.

   (D) All of the above.

14. Why use volume oscillators when volume displayed as a histogram is very helpful?

   (A) Because volume oscillators can emphasize certain characteristics that cannot be easily spotted in a histogram format.

   (B) Because volume oscillators are always at an overbought or oversold extreme.

   (C) Because volume normally leads price.

   (D) None of the above.

15. If the volume oscillator has peaked in this chart, what is the most likely outcome?

   (A) The price has bottomed, at least for the time being.

   (B) The price will continue to decline.

   (C) None of these answers is correct because the question has been incorrectly worded.

   (D) The price will rally and then quickly fall much further.

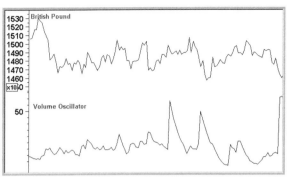

16. This is a buying opportunity because:

   (A) The volume oscillator has shrunk to its lowest reading in years, indicating a total lack of selling pressure.

   (B) The volume oscillator is low and the price has reached a support trendline.

   (C) This is a kind of double bottom because the volume oscillator indicated a selling climax in June.

   (D) B and C.

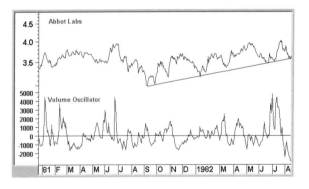

17. What factor suggests that this trendline is n danger of being violated?

    (A) The volume oscillator was declining during the late July, early August rally.

    (B) A and D.

    (C) There is nothing in the chart that warns of danger.

    (D) Volume expands as the price starts to decline in August.

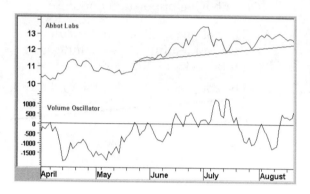

18. Which of these letters offers the best example of a selling climax?

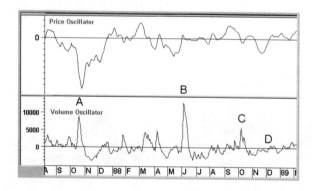

19. This situation is a:

    (A) Buy.

    (B) Sell.

    (C) Hold.

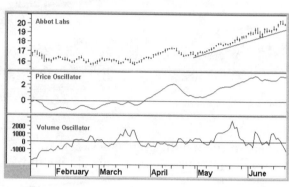

20. The price is in a trading range. In which direction is it likely to break out according to your interpretation of the ROC of volume?

    (A) Up.

    (B) Down.

    (C) No indication is given.

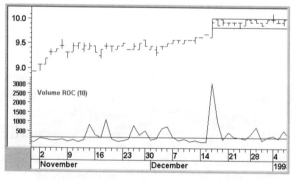

21. These two volume ROCs have a different appearance. This is because:

    (A) They are calculated from different time spans.

    (B) One is calculated using the percent method and the other with a subtraction method.

    (C) One uses ratio scale, the other arithmetic.

    (D) One of them is plotted with a more sophisticated formula.

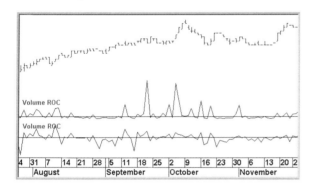

22. In considering the following combinations of moving averages used in a volume oscillator, which is the most suitable for monitoring intermediate trends?

    (A) 2/200-day combination.

    (B) 20/25-day combination.

    (C) 10/25-day combination.

    (D) 25/75-week.

23. How do the Chaikin money flow, Klinger oscillator, and demand index all differ from the ROC and RSI indicators?

    (A) They are all smoothed oscillators, whereas the ROC and RSI are jagged.

    (B) They are all constrained by the 0/100 barrier.

    (C) They require volume figures for the calculation.

    (D) None of the above.

24. Which of the following are appropriate for the interpretation of the demand index?

    (A) Divergence analysis.

    (B) Zero crossovers, trendline, and price pattern analysis.

    (C) Overbought and oversold crossovers.

    (D) All of the above.

25. Looking at this nice breakout in the demand index, this security is:

    (A) Buy.

    (B) Sell short.

    (C) Maintain a long position.

    (D) None of the above.

26. Which of the following methods of interpretation look as if they apply to this security and its demand index?

    (A) Overbought/oversold crossovers and trendlines.

    (B) Overbought/oversold crossovers.

    (C) Zero crossovers and overbought/oversold crossovers.

    (D) A and C.

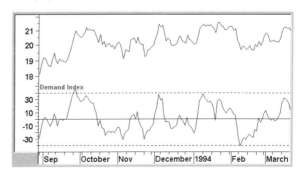

27. The Chande momentum oscillator is a modified version of the RSI. Which of the following are its advantages over the RSI?

    (A) It lends itself better to trendline analysis.

    (B) It experiences more mega overbought/oversold signals.

    (C) None of these answers.

    (D) It experiences more extreme short-term swings and, therefore, triggers more overbought and oversold crossovers.

28. What is the major difference between the dynamic momentum indicator (DMI) and the RSI, from which it is derived?

    (A) The DMI is smoother.

    (B) The DMI is not constrained by the 0/100 barrier, as is the RSI.

    (C) It turns faster than the RSI.

    (D) It is more volatile than the RSI.

29. Does the period between January and March qualify for the DMI cluster rule?

    (A) Yes.

    (B) No.

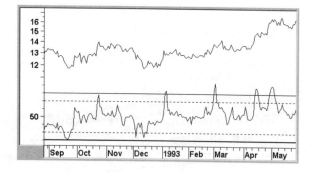

30. Does the March/May period qualify for the DMI cluster rule?

    (A) Yes.

    (B) No.

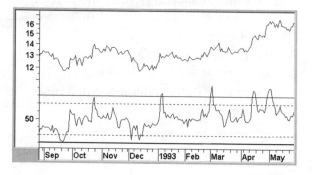

31. The Klinger oscillator incorporates volume and price.

    (A) True.

    (B) False.

32. Which is the relatively best method of interpreting the Klinger oscillator?

    (A) Signal line crossovers.

    (B) Zero crossovers of the signal line.

    (C) When the oscillator is deeply oversold and the price is close to its 89-day EMA.

    (D) None of the above.

33. One relatively better way to interpret the Klinger oscillator is to be on

    the lookout for divergences.

    (A) True.

    (B) False.

34. The relative momentum index (RMI) is a variation of the RSI. Which of the following characteristics is true?

    (A) The RMI is not constrained by the 0 on the downside and 100 on the upside.

    (B) They both use one parameter, the time span.

    (C) The RMI is smoother and experiences more rhythmic fluctuations.

    (D) None of the above.

35. The RMI can be used with many interpretive techniques, but in a relative sense, which is the best?

    (A) Overbought/oversold crossovers.

    (B) Mega overboughts and oversolds.

    (C) Extreme swings.

    (D) Trendline analysis.

36. Looking at this RMI you can see that there are lots of whipsaw overbought/ oversold crossovers. How can these be reduced in number?

    (A) By applying a linear regression line.

    (B) By running a 200-day moving average through the data.

    (C) By doubling the width between these lines and the equilibrium level.

    (D) By calculating the RMI with a slightly longer time span.

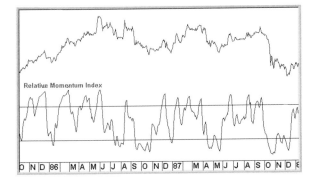

QUIZ CHAPTERS 30–42

1. Which securities can the Herrick payoff be calculated for?

    (A) General Motors and Microsoft

    (B) Spot gold, spot silver, and soybeans.

    (C) The S & P and the Dow.

    (D) The S & P Futures, gold futures, and bond futures.

2. Which are appropriate methods of interpretation for the payoff index?

    (A) Overbought/oversold crossovers.

    (B) Zero crossovers.

    (C) Trendline and price pattern analysis.

    (D) A, B, and C.

3. Which letter identifies a bearish extreme swing?

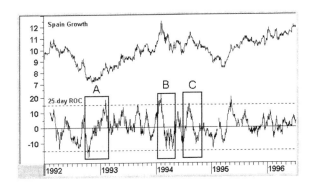

4. What is the difference between a 21-day inertia and a 21-period linear regression indicator of the RVI?

    (A) The inertia is far more volatile.

    (B) The linear regression of the RVI experiences far more whipsaws.

    (C) None whatsoever.

    (D) None of the above.

5. What assumption should be made for the future price of the following security?

   (A) It will continue to fluctuate.

   (B) It will find support and rally.

   (C) It will continue to decline.

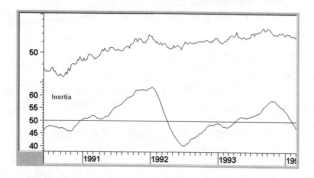

6. The Qstick indicator places special emphasis on:

   (A) The high, low, and close.

   (B) The high and low.

   (C) The open and close.

   (D) None of the above.

7. Put in a simple way, the Qstick is calculated from:

   (A) The difference between the high and low for the day.

   (B) The high, plus the low, divided by the close.

   (C) None of these answers is correct.

   (D) A simple moving average of the difference between the opening and closing prices.

8. If you were trying to plot a Qstick from a data series that contains the high, low, close, volume, and open interest, you would choose:

   (A) Any time span because the Qstick is a very versatile indicator.

   (B) Only weekly time spans because the Qstick is better at measuring intermediate trends.

   (C) Only daily time spans because the Qstick is a short-term indicator.

   (D) None of the above.

9. Because the TRIX indicator is so smooth, it is never possible to draw meaningful trendlines.

   (A) True.

   (B) False.

10. The TRIX bottoms out at the vertical line, after the price has already made its low. Is this a positive reverse divergence?

    (A) Yes.

    (B) No.

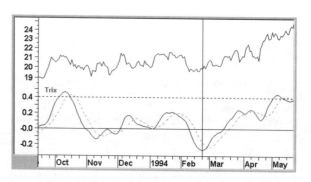

11. Directional movement is a concept that:

    (A) Tells us whether a market is oversold or overbought.

    (B) Measures the difference between yesterday's low and today's low.

    (C) Tells us whether a security price is in a trending or nontrending mode.

    (D) Requires volume figures in the calculation.

12. The ADX tells us whether a security's price is trending; the DIs tell us in which direction.

    (A) True.

    (B) False

13. If the ADX is at an extreme high reading and trending down, you should:

    (A) Assume that the prevailing trend will continue.

    (B) Assume that the prevailing trend will reverse.

    (C) Assume that there will be a change in the prevailing trend.

    (D) Assume that the prevailing trend will continue and change much later on.

14. In this chart, the ADX starts to rally at the dashed vertical line. What is the most likely outcome for the price?

    (A) It will rally, too.

    (B) It will decline.

    (C) It will be trendless.

    (D) It will either experience a rally or a reaction.

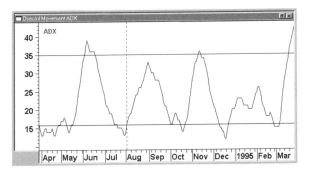

15. The DIs reflect:

    (A) Up and down directional movement over a specific time span, which is usually 14 days.

    (B) Up and down volume over a specific time span, which is usually 14 days.

    (C) The average directional movement over a specific time span.

16. Looking at the following chart, which is the -DI?

    (A) The solid line.

    (B) The dashed line.

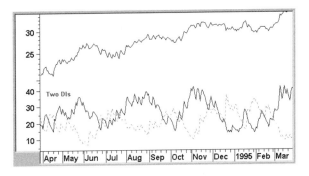

17. In the following chart, the ADX peaks out at point A. What is the most likely outcome?

    (A) The price changes trend.

    (B) The price declines.

    (C) The price rallies.

    (D) None of the above.

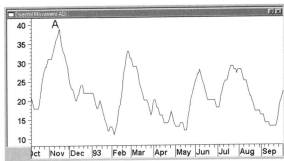

18. If the ADX reaches 150 and reverses and the previous high in the last 5 years was 85, the price is likely to:

    (A) Experience a major trend reversal.

    (B) None of these answers are correct because the question is improperly worded.

    (C) Experience a major change in trend.

    (D) There is no way of knowing how big the trend change will be.

19. Buy signals are given by the DIs when:

    (A) The +DI crosses above the -DI.

    (B) The ADX reverses from a high reading.

    (C) The ADX reverses from a low reading.

    (D) The +DI crosses above zero.

20. What is the most probable outcome given the following technical situation?

    (A) The price will rally back above the trendline.

    (B) The price will experience a trading range.

    (C) The price will decline.

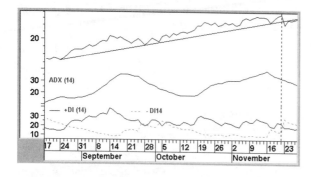

21. The CSI was originally designed to filter out the commodity that will give the trader the greatest bang for his buck, but an alternative interpretation is:

    (A) To use reversals in extreme overextended readings to signal probable trend changes.

    (B) To signal overbought and oversold conditions before they happen.

    (C) To use zero crossovers as buy and sell signals.

    (D) To use reversals in extreme overextended readings to signal probable trend reversals.

22. Looking at the following chart, what is the most probable outcome?

    (A) The price has bottomed.

    (B) The price will continue to decline.

    (C) The price will either continue to decline or experience a trading range.

    (D) None of the above.

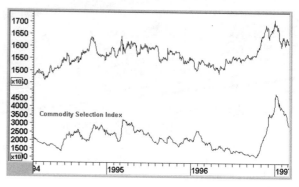

23. The parabolic system is good for:

    (A) Defining unusual overbought/oversold situations.

    (B) Setting stop points.

    (C) Calculating moving averages.

    (D) Identifying future price moves that will end in a parabola.

24. As a day trader, if you are going to go short, the best spot to place your first stop using the parabolic system is:

    (A) Above the previous strong area of minor resistance.

    (B) Below the previous strong area of minor resistance.

    (C) Below the previous strong area of minor support.

    (D) None of the above.

25. If you have a strong reason to believe that this security is in a primary uptrend, where should you place the stop for a short sale?

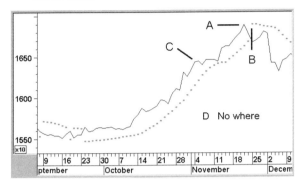

26. Which of the following parabolic lines has the largest initial acceleration factor?

    (A) The solid line.

    (B) The dashed line.

    (C) They are both the same; it is the maximum acceleration factor that causes the difference.

    (D) None of the above.

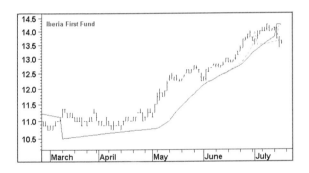

27. Where would be the best point to place a parabolic short stop, given the opportunity?

    (A) Place it immediately as the system triggers a signal, even though it is a long way from the entry point.

    (B) Wait for the price to rally to limit the risk.

    (C) Wait for the price to rally toward the parabolic line, which is also now within the vicinity of a downtrend line.

28. When does the price move outside of the price projection band?

    (A) Whenever it makes a new high for the calculated timespan.

    (B) Whenever the price rises or falls by more than 30 percent.

    (C) Never.

    (D) Soon after it crosses a moving average.

29. The price projection oscillator is:

    (A) The derivative of the stochastic indicator.

    (B) A way of displaying the price projection band, but as an oscillator.

    (C) A derivative of the RSI.

    (D) An oscillator derived from a deviation from a simple moving average.

30. What is the best way to use a price projection oscillator?

    (A) With trendline analysis, and overlaying two oscillators calculated with similar time spans.

    (B) With overbought/oversold crossovers.

    (C) With peak-and-trough analysis.

    (D) With trendline, overbought/oversold bands, and the overlaying of two oscillators calculated with widely differing time spans.

31. What benefit is derived from considering an r-squared indicator along with a price projection band?

    (A) They offer two pieces of evidence that a trend may be in the process of changing.

    (B) They offer two pieces of evidence that the trend has reversed.

    (C) Because the r-squared is an almost infallible indicator.

    (D) Because reversals in the r-squared from a high reading always result in a trend reversal, however small.

Index

About the Author

Martin J. Pring is the highly respected president of Pring Research (www.pring.com). A pioneer in the field of technical analysis, Pring is probably best known for his seminal *Technical Analysis Explained*, used by many technical societies around the world as a teaching tool for certification programs. In addition to 14 books and numerous articles (including contributions to Barron's and other national publications), he has held workshops for traders in Asia, Australia, Africa, Europe, and North America and has lectured at several universities, including Harvard Medical School, the Darden Business School, Golden Gate University, and the University of Richmond. He is also editor of *The Intermarket Review*, a monthly technical letter that forecasts the world's principal financial markets from a long-term perspective. He was awarded the Jack Frost Memorial Award from the Canadian Technical Analysts Society, as well as the Traders' Library Hall of Fame Lifetime Achievement Award for his groundbreaking contributions to the field.

B

Marketplace Books is the preeminent publisher of trading, investing, and finance educational material. We produce professional books, DVDs, courses, and electronic books (ebooks) that showcase the exceptional talent working in the investment world today. Started in 1993, Marketplace Books grew out of the realization that mainstream publishers were not meeting the demand of the trading and investment community. Capitalizing on the access we had through our distribution partner Traders' Library, Marketplace Books was launched, and today publishes the top authors in the industry; where household names like Jack Schwager, Oliver Velez, Larry McMillan, Sheldon Natenberg, Jim Bittman, Martin Pring, and Jeff Cooper are just the beginning. We are actively acquiring some of the brightest new minds in the industry including technician Jeff Greenblatt and programmers Jean Folger and Lee Leibfarth.

From the beginning student to the professional trader, our goal is to continually provide the highest quality resources for those who want an active role in the world of finance. Our products focus on strategic information and cutting edge research to give our readers the best education possible. We are at the forefront of digital publishing and are actively pursuing innovative ways to deliver content. At our annual Traders' Forum event, our readers get the chance to learn and mingle with our top authors in a way unprecedented in the industry. Our titles have been translated in most every major world language and can be shipped all over the globe thanks to our preferred online bookstore, TradersLibrary.com.

Visit us today at
www.marketplacebooks.com and www.traderslibrary.com

473

This book, and other great products, are available at significantly discounted prices. They make great gifts for your customers, clients, and staff. For more information on these long-lasting, cost-effective premiums, please call (800) 272-2855, or email us at sales@traderslibrary.com.

SOFTWARE AND INFORMATION LICENSE

The software and information on this diskette (collectively referred to as the "Product") are the property of Marketplace Books, and are protected by both United States copyright law and international copyright treaty provision. You must treat this Product just like a book, except that you may copy it into a computer to be used and you may make archival copies of the Products for the sole purpose of backing up our software and protecting your investment from loss.

By saying "just like a book," Marketplace Books means, for example, that the Product may be used by any number of people and may be freely moved from one computer location to another, so long as there is no possibility of the Product (or any part of the Product) being used at one location or on one computer while it is being used at another. Just as a book cannot be read by two different people in two different places at the same time, neither can the Product be used by two different people in two different places at the same time (unless, of course, Marketplace Books' rights are being violated).

Marketplace Books reserves the right to alter or modify the contents of the Product at any time.

This agreement is effective until terminated. The Agreement will terminate automatically without notice if you fail to comply with any provisions of this Agreement. In the event of termination by reason of your breach, you will destroy or erase all copies of the Product installed on any computer system or made for backup purposes and shall expunge the Product from your data storage facilities.

LIMITED WARRANTY

Marketplace Books warrants the physical diskette(s) enclosed herein to be free of defects in materials and workmanship for a period of sixty days from the purchase date. If Marketplace Books receives written notification within the warranty period of defects in materials or workmanship, and such notification is determined by Marketplace Books to be correct, Marketplace Books will replace the defective diskette(s). Send request to:

Customer Service
Marketplace Books
9002 Red Branch Road
Columbia MD 21045

The entire and exclusive liability and remedy for breach of this Limited Warranty shall be limited to replacement of defective diskette(s) and shall not include or extend any claim for or right to cover any other damages, including but not limited to, loss of profit, data, or use of the software, or special, incidental, or consequential damages or other similar claims, even if Marketplace Books has been specifically advised as to the possibility of such damages. In no event will Marketplace Books's liability for any damages to you or any other person ever exceed the lower of suggested list price or actual price paid for the license to use the Product, regardless of any form of the claim.

MARKETPLACE BOOKS SPECIFICALLY DISCLAIMS ALL OTHER WARRANTIES, EXPRESS OR IMPLIED, INCLUDING BUT NOT LIMITED TO, ANY IMPLIED WARRANTY OF MERCHANTABILITY OR FITNESS FOR A PARTICULAR PURPOSE. Specifically, Marketplace Books makes no representation or warranty that the Product is fit for any particular purpose and any implied warranty of merchantability is limited to the sixty day duration of the Limited Warranty covering the physical diskette(s) only (and not the software or information) and is otherwise expressly and specifically disclaimed.

This Limited Warranty gives you specific legal rights; you may have others which may vary from state to state. Some states do not allow the exclusion of incidental or consequential damages, or the limitation on how long an implied warranty lasts, so some of the above may not apply to you.

This Agreement constitutes the entire agreement between the parties relating to use of the Product. The terms of any purchase order shall have no effect on the terms of this Agreement. Failure of Marketplace Books to insist at any time on strict compliance with this Agreement shall not constitute a waiver of any rights under this Agreement. This Agreement shall be construed and governed in accordance with the laws of Maryland. If any provision of this Agreement is held to be contrary to law, that provision will be enforced to the maximum extent permissible and the remaining provisions will remain in force and effect.

Installation Instructions

This CD has an Autorun feature. Insert the CD into the CD-ROM drive and it will start automatically. Please allow sufficient time for loading.

   If the Autorun feature does not work, insert the CD, open your CD-ROM drive and double-click on the Setup.exe icon. Then, access the program by clicking on Start, Programs, Pring and locate the icon for the tutorial title you are playing in the flyout.

1. We recommend not changing the default installation settings.

2. This program is best viewed using small fonts.

3. This CD is best viewed in 800 X 600 pixels and 256 colors.

4. For additional support, please go to Support at www.pring.com.

Advanced Technical Analysis CD Tutorials:
Learning the KST
Intro to Candlestick Charting
Tech's Guide to Day Trading
Breaking the Black Box
How to Select Stocks

MetaStock CD Tutorials:
Exploring MS Basic
Exploring MS Advanced
Super CD Companion
Indicator Companion
Market Analysis Companion
Selecting Stocks Using MetaStock

Visit *http://www.pring.com* for info on these and other products.

Pring Research, Inc.
4830 Sweetmeadow Circle, Sarasota, FL 34238
941-926-9664 • Fax: 941-870-0642
Web Site: www.pring.com • E-mail: info@pring.com